THE CHEF'S COMPENDIUM
OF PROFESSIONAL RECIPES

THE CHEF'S COMPENDIUM
OF PROFESSIONAL RECIPES

John Fuller

and

Edward Renold

HEINEMANN : LONDON

William Heinemann Ltd
15 Queen Street, Mayfair, London W1X 8BE
LONDON MELBOURNE TORONTO
JOHANNESBURG AUCKLAND

First published 1963
Reprinted 1966, 1968, 1971
Second edition 1972
Reprinted 1973, 1975
Reprinted (with revisions) 1978
434 90586 0

Printed Offset Litho and bound in Great Britain
by Cox & Wyman Ltd,
London, Fakenham and Reading

Preface

The aim of this book is to provide a range of principal recipes currently used in hotels, restaurants, and in other catering establishments. It has been called a *Compendium* because a degree of selection has been involved, and the temptation to include every possible recipe has been resisted. The authors have chosen typical examples that they hope will enable the user to understand and prepare the majority of dishes, even those that are not listed.

Much of the technical jargon of the kitchen is French and some translations of French terms are cumbersome. In some cases, however, the French title of a dish is followed by an English description but where this description is not given in the recipe heading because no adequate translation is available (e.g for words like mirepoix), it is hoped that the recipe or note makes the meaning apparent. Other terms are given in the brief glossary.

The fact that the *Compendium* covers the normal scope of hotel and restaurant styles of cooking does not mean that the recipes are not suitable for use in other establishments, including institutions like hospitals, schools, and those catering for industry. On the contrary, it is thought that the determined and constant efforts to lift the level of general catering makes these professional methods of interest and use in a wide range of kitchens.

The 'Compendium' is designed for working chefs and cooks but particular care has been taken to ensure that it will also meet the requirements of apprentices, trainees, and students preparing for National Diplomas and Certificates, in particular the City and Guilds of London Institute's examination 706, Cookery for the Catering Industry (basic and advanced). It is for this reason that in most recipes, the ingredients are for 'four covers' as this figure is commonly used for practical tests devised for training and examination purposes.

While it is assumed that users of the *Compendium* will have a basic knowledge of cookery (gained from a year's preliminary trade cookery; or training in a technical institution; or in the first year of apprenticeship or traineeship) most recipes have been reduced to steps sufficiently simple for comprehension by beginners as well as by practising chefs. Though recipe instructions have been kept concise, an attempt has been made to include each step in each individual recipe. Indeed, even elementary points are reiterated in some recipes in order to ensure that every stage may readily be followed and excessive cross-references to other sections can be avoided.

A guide to oven temperatures and readings is given which relates general descriptions such as 'cool', 'hot', etc. to degrees Celsius and Fahrenheit or gas 'marks' so that these need not be incorporated in each recipe. Accuracy in this regard is important especially in, for example, pâtisserie work and a distinguishing mark of the professional chef is his ability to gauge times and temperatures in relation to the varying size of items such as meat joints, pies, and so on, and the age and quality of vegetables; but it would be naïve to believe that even the most explicit recipes and precise formulae can ever entirely replace the skills derived from the day-to-day experience of handling, preparing and cooking foods, in a working-kitchen. The authors emphasize that the *Compendium* is aimed to augment and aid work in practical cuisine and not to replace it.

Though the scope of the work may be thought to be largely traditional in that it covers professional cookery in the conventional French style, the authors, believing that the understanding of underlying principles of first-class cookery is gained through knowledge of and practice in this tradition, have, nevertheless, not hesitated to incorporate reforms and simplifications where these have become accepted trade practice.

The development of processed foods such as, particularly, quick-frozen vegetables continues to bring changes into kitchens and into kitchen organization, but it will be apparent that the accomplished chef, who has a sound grasp of good professional cookery, will be able to use his skills to adapt recipes of the best tradition to the manufacturer's or processor's instructions regarding reconstitution, defrosting and so on. Indeed, the fact that some forms of processing tend to encourage the reappearance over a longer season of some popular vegetables makes it all the more necessary, in the authors' opinion, that chefs should be no less versatile and skilled than formerly in applying sauces, garnishes, and varied dressings to vegetables as well as other processed food commodities.

Because the *Compendium* concentrates on providing recipes, the principles of cookery have been incorporated in them rather than by exhaustive coverage in separate sections; though, in order adequately to link the text and to aid appreciation and interpretation of recipes, some notes on general culinary processes have been included.

The authors gratefully acknowledge the assistance (especially in checking and proof-reading) of Mr Charles Jarvie, FCFA, MHCI, Mr Gordon Sinclair, MHCI, both Lecturers at the Scottish Hotel School and of Mr Iain T. Marshall, MHCI, Lecturer at the Scottish Hotel School, for his contribution to and general assistance with Chapter 8, 'Pastry and Sweets'.

For this Second Edition metric quantities have been added alongside the more familiar Imperial amounts. The transition towards complete metrication is gathering momentum in our daily lives as we write and it is our belief that this addition to the *Compendium* will make it of even greater utility.

J. F.
E. R.

Contents

Metric Conversion
Approximate Equivalents

Mass or Weight

$\frac{1}{4}$ oz = 7g
$\frac{1}{2}$ oz = 15 g
1 oz = 30 g
16 oz = 480 g (500 g in large-scale recipes)
2 lb = 1 kg
10 lb = 5 kg

Capacity or Volume

1 fluid ounce = 25 ml
$\frac{1}{4}$ gill = 30 ml
1 gill = 125 ml
1 pint = 500 ml
1 quart = 1000 ml = 1 litre (l.)

Spoon Measures

British Standard 1348 measures available as a complete set:

1·25 ml = $\frac{1}{4}$ teaspoon
2·50 ml = $\frac{1}{2}$ teaspoon
5·00 ml = 1 teaspoon
10·00 ml = 1 dessertspoon
15·00 ml = 1 tablespoon
20·00 ml = 4 teaspoons

Length

$\frac{1}{8}$ inch = 0·3 cm
$\frac{1}{4}$ inch = 0·5 cm
$\frac{1}{2}$ inch = 1·0 cm
1 inch = 2·0 cm

All Recipes are Designed for 4 Covers

In day-to-day working in a professional kitchen French jargon, as well as English equivalents of French terms, for commodities, utensils, and preparations is commonly used. Chefs and cuisiniers are as likely to speak of 'demi-glace' as of 'half-glaze', or of 'lié' as frequently as 'thickened'; and to refer to 'maître d'hôtel butter' (a mixture of French and English) as often as 'parsley butter'. At the risk of offending purists, recipes in this Compendium reflect normal working usage by including terms either in their French or English versions, French words (or their semi-anglicized equivalents) being allowed to appear freely in the English narrative. It has been thought logical to record the processes in a manner to which chefs are habituated – or to which they must inevitably become habituated.

Oven Temperatures

	Gas Mark	Degrees Celsius	Degrees Fahrenheit
Very cool	$\frac{1}{4}$	115	240
	$\frac{1}{2}$	120	250
Cool	1	135	275
	2	150	300
Warm	2	150	300
	3	160	325
Moderate	3	160	325
	4	175	350
Moderately hot	5	190	375
	6	200	400
Hot	7	215	425
	8	230	450
Very hot	9	245	475

1. Culinary Basics, Stocks, and Sauces

DURING the past quarter of a century many changes have taken place in professional kitchens. Not only those catering for industry, hospitals, and schools, but even hotel and restaurant kitchens organized along traditional *partie* (or sectional) lines, have been affected.

Some of the changes tend to simplify the concept of basic culinary preparations. This has been due to two main influences: the cost factor – the need to make economical use of skilled kitchen labour has become just as important as economizing in ingredients; and, a changing public demand that, under present social and economic conditions, generally favours simpler and shorter meals, but well prepared and presented.

Actual changes in kitchen practices have not, however, always been accurately reflected in professional cookery manuals and large numbers of chefs have paid, and even continue to pay, lip-service to classic recipes that are seldom carried out in full in the kitchens of today.

Yet first-class work still requires properly prepared stocks and similar culinary basics, though, nowadays, stocks may not always contain the high proportion of poultry and butcher's meat that was considered essential in former times. It is also recognized that modern methods, in certain operations, make use of pre-processed bases for stocks, soups, and sauces. These factory-made products are being exploited to a marked extent in many kitchens, particularly in America. Nevertheless, kitchens of the finest grade, even those run on modest lines, must still use basic preparations that are produced by their own staff. Therefore, a sound knowledge of culinary foundations is essential for all who intend to practise the art of good cooking.

Mise-en-place. Despite the changes, traditional kitchen methods, whether for table d'hôte or à la carte service, still include the idea of mise-en-place; that is, the preparation of culinary items in advance. By this means dishes can be assembled at service time with the minimum fuss and bother, the maximum efficiency, and attractively presented.

Fonds de cuisine. The most basic elements of the chef's mise-en-place are described as 'fonds de cuisine' of which a literal translation might be 'foundations of the kitchen or of cookery'. The following recipes for fonds de cuisine are based on the principles of traditional cooking modes, though reconciled with the realities of present-day practice and possibilities, in the belief that the careful building of good cookery on sound foundations still remains of the utmost importance.

(Basic preparations for fish and fish sauces are dealt with in Chapter 5; larder preparations and those for cold cookery appear in Chapter 2.)

BASIC FLAVOURINGS FOR STOCKS, SAUCES, AND SOUPS

In his work the chef uses many seasonings; these various aromatics, spices, and herbs are specified in all the recipes, but there are a few basic, composed flavourings used so frequently in savoury liquors that it is convenient to list them here,

1 Bouquet garni

1 *sprig thyme*	15 g (½ oz) *parsley stalk*	1 *piece celery*
1 *bay-leaf*	2 *pieces green leek*	

1 Bunch together the thyme, bay-leaf, celery and parsley stalk.
2 Wrap the green of leek round the bundle and tie with fine string.

Used for stocks, soups, sauces and entrées.

2 Mirepolx

240 g (½ lb) *carrots*	240 g (½ lb) *celery*	120 g (¼ lb) *onions*
1 *bay-leaf*	1 *sprig thyme*	60 g (2 oz) *diced fat pork*

1 Cut all vegetables into medium dice.
2 Fry-off pork to extract fat.
3 Add the vegetables and herbs.
4 Cook to a light golden colour.

Used in soups, sauces, stews, and for braising.

3 Matignon (for large joints)

240 g (½ lb) *carrots*	240 g (½ lb) *celery*	3 *large onions*
1 *bay-leaf*	1 *sprig thyme*	6 *crushed peppercorns*

1 Cut the vegetables in large thick slices.
2 Place under large joints.

Used in roasting, poêlé, and the subsequent flavouring of jus or sauce.

4 Mirepoix Bordelaise

240 g (½ lb) *carrots*	240 g (½ lb) *white celery*	240 g (½ lb) *onions*
30 g (1 oz) *raw, lean ham*	30 g (1 oz) *butter*	1 *bay-leaf*
1 *sprig thyme*		

1 Dice the vegetables as brunoise.
2 Stew the raw ham and butter.
3 Add the vegetables and herbs and continue to sweat until soft.

Used for chicken, game, etc., and for the subsequent flavouring of jus (gravy) or sauce.

5 Oignon clouté (or piqué) – Studded onion

1 *large onion*	4 *cloves*	1 *blade bay-leaf*

Stud the peeled onion with the spices, impaling the bay-leaf to the onion with cloves.

Used generally; e.g., for infusing in milk or other liquors for sauces, particularly white sauces.

STOCKS

General Directions. As the function of stock is to add to the flavour and to give 'body' (that is, a gelatinous consistency) to the soups and sauces for which it is used, it will be obvious that a stock-pot should not be considered a dumping ground for any old kitchen scraps and left-overs. Moreover, as stocks are prepared in advance for later use they invariably have to be stored in the kitchen. Measures have to be taken, therefore, to prevent the souring or 'turning' of stock during storage. With these two factors in mind the following general points in stock-making should be remembered:

i Choose sound ingredients ensuring that they are fresh and cleaned.

ii Ensure that stock-pots and utensils are scrupulously clean.

iii Break bones into small sizes to aid in extracting the maximum flavour, calcium, and gelatine.

iv Use cold water (normally about twice as much water as the bulk of solid ingredients) and bring slowly to the boil for maximum extraction.

v Carefully skim all scum and fat as they rise to the surface, particularly before the stock actually boils. (This fat may be clarified and used for savoury pastry, e.g. Cornish Pasty.)

vi Simmer gently, continuing to skim as required.

vii Do not allow vegetables to remain in stock longer than is needed for extracting flavour otherwise they merely re-absorb flavour from the liquor.

viii Observe storage precautions to prevent sourness by careful skimming and straining, and by leaving the stock-pot raised on its storage surface to allow air to circulate.

ix Store stock in cool place and bring to the boil daily, and after any storage period.

Note. Various types of commercial bouillons can be used as an aid to stock-making.

6 Fond blanc – White stock [to yield 10 litres (10 quarts)]

10 *kg* (20 *lb*) *beef bones*	500 *g* (1 *lb*) *leeks*	4 *onions cloutés*
1 *kg* (2 *lb*) *whole carrots*	1 *bouquet garni*	14 *l* (14 *qt*) *cold water*
500 *g* (1 lb) *celery*		

1 Chop or saw the bones small; clean and prepare the vegetables.

2 Place bones in large saucepan or stock-pot with the water.

3 Bring to the boil slowly; remove scum as it rises.

4 Add the vegetables and bouquet garni.

5 Simmer for at least 4 hours, skimming frequently. (Simmering throughout the day, i.e. up to 8 hours, is customary. But excessive cooking fulfils no useful purpose.)

6 Remove all fat; strain and reserve for use.

Used for soups, sauces, and white stews.

7 Fond brun ordinaire – Ordinary brown stock [to yield 10 litres (10 quarts)]

> 10 *kg* (20 *lb*) *beef bones*   1 *bouquet garni*   120 *g* (4 *oz*) *stock fat*
> 500 *g* (1 *lb*) *pork rind*   1 *kg* (2 *lb*) *carrots*   1 *kg* (2 *lb*) *onions*
> 12 *l* (12 *qt*) *water*

1 Chop the bones small.
2 Cut the vegetables into large dice.
3 Place bones, pork rind, stock fat, and vegetables in the oven and cook until golden brown.
4 Add bones and vegetables to the water.
5 Bring to the boil, skim, add bouquet garni and simmer for 8 hours.
6 Strain and reserve for use.

This ordinary brown stock is the one most commonly used in trade practice when a brown stock is required.

8 Estouffade – Brown stock [to yield 10 litres (10 quarts)]

> 5 *kg* (10 *lb*) *shin of beef*   750 *g* (1½ *lb*) *pork rind*   1 *kg* (2 *lb*) *onions*
> (*bone and meat*)   (*diced*)   12 *l* (12 *qt*) *water*
> 5 *kg* (10 *lb*) *shin of veal*   1 *kg* (2 *lb*) *carrots*
> (*bone and meat*)

1 Bone the meat and break bones finely.
2 Brown the bones in the oven with stock fat.
3 Place in large stock-pot with roughly sliced pork-rind, onions, carrots, bouquet garni; add the cold water.
4 Bring to the boil and skim; cover with lid and simmer for 8 hours.
5 Remove all fat; strain and allow to cool.
6 Place the meat in a saucepan with a little stock fat and brown over a brisk heat.
7 When brown, drain off the fat and add 1 litre (2 pints) of the stock; simmer under cover until the stock has nearly reduced, taking care to turn the meat during this process.
8 Pour on the remainder of the stock; bring to the boil and simmer with the lid off till the meat is cooked.
9 Remove fat; strain and reserve for use.

Used for braisings (including vegetables) and the preparation of basic sauces and gravies.

9 Fond de veau – Veal stock [to yield 10 litres (10 quarts)]

> 10 *kg* (20 *lb*) *shin of veal*   750 *g* (1½ *lb*) *carrots*   360 *g* (¾ *lb*) *celery*
> (*bone and meat*)   4 *onions cloutés*   14 *l* (14 *qt*) *cold water*
> 4 *raw fowl's*   360 *g* (¾ *lb*) *leeks*
> *carcases*   1 *bouquet garni*

1 Bone the shin of veal and break the bones into small pieces.
2 Place the bones and chicken-carcases in the water; bring to the boil; skim and simmer for 4 hours, skimming frequently.

3 Strain the stock in a clean saucepan; add the meat, whole vegetables, and bouquet garni and simmer for 4 hours.
4 Skim off all fat; strain and use as required.

Used for chicken poêlé, blanquettes, fricassées, etc.

10 Fond de veau brun – Brown veal stock [to yield 10 litres (10 quarts)]

Ingredients: as for White Veal Stock; Method: as for Estouffade.

Used for jus lié (thickened gravy), and braisings (including vegetables).

11 Fond de volaille – Chicken stock [to yield 10 litres (10 quarts)]

1 *old fowl* [2·5 *kg* (5–6	1 *kg* (2 *lb*) *whole carrots*	360 *g* (¾ *lb*) *leeks*
lb approx.)]	4 *onions cloutés*	1 *bouquet garni*
5 *kg* (10 *lb*) *veal bones*	360 *g* (¾ *lb*) *celery*	14 *l* (14 *qt*) *cold water*

1 Break the bones into small lengths [approximately 4 cm (2 inches)].
2 Cover with cold water and simmer for 4 hours.
3 Strain the stock into a clean saucepan; add the fowl, vegetables, and bouquet garni and simmer for 4 hours.
4 Skim off all fat; strain through muslin and reserve for use.

Used for clear soups, veloutés, cream soups, aspic and chaud-froid sauces.

12 Fond de gibier – Game stock [to yield 10 litres (10 quarts)]

4·5 *kg* (9 *lb*) *neck or*	240 *g* (½ *lb*) *diced carrots*	1 *bouquet garni*
breast of venison	480 *g* (1 *lb*) *mushrooms*	2 *onions cloutés**
1·5 *kg* (3 *lb*) *hare*	(*diced*)	12 *l* (12 *qt*) *cold*
trimmings	240 *g* (½ *lb*) *leeks* (*diced*)	*water*
4 *old pheasants*	240 *g* (½ *lb*) *celery* (*diced*)	

1 Chop the venison, hare, and pheasant into small pieces.
2 Brown these same pieces with the carrots in the oven to a golden colour.
3 Place all in a large saucepan, cover with water, bring to the boil and remove the scum.
4 Add the mushrooms, celery, leeks, bouquet garni, and onions cloutés.
5 Simmer under cover for 4 hours.
6 Skim the stock and pass through muslin and allow to cool.

Used for game sauces, aspic, soups.

[*Essences*. An Essence is stock reduced to half its quantity.]

GLACES – GLAZES

Glazes are used in good-class cookery mainly for enriching sauces, though in some instances a thread of glaze added at a dish's finishing point may also have

* Brown onions in the oven before sticking in cloves.

the effect of enhancing its appearance. Glazes are prepared by reducing stock until a thick and barely flowing liquid is achieved. Proprietary extracts of beef and poultry are on the market and have been substituted for glazes made by the chef in his own kitchens. However, it will become apparent that these substitutes have their limitations if fine, individual work in the classic tradition is sought.

Yield of Glazes from Stock

Glaze	Stock and Quantity Required	Yield
13 **Glace de viande** – meat glaze	8 l. (8 qt) meat stock	250 ml (½ pint)
14 **Glace de volaille** – chicken glaze	9 l. (9 qt) chicken stock	375 ml (¾ pint)
15 **Glace de gibier** – game glaze	8 l. (8 qt) game stock	250 ml (½ pint)
16 **Glace de veau** – veal glaze	9 l. (9 qt) veal stock	375 ml (¾ pint)

1 Boil the stock in a thick pan.
2 Reduce on moderate fire for 3½ to 4 hours.
3 Reduce to given amount; when ready, the glaze should be sticky to the touch.
4 Pour in jars when hot.
5 Store for use as required.

GRAVIES

17 Jus – Gravy

The importance of accompanying simpler dishes, such as roasts, with good gravy is frequently underestimated. In modest establishments too great a reliance is often placed on packaged aids rather than on correct methods that capture the true flavour of the main item which the gravy accompanies. When roasting small joints or birds, it is important to place them on a bed of roots and aromates embodying the principle of the mirepoix and matignon (see Recipes 3 and 4), for this enriches the residue after cooking and improves the gravy.

Jus lié – *thickened gravy*
See Recipe 30.

18 Jus rôti – Roast gravy

500 *ml* (1 *pt*) *brown stock*

1 After cooking the joint, poultry or game, pour away surplus fat, retaining the residue.
2 Add a pinch of salt and pour in sufficient brown stock for the number of persons.
3 Strain through muslin.
4 Remove all fat.

Note. Never add flour to jus rôti to thicken.

THICKENINGS AND BINDING AGENTS

Most sauces are given body and consistency by combining their flavoursome liquor with a thickening agent. Similarly, thickening agents can be used to give body to soups. They may, therefore, be regarded as basic or fundamental kitchen preparations.

19 Beurre manié – Manipulated butter [to thicken 1 litre (1 quart)]

    120 g (4 oz) butter   90 g (3 oz) sifted flour

1 Mix the butter and sieved flour together with palette knife to a smooth paste.
2 Add to the liquor to be thickened, just prior to service.
3 Avoid boiling after addition of beurre manié as the sauce would acquire a disagreeable taste.

Used for quick liaison, i.e., matelotes, vegetables and fish sauces.

20 Fécule thickening – Potato-starch thickening [to thicken 1 litre (1 quart)]

    45 g (1½ oz) fécule   125 ml (¼ pt) cold water

1 Dilute fécule in water to a smooth paste.
2 Strain into boiling-liquid and simmer.

Used to thicken sauces and gravy (jus lié).

21 Liaison œuf et crème – Egg and cream liaison [to thicken 1 litre (1 quart)]

    250 ml (½ pt) fresh cream   3 egg yolks

1 Beat egg yolks with cream.
2 Add to boiling liquid but do not allow to boil after the addition.
3 Mix well and draw to side of fire.

Note. Liaison may also be effected with egg yolks alone. Soups may similarly be enriched with butter and cream: 30 g (1 oz) butter, 125 ml (1 gill) cream to 1 litre (1 quart) soup.

Used for chicken and fish sauces, entrées, and soups, etc.

22 Liaison au sang – Blood thickening [to thicken 1 litre (1 quart)]

    500 ml (1 pt) blood   125 ml (1 gill) water

1 This liaison is added at the last minute.
2 Mix blood with water with a whisk.
3 Add to the sauce and draw to the side of the stove-top away from the intense heat.

Used for thickening game soups and dishes such as jugged hare.

ROUX

Although equal quantities of fat and flour are given in roux recipes following, reducing the proportion of flour [to 100 g (3½ oz) in these recipes] results, in the author's experience, in a smoother sauce.

23 Roux blanc – White roux [to thicken 1 litre (1 quart) of white sauce)]

    120 g (4 oz) flour   120 g (4 oz) butter or margarine

1 Melt the butter in a thick saucepan.
2 Sift and add the flour; mix well with wooden spoon.

3 The cooking must be limited to a few minutes, sufficient only to do away with the taste of the flour.
4 Cook on low heat.

Used for white sauces, Béchamel and derivatives.

24 Roux blond – Blond roux [to thicken 1 litre (1 quart of velouté sauce)]

   120 *g* (4 *oz*) *flour*   120 *g* (4 *oz*) *butter or margarine*

1 Melt the butter in a thick saucepan.
2 Sift the flour and add to the butter and mix well with wooden spoon.
3 Cook on low heat.
4 Cooking must cease as soon as the colour of the roux begins to change.

Used for veloutés.

25 Roux brun – Brown roux [to thicken 1 litre (1 quart)]

   120 *g* (4 *oz*) *flour*   120 *g* (4 *oz*) *dripping*

1 Melt the fat, add the flour using a thick saucepan.
2 Place in moderate oven or on side of stove.
3 Stir often with wooden spoon until a light brown colour and a scent resembling hazel nut exudes.

Note. If the roux is cooked too quickly the flour burns. In addition to this fault imparting a burnt taste it also makes it difficult to obtain the right consistency.

Used for Espagnole and other brown sauces.

SAUCES

The importance of sauces in good cookery hardly needs emphasis. The true value of most important dishes depends upon the contribution made by the sauce. Some sauces may be regarded as a vehicle for capturing the basic flavour of the food they are to enhance. While certain sauces may act as a foil, others may complement a food.

Common and obvious examples of the way in which a sauce completes a dish is where a rich, fatty food such as pork or goose is off-set by a sharper or more piquant sauce; or contrarywise, where a completely fatless food, like white fish, is enriched by the presence of an emollient sauce in which butter or oil has been emulsified. It is natural, therefore, that the basic sauces should be regarded as fonds de cuisine – foundations of cookery.

Sauces are so implicit in good professional cookery that excellent, simple sauces have been adapted by a variety of means including changes of flavours and colour to meet the needs of different dishes and foods. The principal sauces from which variants are derived have come to be regarded as basic or mother sauces. To master the making of principal 'mother' sauces, that also have their

own uses in many dishes, is vital to the development of a full, cookery reper-tory. The main kinds of basic sauces are:
i Roux-thickened white sauce such as Béchamel and Velouté.
ii Roux-thickened brown sauce such as Espagnole and demi-glace.
iii Warm egg and butter-emulsion sauce, basic Hollandaise.
iv Cold egg and oil-emulsion sauce, basic Mayonnaise. (See 'Larder Pre-parations' Chapter 2.)
v The 'hard' sauce or flavoured cold butter, such as Maître d'Hôtel.

Note. There are, of course, sauces such as vinaigrette and sweet sauces which are not made from the foregoing basics; just as jus liés, thickened gravies, are similarly fundamental to good cookery but not derivative from the foregoing. Some of the miscellaneous savoury sauces are used sufficiently frequently by themselves, or in combination with other sauces, for them to be listed below as secondary or non-derivative sauces. The principal basic sauces in common use are:

BASIC SAUCES FROM STOCKS

VELOUTÉS

Veloutés classified here as derived from stocks are also regarded as con-stituting a basic white sauce, though Béchamel and Butter Sauce have wider use in forming true white sauces.

26 Velouté de veau – Veal velouté [to yield 1 litre (1 quart)]

1·5 *l* (1½ *qt*) *veal stock* (*Recipe 9*)	12 *ground peppercorns*	120 *g* (4 *oz*) *butter or*
1 *bouquet garni*	120 *g* (4 *oz*) *sifted flour*	*margarine*
		15 *g* (½ *oz*) *mushroom peelings*

1 Bring the veal stock to the boil.
2 Make a blond roux (Recipe 24).
3 Allow roux to cool slightly and mix in stock slowly using a wooden spoon.
4 Continue to boil, skimming carefully.
5 Add peppercorns, mushroom peelings and bouquet garni.
6 Simmer over low heat until reduced to 1 litre (1 quart), strain and reserve for use.

27 Velouté de volaille – Chicken velouté [to yield 1 litre (1 quart)]
Ingredients and method as for Velouté de veau, substituting white chicken stock (Recipe 11).

BROWN SAUCES

28 Espagnole – Basic brown sauce [to yield 1 litre (1 quart)]

120 *g* (4 *oz*) *dripping*	120 *g* (4 *oz*) *diced carrots*	2·5 *l* (2½ *qt*) *estouffade*
120 *g* (4 *oz*) *flour*		480 *g* (1 *lb*) *fresh tomatoes or*
30 *g* (1 *oz*) *diced fat bacon*	120 *g* (4 *oz*) *diced onions*	125 *ml* (1 *gill*) *tomato purée*
		15 *g* (½ *oz*) *mushroom peelings*

1 Make a brown roux (Recipe 25).
2 Allow to cool and add the boiling estouffade, slowly mixing to smoothness with a wooden spoon.
3 Bring slowly to the boil. Add tomato.
4 Remove all scum by careful skimming.
5 Fry the bacon to extract the fat. Add the vegetables and cook to a golden-brown colour.
6 Add the vegetables to the sauce and simmer 4 hours, skimming frequently.
7 Strain through fine chinois and reserve for use.

29 Demi-glace – Half-glaze (or refined basic brown sauce) [to yield 1 litre (1 quart)]

1 *l* (1 *qt*) *estouffade* (*Recipe* 8)   25 *ml* (1 *fluid oz*) *truffle essence*
1 *l* (1 *qt*) *espagnole* (*Recipe* 28)

1 Mix together both liquids and essence.
2 Reduce by boiling to 1 litre (1 quart).
3 Strain and season.

SECONDARY OR NON-DERIVATIVE SAUCES

30 Jus lié – Thickened gravy [to thicken 1 litre (1 quart)]

1·5 *l* (1½ *qt*) *brown veal*   15 *g* (½ *oz*) *diced bacon* 45 *g* (1½ *oz*) *fécule*
 stock (*Recipe* 10)   *rind*   12 *crushed pepper-*
120 *g* (4 *oz*) *meat*   1 *bouquet garni*   *corns*
 trimmings   240 *g* (½ *lb*) *fresh*   30 *g* (1 *oz*) *mushroom*
60 *g* (2 *oz*) *diced onions*   *mashed tomatoes or*   *peelings*
60 *g* (2 *oz*) *diced carrots*   125 *ml* (1 *gill*) *tomato*   *salt*
                                   purée

1 Fry off the bacon rind to extract the fat.
2 Continuing to fry, add the diced meat and allow to brown.
3 Add the vegetables and colour slightly.
4 Strain off surplus fat.
5 Add the meat and vegetables to the stock. Bring to the boil and skim.
6 Add the bouquet garni, tomato, peppercorns and mushroom peelings.
7 Simmer 45 minutes, skimming frequently.
8 Dilute fécule with water and add to the liquid; re-boil, skim, season and strain through fine chinois.

31 Sauce bigarade [to yield 1 litre (1 quart)]

Juice of 3 *oranges*   *zest of* 1 *orange*   1 *l* (2 *pts*) *thickened braising*
Juice of ½ *lemon*   *zest of* 1 *lemon*   *stock**

1 Strain the braising-liquor and remove all fat.
2 Add the orange and lemon-juice and reduce to 1 litre (2 pints).
3 Strain through a muslin cloth.
4 Cut the zest of orange and lemon into fine julienne and blanch for 2 minutes.
5 Season the sauce and add the julienne of lemon and orange.

   * This sauce is used to accompany braised and poêléd ducklings and the braising-stock, being thickened, constitutes a sauce.

32 Sauce kari – Curry sauce [to yield 1 litre (1 quart)]

60 g (2 oz) margarine or butter
60 g (2 oz) sifted flour
15 g (½ oz) curry powder
65 ml (½ gill) tomato purée
15 g (½ oz) chopped chutney
1 finely chopped apple

90 g (3 oz) finely-chopped onions
125 ml (1 gill) cold milk
7 g (¼ oz) desiccated coconut
65 ml (½ gill) warm, fresh cream

¼ clove garlic
1 bouquet garni
salt and pepper
pinch cayenne
1 l (1 qt) brown stock (Recipe 8)

1 Sweat the onions in butter.
2 Add the curry powder continuing to sweat.
3 Blend in the flour and cook for a few minutes at the side of the stove (or over low heat).
4 Mix in thoroughly the tomato purée.
5 Add the stock; mix smoothly; allow to boil and skim.
6 Add the crushed garlic, bouquet garni, chopped apple and chutney.
7 Simmer 1 hour skimming frequently; then remove bouquet garni.
8 Soak the coconut in the cold milk for ½ hour and squeeze the resulting liquid out.
9 Add this coconut liquor to the sauce and simmer for a further few moments; season and finish off with cream.
10 The sauce need not be strained.

Note. This is not intended to represent a true Indian curry but typifies the curry-flavoured sauce used not only alone but to flavour other sauces in professional Western cookery.

33 Sauce provençale I

60 g (2 oz) finely-chopped shallots
1 clove crushed garlic

15 g (½ oz) fines herbes
100 ml (⅛ pt) olive oil
125 ml (¼ pt) white wine

120 g (¼ lb) butter
725 g (1½ lb) tomato concassé

1 Sweat off the shallots and garlic in the oil.
2 Add the wine and make a reduction.
3 Add the tomato concassé and fines herbes.
4 Cook for approximately 10 minutes on the side of the stove.
5 Blend in the butter and season; do not strain.

33a Sauce provençale II

60 g (2 oz) finely-chopped shallots
1 clove crushed garlic
125 ml (¼ pt) white wine

480 g (1 lb) tomato concassé
250 ml (½ pt) tomato sauce

120 g (¼ lb) butter
15 g (½ oz) fines herbes
15 g (½ oz) meat glaze (Recipe 13)

1 Sweat off the shallots in 30 g (1 oz) butter.
2 Make a reduction of the wine
3 Add the tomato concassé and garlic and stew for a few minutes.

4 Add the tomato sauce and fines herbes and simmer for 10 minutes.
5 Add the meat glaze.
6 Blend in the butter and adjust seasoning; do not strain.

34 Sauce tomate – Tomato sauce

60 g (2 oz) diced fat pork	240 g (½ lb) tomato	7 g (¼ oz) sugar
15 g (½ oz) butter	purée or	1 sprig thyme
60 g (2 oz) flour	1 kg (2 lb) raw mashed	1 clove crushed garlic
1½ diced onions	tomatoes	salt and pepper
45 g (1½ oz) diced	1·25 l (2½ pt) fond blanc	1 bay-leaf
carrots	(Recipe 6)	

Note. When using fresh tomato in lieu of purée, reduce quantity of fond blanc (white stock) to 750 *ml* (1½ pt).

1 Fry the diced pork in butter.
2 Add the vegetables and sweat on.
3 Add the flour, thus making a blond roux.
4 Add the tomatoes and mix well.
5 Blend in the stock; boil and skim.
6 Add the garlic, herbes and seasoning.
7 Cook under cover in a moderate oven for 1½ hours.
8 Pass through chinois; butter the surface to avoid the formation of a skin.

DERIVATIVE BROWN SAUCES

In the following group of sauces, demi-glace plays an important role, although in some instances sauces are 'doubly derivative'; e.g., sauce Charcutière which is an elaboration of sauce Robert.

35 Sauce bordelaise

60 g (2 oz) finely-chopped	1 sprig of thyme	30 g (1 oz) diced marrow
shallots	30 g (1 oz) meat	750 ml (1½ pt) demi-glace
250 ml (½ pt) red wine	glaze	(Recipe 29)
6 crushed peppercorns	(Recipe 13)	90 g (3 oz) butter
1 bay-leaf		

1 Sweat off the shallots and peppercorns in 30 g (1 oz) butter.
2 Add the thyme and bay-leaf and make a reduction of the wine.
3 Add the demi-glace and simmer to 500 ml (1 pint).
4 Strain the sauce and add the diced marrow which has been soaked in a little warm stock.
5 Add butter, meat glaze, and season.

36 Sauce bourguignonne

500 ml (1 pt) demi-glace (Recipe 29)	250 ml (½ pt) red wine
12 crushed peppercorns	30 g (1 oz) finely-chopped shallots
1 bay-leaf	1 sprig thyme
120 g (4 oz) butter	

1 Sweat off the shallots and peppercorns in 30 g (1 oz) butter.
2 Add bay-leaf and thyme, pour on red wine and make a reduction.

3 Moisten with demi-glace and reduce to 375 ml (¾ pint).

4 Strain the sauce; blend in the remainder of butter and season.

Note. See also Sauce bourguignonne for fish in Chapter 5, Recipe 381.

37 Sauce charcutière

> 500 *ml* (1 *pt*) *sauce Robert* (*recipe* 49) 30 *g* (1 *oz*) *julienne of gherkins*

Toss the julienne of gherkins in a little butter and add to the sauce Robert as a garnish; do not strain.

38 Sauce chasseur

> 250 *ml* (½ *pt*) *demi-glace* (*Recipe* 29)
> 125 *ml* (¼ *pt*) *tomato sauce* (*Recipe* 34)
> 15 *g* (½ *oz*) *meat glaze* (*Recipe* 13)
>
> 240 *g* (½ *lb*) *tomato concass*; 8 *medium mushrooms* 15 *g* (½ *oz*) *diced onions* 15 *g* (½ *oz*) *fines herbes*
>
> 1 *small liqueur-glass brandy* 250 *ml* (½ *pt*) *white wine* 90 *g* (3 *oz*) *butter seasoning*

1 Sweat the onions in 30 g (1 oz) butter.

2 Peel and slice mushrooms and add to onions and cook for a few minutes.

3 Make a reduction of the wine and brandy.

4 Add the tomato concassé, moisten with demi-glace and tomato sauce and simmer for 10 minutes.

5 Add the meat glaze and fines herbes.

6 Thicken with butter – season but do not strain.

39 Sauce Châteaubriand

> 60 *g* (2 *oz*) *finely-chopped shallots*
> 60 *g* (2 *oz*) *mushroom peelings*
> 1 *sprig thyme*
>
> 2 *bay leaves* 180 *g* (6 *oz*) *parsley butter* (*Recipe* 89) 15 *g* (½ *oz*) *chopped tarragon*
>
> 500 *ml* (1 *pt*) *demi-glace* (*Recipe* 29) 250 *ml* (½ *pt*) *white wine*

1 Sweat off shallots in 30 g (1 oz) butter.

2 Add the bay-leaves, thyme and make a reduction of the wine.

3 Moisten with demi-glace and reduce by one-third.

4 Strain, blend with the parsley butter.

5 Season and garnish with the chopped tarragon.

6 Add the mushroom peelings while making the reduction of demi-glace.

40 Sauce diable – Devilled sauce

> 60 *g* (2 *oz*) *finely-chopped shallots*
> 12 *crushed peppercorns*
> 90 *g* (3 *oz*) *butter*
> 165 *ml* (⅓ *pt*) *white wine*
>
> 165 *ml* (⅓ *pt*) *wine vinegar* 375 *ml* (¾ *pt*) *half-glace* (*Recipe* 29)
>
> 1 *sprig thyme seasoning* pinch cayenne pepper 1 *bay-leaf*

1 Sweat off shallots and peppercorns in 30 g (1 oz) butter.

2 Add the thyme and bay-leaf.

3 Make a reduction of the wine and vinegar.

4 Add the demi-glace and simmer to 250 ml (½ pint).
5 Strain and season – blend in the butter.

41 Sauce grand veneur

30 g (1 oz) meat glaze   500 ml (1 pt) game stock   125 ml (¼ pt) fresh
  (Recipe 13)   (Recipe 12)   cream
500 ml (1 pt) sauce   3 × 20 ml spoon [4   120 g (¼ lb) butter
  poivrade   tablespoons] red-
  (Recipe 47)   currant jelly

1 Reduce sauce poivrade and game stock to 500 ml (1 pint).
2 Dissolve red-currant jelly and meat glaze in the sauce.
3 Finish with the cream and butter.

42 Sauce italienne

240 g (½ lb) dry duxelle (Recipe 101)   90 g (3 oz) butter
60 g (2 oz) diced lean cooked ham   375 ml (¾ pt) half-glaze
30 g (1 oz) finely-chopped shallots   (Recipe 29)
125 ml (¼ pt) tomato sauce (Recipe 34)   7 g (¼ oz) fines herbes
¼ clove crushed garlic

1 Sweat the shallots in 30 g (1 oz) butter.
2 Add the garlic and finely chopped ham.
3 Add the duxelle and cook for a few minutes.
4 Moisten with the two sauces.
5 Simmer for 10 minutes; skim; add the fines herbes and blend in the butter.
6 Season but do not strain.

43 Sauce lyonnaise

120 g (4 oz) thinly-sliced   125 ml (¼ pt) white   750 ml (1½ pt) demi-
  onions   wine   glace
90 g (3 oz) butter   125 ml (¼ pt) wine   (Recipe 29)
                               vinegar

1 Stew the onions gently in 60 g (2 oz) butter to a light colour.
2 Make a reduction of the wine and vinegar.
3 Moisten with the demi-glace and simmer to 500 ml (1 pint).
4 Skim and season; thicken with 30 g (1 oz) butter; do not strain.

44 Sauce madère – Madeira sauce

750 ml (1½ pt) demi-glace (Recipe 29)   60 g (2 oz) butter
100 ml (⅛ pt) Madeira wine   seasoning

1 Reduce the demi-glace to 500 ml (1 pint).
2 Add the Madeira wine.
3 Season, blend in the butter and strain.

45 Sauce Périgueux

500 ml (1 pt) sauce madère (Recipe 44)   85 ml (⅙ pt) truffle essence
90 g (3 oz) chopped truffles

Add the truffles and truffle essence to 500 ml (1 pint) of prepared sauce
madère.

46 Sauce piquante

250 ml (½ pt) sauce diable (Recipe 40)   30 g (1 oz) chopped capers
60 g (2 oz) chopped gherkins   15 g (½ oz) fines herbes

Add the chopped gherkins, capers and fines herbes to the basic sauce diable.

47 Sauce poivrade

480 g (1 lb) fine mirepoix   750 ml (1½ pt) demi-   2 bay-leaves
(Recipe 4)   glace (Recipe 29)   1 sprig thyme
120 g (4 oz) butter   ½ clove crushed garlic   30 g (1 oz) meat glaze
125 ml (¼ pt) vinegar   250 ml (½ pt) red wine   (Recipe 13)
18 crushed peppercorns

1 Fry off mirepoix in butter.
2 Make a reduction of the wine and vinegar with the bay-leaves and thyme.
3 Add the demi-glace and simmer to 500 ml (1 pint).
4 Add the peppercorns and simmer for 5 minutes.
5 Strain the sauce and skim.
6 Season and thicken with butter.

48 Sauce Reform

500 ml (1 pt) demi-glace   250 ml (½ pt) sauce   3 × 20 ml spoon [4
(Recipe 29)   poivrade (Recipe 47)   tablespoons] red-
4 chopped shallots   240 g (½ lb) butter   currant jelly
250 ml (½ pt) red wine

1 Sweat shallots in 30 g (1 oz) butter.
2 Make a reduction of the red wine.
3 Moisten with the 2 sauces and reduce to 500 ml (1 pint).
4 Add the red-currant jelly and dissolve well.
5 Season; thicken with butter (monter au beurre).
6 Strain.

Used with côtelette d'agneau (lamb cutlet Reform incorporating the following garnish: *Julienne of ham, tongue gherkin, cooked egg-white, beetroot, truffles.*

49 Sauce Robert

60 g (2 oz) finely-chopped   750 ml (1½ pt) half-   30 g (1 oz) meat glaze
onions   glaze (Recipe 29)   (Recipe 13)
165 ml (⅓ pt) white wine   5 ml spoon [1 teaspoon]   60 g (2 oz) butter
English mustard

1 Fry the onions gently in butter but do not colour.
2 Make a reduction of the white wine.
3 Add the demi-glace and reduce to 500 ml (1 pint).
4 Finish off with diluted mustard and meat glaze.
5 Blend in the butter and season; do not strain.

50 Sauce salmis

750 ml (1½ pt) demi-glace   65 ml (½ gill) truffle   240 g (½ lb) game
(Recipe 29)   essence   bones
150 g (5 oz) fine mirepoix   125 ml (¼ pt) sherry   120 g (4 oz) butter
(Recipe 4)   125 ml (¼ pt) mushroom
essence

1 Fry off the game bones and mirepoix in butter to golden colour.
2 Add the mushrooms, truffle essence, and demi-glace.
3 Reduce to 500 ml (1 pint).
4 Add the sherry and adjust the seasoning.
5 Pass through a fine chinois.

Use with venison and other game.

BASIC WHITE SAUCE

In addition to the veloutés, the following white sauces may be considered basic or mother sauces for savoury purposes and they are used to provide variants.

51 Béchamel sauce – Basic white savoury sauce [to yield 1 litre (1 quart)]

120 g (4 oz) butter	1 l (1 qt) milk	1 bouquet garni
120 g (4 oz) sifted flour	1 onion clouté	salt and pepper

1 Make an infusion by boiling the milk with the onion clouté.
2 Make a white roux (Recipe 23) with the butter and flour and allow to cool.
3 Remove the onion from the infused milk.
4 Add the milk slowly to the roux mixing with a wooden spoon to a smooth sauce.
5 Add the bouquet garni.
6 Bring to boil slowly in moderate heat.
7 Simmer 20 minutes; season, strain and cover top with greased paper.

52 Sauce au beurre – Butter sauce [to yield 1 litre (1 quart)]

60 g (2 oz) melted butter	7 g (¼ oz) salt	150 g (5 oz) butter
60 g (2 oz) sifted flour	6 egg yolks	125 ml (¼ pt) cream
1 l (1 qt) boiling water	juice of ½ lemon	

1 Melt butter and stir in flour in a thick pan over low heat and without allowing to cook.
2 Add the boiling water with salt added and whisk to make a smooth sauce but do not boil.
3 Immediately add the egg yolks mixed with the cream and then follow with the lemon-juice and mix thoroughly.
4 Finish off the sauce by adding walnut-size pieces of butter, blending well.

DERIVATIVE WHITE SAUCES (FROM BÉCHAMEL AND VELOUTÉ)

53 Sauce Albufera (or Sauce Ivoire) [to yield 1 litre (1 quart)]

1 l (1 qt) sauce suprême (Recipe 63)   45 g (1½ oz) meat glaze (Recipe 13)

Add the warm meat glaze to sauce suprême and strain.

54 Sauce allemande [to yield 1 litre (1 quart)]

750 ml (1½ pt) white veal stock (Recipe 9)
750 ml (1½ pt) veal velouté (Recipe 26)

1 bay-leaf
juice of ½ lemon
5 egg yolks
60 g (2 oz) mushroom peelings

250 ml (½ pt) fresh cream
salt and cayenne pepper
24 crushed peppercorns

1 Mix stock with velouté and add peppercorns, bay-leaf and mushroom peelings.
2 Reduce liquid to 1 litre (1 quart).
3 Season with salt, cayenne pepper and lemon juice.
4 Draw to side of stove.
5 Beat egg yolks with cream and add to sauce.
6 Strain and cover with buttered paper.
7 Do not allow to boil after adding egg yolks and cream.

55 Sauce aurore [to yield 1 litre (1 quart)]

750 ml (1½ pt) chicken velouté (Recipe 27)
180 g (6 oz) butter

125 ml (¼ pt) fresh cream
salt and pepper

250 ml (½ pt) basic tomato sauce (Recipe 34)

1 Mix chicken velouté and basic tomato sauce together.
2 Simmer for a few minutes; add cream.
3 Season and pass through tammy-cloth.
4 Blend in the butter.

56 Sauce Bonnefoy [to yield 1 litre (1 quart)]

60 g (2 oz) finely-chopped shallots
250 ml (½ pt) white wine
150 g (5 oz) butter

250 ml (½ pt) chicken velouté (Recipe 27)
5 ml spoon (1 teaspoon) chopped tarragon

1 Sweat off the shallots in 30 g (1 oz) butter.
2 Add the white wine and reduce to half.
3 Moisten the reduction with the chicken velouté and reduce to 125 ml (¼ pint).
4 Rub through a tammy-cloth.
5 Blend in the butter slowly, garnish with chopped tarragon and season.

Serve separately with grilled fish or grilled white meat.

57 Sauce hongroise [to yield 1 litre (1 quart)]

90 g (3 oz) finely-chopped onions
250 ml (½ pt) white wine
1 l (1 qt) well-reduced chicken velouté (Recipe 27)

120 g (4 oz) butter
15 g (½ oz) paprika
1 small bouquet garni
250 ml (½ pt) cream

1 Take 30 g (1 oz) of the butter and gently cook the onions without colouring.
2 Add the paprika to the onions and cook for a few minutes.
3 Add the white wine and the bouquet garni and reduce the wine to one-third of its volume.

4 Add the velouté and simmer for approximately 10 minutes.
5 Add the cream; blend in the butter.
6 Strain and season.

Note. When required for fish, substitute fish velouté for chicken.

Sauce Ivoire
see Recipe 53.

58 Sauce Mornay [to yield 1 litre (1 quart)]

1 *l* (1 *qt*) *Béchamel*	65 *ml* (⅛ *pt*) *fresh cream*	*salt and pepper*
(*Recipe* 51)	2 *egg yolks*	*pinch cayenne*
60 *g* (2 *oz*) *grated gruyère*	60 *g* (2 *oz*) *grated*	
cheese	*parmesan*	

1 Stir the cheese into the Béchamel with a whisk until the cheese is melted and thoroughly blended.
2 Effect a liaison with the egg yolks and cream and add this at the last minute to the sauce.

The above sauce is used for vegetables and for general purposes. If required for fish, a little fish glaze should be added.

59 Sauce poulette [to yield 1 litre (1 quart)]

1 *l* (1 *qt*) *sauce allemande* (*Recipe* 54)	5 *ml spoon* [1 *teaspoon*] *chopped*
120 *g* (4 *oz*) *butter*	*parsley*
strained juice of ½ *lemon*	25 *ml* (1 *fluid oz*) *mushroom liquor*

Blend the butter, parsley, lemon juice and mushroom liquor into the sauce allemande.

60 Sauce soubise

1 *kg* (2 *lb*) *onions*	125 *ml* (¼ *pt*) *cream*	5 *ml spoon* [1 *teaspoon*]
250 *ml* (½ *pt*) *thick*	120 *g* (4 *oz*) *butter*	*caster sugar*
Béchamel (*Recipe* 51)		*salt and pepper*

1 Chop the onions finely.
2 Blanch for 3 minutes and drain well.
3 Stew the onions in the butter but do not allow them to colour.
4 Add the Béchamel; mix well; season and add the sugar.
5 Cook gently for ½ hour; rub first through a fine sieve and then through a tammy-cloth.
6 Finish off by adding cream.

61 Soubise au riz

1 *kg* (2 *lb*) *onions*	120 *g* (¼ *lb*) *Carolina*	120 *g* (4 *oz*) *butter*
350 *g* (¾ *lb*) *streaky bacon*	*rice*	125 *ml* (¼ *pt*) *cream*
rashers	500 *ml* (1 *pt*) *white stock*	*salt and pepper*
5 *ml spoon* [1 *teaspoon*]	(*Recipe* 6)	
caster sugar		

1 Chop the onions finely; blanch for 3 minutes and drain well.
2 Stew the blanched onions in 60 g (2 oz) butter but do not allow to colour.

3 Line a medium stew-pan with rashers of bacon.
4 Mix the onions with rice and season with sugar, salt and pepper.
5 Place the onions and rice in the bacon-lined pan; add the stock; cover with
   lid and cook until the purée stage in a slow oven.
6 Pass this mixture through a fine sieve.
7 Finish off with cream and butter.

62 Sauce soubise tomatée

> Basic recipe sauce soubise   2 × 15 ml spoon [2 tablespoons] tomato
>   (Recipe 60)   pulp
> 150 ml (¼ pt) fresh tomato purée ¼ teaspoon paprika

Add the three additional ingredients to the basic sauce soubise.

63 Sauce suprême

> 1·5 l (1½ qt) chicken   500 ml (½ qt) fond de   125 ml (¼ pt) mushroom
>   velouté (Recipe 27)   volaille   stock
> 250 ml (½ pt) fresh cream   (Recipe 11)   120 g (4 oz) butter
>   (Recipe 11)

1 Reduce the chicken stock to ⅓ of its volume.
2 Add the velouté and mushroom stock. Reduce the total liquid to 1 litre (1
  quart).
3 Blend in the cream and butter.
4 Season and pass through tammy-cloth.

ENGLISH-STYLE WHITE SAUCE DERIVATIVES

64 Caper Sauce

> 500 ml (1 pt) velouté (as   60 g (2 oz) butter   seasoning
>   Recipe 26 but using   125 ml (1 gill)   30 g (1 oz) capers
>   mutton stock)   cream   (whole)

1 Add the whole capers to the velouté.
2 Blend in the butter and cream; season.

Note. When making caper sauce for fish use 500 ml (1 pint) of Béchamel in
place of mutton velouté.

65 Cream Sauce

> 500 ml (1 pt) Béchamel (Recipe 51)   60 g (2 oz) butter
> 125 ml (¼ pt) fresh cream   seasoning

1 Add the cream to the Béchamel and reduce to 500 ml (1 pint).
2 Add the butter, season and strain.

66 Egg sauce

> 500 ml (1 pt) Béchamel   60 g (2 oz) butter   125 ml (1 gill) cream
>   (Recipe 51)   3 hard-boiled eggs   seasoning

1 Chop the hard-boiled eggs small.
2 Add the eggs to the Béchamel.
3 Blend in the cream and butter.
4 Season.

67 Mustard sauce I – (English style)

> 500 *ml* (1 *pt*) *Béchamel*   30 *g* (1 *oz*) *butter*   15 *ml* spoon [1 *table-*
> (*Recipe* 51)   *salt and pepper*   *spoon*] *mustard*
> 25 *ml* [1 *fluid oz*] *water*

1 Dilute mustard in 25 ml (1 fluid oz) water.
2 Place in sauté-pan and reduce by half.
3 Add the Béchamel and mix well.
4 Strain, blend in butter and season; heat but do not boil.
5 Keep in bain-marie; butter the top to avoid skin formation.

68 Mustard sauce II – (Classic style)

Proceed as Method I above but substitute 500 ml (1 pint) of butter sauce (Recipe 52) for the pint of Béchamel.

69 White onion sauce

> 500 *ml* (1 *pt*) *Béchamel*   30 *g* (1 *oz*) *butter*   *salt and pepper*
> (*Recipe* 51)   125 *ml* (1 *gill*) *cream*   *little grated nutmeg*
> 120 *g* (4 *oz*) *diced onions*   250 *ml* (½ *pt*) *water*

1 Simmer the onions with the water and butter until soft.
2 Add the cooked onions and liquid to 500 ml (1 pint) of stiff Béchamel.
3 Warm the cream and add to the sauce.
4 Season.
5 Serve without straining.

70 Parsley sauce I

> 500 *ml* (1 *pt*) *cream sauce* (*Recipe* 65)   30 *g* (1 *oz*) *butter*
> 15 *g* (½ *oz*) *blanched chopped parsley*   *seasoning*

1 Blanch and chop the parsley.
2 Blend the cream and butter into the cream sauce and season.
3 Add the blanched chopped parsley.
Note. Blanching the parsley ensures that the sauce has a nice colour.

71 Sauce persil – Parsley sauce II

> 500 *ml* (1 *pt*) *butter sauce*   15 *g* (½ *oz*) *blanched chopped*
> (*Recipe* 52)   *parsley*

Mix all ingredients; do not boil.

Note. Further white sauce derivatives are included in Chapter 5.

HOLLANDAISE SAUCE AND DERIVATIVES

In the preparation of warm dishes, Hollandaise is the mother of the classic egg-and-butter emulsion sauces; just as in cold cookery, Mayonnaise (see Chapter 2) is the parent egg-and-oil emulsion sauce. Hollandaise and some of its derivatives are extensively used with fish dishes such as Poached turbot Sauce Hollandaise, and they are also widely used with vegetables and garnishes.

72 Sauce hollandaise

480 g (1 *lb*) *melted butter*	50 *ml* (2 *fluid oz*) *water*	*pinch cayenne*
6 *egg yolks*	12 *crushed peppercorns*	*pinch salt*
25 *ml* (1 *fluid oz*) *vinegar*	*juice of* ½ *lemon*	*and pepper*

1 Reduce vinegar and peppercorns in a sauteuse.
2 Allow to cool and add cold water.
3 Whisk in the egg and cook to ribbon stage, whisking all the time in the bain-marie.
4 Add the melted butter in a thin stream, whisking all the time.
5 Add the lemon juice and season.
6 Strain through muslin; keep warm.

Note. When the sauce is finished do not expose it to fierce heat or it will curdle.

DERIVATIVES OF SAUCE HOLLANDAISE

73 Sauce béarnaise

300 g (10 *oz*) *melted* *butter*	60 *ml* [4 *tablespoons*] *vinegar*	15 g (½ *oz*) *chopped tarragon*
5 *egg yolks*	15 *ml* spoon [1 *table-spoon*] *water*	*juice of* ½ *lemon*
12 *crushed peppercorns*	30 g (1 *oz*) *tarragon*	7 g (¼ *oz*) *chopped chervil*
cayenne pepper	*stalks*	
15 g (½ *oz*) *finely-chopped shallots*		*salt*

1 Make a reduction of the vinegar, peppercorns, shallots and tarragon stalks.
2 Cool pan, add water and egg yolks.
3 Cook to ribbon stage in the bain-marie, whisking all the time.
4 Add the melted butter slowly, whisking to form an emulsion.
5 Season with lemon juice, salt and cayenne.
6 Strain through muslin.
7 Garnish with the chopped tarragon and chervil.

74 Sauce Choron

Basic béarnaise (*Recipe* 73) *plus one-third pint fresh tomato purée.**

Mix warm tomato purée well with béarnaise.

* *To make fresh tomato purée.* Blanch tomatoes, remove all seeds, toss in butter and rub through fine sieve.

Sauce divine:

To sauce hollandaise (Recipe 72) add a reduction of sherry (1 sherry glassful reduced to half). Fold in 125 ml (¼ pint) whipped cream before serving.

75 Sauce Foyot (or Sauce valoise)

> *Basic béarnaise (Recipe 73) plus* 3 × 15 *ml spoon* [3 *tablespoons*] *of warm meat glaze (Recipe 13).*

Blend the meat glaze with Béarnaise and put a thread of meat glaze on top before serving.

76 Sauce maltaise

> *Basic hollandaise   juice of 2 small blood   grated zest of ½ orange*
> *(Recipe 72)   oranges*

Add the strained orange juice and grated zest to basic hollandaise.

77 Sauce mousseline

> *Basic hollandaise (Recipe 72) plus 125 ml (¼ pint) stiffly whipped fresh cream.*

Fold cream gently into hollandaise sauce.

78 Sauce noisette

> *Basic hollandaise (Recipe 72) plus 60 g (2 oz) beurre noisette (Recipe 82).*

Blend in the warm noisette butter with hollandaise just before serving.

79 Sauce valoise

(As Sauce Foyot, Recipe 75 above)

WARM BUTTERS

Butter is widely used as an emollient and as a flavoursome accompaniment with many vegetable, fish, meat, and poultry dishes in good cookery. Therefore, in effect, prepared butters may be classified as sauces.

80 Beurre fondu – Melted butter

> 120 *g* (¼ *lb*) *best butter   few drops lemon juice*

1 Melt butter slowly, add lemon juice.
2 Strain off the whey.

81 Beurre noir – Black butter

> 120 *g* (4 *oz*) *butter   juice of ½ lemon*
> 15 *g* (½ *oz*) *chopped parsley   15 ml spoon* [1 *tablespoon*] *vinegar*

1 Brown the butter in a frying-pan.
2 Add the vinegar lemon juice, and parsley.

82 Beurre noisette

120 *g* (4 *oz*) *butter*   *juice of* ½ *lemon*

Brown butter in a frying-pan and add lemon juice.

83 Beurre meunière

Same as noisette plus a little chopped parsley.

Note. It is sometimes the custom when using beurre meunière to surround the article with a thread of jus lié before pouring the beurre meunière on top. This constitutes a type of meunière sauce.

84 Clarified butter

Though clarified butter is used more as a cooking medium than as an accompaniment, its function may conveniently be noted here. This form of butter is cooked slowly until all the whey in the butter has evaporated, and the pure butter-fat is separated from any milk solids. Clarified butter is used for making omelettes and for fine types of griddle-frying.

BEURRE COMPOSÉ

Composed butters or 'Hard sauces'. Butter blended with other flavouring agents is widely used, particularly to accompany grilled meats and fish. In most cases the butter, when completed with its additives, is rolled in grease-proof or butter paper into a cylindrical shape and chilled. Roundels are sliced off as required. These slices are normally served in a sauce-boat containing iced water. (For butters with fish flavourings, see the section on fish sauces in Chapter 5.)

85 Beurre Bercy I

30 *g* (1 *oz*) *finely-chopped shallots*   125 *ml* (¼ *pt*) *white wine*
30 *g* (1 *oz*) *meat glaze (Recipe* 13)   5 *ml spoon* [1 *teaspoon*] *chopped*
240 *g* (½ *lb*) *butter*   *parsley*
30 *g* (1 *oz*) *diced marrow*   *juice of* ¼ *lemon*

1 Cream the butter and soften marrow in a little warm stock.
2 Reduce the shallots in the white wine, allow pan to cool.
3 Blend in the butter, marrow, meat glaze, parsley, and lemon juice.
4 Strain marrow before adding.

Note. This butter should not be melted and is used for grilled meats.

86 Beurre Bercy II

120 *g* (4 *oz*) *butter*   15 *g* (½ *oz*) *chopped*   30 *g* (1 *oz*) *chopped shallots*
5 *ml spoon* [1 *teaspoon*]   *parsley*   *pinch cayenne*
   meat glaze   ¼ *clove chopped*   *juice of* ½ *lemon*
                              garlic

1. Blanch and refresh shallots.

2 Work the shallots, garlic, cayenne, parsley, meat glaze, and butter together.
3 Roll in greaseproof paper and keep until required.

Used for escargots – snails.

87 Beurre diable – Devilled butter

120 g (4 oz) butter	*2·5 ml [½ teaspoon]*	*juice of ½ lemon*
2·5 ml spoon [½ teaspoon]	*curry powder*	*pinch cayenne*
paprika pepper		

1 Mix all ingredients well.
2 Roll in greaseproof paper and keep until required.

88 Beurre echalote – Shallot butter

120 g (4 oz) finely-chopped shallots	*juice of ½ lemon*
120 g (4 oz) butter	*pinch of cayenne pepper*

1 Blanch and refresh shallots.
2 Work shallots into butter with lemon juice and cayenne pepper.
3 Roll in greaseproof paper and keep until required.

89 Beurre maître d'hôtel – Parsley butter

120 g (4 oz) butter	*15 g (½ oz) chopped parsley*
juice of ½ lemon	*pinch of cayenne pepper*

1 Work the lemon juice, parsley, and cayenne into the butter.
2 Roll in greaseproof paper and keep until required.

90 Beurre Madras

120 g (4 oz) butter	*juice of ½ lemon*
60 g (2 oz) chopped chutney	*pinch of cayenne pepper*

1 Pound the chutney and butter.
2 Add lemon juice, cayenne, and salt.
3 Roll in greased paper and keep in refrigerator till required.

91 Beurre de moutarde – Mustard butter

120 g (4 oz) butter	*juice of ½ lemon*
5 ml spoon [1 teaspoon] mustard	*pinch cayenne*

1 Work mustard, pepper and lemon juice into the butter.
2 Roll in greaseproof paper and leave until required.

92 Beurre Montpellier

30 g (1 oz) parsley	*7 g (¼ oz) capers*	*4 hard-boiled eggs*
60 g (2 oz) cooked	*15 g (½ oz) tarragon*	*cayenne pepper*
spinach	*and chervil*	*120 g (4 oz) butter*
2 boned anchovies	*15 g (½ oz) chives*	*2 gherkins*

1 Blanch and refresh parsley, spinach, tarragon, chives, chervil.
2 Drain well.
3 Pound the anchovies and the herbs in the mortar.
4 Add the butter, eggs, chopped gherkins, capers.
5 Pound the whole mixture to a smooth paste.
6 Rub through a medium sieve.
7 Roll in greaseproof paper, keep until required.

93 Beurre au paprika

   120 g (4 oz) butter   5 ml spoon [1 teaspoon] paprika   juice of ½ lemon

1 Work the lemon juice and paprika well into butter.
2 Roll in greaseproof paper and keep in refrigerator until required.

94 Beurre de raifort – Horse-radish butter

   120 g (4 oz) butter   juice of ½ lemon
   15 g (½ oz) horse-radish   pinch salt and cayenne pepper

1 Chop the horse-radish finely.
2 Work the butter, horse-radish, lemon juice, salt and cayenne together.
3 Roll in greaseproof paper and keep until required.

UNCLASSIFIED ENGLISH SAUCES

Although one or two of the non-classified sauces might appear in the following chapter, 'Larder Preparations', it was thought more convenient to group them together in this section. Many are known by their French designations, but they constitute a miscellaneous collection of sauces belonging to the British tradition of cookery.

95 Apple sauce – Sauce pommes

   750 g (1½ lb) apples   30 g (1 oz) sugar   juice of ¼ lemon
   30 g (1 oz) butter   125 ml (1 gill) water

1 Peel and core apples and cut.
2 Add the water.
3 Cook quickly under cover till soft.
4 Pass through a medium sieve.
5 Add the butter, lemon juice and mix well.

The sauce may be served hot or cold as appropriate with hot or cold roast pork, duck, goose.

96 Bread sauce

   500 ml (1 pt) milk   1 onion clouté   salt and pepper
   90 g (3 oz) breadcrumbs   60 g (2 oz) butter

   Boil milk with onion clouté.

2 Remove the onion and stir in the crumbs; mix well for the sauce must be of a smooth texture.
3 Simmer for a few minutes at the side of the stove.
4 Blend in the butter and season.
5 Keep warm in the bain-marie.
6 Cover with butter paper.

Served warm with roast poultry or feathered game (though butter-fried breadcrumbs are a preferred alternative with game).

97 Cranberry sauce – Sauce airelles

480 g (1 *lb*) *cranberries*   250 *ml* (2 *gills*) *water*
45 g (1½ *oz*) *caster sugar*   *pinch salt*

1 Wash cranberries.
2 Add the sugar, water, and salt to cranberries.
3 Cook quickly under cover.
4 Pass through a sieve.

The sauce may be served hot or cold. Usually accompanies turkey or game.

98 Cumberland Sauce

2·5 *ml* [½ *teaspoon*] *English mustard*   65 *ml* (½ *gill*) *orange juice*
240 g (½ *lb*) *half-melted red-currant*   *juice of* ½ *lemon*
  jelly   *zest of* ½ *orange cut in julienne*
65 *ml* (½ *gill*) *port wine*   15 g (½ *oz*) *finely-chopped shallots*

1 Place in a china bowl the half-melted red-currant jelly.
2 Add the English mustard and whisk in the port wine and the orange juice.
3 Blanch and refresh the shallots and add to the emulsion.
4 Complete the sauce with the julienne of the zest of orange.

Serve cold with cold meat (particularly venison), cold chicken or duck.

99 Horse-radish sauce – Sauce raifort

1 *stick horse-radish*   125 *ml* (¼ *pt*) *lightly*   125 *ml* (1 *gill*) *milk*
25 *ml* (1 *fluid oz*) *vinegar*   *whipped cream*   *salt and pepper*
120 g (4 *oz*) *fine white*   1 *ml* [¼ *teaspoon*] *diluted*
  breadcrumbs   *mustard*

1 Scrub and peel carefully the horse-radish.
2 Grate finely into china bowl.
3 Pour on the vinegar and mix in the mustard.
4 Soak the breadcrumbs in 125 ml (one gill) of milk.
5 Allow this mixture to stand for 1 hour.
6 Squeeze the milk from the crumbs and mix into the marinated horse-radish.
7 Fold in the cream and season.

Serve cold in sauce-boat with roast beef (hot or cold).

100 Mint sauce – Sauce à la menthe

For 1 litre (1 quart)

1 *l* (1 *qt*) *malt vinegar*   30 *g* (1 *oz*) *caster sugar*
120 *g* (4 *oz*) *chopped mint*   *juice of* ½ *lemon*

1 Pick leaves from stalks and wash well and chop finely with the sugar.
2 Add the sugar and mint to vinegar and allow to stand for 1 hour.
3 Add the lemon juice and mix well.

Serve cold with hot or cold roast lamb.

Note. If using dried mint use 45 g (1½ oz) and bring to boil in the vinegar and allow to get cold before using.

DUXELLE

Duxelle has a wide culinary use, particularly as a base for stuffing vegetables, and in completing the garnish for meat entrées, fish, and vegetable dishes. A culinary basic, Duxelle is normally part of the kitchen mis-en-place.

101 Duxelle

1 *large finely-chopped onion*   30 *g* (1 *oz*) *chopped parsley*
480 *g* (1 *lb*) *freshly-chopped*   *nutmeg, pinch salt, pepper*
  mushroom débris (stalk   30 *g* (1 *oz*) *butter* 12 *ml* (½ *fluid*
  and peel)   *oz) oil*

1 Fry the onions in butter and oil without colouring.
2 Squeeze mushrooms in kitchen cloth to remove moisture.
3 Add mushrooms to onions and continue to cook until dry.
4 Add seasoning and chopped parsley.
5 Retain in china bowl covered with buttered paper until required.

102 Duxelle for stuffing vegetables

1 Mix Duxelle with 120 *g* (¼ *lb*) white breadcrumbs, moisten with tomatéd demi-glace and white wine.
2 Flavour with crushed, chopped garlic and simmer until reduced to consistency desired.

SALPICONS

A simple *salpicon* is a single item such as chicken, diced and combined with sauce. Salpicons may be compounded of a variety of ingredients but always diced and always blended with a sauce. Mainly composed of cooked meat, poultry, and quenelles, they are commonly used to fill vol-au-vent, bouchés, croustades, etc. Combined with sauces given in previous recipes, salpicons may be considered one of the basic preparations for many different dishes. Examples of salpicon for fish are included in Chapter 5.

103 Financière

quenelles of veal	mushrooms	stoned olives
(*Recipe* 194)	sweetbread	diced ham (*lean*)
diced tongue		may be added

Sweat ingredients in butter and cohere with demi-glace (Recipe 29).

104 Godard

chicken quenelles	mushrooms	lamb's sweetbreads
(*Recipe* 194)	diced truffle	

Sweat ingredients in butter and cohere with sauce madère (Recipe 44).

105 Régence

truffles	quenelles of veal	diced white part of
	(*Recipe* 194)	boiled fowl

Sweat ingredients in butter and cohere with sauce suprême (*Recipe* 63). Garnish with sliced truffles.

106 Reine

diced, cooked chicken	truffles	sweetbreads
mushrooms		

Sweat ingredients in butter, cohere with sauce suprême (Recipe 63).

107 Royale

diced foie-gras	chicken	sweetbreads
mushrooms		

Sweat ingredients in butter, cohere with sauce crème (Recipe 65).

108 St Hubert

truffles	mushrooms	dice of cooked game

Sweat ingredients in butter and cohere with sauce salmis (Recipe 50).

109 Toulousaine

chicken quenelles	mushrooms	slices of truffle
(*Recipe* 194)	sweetbreads	

Sweat ingredients in butter, cohere with sauce suprême (Recipe 63); garnish with slices of truffle.

Note. Pre-prepared vol-au-vents, etc. may be used with any of these fillings.

2. Larder Preparations

THE LARDER or garde manger in a professional kitchen is a leading *partie* or section. Its significance is not always apparent to laymen who associate the word larder with its domestic use as a food-storing place, but it can well be described as the nerve-centre of the kitchen. The garde manger is responsible for the vital work of portioning and pre-preparing meat, fish, poultry, and game items for other sections as well as for its own function in cold cookery, buffet dishes, and salad making, hors d'œuvre preparation, and so on. As in other sections of cuisine, basic preparations and sauces are of great importance.

COLD SAUCES AND LARDER BASICS

MAYONNAISE

While mayonnaise and its derivative sauces have a widespread application in cold cookery, the use of them with hot fried and grilled fish is, of course, a major one.

110 Sauce mayonnaise [to yield 1 litre (1 quart)]

6 egg yolks	2·5 ml spoon [½ teaspoon]	5 ml spoon [1 tea-
5 ml spoon [1 teaspoon]	salt	spoon] ground
English mustard	1 l (1 qt) salad oil	pepper
65 ml (½ gill) vinegar	juice of ½ lemon	

1 Place egg yolks in basin.
2 Add half the vinegar with the salt, pepper and mustard.
3 Whisk briskly.
4 Whisking all the time add the oil in a thin stream.
5 Add the lemon juice.

Note. If the sauce becomes too thick add up to 2 × 15 ml spoon [2 tablespoons] boiling water and a little vinegar. A well-made sauce should keep its shape when heaped on a spoon.

DERIVATIVES OF SAUCE MAYONNAISE

111 Cambridge sauce [to yield 1 litre (1 quart)]

6 hard-boiled eggs	15 g (½ oz) capers
30 g (1 oz) anchovy fillets	15 g (½ oz) blanched and refreshed chervil,
7 g (¼ oz) chopped parsley	tarragon, chives
pinch cayenne pepper	1 l (1 qt) mayonnaise (Recipe 110)

Pass the hard-boiled eggs through a medium sieve.

2 Pound in a mortar to a smooth paste the following: sieved eggs, anchovies, chives, chervil and tarragon.
3 Pass the resulting purée through a fine sieve.
4 Add the mixture to 1 litre (1 qt) basic mayonnaise.
5 Mix well and season – garnish with chopped parsley.

112 Gloucester sauce [to yield 1 litre (1 quart)]

1 *l* (1 *qt*) *basic mayonnaise* (*Recipe* 110)	250 *ml* (½ *pt*) *sour cream*	15 *g* (½ *oz*) *chopped fennel*

Add to the basic mayonnaise the sour cream and chopped fennel.

Use with cold meats, particularly pork and duck.

113 Sauce remoulade [to yield 1 litre (1 quart)]

1 *l* (1 *qt*) *basic mayonnaise* (*Recipe* 110)	30 *g* (1 *oz*) *chopped capers*	10 *ml spoon* [2 *teaspoons*] *French*
15 *ml spoon* [1 *tablespoon*] *anchovy essence*	30 *g* (1 *oz*) *chopped gherkins*	(*preferably Dijon fort*) *mustard*

Add anchovy-essence, capers, gherkins, French mustard to basic mayonnaise.

Use with cold eggs, fried fish, grilled meats.

114 Sauce tartare [to yield 1 litre (1 quart)]

30 *g* (1 *oz*) *finely-chopped shallots*	1 *l* (1 *qt*) *basic mayonnaise* (*Recipe* 110)	15 *g* (½ *oz*) *tarragon*
30 *g* (1 *oz*) *chopped gherkins*		15 *g* (½ *oz*) *chopped parsley*
60 *g* (2 *oz*) *chopped capers*	15 *g* (½ *oz*) *chopped chives*	15 *g* (½ *oz*) *chopped chervil*

Add the finely-chopped gherkins, capers, tarragon, parsley, chervil and chives to 1 l (1 qt) basic mayonnaise.

Used particularly with fried and grilled fish.

115 Sauce tyrolienne [to yield 1 litre (1 quart)]

1 *l* (1 *qt*) *basic mayonnaise* (*Recipe* 110)	240 *g* (½ *lb*) *tomato concassé*	1 *bay-leaf*
30 *g* (1 *oz*) *finely-chopped shallots*	12 *ml* (½ *fluid oz*) *salad oil*	½ *clove, chopped garlic*
		15 *g* (½ *oz*) *chopped fines herbes*

1 Sweat the shallots and garlic in oil.
2 Add the tomato concassé and bay-leaf.
3 Sweat the above under cover till a purée is made.
4 Pass through a fine sieve.
5 Allow to cool, add to basic mayonnaise and finish with the fines herbes.

Use with fried fish and with cold meats.

116 Sauce verte

1 *l* (1 *qt*) *basic mayonnaise*   90 *g* (3 *oz*) *blanched leaves of spinach, water-*
   (*Recipe* 110)   *cress, tarragon, chervil and chives*

1 Squeeze the blanched and refreshed leaves free of all water.
2 Pound in mortar, pass through a fine sieve.
3 Mix this purée with basic mayonnaise.
Use particularly with cold fish, fried and grilled fish.

117 Sauce Vincent

500 *ml* (1 *pt*) *sauce verte*   500 *ml* (1 *pt*) *sauce tartare*
   (*Recipe* 116)   (*Recipe* 114)
Mix both sauces together.
Use particularly with cold and fried fish.

Salad dressings. The basic blend of oil and vinegar (sauce vinaigrette) and its possible permutations are used, of course, not only to dress lettuce and leaf salads, potato and other vegetable salads, but shredded .meats, fish, and similar dishes for hors d'œuvre and other dishes for cold service.

OIL AND VINEGAR DRESSINGS

118 Sauce vinaigrette [to yield 1 litre (1 quart)]

750 *ml* (1½ *pt*) *salad oil*   10 *ml spoon* [2 *teaspoons*] *French mustard*
250 *ml* (½ *pt*) *wine vinegar*   1·25 *ml spoon* [¼ *teaspoon*] *ground*
½ *teaspoon salt*   *pepper*

1 Place mustard, salt, pepper and vinegar in a bowl.
2 When the salt has dissolved add the salad oil, gradually whisking till it forms an emulsion.
Note. This is basic vinaigrette. To it many chefs may add a garnish of one or all of the following: chopped capers, parsley, chervil, tarragon, shallot, e.g when serving with calf's head (see Recipe 650).

119 Sauce ailloli – Garlic dressing [to yield 1 litre (1 quart)]

4 *small cloves*   4 *raw egg yolks*   1·25 *ml spoon* [¼ *tea-*
   crushed garlic   750 *ml* (6 *gills*) *oil*   *spoon*] *ground pepper*
12 *ml* (½ *fluid oz*) *water* 25 *ml* (1 *fluid oz*) *wine* 2·5 *ml spoon* [½ *tea-*
                             vinegar   *spoon*] *salt*

1 Pound the garlic finely in a mortar.
2 Add the raw egg-yolks, salt, pepper and work the mixture well.
3 Gradually add the oil in a thin stream.
4 Finally add a few drops of water 10 ml spoon (½ fluid oz) to prevent curdling.
5 Pass sauce through fine muslin.

120 Sauce ravigote [to yield 1 litre (1 quart)]

1 *l* (1 *qt*) *basic vinaigrette* (*Recipe* 118)   30 *g* (1 *oz*) *chopped tarragon,*
30 *g* (1 *oz*) *finely-chopped shallots*   *chervil, chives, parsley*
30 *g* (1 *oz*) *chopped capers*

1 Blanch and refresh chopped shallots and dry on cloth.
2 Blend shallots, herbs and chopped capers with vinaigrette.
Use for calf's head and other meat salads.

121 Thousand Island dressing [to yield 1 litre (1 quart)]

1 *l* (1 *qt*) *basic dressing* (*Recipe* 118)   15 *g* (½ *oz*) *chopped parsley*
4 *chopped hard-boiled eggs*   15 *g* (½ *oz*) *chopped tarragon*
15 *g* (½ *oz*) *lobster coral* (*cooked*)   30 *g* (1 *oz*) *finely-chopped shallots*
125 *ml* (1 *gill*) *tomato ketchup*

1 Dry the lobster coral and chop finely.
2 Blanch and refresh the shallots.
3 Add the coral, chopped eggs, parsley, tarragon and tomato ketchup to the basic vinaigrette.
4 Mix well. (This may also be used as a sea-food cocktail sauce.)
This sauce can also be made using 750 ml of basic mayonnaise instead of dressing.

ASPICS

Aspic is widely used in cold cookery. Its clear, solid consistency allows it to be cut into decorative shapes and it is, of course, used to glaze over cold items, for lining moulds, or for incorporation into pâtés and pies to fill up crevices with its rich gelatinous material. The common faults to avoid in making aspic and when using the following recipes are:
 i Forgetting the preliminary soaking of gelatine in water.
 ii Boiling too fast.
 iii Not ladling gently when passing the aspic through muslin.
General guidance. For every litre (quart) of good, gelatinous stock of veal, chicken or fish, use 60 to 120 g [2 to 4 oz (according to warmth of weather)] of good gelatine (leaf gelatine for preference) and 1 raw egg-white. *Strong for heavy aspic.* For 'heavy' aspic, i.e. for pressed brisket (Recipe 206) the proportion of gelatine is further increased.

122 Stock for aspic jelly [to yield 10 litres (10 quarts)]

5 *kg* (10 *lb*) *chopped veal*   2 *large onions*   45 *g* (1½ *oz*) *salt*
    knuckle-bone   1 *leek*   12 *l* (12 *qt*) *water*
2 *kg* (4 *lb*) *shin of beef*   1 *stick celery*   1 *bouquet garni*
    minced   2 *calf's feet*   4 *large carrots*

1 Blanch and bone the calf's feet.
2 Oven-brown the veal knuckle-bone lightly to uniform colour.
3 Draw fat from bones and place in a large pan with the minced shin of beef.
4 Mix well with water; add the calf's feet, bring slowly to the boil; add the salt.
5 When boiling remove the scum and place in the vegetables.
6 Simmer for 4 to 5 hours, taking care to remove vegetables when they are cooked.
7 Remove fat often from the surface.
8 When cooked, pass through muslin-cloth and cool.
9 To make aspic from this base, add gelatine in accordance with the notes in General Guidance above.
Note. Flavouring of aspic jelly may be appropriately varied by using chicken and game stocks.

123 Fish aspic [to yield 10 litres (10 quarts)]

1 *kg* (30 *oz*) *gelatine leaf*	1 *bouquet garni*	500 *g* (1 *lb*) *diced carrots*
10 *l* (10 *qt*) *fish stock* (*Recipe* 374)	4 *sprigs tarragon*	500 *g* (1 *lb*) *diced onions*
1 *bottle white wine*	22 *crushed peppercorns*	10 *egg whites*
	½ *bottle sherry*	

1 Allow fish stock to become very cold and remove all scum.
2 Beat the egg whites to a froth and add the cold stock. Add the white wine.
3 Soak the leaf-gelatine until soft in cold water; when soft, squeeze out all the water.
4 Add the vegetables, gelatine, peppercorns, to the stock and bring quickly to the boil, stirring all the time.
5 When boiling, add the bouquet garni and tarragon leaves and simmer slowly until the clarification is complete (approximately 1 hour).
6 Add the sherry and strain carefully through muslin.
7 Remove all fat and season.
8 Use a kitchen paper to remove any surplus fat that may be on the surface.

MARINADE

A marinade is a liquor which flavours and helps to make tender the flesh of meat or fish. Marinading could be described as a mild form of pickling. It is used more often for meat than fish and has special value in dealing with game such as hare.

124 Marinade cuit – Cooked marinade [to yield 2 litres (2 quarts)]

1·5 *l* (3 *pt*) *red wine*	1 *sliced onion*	2 *blades mace*
250 *ml* (½ *pt*) *malt vinegar*	1 *sliced carrot*	2 *sprigs marjoram*
125 *ml* (1 *gill*) *brandy*	*juice of* ½ *lemon*	1 *sprig thyme*
125 *ml* (1 *gill*) *olive oil*	60 *g* (2 *oz*) *green celery*	½ *clove crushed garlic*
3 *cloves*	12 *crushed peppercorns*	30 *g* (1 *oz*) *parsley stalks*
2·5 *ml spoon* [½ *teaspoon*] *salt*		2 *bay-leaves*

1 Boil the vinegar and wine.
2 Pour over the other ingredients.
3 Allow to cool.
4 Season the meat with salt before marinading.
5 Turn over the items daily in marinade.
Used for game, meat, venison.

125 Marinade instantanée – Instant marinade [to yield 1 litre (1 quart)]

1 *l* (1 *qt*) *oil*	60 *g* (2 *oz*) *finely-minced shallots*	2·5 *ml spoon* [½ *teaspoon*] *salt*
240 *g* (½ *lb*) *thinly-sliced onion*	*juice of* 1 *lemon*	1·25 *ml spoon* [¼ *teaspoon*] *ground pepper*
5 *ml spoon* [1 *teaspoon*] *powdered thyme*	15 *g* (½ *oz*) *chopped chives*	2 *bay-leaves*
	15 *g* (½ *oz*) *chopped parsley*	

1 Mix all ingredients.
2 Allow to stand 2 hours before use.
Used with fish before frying, e.g., Filet de Sole à l'Orly and à la juive.

126 Marinade for braised beef [to yield 1 litre (1 quart)]

500 *ml* (1 *pt*) *red wine*	½ *clove, crushed garlic*	1 *sprig thyme*
125 *ml* (1 *gill*) *brandy*	30 *g* (1 *oz*) *parsley*	1·25 *ml spoon* [¼
120 *g* (¼ *lb*) *diced celery*	*stalks*	*teaspoon*] *salt*
12 *crushed peppercorns*	120 *g* (¼ *lb*) *sliced carrots*	125 *ml* (1 *gill*)
120 *g* (¼ *lb*) *diced onions*	2 *bay-leaves*	*olive oil*

1 Mix all ingredients together in a large china bowl.
2 Allow to stand for 1 hour before use.
3 Keep in very cold place.
Use for large pieces of braising-beef (salt-seasoned before marinading). **Turn in the marinade each day.**

127 Marinade for soused herring [to yield 1 litre (1 quart)]

750 *ml* (1½ *pt*) *malt vinegar*	15 *g* (½ *oz*) *chopped*	5 *ml spoon* [1 *tea-*
250 *ml* (½ *pt*) *water*	*parsley*	*spoon*] *salt*
60 *g* (2 *oz*) *carrots*	2 *cloves*	1·25 *ml spoon* [¼
(*paysanne cut*)	1 *bay-leaf*	*teaspoon*] *pepper*
60 *g* (2 *oz*) *thin onion rings*	*pinch sugar*	6 *black peppercorns*
6 *chillies*	*pinch allspice*	2 *slices lemon*

1 Mix all ingredients.
2 Bring to boil.
3 Pour in china bowl and allow to cool; do not strain.

128 Marinade for Bismark herring [to yield 1 litre (1 quart)]

750 *ml* (1½ *pt*) *white vinegar*	1·25 *ml spoon* [¼ *tea-*	2 *black peppercorns*
250 *ml* (½ *pt*) *dry white wine*	*spoon*] *salt*	8 *white peppercorns*
60 *g* (2 *oz*) *thinly-sliced*	8 *chillies*	*juice of* ½ *lemon*
onion	*pinch allspice*	2 *cloves*
	2 *bay-leaves*	

Mix all the ingredients, allow to cool, then strain.
Used to pickle raw herring.

129 Marinade à la grecque – Marinade Greek style [to yield 1 litre (1 quart)]

1 *l* (1 *qt*) *water*	1 *sprig thyme*	125 *ml* (1 *gill*) *oil*
juice of 4 *lemons*	2 *bay-leaves*	¼ *root of fennel*
10 *ml spoon* [2 *teaspoons*]	12 *crushed pepper-*	4 *celery sticks*
salt	*corns*	

1 Boil the lemon juice and water with the ingredients until they are cooked before adding the oil.
2 Cook in the resultant 'cuisson' whatever you wish to cook in the style 'à la grecque', i.e., cauliflower, onions, artichoke, marrow, etc.

130 Marinade à la portugaise [to yield 1 litre (1 quart)]

Add to the above recipe:

15 *ml spoon* [1 *tablespoon*] *tomato*   1 *clove crushed garlic*
   purée   480 *g* [1 *lb* (*net*)] *tomato concassé*

131 Spiced vinegar [to yield 1 litre (1 quart)]

7 *g* ($\frac{1}{4}$ *oz*) *allspice*   7 *g* ($\frac{1}{4}$ *oz*) *mace*   7 *g* ($\frac{1}{4}$ *oz*) *cinnamon*
7 *g* ($\frac{1}{4}$ *oz*) *cloves*   7 *g* ($\frac{1}{4}$ *oz*) *black*   *bark*
7 *g* ($\frac{1}{4}$ *oz*) *root-ginger*   *peppercorn*   1·5 *l* (1$\frac{1}{2}$ *qt*) *vinegar*

1 Bruise all ingredients by crushing with a rolling-pin.
2 Tie in a muslin-bag.
3 Boil the vinegar; infuse the crushed ingredients in the vinegar just off the boil; allow to cool.

Used for pickling red cabbage, cauliflower, onions, etc.

BRINE

General points in brine-making. Brine joints such as silverside of beef for 4 to 5 days. (Ox-tongues because of tough skin may take about three weeks unless injection method is used):
i Wash and dry meat before putting it into brine.
ii After removing the meat from the brine, run cold-tap water over it.
iii Keep in very cold place.
iv Wash the tub scrupulously after use.

132 Sweet brine [to yield 9 litres (2 gallons)]

9 *l* (2 *gallons*) *water*   360 *g* ($\frac{3}{4}$ *lb*) *brown sugar*
3 *kg* (6 *lb*) *bay-salt*   45 *g* (1$\frac{1}{2}$ *oz*) *saltpetre*

Place all ingredients in a pan and boil for 20 minutes.
Allow to get cold and pour into porcelain or wooden-type tub; keep covered.

Use for salt beef, pork, tongues, ham.

133 Dry pickle [sufficient for 7 kg (14 lb of meat)]

750 *g* (1$\frac{1}{2}$ *lb*) *salt*   120 *g* ($\frac{1}{4}$ *lb*) *brown sugar*
30 *g* (1 *oz*) *saltpetre*   120 *g* ($\frac{1}{4}$ *lb*) *allspice*

Rub meat in sugar and let it stand for 2 hours.
Rub on a little saltpetre, allspice and salt a little at a time.
Turn and knead the meat well.
Let it lie for about 10 weeks in a very cold place, turning daily.

Note. Dry pickling certainly does not involve the use of culinary liquor but is included here as it is often used as an alternative to pickling in brine; particularly for Belly of Pork, Bath Chaps, Silverside of Beef.

CHAUD-FROID SAUCES

The chaud-froid sauces (literally, hot-cold sauces) are those which, though cooked and thus, initially hot, are intended specifically for cold use as buffet items and similar purposes.

Points to note in making and using chaud-froid sauces. When cooling, stir often to avoid lumps for the sauce must be a smooth texture while coating. Chaud-froid can also be reheated slowly in the bain-marie; re-strain before using.

134 Chaud-froid blanc – White chaud-froid [to yield 1·5 litres (3 pints)]

1 *l* (2 *pt*) *chicken velouté*   500 *ml* (1 *pt*) *chicken aspic-jelly*
  (*Recipe* 27)   (*Recipe* 123 *made with chicken*
250 *ml* (½ *pt*) *fresh cream*   *stock*)
250 *ml* (½ *pt*) *chicken stock* *seasoning*
  (*Recipe* 11)

1 Mix the velouté with chicken stock and reduce on quick fire.
2 While the sauce is reducing, add the aspic, 125 ml (1 gill) at a time; yield after total reduction should be 1·25 l (2½ pints).
3 Season, blend in the cream and strain through muslin.

Note. To make a quick type add 45 g (1½ oz) leaf gelatine softened in water to 1 litre (1 quart) of sauce allemande (Recipe 54). Be sure to allow the gelatine to melt thoroughly and to strain it through a muslin.

135 Chaud-froid à l'aurore – Pink, tomaté chaud-froid [to yield 1 litre (1 quart)]

  1 *l* (1 *qt*) *white chaud-froid* (*Recipe* 134)   125 *ml* (1 *gill*) *fine tomato-pulp*

Add 125 ml (1 gill) of fine tomato-pulp to basic chaud-froid while hot and strain through muslin.

This pink chaud-froid is used in dishes such as Poularde Rose de Mai.

136 Chaud-froid brun – Brown chaud-froid [to yield 1 litre (1 quart)]

1·25 *l* (2½ *pt*) *demi-glace* (*Recipe* 29)   100 *ml* (⅛ *pt*) *truffle essence*
1 *glass Madeira wine*   500 *ml* (1 *pt*) *aspic jelly*
seasoning

1 Add the truffle-essence to demi-glace and reduce on quick fire.
2 While the sauce is reducing add the aspic jelly, 125 ml (1 gill) at a time [Yield of total reduction should be 1 litre (1 quart).]
3 Add the Madeira wine and season.

The use of this type of aspic jelly is determined by the article to be coated, i.e. for game, use game aspic-jelly.

137 Chaud-froid blanc de poisson – White fish chaud-froid [to yield 1 litre (1 quart)].

Same recipe and method as white chaud-froid but using fish velouté (Recipe 377) instead of chicken velouté.

138 Chaud-froid au vin rouge (for fish) – Red wine chaud-froid (fish) [to yield 1 litre (1 quart)]

Same method as chaud-froid brun, using 1·25 l (2½ pints) Genevoise Sauce (Recipe 385), and 500 ml (1 pint) of fish aspic (Recipe 123) instead of demi-glace and ordinary aspic.

HORS D'ŒUVRE

Hors d'œuvre are meant to stimulate the appetite. Therefore, their presentation is as important as taste: items must be dainty, petite, and fresh with eye-appealing colour contrasts. But simplicity should be the watchword; do not over-elaborate. Left-overs may be used, but hors d'œuvre should not depend entirely on these elements, and certainly they must never look like left-overs. Merely pouring oil and vinegar on to vegetables will not make an hors d'œuvre.

An hors d'œuvre may be a single item (or a single item with simple accompaniments) or a variety of items. Examples of single hors d'œuvre are: caviar, oysters, lobster, smoked ham, foie gras, pâtés and terrines, smoked salmon, trout, and smoked poultry; potted or cocktail shrimps, or other sea-food cocktails; fruits such as melon, avocado pear, grapefruit, and fruit cocktails; cold asparagus or artichoke with vinaigrette. Even fruit and tomato juices may be served as an appetizer course.

Recipes for mixed and plain hors d'œuvre are practically inexhaustible. It would, indeed, be easier to compile a list of food that should not be used. Discretion, commonsense, imagination, and good taste should determine the selection.

A few of the standard hors d'œuvre expected in a selection include: salads (particularly potato, tomato, cucumber, Russian); vegetables (especially cauliflower, onions, mushrooms) and fish cooked à la grecque, i.e. in the à la grecque marinade (Recipe 129); other fish like soused, pickled, and smoked herrings, anchovies and sardines; egg mayonnaise, salami, celery, cheese, and olives.

Grapefruit or oysters are normally served as single appetizers, but many of the dishes in this section may also be featured as part of a selection of hors d'œuvre variés. Although most hors d'œuvre are served cold, there are also hot appetizers; one or two of these are included in this chapter.

FRUITS AND FRUIT JUICES

AVOCAT – AVOCADO PEAR

Avocado pear has widespread use as an appetizer. To prepare, halve the fruit, remove the centre stone, carefully scoop out the soft flesh and cut into small dice, then blend with a dressing and replace the flesh in the half-shell of skin. The diced pear may, of course, be combined with other ingredients (as in the examples which follow) and may also be used in mixed salads.

139 Avocat épicure

2 *avocado pears*	15 *g* (½ *oz*) *walnuts*	62 *ml* (½ *gill*) *mayon-*
4 *pickled walnut*	30 *g* (1 *oz*) *gherkins*	*naise*
halves	*paprika*	(*Recipe* 110)

1 Halve the pears, remove stone and flesh, taking care not to break the skin.
2 Dice the pear flesh and combine with diced gherkins, walnuts, and mayonnaise; season with paprika.
3 Garnish the top with half a pickled walnut.
4 Present on a bed of crisp lettuce-hearts.

140 Avocat Singapore

2 *avocado pears*	62 *ml* (½ *gill*) *mayonnaise*	*lemon juice*
60 *g* (2 *oz*) *flaked, white*	(*Recipe* 110)	*cayenne pepper*
crab meat	7·5 *ml* [½ *tablespoon*]	
	whipped cream	

1 Cut the pears in half, lengthwise, and remove the stone.
2 Dice the flesh and sprinkle with a few drops of vinegar.
3 Mix the crab meat, mayonnaise, cream, and lemon juice together and
replace in the half-pear shells.
4 Serve on crushed ice with quarters of lettuce and slices of lemon.

MELON

141 Cantaloup or Honeydew melon

1 Cut into sections and remove seeds.
2 Serve on crushed ice.
3 Decorate with orange slivers and/or cherries impaled on cocktail sticks, and
also frills for melon-end points.
4 Ground ginger and caster sugar served separately.

142 Melon de Charente au porto – Charentais melon with port wine

1 Cut small piece from top in form of lid.
2 Remove seeds – macerate with port wine.
3 Replace lid and serve on crushed ice.

PAMPLEMOUSSE – GRAPEFRUIT

Grapefruit may be served plainly in halves with the segments loosened to
facilitate eating. Grapefruit juice may be served chilled in goblets (or double
vessels with ice liner) as an appetizer.

143 Demi-pamplemousse frappé au kirsch – Chilled half grapefruit, kirsch-flavoured

1 Prepare grapefruit in halves.
2 Add a little kirsch and a 5 ml spoon [teaspoon] of caster sugar to each half.
3 Serve on crushed ice; garnish with cocktail cherries.

144 Grapefruit cocktail

| 4 *grapefruit* | 125 *ml* (¼ *pt*) *stock* | 30 *ml* (¼ *gill*) *kirsch* |
| 4 *cherries* | *syrup* (*Recipe* 992) | 4 *goblets* |

1 Rim goblets with sugar as follows: (a) colour the sugar or leave plain as desired; (b) dip the rim of glass into egg-white and then in sugar.
2 Skin and fillet grapefruit.
3 Place the fillets in the stock syrup with the kirsch.
4 Serve very cold in goblets. Garnish with cocktail cherries.

144a Cocktail Florida

Combine equal parts of orange fillets with grapefruit to make this variant cocktail.

145 Pamplemousse mexicaine – grapefruit Mexicaine (hot)

| 2 *grapefruit* | 15 *g* (½ *oz*) *caster sugar* |
| ½ *glass sherry* | 1 *pimentoe* |

1 Prepare grapefruit in halves.
2 Add 7·5 ml spoon [½ tablespoon] of brown sugar and 7·5 ml spoon [½ tablespoon] sherry. All to stand 1 hour.
3 Sprinkle some caster sugar on top of each, brown under the grill.
4 Garnish with pimentoe. Serve hot.

146 Fresh tomato juice

12 *blanched tomatoes*	1 *piece bruised celery*
15 *ml spoon* [1 *tablespoon*]	*juice of* 1 *lemon*
Worcester sauce	

1 Squeeze all tomatoes through fine sieve.
2 Add Worcester sauce, bruised celery, half-pint of cold water, lemon juice and strain.
3 Season and mix well; serve chilled.
Note. Orange juice and pineapple juice may also be served chilled, as for grapefruit juice.

FISH AND FISH PRODUCTS

147 Anchois niçoise or filets d'anchois niçoise – Anchovy fillets (Nice style)
1 Using a sharp knife, trim and prepare fillets, and cut them full length.
2 Arrange them in a form of a grille on a ravier and decorate with a few capers, sieved yolk and white of hard-boiled egg, chopped parsley, and lobster coral.
3 Add a few drops of oil.

148 Anguille fumée – Smoked eel
1 Skin. Slice in thin fillets.
2 Dress on a ravier.
3 Serve with lemon and sour cream.

CAVIAR

The most renowned caviar comes from the delta of the Volga in the Caspian Sea – the area known as the Astrakan. The species are:
Beluga – Supreme quality: large grained and slightly salty.
Ocietrova Malossol – Small grained and less costly.
Secruga Malossol – Two-thirds of the price of Beluga.

149　Caviar

To serve:
1　See that it is in a perfectly fresh condition. (Caviar is perishable and loses its quality on ageing.)
2　Encrust it in ice and use a bone or ivory spoon for service.
3　Accompany the dish with: finely-chopped onions, halves of lemon, slices of rye bread or toast; or Blinis – small pancakes of buckwheat (Recipe 1095). (Sour cream may also be served with Blinis.)

HARENGS – HERRINGS

150　Bismark herrings

Ingredients as for Marinade (Recipe 128).
1　Bone fresh herrings and sprinkle them with salt; leave over night.
2　Wash off surplus salt by letting cold water run over them for 2 hours.
3　Place the boned herrings flat in crocks with marinade (Recipe 128) including sliced onions, mustard seed, bay-leaves, peppercorns, chillies, sliced lemon and sliced salt-cucumbers and 250 ml ($\frac{1}{2}$ pint) water.
4　Store in a cool place for a few days and keep well covered.

151　Rollmops

1　Prepare as Bismark herring (Recipe 150).
2　Roll herring around a slice of salt cucumber (or dill pickle) and a little mustard seed.
3　Secure in position with cocktail stick or small skewer.

152　Soused herrings

1　Pour marinade (Recipe 127) over the gutted fish.
2　Bake in dish in the oven till cooked.

Note. Trout or mackerel can be treated in the same way.

153　Smoked herring fillets in oil

If prepared canned fillets are not used, the following is an alternative:

4 *large kippers*	6 *peppercorns*
1 *bay-leaf*	250 *ml* ($\frac{1}{2}$ *pt*) *oil*

1　Place kippers on stove upside-down for a few minutes to remove skin.

2 Ease the bones out with the fingers.
3 Store the flesh in earthenware terrines with bay-leaves and peppercorns interspersed among the fillets.
4 Pour over the oil and leave over night.

154 Salade de poisson – Fish salad

1 Use left-over fish of firm texture.
2 Cut into small cubes.
3 Add the same amount of cold, boiled, sliced or diced potatoes and a few pieces of peeled and seeded tomatoes.
4 Bind with tomato-flavoured mayonnaise.

155 Sardines à l'huile – Sardines (canned) in oil

To serve:
1 These may be served direct from the tin.
2 May also be served dressed fanwise on a ravier with the tails pointing one way.
3 Serve a little oil on top and garnish with parsley.

Note. May be served à la niçoise (as Recipe 147).

156 Saumon fumé – Smoked salmon

250 g (½ lb) smoked salmon   2 lemons   15 g (½ oz) capers

1 Slice salmon very thinly.
2 Garnish with capers, parsley sprigs and half-lemons.
3 Serve with brown bread and butter. Moulin (peppermill) and cayenne should be 'en place'.

157 Truite fumée – Smoked trout

4, 200 g (6 oz) trout   2 lemons   125 ml (¼ pt) sour cream

1 Skin both sides of the trout.
2 Garnish with slices of lemon and parsley.
3 Serve separately, from sauce-boat, acidulated cream or sauce raifort (Recipe 99).

158 Thon à l'huile – Tunny fish in oil

To serve:
1 Remove from can and slice thickly.
2 Garnish with onion rings and dress with a little salad oil.

159 Pickled left-over white fish, salmon, etc.

1 If the fish has been fried or meunière remove brown coating.
2 Arrange the fish in a dish, season, add some sliced onions and cover with vinaigrette.

CHARCUTERIE: CURED OR SMOKED MEATS AND SAUSAGES

160 Saucisson (Salami) – Smoked or prepared sausage

To serve:

1 Sausage of French type such as Saucisson de ménage, Saucisson de ménage fumé, Saucisson d'Arles, Saucisson de Lyons, etc., and Italian type such as Salami di Milano: slice thinly and dress the slices overlapping on a salver.
2 Types such as Mortadella (Italian) and Andouille de Vire (French): these slices should be slightly thicker, because of their larger diameter.
3 Saucisson á l'ail (Garlic sausage) and Leberwurst (Liver sausage): here again slices should be thicker because of the softer texture.

161 Jambon cru – Raw, salt ham

161a Jambon fumé – Smoked ham (such as Jambon de Bayonne – Bayonne ham)

Cut very thin: serve with lettuce, tomato and gherkin.

161b Jambone de Parme – Parma ham

This is served in a similar style to Bayonne ham.

162 Jambon cru au melon

Cured and smoked hams for eating without further preparation, other than slicing, may also be accompanied by melon. Parma ham is especially served in this style.

Other Smoked and Cured Meats. Westphalia ham, Bundnerfleisch (Swiss cured) dried beef-fillet, bœuf fumé Hamburg, smoked fillet of pork, smoked tongue and similar hams are similarly served thinly-sliced with gherkin and parsley sprig garnish.

EGGS

163 Œufs à la mayonnaise – Egg mayonnaise

1 Cold hard-boiled eggs.
2 Cut into halves and dress on a bed of shredded lettuce.
3 Coat with mayonnaise thinned to coating consistency and garnish with capers, anchovies, and lettuce hearts.
4 Sprinkle a little lobster coral on top for decoration.

164 Plovers' eggs

Seldom encountered in post-war service; these are served hard-boiled within a 'nest' – usually of mustard and cress.

PÂTÉS AND TERRINES

165 Foie gras or pâté de foie gras

1 Serve from terrine embedded in ice.
2 Warm toast or brioche normally accompanies.
3 Chopped hard-boiled egg may also be served.

165a Chaud-froid de foie gras en caisses

½ *tin natural foie gras*	250 *ml* (½ *pt*) *aspic*	*blanched chervil*
30 *ml* (¼ *gill*) *sherry*	*jelly*	*leaves*
125 *ml* (¼ *pt*) *white*	(*Recipe* 122)	4 *small soufflé cases*
chaud-froid	1 *truffle*	90 *g* (3 *oz*) *fine*
(*Recipe* 134)		*Russian salad*

1 Remove foie gras from tin and trim all fat. Cut into slices the same size as the soufflé cases.
2 Mask with chaud-froid and decorate with truffle and chervil.
3 Place a small quantity of Russian salad in the bottom of each case, place the foie gras on top.
4 Serve a suitable salad separately.

165b Darioles de foie gras Vatel

4 *fluted dariole moulds*	250 *ml* (½ *pt*) *aspic*	1 *white of hard-boiled egg*
125 *g* (¼ *lb*) *foie gras*	(*Recipe* 122)	1 *small truffle*

1 Mask the dariole moulds with aspic jelly, decorate the sides and bottom with decorative cuts of truffle and egg white.
2 Work the foie gras into a purée and pipe into each dariole mould, cover with aspic jelly.
3 Set on ice until required. Turn out and serve with salad.

165c Médaillons de foie gras

1 Slices of foie gras decorated and coated with aspic.
2 May also be served with warm brioche or hot on toast.

166 Paté de foie – Liver pâté

750 *g* (1½ *lb*) *chicken livers*	1 *sprig thyme*	120 *g* (¼ *lb*) *melted butter*
250 *g* (½ *lb*) *lean pork*	2 *bay-leaves*	125 *ml* (1 *gill*) *fresh*
30 *g* (1 *oz*) *chopped onions*	*seasoning*	*cream*

1 Dice the pork and fry gently in pan.
2 Add the onions and colour slightly.
3 Add the thyme, bay-leaf and chicken livers and fry the livers till cooked.
4 Season, pass through fine mincer and rub through a sieve.
5 Allow to go cold, place in basin and blend in the melted butter and cream.

167 Pâté de jambon – Ham pâté

750 g (1½ lb) lean cooked ham
250 g (¼ lb) melted butter
2·5 ml spoon [½ teaspoon] paprika

125 ml (1 gill) cold Béchamel (Recipe 51)

125 ml (1 gill) fresh cream
seasoning

1 Mince the ham finely and rub through a sieve.
2 Place in a basin, add the béchamel and paprika and beat well.
3 Place the basin on ice and gently beat in the butter and cream. Season.

168 Pâté maison – Pâté in the style of the house

1 kg (2 lb) chicken livers
250 g (½ lb) lean pork
250 g (½ lb) lean bacon
1 clove, crushed garlic

60 g (2 oz) finely-chopped onion
seasoning
2 bay-leaves

500 g (1 lb) streaky bacon
1 sprig thyme
1 glass brandy
2 eggs

1 Dice the lean ham and pork and fry with the chopped onions and herbs.
2 Add chicken livers. Fry until cooked and season.
3 Pass through a fine mincer and then rub through a sieve.
4 Bind with the eggs and add the brandy.
5 Line a casserole with the streaky bacon and place the mixture in over-lapping the bacon on top.
6 Place on lid and cook in the oven in a bain-marie slowly.
7 Allow to get cold and slice as required.

169 Terrine Bonne Femme

500 g (1 lb) lean pork (diced)
500 g (1 lb) veal (diced)
1 boned hare (diced)
1 filleted chicken (diced)

2 boned grouse (diced)
seasoning
60 g (2 oz) chopped onions
15 g (½ oz) chopped parsley

1 sprig thyme
1 broken bay-leaf
1 glass Madeira
1 glass white wine

1 Fry meat and game in a little butter to stiffen but not to cook.
2 Mix in the onions and herbs; season.
3 Place the mixture in a terrine, and add the Madeira and white wine and put aside until next day.
4 Place in the oven with cover and cook slowly.
5 When cooked, allow to get cold and finish off with a good game aspic.

VEGETABLE HORS D'ŒUVRE

Only a few examples of vegetable hors d'œuvre are given. These illustrate the typical preparation of vegetables for use as hors d'œuvre.

General points.
 i Cut and shape vegetables with care to ensure uniformity and daintiness.
ii Before adding sauce or dressing, drain the vegetables well to ensure that all moisture is removed – this facilitates the adherence of the dressing and prevents its dilution.

170 Artichauts vinaigrette – Whole artichokes vinaigrette

1 Trim and cook for 20 minutes in salted water with lemon juice.
2 Remove centre part (the choke) and dress on a serviette.
3 Serve separately with a sauce-boat of vinaigrette.

Asparagus or asparagus tips may be similarly served.

171 Fonds d'artichauts à la grecque – Artichokes in à la grecque marinade

1 Trim and cut artichoke bottoms into quarters.
2 Cook until tender in à la grecque marinade (Recipe 129). Allow to go cold.

Mushrooms, button onions, celeriac (cut into jardinière) and other vegetables may be prepared in this style.

172 Betterave – Beetroot (pickled)

1 Cook in pan or steamer until tender.
2 Remove skin carefully.
3 Leave whole or slice.
4 When cold, cover with spiced vinegar (Recipe 131).
5 May be served sliced or diced and mixed with cream for hors d'œuvre.

173 Choux rouge – Red cabbage (pickled)

1 Select firm cabbage of good colour.
2 Remove the hard mid-rib and shred the cabbage finely.
3 Sprinkle the shreds with coarse salt and leave for a day.
4 Drain. Pack into jars.
5 Cover with cold, spiced vinegar, (Recipe 131), add a few juniper berries.
6 Tie a paper over each jar.
7 May be used after 4 hours' pickling.

174 Maïs à la crème – Creamed sweetcorn

Remove the ears from the cooked sweetcorn and mix the grains with cream.

175 Corn on the cob (Hot sweetcorn)

As an appetizer course.

Boil the whole sweetcorn for 20 minutes in salt water containing a little milk.
Melted butter is served separately.

176 Piment provençale

Remove seeds and shred.
Cook in basic à la grecque marinade (Recipe 129) with equal parts of tomato concassé and one crushed clove of garlic; season.
Allow to cool.

SALADS FOR HORS D'ŒUVRE

177 Salade de céleri–rave – Celeriac salad

1 Wash celeriac and peel.
2 Cut into thin slices with the mandolin and then cut into fine julienne.
3 Place in salted water to which lemon juice has been added.
4 Drain, mix with mayonnaise (Recipe 110) and season.

178 Salade de concombres – Cucumber salad

1 Peel thinly.
2 Slice very thinly and sprinkle with a little salt and vinegar.
3 Garnish with chopped parsley.

179 Salade de haricots blancs – Haricot bean salad

1 Soak beans for 12 hours – rinse.
2 Cook with plenty of water with a carrot, onion piqué and bouquet garni. Season.
3 When cooked allow to go cold and drain from liquor.
4 Add some finely chopped onion and season with vinaigrette (Recipe 118) and chopped parsley.
5 Serve on a ravier and garnish with a little sliced gherkins.

Flageolets and other types of beans may be similarly prepared.

180 Salade de haricots verts et tomates – French bean and tomato salad

1 Use small French beans. Top and tail.
2 Cook in boiling salt water and refresh.
3 Mix with vinaigrette (Recipe 118). Season.
4 Heap in the centre of a salad bowl.
5 Surround with blanched, sliced tomatoes.

181 Salade de pommes de terre – Potato salad

1 Steam potatoes in jacket.
2 When cold peel and dice.
3 Pour over 250 ml ($\frac{1}{2}$ pt) of cold consommé (Recipe 227).
4 Allow to stand for 1 hour.
5 Mix with finely-chopped onions, mayonnaise and a little chopped parsley. Season.

Note. Alternatively, potato salad may be mixed with vinaigrette (Recipe 118).

182 Salade de piment – Pimento salad

1 Blanch and skin.
2 Remove seeds and shred.
3 Mix with vinaigrette (Recipe 118).

183 Salade russe (maigre) – Russian salad

250 g (½ lb) carrots	250 g (½ lb) green peas	250 ml (½ pint)
250 g (½ lb) turnips	120 g (¼ lb) diced,	mayonnaise
250 g (½ lb) French beans	cooked potatoes	(Recipe 110)

1 Cut the carrots and turnips into jardinière.
2 Cut the French beans into lozenge shapes.
3 Cook the vegetables separately in boiling salt water.
4 Refresh and blend with mayonnaise; season.

184 Salade de tomates – Tomato salad

1 Blanch and slice thinly.
2 Season; marinate with vinaigrette (Recipe 118).
3 Garnish with sliced onions and chopped parsley.

185 Radis – Radishes

1 Wash well and trim green part.
2 Cut the end into tulip shape.
3 Serve on crushed ice.

186 Riz – Rice (for hors d'œuvre)

1 Prepare ordinary rice pilaff (Recipe 366).
2 Garnish with diced pimentoes and peas and diced, cooked chicken's liver.
3 Season with vinaigrette (Recipe 118).

Italian pastas (macaroni, etc.) may be similarly treated.

FINGER HORS D'ŒUVRE AND SNACKS

187 Carolines and Duchesses, Eclairs

Both Carolines and Duchesses are used as appetizers. The former are small eclairs shaped like the letter 'C' and are 3 cm (1½ inches) long. The latter are small eclairs, of customary shape, also 3 cm (1½ inches) long. Both may be filled with various purées,' i.e., cheese, ham or liver. They are then coated with chaud-froid, according to the filling, and finished with aspic.

188 Barquettes, Croustades, and Tartelettes

These are made by simply lining different shapes of small patty tins with short paste. Various fillings may be used as for Duchesses and Carolines. (They are also used to garnish hot dishes).

189 Cassolettes

These can also be garnished with appetizer fillings. They are made by using a special iron mould, dipped into batter and deep-fried until crisp.

FARCES AND MOUSSES

The finer forcemeats in this section, normally prepared in the larder, are not to be confused with hot stuffings such as those served with roast duck prepared in the English style. Stuffings are more appropriately included in Chapters 6 and 7.

PANADAS

Panadas are preparations which form the thickening or binding of forcemeat. They are not necessary for all forcemeats and the most delicate do not need a panada. There are 3 types of panada:

190 Bread panada

    500 *ml* (1 *pt*) *milk*   250 *g* ($\frac{1}{2}$ *lb*) *breadcrumbs*

Pour boiling milk over the breadcrumbs and cook until all the milk has been absorbed and the mixture has become too thick to adhere to the spatula.

191 Flour panada

    250 *ml* ($\frac{1}{2}$ *pt*) *water*   60 *g* (2 *oz*) *butter*   150 *g* (5 *oz*) *sifted flour*

1 Boil the water with the butter; then add the sifted flour.
2 Cook together until the mixture no longer sticks to the spatula.

192 Frangipan panada

    90 *g* (3 *oz*) *flour*   90 *g* (3 *oz*) *melted butter*
    4 *egg yolks* $\frac{1}{2}$ *pint milk*

1 Blend together flour, egg yolks, melted butter and milk.
2 Mix well, strain and bring slowly to the boil.
3 Allow to cook slowly for 5 minutes stirring frequently.

Note. All panadas must be allowed to become cold before use after cooking. Butter the surface to prevent a crust forming while cooling.

193 Godiveau – Poached veal forcemeat balls

    500 *g* (1 *lb*) *veal*   4 *eggs*   *seasoning*
    1 *kg* (2 *lb*) *beef fat*   350 *ml* (14 *fluid oz*) *iced water*

1 Remove sinews from veal and fat.
2 Mince finely and pound in mortar.
3 Season; add eggs one at a time and mix well.
4 Allow to stand in cool place.
5 Add the iced water to required consistency.
6 Shape in balls by means of two spoons and poach gently.

194 Quenelles – Poached forcemeat balls

This is the name given to completed forcemeats that are shaped to the required size by means of two spoons – or by moulding with the hands. The forcemeat for quenelles is made by mixing a panada with the required ingredients. Finely pounded chicken or fish, etc., may be used. Quenelles are used to garnish soups, sauces, and vol-au-vents, etc.

195 Farce fine de porc – Fine pork forcemeat

250 g (½ *lb*) *lean pork*	*Seasoning of salt, ground*
250 g (½ *lb*) *veal*	*mace, pepper*
250 g (½ *lb*) *pork fat*	1 *glass brandy*

1 Macerate the meats in the brandy for 1 hour.
2 Pass through a fine mincer, rub through sieve, and season.

196 Mousse de jambon – Cold ham mousse

480 g (1 *lb*) *lean cooked ham*	125 *ml* (¼ *pt*) *aspic jelly* (*Recipe* 122)
165 *ml* (⅓ *pt*) *cold velouté* (*Recipe* 26)	320 *ml* (⅔ *pt*) *half-beaten cream*

1 Mince ham finely and pound in the mortar with the velouté.
2 Rub through fine sieve.
3 Place mixture in a bowl of ice.
4 Gradually beat in the cream and the aspic jelly. Season.
5 Place mixture in an aspic-lined mould or soufflé dish.

Note. Mousse of chicken, fish, etc., can be made by using the same quantities as above: substitute chicken or fish for ham and use a chicken or fish velouté. A hot fish mousse and mousseline is included in the fish recipes (Chapter 5).

COLD COOKERY

As indicated in the introductory paragraph to this chapter, the work of the chef garde manger is important and extensive. This *Compendium* of recipes does not, of course, aim to cover work such as meat dissection and the preparation of small cuts, poultry, and fish. Dishes listed below, however, typify the actual cold cookery carried out in the larder but it should also be noted that many of the meat, poultry, game, and fish dishes from other chapters, when cold, can be treated by the garde manger for buffet and assiette-anglaise service. Cold dishes are also included in Chapters 4, 5 and 6.

FISH

197 Saumon poché froid – Cold salmon

5 *kg* (10 *lb*) *salmon* 9 *l* (2 *gall. approx.*) *court-bouillon* (*Recipe* 371)   *salt*

1 Gut, scale, and trim fine.
2 Tie into shape.

3 Cover with cold court-bouillon.
4 Cover and bring to boil; allow to simmer for 10 minutes.
5 Allow to go cold with lid on.
6 When cold, skin both sides.
7 Decorate and coat with fish aspic (Recipe 123).
8 Garnish with lettuce, cucumbers and stuffed eggs.

Note. Salmon may be coated with chaud-froid (Recipes 134 or 135) if desired or a mayonnaise (Recipe 110) cohered with aspic. Individual portion cuts of salmon may be treated in the same way.

198 Truite saumonée froide – Cold salmon-trout

1 Scale, gut, and trim fins.
2 Poach gently in court-bouillon (Recipe 371) and allow to go very cold.
3 Proceed as for salmon.

199   Turbot farci en aspic – Cold stuffed turbot in aspic

1 Clean and gut the turbot. Remove eyes but leave head on.
2 As for Sole Colbert, cut the flesh on the dark skin side of the turbot down the back bone.
3 Detach, without removing, the fish flesh from the spine bone. Then remove all the bones carefully so as not to destroy the fish's shape.
4 Stuff the cavity evenly with fish mousseline (Recipe 460). Place in buttered poaching dish. Cover with white court-bouillon (Recipe 370) and then place a *cartouche* (buttered grease-proof paper) over the fish.
5 Place in moderate oven and poach gently (essential in order to preserve shape).
6 Allow to cool in own liquor, Drain, trim, place on wire rack and coat with mayonnaise (Recipe 110) cohered with aspic or fish chaud-froid (Recipe 137).
7 Decorate, glaze with fish aspic (Recipe 123). Add a fine garnish.

HAM, VEAL, AND BRAWN DISHES

200 Ham

To Boil:
1 Soak in cold water overnight.
2 Cook for approximately 4 hours.
3 Allow to go cold in its own cooking-liquor.
4 Remove skin and trim.
5 Coat with chaud-froid (Recipe 134); decorate, and glaze with aspic (Recipe 122).

Note. Traditionalists may not approve of coating ham with chaud-froid but the alternative method of carving the fat decoratively is tending to disappear. For economical service the fat may be plainly coated with brown breadcrumbs.

201 Brawn

½ pickled pig's head	1 carrot	bouquet garni
120 g (4 oz) cooked bacon	1 onion	peppercorns
1 hard-boiled egg	2 cloves	

1 Wash the head in several waters, remove brains, veins and bone splinters.
2 Cook the head in saucepan with enough water to cover. Add a little salt, onion piqué, bouquet garni and peppercorns. Cook 2 hours.
3 Skim frequently. Remove meat from bones and reduce liquor with bones.
4 Cut the meat and bacon in small dice.
5 Slice the egg and decorate the bottom of charlotte mould.
6 Fill the mould with the pig's head and bacon. Press lightly.
7 Add a reduced pint of the liquid.
8 Place in a refrigerator to set for 12 hours.
9 Warm mould in warm water before turning out.

202 Veal and ham pie (cold)

750 g (1½ lb) nut-veal	seasoning	8 leaves soaked gelatine
750 g (1½ lb) thickly-sliced raw ham [0·5 cm (¼ inch) thick]	30 g (1 oz) finely-chopped onions	15 g (½ oz) chopped parsley
4 hard-boiled eggs	500 g (1 lb) streaky bacon	Puff paste (Recipe 994)

1 Cut veal into 0·5 cm (¼ inch) thick escalopes.
2 Line the pie-dish with the streaky bacon.
3 Build the pie by adding alternate layers of ham, veal and gelatine.
4 Place in the middle a line of hard-boiled egg, onions, and chopped parsley.
5 Season each layer.
6 Cover with puff paste and decorate.
7 Cook, and when cold, fill with aspic jelly (Recipe 122).

BEEF DISHES

203 Galantine de bœuf – Beef galantine

| 750 g (1½ lb) lean beef | 2 eggs | bouquet garni |
| 125 ml (1 gill) white stock (Recipe 6) | 180 g (6 oz) bread-crumbs | 250 g (½ lb) bacon seasoning |

1 Cut the bacon and beef into very small dice.
2 Put the meat and bacon into a basin with the breadcrumbs and seasoning.
3 Beat the eggs with the stock, add to other ingredients and mix well.
4 Shape into a short roll and tie in greased, floured cloth.
5 Cook in boiling white stock with the bouquet garni for 2½ hours.
6 When cooked, press lightly until cold, glaze with aspic (Recipe 122) and decorate.

204 Langue de bœuf froide – Cold ox-tongue

1 If pickled or salted, soak in cold water overnight and boil in water.
2 When cooked, skin, remove bones, and press.

205 Pièce de bœuf rôtie froide – Joint of cold roast beef

1 Remove chine bone.
2 Trim rib-bone ends.
3 Glaze with brown aspic (Recipe 122 with colouring).
4 Garnish with grated horse-radish.

206 Pressed brisket

1 Bone brisket and place in pickle (Recipe 132) for at least 5 days.
2 Wash off; place in boiling water and simmer until cooked (approximately 20 minutes per 500 g or lb).
3 Drain and place in the press while hot and squeeze until firm.
4 Allow it to become cold; remove from press, trim and glaze with double-strength aspic (normally coloured red or reddish brown).

POULTRY AND GAME DISHES

207 Suprême de volaille en chaud-froid – Cold supreme of chicken

1 Poach chicken gently and when cold, carefully remove the supremes.
2 Make a farce by rubbing through a sieve equal parts of foie gras and white meat of chicken.
3 Spread a layer of farce on the top of each supreme.
4 Coat each supreme with chaud-froid (Recipe 134) and decorate with truffles and glaze with aspic jelly (Recipe 122).
5 Serve with small darioles of salade Russe (Recipe 183) cohered with aspic jelly.

208 Galantine de volaille – Chicken galantine

1, 2·5 kg (5 lb) fowl	90 g (3 oz) pork fat	1 hard-boiled egg
750 g (1½ lb) fine pork or	½ glass sherry	2 whole truffles
veal forcemeat	90 g (3 oz) ham	2 gherkins
(Recipe 195)	15 g (½ oz) pistachio	salt
90 g (3 oz) tongue	nuts	pepper

1 Skin the bird completely without holes.
2 Take off the supremes and cut into fingers.
3 Bone out the legs and pass through fine mincer and rub through sieve and add to the pork forcemeat.
4 Spread the skin on a damp cloth and place a layer of forcemeat in the centre. Cut the ham, tongue and gherkins into strips and marinate in sherry. Then garnish each layer of farce with fillets of chicken, tongue, ham, fresh fat pork, egg quarters, gherkin strips, pistachio nuts and truffles.
5 Roll up, tie in damp cloth and cook in chicken stock (Recipe 11), allowing 20 minutes per 500 g or lb).
6 When cooked let it cool slightly; re-tie and press under a board.
7 When cold, remove cloth and string; coat with chaud-froid (Recipe 134) decorate, and glaze with aspic (Recipe 122).

209 Game cutlets

300 g (10 *oz*) *diced, cooked game*	125 *ml* (1 *gill*) *brown stock*	30 g (1 *oz*) *flour*
60 g (2 *oz*) *diced, cooked ham*	(*Recipe* 7 *or* 8) *seasoning*	30 g (1 *oz*) *butter*
		2 *egg yolks*

1 Make a panada with the flour, butter, and stock (Recipe 191).
2 Add the game and ham, finely diced, to the panada.
3 Bind with egg yolks and season.
4 Place the mixture on greased tray and allow to get cold.
5 Shape as cutlets, flour, egg and crumb and sauter in butter.

210 Chicken cutlets

Use chicken stock (Recipe 11) and diced chicken instead of game and brown stock.

211 Raised grouse pie

Pie mould 15 cm × 10 cm (5½″ × 4″)	250 g (½ *lb*) *chicken livers*	1 *glass of brandy*
750 g (1½ *lb*) *hot-water paste* (*Recipe* 997)	*seasoning*	30 g (1 *oz*) *finely-chopped onions*
5 *old grouse*	750 g (1½ *lb*) *pork sausage-meat*	500 g (1 *lb*) *streaky bacon*

1 Line the pie mould with paste and see there are no cracks.
2 Reserve enough paste for the cover and decoration.
3 Line the inside with streaky bacon.
4 Remove the supremes from the grouse and soak in brandy.
5 Bone the legs and mince finely with the sausage-meat, liver and onions.
6 Place in layers of sausage-meat on the bacon, then the raw grouse fillets.
7 Continue until the pie is full, making sure the last layer is one of sausage-meat filling.
8 Cover with paste and decorate; egg-wash and bake in oven.
9 When cold, fill with game aspic (Recipe 122 with game stock).

SALADS TO ACCOMPANY MAIN DISHES

Examples of salads, mostly 'single' ones, suitable for hors d'œuvre, tray or trolley raviers, have been listed earlier in the hors d'œuvre section. The ingredients for salads served with cold meat, fish, poultry, pies, and game are capable of infinite variations and permutations. Such mixed salads are commonly of the à la française (French salad) type included below. Many salads are, however, suitable (and correct) for service with hot roasts, particularly poultry and game. Plain lettuce and other green stuffs are customarily dressed with vinaigrette (Recipe 118).

212 à la française

Lettuce hearts, beetroot, tomatoes, hard-boiled eggs, dressed with vinaigrette and chopped tarragon.

213 Allemande

Diced apples, potatoes, gherkins, smoked herrings, onions, chopped parsley, vinaigrette-dressed, decorated with beetroot.

214 Carmen

Pimentoes, dice of chicken, peas, rice, dressing of vinaigrette with mustard and chopped tarragon.

215 Chicago

Tomatoes, asparagus tips, French beans, slices of foie gras, julienne of carrots, mushrooms, mayonnaise sauce.

216 Cressonnière

Slices of potatoes, watercress leaves sprinkled with parsley and hard-boiled eggs.

217 Dalila

Bananas, apples, julienne of celery, and mayonnaise.

218 Égyptienne

Rice pillaf with chicken livers, ham, mushrooms, pimentoes, peas, served in artichoke bottoms.

219 Fanchette

Julienne of chicken, raw mushrooms, chicory, julienne of truffles, vinaigrette.

220 Indienne

Rice, asparagus, julienne of pimentoes, dice of apples, and curried cream-dressing.

221 Japonaise

Dice of fresh fruit, mixed with acidulated cream, served with fresh lettuce or in half an orange.

222 Jockey club

Asparagus tips, julienne of truffle dressed with vinaigrette or with mayonnaise on hearts of lettuce.

223 Mimosa

Half-lettuce hearts garnished with orange fillets, grapes, bananas, and acidulated cream.

224 Niçoise

French beans, tomatoes, potatoes, anchovies, olives, capers, lettuce, vinaigrette dressing.

225 Tourangelle

Julienne of potatoes, French beans, flageolets beans, mayonnaise with cream, and chopped tarragon.

226 Waldorf

(a) Diced celeriac, apples, walnuts dressed with thin mayonnaise; or (b) Celery, apples, bananas, walnuts, served in scooped-out apples.

3. Soups

CLASSIFICATION of the different types of soup can be effected in more than one way; witness the waitress's naïve 'thick or clear'. In considering the recipes of the chef potager, the soup chef in the traditional kitchen brigade who is responsible for all soups, it has been thought simple and convenient to group them into the following categories:

Classification of soups

Consommés – Clear soup of refined type, mainly used for dinner (and late supper) service.

Bouillons and Broths – Clear soup of natural liquor base. Clear in the sense of being unthickened, but with garnishes and ingredients possibly clouding the clarity. Such soups tend to be used for luncheon or family supper purposes.

Thickened Brown Soups – Savoury or meaty soups mainly for luncheon service.

Bisque and Chowders – Fish soups suitable for luncheon and dinner.

Purées – Vegetable soups with the ingredients themselves providing most or all of the thickening. These are mainly used for luncheon service.

Creams and Veloutés – This group includes purées finely finished with cream, and high-quality thickened cream soups (veloutés) such as chicken. They are suitable for dinners, though possibly not so widely used as consommés for formal functions.

Cold Soups – Soups suitable for service cold are chiefly found among the clear soups (Consommé and Bortch for example) and creams. Cold fruit soups are not included.

Bread Accompaniments with Soup

Flutes – Thin slices from French bread of long, thin flute-shape and size, yielding small neat ovals or roundels for drying or toasting.

Croûtons or Sippets – Small dainty dice of bread tossed in butter to a golden brown and seasoned.

CONSOMMÉS

227 Clarified consommé [to yield 1 litre (1 quart)]

1·5 *l* (1½ *qt*) *fond blanc* (*cold*) (*Recipe 6*)	250 *g* (½ *lb*) *mirepoix* (*Recipe 2 but omit pork*)	1 *small chopped bay-leaf*
350 *g* (¾ *lb*) *minced shin of beef*	*seasoning* 2 *egg whites*	1 *chicken carcass*

1 Roast the chicken carcase and vegetable in a little fat.
2 Mix minced beef and egg whites thoroughly with a little cold stock. See note on clarification.
3 Drain the bones free of fat and place in a large thick-bottomed saucepan.
4 Add the clarification (minced beef, etc.) and gradually add the cold stock until all is well mixed.
5 Put the pan to boil and stir often to prevent burning.
6 When boiling draw to the side (or reduce heat) and simmer for 1 hour.
7 Carefully remove all fat and strain gently through muslin into another pan.
8 Re-boil and remove all grease with greaseproof paper. Adjust seasoning.

Note. For clarification:
  i Use the meat of old animals. This gives better flavour. The stock should be free of all fat. See the egg whites and minced shin of beef are mixed well. Damp the muslin before straining.
 ii Consommé can be clarified with blood using 250 ml (½ pint) to 1 litre (1 quart) of consommé.
iii When straining consommé, dip ladle gently in at the side to avoid the breaking up of the clarification mixture.

227a Simplified consommé [to yield 1 litre (1 quart)]

500 *ml* (1 *pt*) *cold white stock* (*Recipe 6*)	250 *g* (½ *lb*) *minced shin of beef*	60 *g* (2 *oz*) *each sliced carrot,*
1 *l* (2 *pt*) *hot brown stock* (*Recipe 7*)	2 *egg whites* ½ *burnt onion* 1 *small bay-leaf* *seasoning*	*leek and celery* 6 *peppercorns; parsley stalks*

1 Mix minced beef thoroughly with the cold white stock. (See note on clarification.)
2 Add the remaining ingredients and stir in the hot brown stock.
3 Bring to boil and stir often to prevent burning.
4 When boiling, reduce heat and simmer for 1 hour.
5 Strain gently through muslin into another vessel.
6 Reboil, remove all grease and adjust for seasoning.

228 Consommé de volaille – Chicken consommé [to yield 1 litre (1 quart)]

1 *kg* (2 *lb*) *roast-fowl carcass*	250 *g* (½ *lb*) *mirepoix* (*omitting pork*)	375 *g* (¾ lb) *minced shin of beef*
2 *l* (2 *qt*) *fond de volaille, cold* (*Recipe 11*)	(*Recipe 2*) *seasoning* 2 *egg whites*	1 *small roasted fowl*

1 Mince the shin of beef and pound the carcases with the egg whites in a mortar.
2 Place this in a thick saucepan and mix well with the cold chicken-stock.
3 Add the vegetable and bring to the boil, stirring frequently.
4 When boiling, add the fowl which has been browned in the oven.
5 Simmer for 1½ hours; strain through muslin and season; bring to the boil and remove all fat with greaseproof paper.

229 Game consommé (pheasant) [to yield 1 litre (1 quart)]

2 *l* (2 *qt*) *fond de gibier, cold*   2 *egg whites*   250 *g* (½ *lb*) *mirepoix*
(*Recipe* 12)   30 *g* (1 *oz*) *diced*   (*omitting pork*)
1 *pheasant*   *mushrooms*   (*Recipe* 2)

1 Bone the pheasant; mince finely and combine with the egg whites and 1 pint of cold game-stock; mix well.
2 Roast the pheasant bones and mirepoix in the oven until golden brown.
3 Place the bones, mushrooms, and minced pheasant in a large stewpan and gradually mix with remaining cold game-stock.
4 Bring to the boil stirring frequently.
5 Draw to the side or reduce heat and simmer for 1 hour.
6 Strain through muslin.
7 Remove all fat.

Note. If the flavour is to be of venison, rabbit or hare, allow 500 g (1 lb) of the appropriate meat for each litre (quart).

230 Consommé au fumet de céleri – Celery-flavoured consommé [to yield 1 litre (1 quart)]

1·5 *l* (1½ *qt*) *chicken consommé*   500 *g* (1 *lb*) *blanched celery*
(*Recipe* 228)   *celery salt*

1 Cut the celery into small pieces.
2 Add the consommé while clarifying.
3 Garnish with batons of cooked celery.

231 Consommé tomate (base for consommé Carmen) – Tomato-flavoured consommé [to yield 1 litre (1 quart)]

30 *g* (1 *oz*) *blanched*   125 *ml* (¼ *pt*) *tomato*   125 *g* (¼ *lb*) *diced*
   pimentoes   *purée*   *tomatoes*
2 *l* (2 *qt*) *consommé de*   15 *ml spoon* [1 *table-*   (*peeled*)
   volaille (*Recipe* 228)   *spoon*] *boiled rice*

1 While clarifying 2 l (2 quarts) of chicken consommé add the tomato purée to give a pink colour.
2 Strain the consommé in the usual way.
3 Garnish with tomatoes, rice, and pimento.

232 Consommé madrilène [to yield 1 litre (1 quart)]

2 *l* (2 *qt*) *consommé de*	125 *ml* ($\frac{1}{4}$ *pt*) *of tomato*	30 *g* (1 *oz*) *blanched*
volaille	*purée*	*pimento*
(*Recipe* 228)	125 *g* ($\frac{1}{4}$ *lb*) *diced,*	30 *g* (1 *oz*) *vermicelli*
500 *g* (1 *lb*) *blanched*	*peeled tomatoes*	15 *g* ($\frac{1}{2}$ *oz*) *shredded*
celery		*sorrel*

1 While clarifying 2 litres (2 quarts) chicken consommé add the tomato purée and celery to give celery flavour.
2 Strain and garnish with the tomato and diced pimento, vermicelli, and julienne of sorrel.

Note. i Cook the vermicelli in a little consommé for 15 minutes.
    ii Sweat the sorrel in a little butter.
    iii This soup may be served cold.
    iv For cold madrilène add 15 g ($\frac{1}{2}$ oz) leaf gelatine soaked in water to 1 litre (1 quart) strong consommé; strain and garnish.

233 Consommè au vin – Consommé with wine

Consommé au madère	Consommé au vin de chypre
Consommé au marsala	Consommé au vin de malvoisie
Consommé au porto	

Add 250 ml ($\frac{1}{2}$ pint) of the chosen wine at the last minute, before service, to 1 litre (1 quart) of consommé.

234 Consommé aux nids d'hirondelles – Swallows' nest consommé [to yield 1 litre (1 quart)]

2 *l* (2 *qt*) *chicken consommé* (*Recipe* 228)   2 *swallows' nests*

1 Prepare and strain 2 litres (2 quarts) chicken consommé.
2 Soak nests in cold water for 24 hours.
3 Remove any feathers from the nest.
4 When nests are clean drain well.
5 Place the nests in the consommé and simmer for 50 minutes.

Note. The gummy parts of the nest will have melted in the consommé giving this consommé its characteristic consistency and flavour. There will only remain visible those portions which constitute the framework of the nest and resemble cooked vermicelli.

235 Consommé froid en gelée – Cold consommé [to yield 1 litre (1 quart)]

A note in Recipe 232 for Consommé madrilène, indicates that a cold version may be made by adding 15 g ($\frac{1}{2}$ oz) soaked leaf-gelatine to 1 litre (1 quart) of strong consommé, followed by straining and in that case, garnishing. Other suitable consommés, for example, 'au porto', may be similarly prepared for cold service.

SELECTED CONSOMMÉ GARNISHES

Vegetables for garnishing consommés should be blanched and cooked in a little consommé au point (just cooked) so as not to cloud the clear soup. A vast number of garnishes exist in addition to those listed below.

Bretonne – Fine julienne of celery, leek and chervil.

Brunoise – Fine dice of mixed vegetables (carrots, turnip, leek, celery).

Carmen – Tomate consommé (Recipe 231) with diamonds of tomato, red pepper and rice.

Caroline – Diamonds of Royale (unsweetened egg-custard), chiffonade of chervil and rice.

Célestine – Fine julienne of thin, cooked savoury pancake (also brunoise of truffle when costing permits). The consommé may be given slight 'body' with tapioca thickening.

Cheveux d'anges – Fine vermicelli; grated Parmesan cheese is served separately.

Clear oxtail soup – Infusion of turtle herbs, garnish small sections of oxtail, batons of vegetables (carrots, turnip, celery). Sometimes lightly lié with fécule.

Demidoff – Mixed spring vegetables, macédoine cut with tiny, fines herbes-flavoured quenelles (Recipe 194).

Diane – Game consommé (Recipe 229) with Madeira. Lean game-flesh in julienne, brunoise of truffle.

Dubarry – Tiny cauliflower sprigs, chiffonade of chervil, Royale roundels, slight tapioca thickening.

Julienne – Fine julienne of mixed vegetables (carrots, leek, celery), with peas, chervil, and sorrel chiffonade.

Monte Carlo – Consommé de volaille (Recipe 228) with coin-size (one penny) shaped garnish of carrots, turnips and truffle (optionally with rolled, stuffed pancakes sliced in rings).

Niçoise – Consommé madrilène (Recipe 232). Diced tomato, French beans and potato.

Olga – Port flavoured. Julienne of gherkin, celeriac, carrot and leek.

Orge perlé – Pearl barley.

Portugaise – Tomato flavoured.

Printanier – Small parisienne spoon-scooped balls of carrots and turnip with peas.

Quenelles – With quenelles flavoured as desired.

Ravioli – Small raviolis.

Royale – Unsweetened egg custard cut into dice or diamonds. (See note below.)

Solange – Pearl barley, julienne of chicken, small squares of lettuce.

236 Ordinary Royale (for consommé garnish)

250 ml (½ pt) *clear consommé (boiling)*	1 *whole egg* 3 *egg yolks*	2·5 *ml spoon* [½ *tea-spoon*] *salt*
15 g (½ oz) *chervil leaves or stalks*		

1 Make an infusion of the consommé and chervil. Allow to stand for 20 minutes.
2 Strain the infusion.
3 Beat all the eggs in a basin with a whisk, pour over the infusion, add salt.
4 Strain through a fine chinois or muslin.
5 Butter some dariole moulds, pour in the mixture, poach in a bain-marie in the oven, taking care it does not boil. (Approximate cooking time, small moulds, 15 minutes.)
6 When cooked allow to cool, trim and cut into diamond shapes or as desired.
Note. This basic Royale may be varied by colouring with vegetable purées and by introducing other flavours.

CLEAR SOUPS

The following clear soups are akin to consommés and have a similar place on menus; in some instances their service at luncheon is appropriate.

236a Bortsch à la russe [to yield 1 litre (1 quart)]

250 ml (½ pt) beetroot juice*	250 g (½ lb) boiling beef	30 g (1 oz) julienne leeks
1, 2 kg (4-lb) duck	12 small duck-patties†	30 g (1 oz) julienne carrots
2 l (2 qt) cold fond blanc (*Recipe* 6)	180 g (6 oz) parsley stalks	30 g (1 oz) julienne cooked beetroot
125 ml (¼ pt) sour cream	2 egg whites	

1 Half-roast the duck on a bed of vegetables.
2 Drain off the fat.
3 Mix the cold fond blanc and egg whites for clarification.
4 Place the duck and vegetables in a large pan and cover with the remaining cold fond blanc.
5 Add the parsley stalks and bring to the boil stirring frequently.
6 Add the boiling beef and 125 ml (¼ pint) of the beetroot juice and simmer until the duck and beef are cooked.
7 Strain through a muslin-cloth.
8 Cook the julienne of vegetables in a little butter and stock; garnish the consommé.
9 Cut the breast of duck and beef into small cubes and add to the consommé.
10 Just before service add the julienne of beetroot.
11 Accompany with a service of sauce-boats of sour cream and beetroot juice plus the small duck-patties.

237 Petite marmite [to yield 1 litre (1 quart)]

1 l (1 qt) strong beef and chicken consommé (*Recipes* 227 and 228)	60 g (2 oz) diced lean boiled beef	8 slices beef-bone marrow
120 g (¼ lb) carrots	60 g (2 oz) white cabbage	1 sauce-boat toasted croûtons
120 g (¼ lb) turnips	30 g (1 oz) julienne of celery	120 g (¼ lb) cooked chicken-dice or winglets
120 g (¼ lb) leeks (white)		

* *Beetroot juice* – Obtain by grating and squeezing raw beetroot.
† *Duck-patties* – These are made from a forcemeat of duck covered in puff paste roughly the size of a shilling.

1 Turn the carrots and turnips very small.
2 Shred the cabbage and leeks into julienne.
3 Cook the carrots, turnips, leeks, cabbage and celery in a little consommé until tender.
4 Add the garnish to the consommé and the beef and chicken.
5 Just before service add the marrow.
6 Serve in earthenware marmite pots accompanied by toasted croûtons. (Grated Parmesan cheese may be offered in a sauce-boat.)

238 Petite marmite béarnaise [to yield 1 litre (1 quart)]

As Recipe 237 adding: 15 g ($\frac{1}{2}$ oz) *cooked rice*
30 g (1 oz) *julienne-cooked potatoes*

239 Poule au pot

A variation of Petite marmite, Recipe 237, plus a fowl cooked in the stock and garnished in the same way.

240 Potage à la tortue clair – Clear turtle soup [to yield 1 litre (1 quart)]

750 *ml* (1$\frac{1}{2}$ *pt*) *chicken consommé* (*Recipe* 228)	120 *g* ($\frac{1}{4}$ *lb*) *dried turtle-meat*	1 *packet turtle herbs* (*Recipe* 240a)
750 *ml* (1$\frac{1}{2}$ *pt*) *beef consommé* (*Recipe* 227)	30 *g* (1 *oz*) *fécule*	250 *ml* ($\frac{1}{2}$ *pt*) *Madeira wine*

Adjuncts: *Cheese straws* (*Recipe* 1188), *lemon.*

1 Soak the dry turtle-meat in water for at least 24 hours.
2 Mix the two consommés and cook the turtle while in the clarifying stage
3 When the turtle is cooked, remove and cut into small dice.
4 Strain the consommé, bring to the boil and add the diluted fécule.
5 Make an infusion of the turtle herbs in 250 ml ($\frac{1}{2}$ pint) of the strained consommé. (This infusion should stand for 10 minutes.)
6 Strain the infusion into the consommé, garnish with the diced turtle-meat add the Madeira. Re-boil and remove all grease.

240a Turtle herbs – dried

Basil	*Sage*	*Thyme*
Marjoram	*Rosemary*	*Coriander*
6 *peppercorns*	1 *bay-leaf*	

Tie in a muslin bag and use 7 g ($\frac{1}{4}$ oz) total of dried herbs to 1 litre (1 quart of turtle consommé.

BOUILLONS

Petite marmite and Poule au pot (see Recipes 237 and 239) may justly be considered refined forms of bouillon. However, the following example typify the unthickened, natural liquor in which meat and poultry have bee simply cooked and from which bouillons originate. This type of soup is suitable for luncheon. Originally, en famille, the boiled meat from the bouillon constituted a main course or further meal.

241 Bouillon de volaille [to yield 1 litre (1 quart)]

1, 2·5 kg (5-*lb*) *old fowl*	1 *onion clouté*	3 *l* (3 *qt*) *cold*
500 g (1 *lb*) *chopped*	2 *whole carrots*	*water*
veal-bones	250 g (½ *lb*)	30 g (1 *oz*)
250 g (½ *lb*) *minced lean beef*	*leeks*	*vermicelli*

1 Blanch the veal bones and clean and truss the fowl.
2 Mix the beef with the cold water and add the fowl.
3 Bring to the boil and remove all scum.
4 Add the vegetables whole.
5 Simmer till the fowl is cooked.
6 Remove all fat; strain through muslin.
7 Season and garnish with cooked vermicelli.

242 Bouillon aux œufs [to yield 1 litre (1 quart)]

As above, Recipe 241, with two fresh eggs beaten and strained into 1 litre (1 quart) bouillon, but do not use vermicelli.

243 Croûte au pot [to yield 1 litre (1 quart)]

1 Prepare Petite marmite, Recipe 237, and similarly garnish but omit the meat and chicken garnish.
2 Serve in marmite pots.

Note. The service of croûtons differs in that they are first dipped in a little stock fat and dried off in the oven.

244 Pot-au-feu [to yield 1 litre (1 quart)]

1 *kg* (2 *lb*) *boiling beef*	250 g (½ *lb*) *whole*	½ *white cabbage*
2 *l* (2 *qt*) *water*	*turnip*	2 *whole leeks*
1 *large onion*	2 *cloves*	1 *bay-leaf*
2 *whole carrots*	120 g (4 *oz*) *celery*	*seasoning*

1 Wash the meat under cold water.
2 Place the meat in a large earthenware pot and add the water.
3 Bring to the boil and remove all scum.
4 Stick the onion with the cloves and tie the cabbage, leeks, celery in single bundles.
5 Add the vegetables to the pot and simmer till the meat and vegetables are cooked.
6 Take out the meat and the vegetables.
7 Strain the stock and season.
8 Slice the vegetables and garnish the broth.
9 The meat can be sliced.
10 Serve toasted croûtons.

BROTHS AND GARNISHED UNTHICKENED SOUPS

The following soups have a base of broth or unthickened liquor. Garnishes in some instances, particularly heavy ones, do have the effect of slight thickening or clouding. These are regarded as luncheon soups.

In all recipes for 'unpassed' soups, vegetable quantities are of prepared weights.

245 Cocky Leeky [to yield 1 litre (1 quart)]

2 *l (2 qt) chicken stock (Recipe* 11)   250 *g* (½ *lb) Julienne white leek*
30 *g* (1 *oz) boiled rice*   1 *bouquet garni*
12 *stewed prunes*   1, 2 *kg* (4-*lb) fowl*

1 Joint the fowl as for sauter.
2 Fry the fowl to a golden colour in butter.
3 Add the fowl to the stock.
4 Boil and skim; add bouquet garni and simmer till the fowl is cooked.
5 Strain the liquid.
6 Cut the fowl in small pieces.
7 Stew the leeks in butter, pour the stock over and cook for 20 minutes.
8 Add the boiled rice and chicken to the soup; remove all fat and season.
9 Prunes are heated in a little stock and added before service.

246 Minestrone [to yield 1 litre (1 quart)]

60 *g* (2 *oz) fat bacon*   60 *g* (2 *oz) leeks*   45 *g* (1½ *oz) rice*
1 *clove, crushed garlic*   *toasted croûtons*   1 *bouquet garni*
60 *g* (2 *oz) broken*   (*flutes*)   60 *g* (2 *oz) onions*
  spaghetti   240 *g* (½ *lb) tomato*   60 *g* (2 *oz) cabbage*
30 *g* (1 *oz) fresh or*   *concassé*   1·5 *l* (1½ *qt) white stock*
  frozen peas   10 *ml spoon* [1   30 *g* (1 *oz) grated*
60 *g* (2 *oz) carrots*   *dessertspoon*]   *Parmesan cheese*
60 *g* (2 *oz) turnips*   *tomato purée*
60 *g* (2 *oz) celery*   30 *g* (1 *oz) French beans*
60 *g* (2 *oz) potato*   (*cut into diamonds*)

1 Dice the bacon to extract the fat.
2 Add the vegetables (cut into paysanne), and garlic, and sweat under cover.
3 Add the stock; boil and skim.
4 Add the bouquet garni and simmer for 20 minutes.
5 Add the tomato purée and tomato concassé, spaghetti, rice and French beans and peas.
6 Simmer for a further 15 minutes.
7 Skim off all fat; remove bouquet garni and season.
8 Serve with cheese and croûtons; do not strain.

247 Mutton broth [to yield 1 litre (1 quart)]

Prepare as Scotch broth, Recipe 252, but halve the quantities of vegetable garnish.

248 Potage bonne femme [to yield 1 litre (1 quart)]

1 *l* (1 *qt*) *fond blanc* (*Recipe* 6)	350 *g* (¾ *lb*) *white of leek* (*paysanne*)	720 *g* [1½ *lb* (*net*)] *diced potato*
125 *ml* (¼ *pt*) *fresh cream*	1 *bouquet garni* *seasoning*	120 *g* (4 *oz*) *butter*

1 Sweat the potatoes and leeks in 60 g (2 oz) butter under cover.
2 Moisten with the fond blanc. Boil and skim. Add bouquet garni and simmer until the vegetables are cooked.
3 Remove bouquet garni and all fat.
4 Season; add the cream and blend in the butter.
5 Sprinkle a little fresh, chopped parsley on the top before service.
6 Served toasted flutes separately or thin slices of toasted, French bread; do not strain.

Note. To the above a liaison of 1 egg yolk and 125 ml (gill) of cream may be added. The cream should be warmed before adding. When this is done, the soup ceases to be an unthickened type.

249 Potage cultivateur [to yield 1 litre (1 quart)]

60 *g* (2 *oz*) *diced, salted pork*	60 *g* (2 *oz*) *turnips*	1 *l* (1 *qt*) *white stock* (*Recipe* 6)
60 *g* (2 *oz*) *carrots*	60 *g* (2 *oz*) *celery*	1 *bouquet garni*
60 *g* (2 *oz*) *onions*	90 *g* (3 *oz*) *potatoes*	15 *ml spoon* [1 *tablespoon*]
90 *g* (3 *oz*) *leeks*	60 *g* (2 *oz*) *butter* *seasoning*	*chopped parsley*

1 Blanch and refresh the pork and fry off.
2 Cut the vegetables into paysanne and sweat in butter under cover.
3 Moisten with the stock, boil, skim; add the bouquet garni and simmer till the vegetables are cooked.
4 Remove the bouquet garni and all fat.
5 Adjust the seasoning, add the fried pork and sprinkle with chopped parsley.
Note. The vegetables should retain their shape in cooking.

250 Potage fermière [to yield 1 litre (1 quart)]

1 *l* (1 *qt*) *fond de volaille* (*Recipe* 11)	60 *g* (2 *oz*) *celery*	1 *bouquet garni*
60 *g* (2 *oz*) *butter*	90 *g* (3 *oz*) *leeks*	*seasoning*
60 *g* (2 *oz*) *carrots*	90 *g* (3 *oz*) *potatoes*	15 *ml spoon* [1 *tablespoon*]
60 *g* (2 *oz*) *turnips*	60 *g* (2 *oz*) *onions*	*chopped parsley*
	60 *g* (2 *oz*) *cabbage*	

1 Cut the cabbage into julienne and the rest of the vegetables into paysanne.
2 Sweat the vegetables in butter under cover.
3 Add the fond de volaille, boil and skim; add the bouquet garni.
4 Simmer till the vegetables are cooked; remove bouquet garni.
5 Remove all fat and season.
6 Sprinkle with fresh chopped parsley.
7 Serve toasted flutes.

Note. The vegetables must retain their shape and not be in the purée.

251 Potage paysanne [to yield (1 litre (1 quart)]

1·25 *l* (1¼ *qt*) *white stock*   15 *g* (½ *oz*) *chervil*   1 *bouquet garni*
    (*Recipe* 6)   *leaves*   60 *g* (2 *oz*) *turnips*
30 *g* (1 *oz*) *fresh peas*   60 *g* (2 *oz*) *carrots*   60 *g* (2 *oz*) *onions*
30 *g* (1 *oz*) *French*   90 *g* (3 *oz*) *butter*   60 *g* (2 *oz*) *leeks*
    beans (*cut into*   15 *ml spoon* [1 *table-*   60 *g* (2 *oz*) *celery*
    diamonds)   *spoon*] *chopped*   60 *g* (2 *oz*) *potatoes*
30 *g* (1 *oz*) *flageolets*   *parsley*   *seasoning*

1 Cut the vegetables into paysanne and sweat in butter under cover.
2 Add the white stock. Boil, skim and add the bouquet garni.
3 Simmer until the vegetables are cooked. They must retain their shape when cooked.
4 Remove bouquet garni and all fat; season.
5 Sprinkle with parsley and chervil leaves before service.
6 Do not strain.

252 Scotch broth [to yield 1 litre (1 quart)]

1·5 *l* (1½ *qt*) *water* (*or*   90 *g* (3 *oz*) *brunoise of*   90 *g* (3 *oz*) *brunoise of*
    white stock (*Recipe* 6   *celery*   *leek*
    from mutton bones)   60 *g* (2 *oz*) *finely-*   30 *g* (1 *oz*) *barley*
350 *g* (¾ *lb*) *scrag of*   *diced onions*   2 × 15 *ml spoon* [2
    mutton   30 *g* (1 *oz*) *dried peas*   *tablespoons*] *chopped*
120 *g* (4 *oz*) *brunoise of*   60 *g* (2 *oz*) *diced*   *parsley*
    carrots   *cabbage*   *seasoning*
60 *g* (2 *oz*) *brunoise of*
    turnips

1 Soak, in separate dishes, the barley and peas in cold water.
2 Boil the water with the scrag of mutton; remove all scum.
3 Add the barley, peas and cook for 20 minutes.
4 Add all the vegetables and simmer till cooked and the meat tender.
5 Cut the meat into small dice.
6 Remove all fat; season, add the diced meat.
7 Sprinkle with chopped parsley.

Note. In some cases of high-quality service, the broth is finished with light cream.

253 Soupe à l'oignon gratinée à la française – Brown onion soup (French style) [to yield 1 litre (1 quart)]

1 *kg* (2 *lb*) *sliced onions*   21 *g* (¾ *oz*) *flour*   *toasted flute*
1·5 *l* (1½ *qt*) *fond brun*   120 *g* (4 *oz*) *butter*   *croûtons*
    (*Recipe* 7 *or* 8)   90 *g* (3 *oz*) *grated*   *seasoning*
1 *clove crushed garlic*   *Gruyère*

1 Fry onions and garlic in the butter to light-golden colour.
2 Blend in the flour and cook for about 3 minutes.
3 Moisten with the stock (good consommé is even better) and simmer till the onions are cooked.
4 Carefully remove all fat and season lightly from the pepper mill, and with salt.

5 Pour the soup into earthenware bowls and spread on the toasted flutes neatly.

6 Sprinkle Gruyère cheese on top and set to brown in the oven.

7 Do not strain.

THICKENED BROWN SOUPS

The following miscellany of soups, having thickened brown stock or a common denominator, are for luncheon service.

254 Brown Windsor soup [to yield 1 litre (1 quart)]

2 *l* (2 *qt*) *estouffade* (*Recipe* 8)	*bouquet garni*	250 *g* (½ *lb*) *mirepoix*
500 *g* (1 *lb*) *chopped beef-bones*	30 *g* (1 *oz*) *cooked macédoine of vegetables*	*of vegetables* (*Recipe* 2)
90 *g* (3 *oz*) *fat*		30 *g* (1 *oz*) *stock fat*
90 *g* (3 *oz*) *flour*		125 *ml* (1 *gill*) *tomato purée*

Brown off the vegetables and bones in the stock fat and drain.

Fry the mirepoix to a golden colour in the fat and add the flour to make a brown roux.

Blend in the tomato purée and mix well with the estouffade.

Boil and skim; add the bouquet garni and simmer for 1½ hours.

Strain, skim and season.

Garnish with the cooked macedoine of vegetables.

Note. Windsor soup was originally a white soup featuring, inter alia, calves' feet. Brown Windsor is a relatively recent (and generally unwelcome) addition to the chef's repertoire. The above is offered as a serviceable formula for a run-of-the-mill lunch-time soup.

255 Potage à la fausse tortue épais – Thick mock-turtle soup [to yield 1 litre (1 quart)]

½ *calf's head*	1 *bouquet garni*	120 *g* (¼ *lb*) *celery*
2 *carrots*	12 *crushed pepper-corns*	1 *small pkt turtle herbs**
1 *onion*	125 *ml* (1 *gill*) *Madeira*	90 *g* (3 *oz*) *butter*
1·5 *l* (1½ *qt*) *brown stock* (*Recipe* 7)		90 *g* (3 *oz*) *flour*
thyme, bay-leaf, cloves	10 *ml spoon* [1 *dessert-spoon*] *tomato purée*	6 *tomatoes*
250 *g* (½ *lb*) *lean ham* (*diced*)		*juice of* ½ *lemon*

1 Bone the head and chop the bones.

2 Cook bones and head in water with 1 onion clouté, 2 whole carrots, 1 sprig thyme and 1 bay-leaf.

3 When cooked remove the head and strain the stock.

4 Dice the head into small pieces and keep warm.

5 Fry off the diced ham in the fat.

6 Add the flour to make a brown roux. When cooked blend in the tomatoes.

7 Moisten with the stock, mix well, boil and skim.

* See Recipe 240a.

8 Add the peppercorns, bouquet garni and simmer for 1 hour.
9 Stand the turtle herbs in 250 ml (½ pint) brown stock for 5 minutes on the side of the stove and add the infusion to the soup.
10 Strain, adjust seasoning, add the lemon juice and Madeira.
11 Garnish with the diced calf's head.

256 Hare Soup [to yield 1 litre (1 quart)]

1·5 *l* (1½ *qt*) *estouffade* (*Recipe* 8)	30 *g* (1 *oz*) *parsley stalks*	125 *ml* (1 *gill*) *tomato purée*
1 *hare*	60 *g* (2 *oz*) *carrot* (*diced*)	*bouquet garni*
250 *ml* (½ *pt*) *port wine*	60 *g* (2 *oz*) *butter*	125 *ml* (1 *gill*) *Madeira wine*
60 *g* (2 *oz*) *celery* (*diced*)		
60 *g* (2 *oz*) *flour*		

1 Cut up the hare retaining the blood and liver.
2 Add the vegetables to the hare and pour on the port wine and stand for 1½ hours.
3 Remove the hare and vegetables and fry off in the fat; add the flour and make a brown roux; when cooked blend in the tomato purée.
4 Moisten with stock and the port wine from the hare; boil and skim; add bouquet garni.
5 Simmer one hour or until the hare is cooked well.
6 Beat the blood with a little water and add to the soup; simmer for a few minutes.
7 Strain, adjust the seasoning and add the Madeira wine.

Note. The soup may be finished with 30 ml spoon (2 tablespoons) of cream.

257 Mulligatawny [to yield 1 litre (1 quart)]

1·25 (1¼ *qt*) *estouffade* (*Recipe* 8)	120 *g* (4 *oz*) *diced onions*	15 *g* (½ *oz*) *chutney* *bouquet garni*
60 *g* (2 *oz*) *butter*	60 *g* (2 *oz*) *diced apples*	15 *g* (½ *oz*) *boiled rice*
60 *g* (2 *oz*) *flour*		125 *ml* (1 *gill*) *cream*
15 *ml spoon* [1 table-spoon] *tomato purée*	15 *g* (½ *oz*) *curry powder*	*seasoning*

1 Melt the butter and sweat the onions.
2 Mix in the flour to make a blond roux.
3 Add the curry powder and cook for 2 to 3 minutes.
4 Blend in the tomato purée.
5 Add the stock, mix well, boil and skim; add the bouquet garni, apple and chutney.
6 Simmer for 1 hour.
7 Strain – adjust seasoning, garnish with boiled rice.
8 Add the warm cream.

258 Oxtail soup (thick) [to yield 1 litre (1 quart)]

750 *g* (1½ *lb*) *oxtail*	90 *g* (3 *oz*) *fat* ⎱ *roux*	
1·5 *l* (1½ *qt*) *estouffade* (*Recipe* 8)	90 *g* (3 *oz*) *flour* ⎰	
	30 *g* (1 *oz*) *tomato purée*	
120 *g* (4 *oz*) *onions* ⎱ *mirepoix*		
120 *g* (4 *oz*) *carrots* ⎰	*bouquet garni*	

Garnish: 30 *g* (1 *oz*) *carrots, leeks, turnips, cut into paysanne.*

1 Remove fat from the oxtail.
2 Cut into small sections.
3 Fry off the sections in the fat to a golden brown.
4 Remove the oxtail from the pan and fry off the mirepoix in the same pan.
5 Add the flour to the mirepoix and make a brown roux. When cooked blend in the tomato purée.
6 Mix well with the stock; boil and skim.
7 Add the oxtail and bouquet garni.
8 Simmer until the oxtail is cooked (approximately 2½ hours).
9 Remove oxtail and cut into small dice.
10 Strain the soup and remove all fat; season.
11 Cook the paysanne of vegetables in a little stock and add to the soup with the diced oxtail.

Note. The soup may be finished with 62 ml (½ gill) of cream.

259 Soupe aux rognons – Kidney soup [to yield 1 litre (1 quart)]

1·25 *ml* (1¼ *qt*) *estouffade* (*Recipe* 8)	62 *ml* (½ *gill*) *tomato purée*	60 *g* (2 *oz*) *brunoise onion*
180 *g* (6 *oz*) *ox-kidney*	60 *g* (2 *oz*) *brunoise carrot*	*bouquet garni*
60 *g* (2 *oz*) *lard*		15 *g* (½ *oz*) *butter*
		60 *g* (2 *oz*) *flour*

1 Brown the kidney in some of the fat.
2 Fry the vegetables in the same fat having removed the kidney.
3 Add flour to make a brown roux and blend in the tomato purée.
4 Add the estouffade and mix well; boil and skim.
5 Add the bouquet garni and the kidney.
6 Simmer till the kidney is cooked; remove and dice.
7 Strain the soup, adjust the seasoning, add the diced kidney and blend in the butter.

Note. A little brunoise of vegetable is also sometimes included in the garnish. A Crème version may be made by stirring in 15 ml spoon (1 tablespoon) cream when finally blending in the butter.

BISQUES AND CHOWDERS

Bisques are made of high-quality fish (usually shellfish) and are thick soups. Chowders, developed in America, are also thick soups owing their consistency to potatoes and biscuit crumbs. Bisques and Chowders differ from the thin-liquor fish-soup stews in being thick and because they are normally made of shellfish.

260 Bisque d'écrevisse – Crayfish bisque [to yield 1 litre (1 quart)]

3 *dozen crayfish*	125 *ml* (1 *gill*) *white wine*	90 *g* (3 *oz*) *rice, Carolina*
12 *anchovy fillets*	125 *ml* (1 *gill*) *brandy*	*bouquet garni*
120 *g* (4 *oz*) *butter*	90 *g* (3 *oz*) *fine mirepoix* (*Recipe* 2)	12 *crushed peppercorns*
15 *l* (1½ *qt*) *fish stock* (*Recipe* 374)		125 *ml* (1 *gill*) *cream*
		juice of ½ *lemon*

1 Pound the crayfish and retain 12 tails for garnish.
2 Fry the mirepoix in butter, add the pounded crayfish and cook till a red colour; flambé with brandy.
3 Add the fish stock, boil and skim; add the rice, bouquet garni, crayfish tails and white wine.
4 Simmer till the rice is cooked and very soft.
5 Rub the whole through a tammy.
6 Re-boil; season with lemon juice, salt and cayenne pepper.
7 Blend the cream and 30 g (1 oz) butter.
8 Garnish with the diced crayfish tails.

Note. Other bisques such as Bisque de crevettes (Shrimp) and Crabes (Crab) maybe, are prepared in the same way as the above.

261 Bisque de homard – Lobster bisque [to yield 1 litre (1 quart)]

1, 750 g (1½-lb) raw lobster	1 glass cognac	6 fresh tomatoes
120 g (4 oz) fine mirepoix (Recipe 4)	1·25 l (2½ pt) fish stock (Recipe 374)	125 ml (1 gill) cream
125 ml (1 gill) white wine	bouquet garni	6 crushed peppercorns
120 g (4 oz) butter	125 ml (1 gill) tomato purée	90 g (3 oz) flour
		juice of ½ lemon
		salt, cayenne pepper

1 Split the lobster down the back.
2 Remove the meat and crack the claws.
3 Pound the lobster and shell in the mortar and mix with the butter.
4 Put all in a stewpan, stir over fire till the lobster turns red and then add mirepoix.
5 Mix in the flour and cook for 2 or 3 minutes.
6 Blend in the tomatoes and moisten with the wine and stock; mix well.
7 Boil, skim; add peppercorns and bouquet garni; simmer for 20 minutes.
8 Remove the claws, take out the meat and dice for garnish; marinate in the brandy.
9 Rub the soup through a tammy.
10 Season with lemon juice, salt and cayenne pepper; add the cream and blend in 30 g (1 oz) butter.
11 Garnish with diced lobster claws.

Note. White veal stock (Recipe 9) may be used in lieu of fish stock.

262 Clam chowder [to yield 1 litre (1 quart)]

18 clams	1 l (1 qt) fish stock (Recipe 374)	60 g (2 oz) butter
500 g (1 lb) small diced potatoes	4 diced white of leek	15 g (½ oz) fines herbes
250 g (½ lb) diced onions	6 water biscuits or cream crackers	125 ml (1 gill) cream
		60 g (2 oz) fat pickled pork

1 Open clams and gently poach in 500 ml (1 pint) of fish stock; when cooked cut into small dice.
2 Sweat the diced pork, onions, and leeks in butter; add the potatoes and sweat under cover for a further few minutes.

3 Moisten with fish stock and the cooking liquid from the clams.

4 Simmer gently until the vegetables are cooked; add the clams, cream, fines herbes, water biscuits (broken into small pieces); season.

262a New England chowder

This may be made by adding 250 g ($\frac{1}{2}$ lb) tomato concassé and a pinch of saffron to the ingredients of Recipe 262.

Note. Other white fish such as cod and haddock may be used in chowder-making.

Fish-soup stews. Bouillabaisse, the celebrated fish-soup stew of the Marseilles coast, is so truly regional that it is unlikely to be featured in good establishments outside its own area, but recipes for it, for matelotes, and for waterzoi are given in Chapter 5 (Recipes 455 to 458). For other fish soups of this kind, culinary encyclopœdias or speciality food books should be consulted.

THICKENED SOUPS: PURÉES, CRÈMES, AND VELOUTÉS

Purées and crèmes.

Starchy vegetables such as haricot beans, lentils, and potatoes when purée-d in soups, usually act as self-thickeners. Soups made from these vegetables need no further thickening ingredient.

Other vegetables like carrots, pumpkins, turnips, celery and leaf greens do need an additional thickening agent as their own purées do not cohere at all. To effect coherence in this kind of vegetable purée, either potatoes or rice may be added: 90 g (3 oz) rice or 300 g (10 oz) potato per 500 g (1 lb) of vegetables.

Both these soups, self-thickened or with added rice- or potato-thickening, are correctly designated purées. For simple service, they may be prepared and served without a cream finish, or milk can be used in lieu of cream.

Vegetable Crèmes.

In some instances purées may be called crèmes. Examples are Crème d'orge (Cream of barley) and, when the vegetable purée is specially named, St Germain, for green-pea purée. The word crème (hence Crème St Germain) is commonly used when the purée has been given a cream finish (but see the following paragraph on crèmes).

Veloutés and Crèmes.

Basic veloutés for sauces have already been described in Chapter 1. Veloutés as soups are similar to other veloutés and, by the same token, differ from purées in that they require a thickening element, a roux. For soup veloutés 90 g (3 oz) of white roux per litre (quart) of the liquid to be thickened is used. Veloutés may be made with a vegetable content, e.g., velouté crécy (carrot purée, roux-cohered) in conjunction with stock or white consommé (or fish stock for a fish velouté). For a velouté de volaille (chicken velouté) and derivatives, thickened white chicken consommé is the dominant element.

Generally, proportions for a velouté soup are $\frac{1}{2}$ basic velouté (as appropriate); $\frac{1}{4}$ purée (of the appropriate main ingredient characterizing the soup);

¼ stock or white consommé used to dilute the mix of purée and velouté to the correct consistency.

Finishing Veloutés.
Correct finishing of velouté is effected with a liaison of beaten egg yolks and cream, using 3 yolks and ⅕ pint (100 ml) cream per 1 litre (1 quart) of soup.

Crèmes–creams.
Cream soups, other than simple purées given a cream finish, are prepared similarly to veloutés with these differences:
  i Whatever the nature of the soup, Béchamel is used instead of velouté.
 ii Milk is used to dilute and achieve correct consistency instead of stock or consommé.
iii Creams are finished with cream. They do not require egg yolk.

Note. An exception is tomato soup which, when not cream-finished, might correctly be designated velouté de tomates for it is roux-thickened. Yet when cream-finished this soup is invariably called crème de tomate – Cream of Tomato Soup (Recipe 288).

General comments. Although there are these differences between purées, veloutés and creams, the use of crème or cream as a common designation for soups made with a cream finish is now so widespread as to constitute accepted usage. What remains important is to use good methods and recipes for the type of soups desired.

Stock and Consommé.
In many of the recipes of master chefs of past generations, white consommés or chicken consommés were specified as the liquid base for most of the thickened soups in the following recipes. For vegetable, farinaceous, and pulse soups, good fond blanc or good fond de volaille are nowadays used for this purpose. The term white consommé did not, in any case, have the significance of the clarified consommés or clear soups and simply implied high-quality fond or stock. Obviously, where white stock is to be used in cream or velouté of chicken, the white stock can be reinforced with chicken (bones and carcass).

THICK VEGETABLE SOUPS

The vegetables soups in this section include veloutés, purées and crèmes. Farinaceous soups of corn, barley and, of course, the pulses, have been grouped under the broad heading of 'vegetable'.

263 Potage ambassadeurs [to yield 1 litre (1 quart)]

30 g (1 oz) white of leek (cut into julienne)
15 g (½ oz) shredded sorrel

15 g (½ oz) shredded lettuce
1 l (1 qt) Crème St Germain (Recipe 285)

1 Stew the lettuce and sorrel in butter.

2 Cook the leek in fond blanc (Recipe 6).

3 Add the garnish to 1 litre (1 qt) St Germain.

Note. This soup can also be made by using dried-pea purée (Recipe 283).

264 Crème argenteuil – Cream of asparagus [to yield 1 litre (1 quart)]

750 g (1½ *lb*) *asparagus tips* 250 ml (½ pt) chicken   30 g (1 oz) butter
750 ml (1½ pt) Béchamel   stock (Recipe 11)   15 g (½ oz) chervil-
  (Recipe 51)   125 ml (¼ pt) cream   leaves

1 Parboil the asparagus heads for 8 minutes and drain.

2 Add the asparagus heads to the Béchamel and continue cooking till soft.

3 Rub through a sieve and adjust the consistency with the stock.

4 Season, blend in the cream and butter.

5 Garnish with small pieces of green asparagus and blanched chervil-leaves

265 Crème bruxelloise [to yield 1 litre (1 quart)]

500 g (1 lb) fresh chicory   750 ml (1½ pt) Béchamel   125 ml (¼ pt)
90 g (3 oz) butter   (Recipe 51)   cream
juice of 1 lemon   250 ml (½ pt) fond blanc 2 Belgian endives
                               (Recipe 6)   (cut into julienne)

1 Stew the chicory in 60 g (2 oz) fresh butter with the lemon juice.

2 Mix the stewed chicory with the Béchamel; when cooked, rub through a fine sieve and return to the pan.

3 Adjust the consistency with fond blanc.

4 Season and blend in the cream and butter.

5 Garnish with julienne of endives stewed in butter.

266 Crème de céleri – Cream of celery [to yield 1 litre (1 quart)]

500 g (1 lb) white celery   125 ml (¼ pt) cream   seasoning
90 g (3 oz) flour   750 ml (1½ pt) chicken   bouquet garni
90 g (3 oz) margarine   stock (Recipe 11)   30 g (1 oz) butter
                            500 ml (1 pt) milk

Garnish: 90 g (3 oz) cooked brunoise of celery

1 Dice the celery and blanch for 8 minutes.

2 Make a white roux.

3 Add the stock and milk, and mix well.

4 Boil, skim, add celery and bouquet garni.

5 Simmer until the celery is a purée, then rub through a fine sieve.

6 Re-boil, season, adjust consistency with a little boiled milk.

7 Blend in the cream and butter.

267 Crème de champignons – Cream of mushroom soup [to yield 1 litre (1 quart)]

60 g (2 oz) diced onions 90 g (3 oz) butter   250 ml (½ pt) milk
360 g (¾ lb) mushroom   750 ml (1½ pt) chicken   2 egg yolks   ⎫
  duxelle (Recipe 101)   stock (Recipe 11)   125 ml (1 gill) ⎬ liaison
90 g (3 oz) flour   seasoning   cream   ⎭

1 Sweat the onions and duxelle in butter; add the flour and make a blond roux.
2 Moisten with the stock and simmer for 20 minutes.
3 Add the boiled milk.
4 Strain through a hair-sieve.
5 Re-boil; add the liaison and season.
6 Add a little diced, cooked mushrooms as a garnish.

268 Purée or Crème condé [to yield 1 litre (1 quart)]

300 g (10 oz) red beans	120 g (4 oz) chopped	90 g (3 oz) butter
500 ml (1 pt) red wine	onions	125 ml (1 gill)
500 ml (1 pt) white stock	120 g (4 oz) diced carrots	cream
(Recipe 6)	bouquet garni	seasoning

1 Soak the beans in water for 6 hours.
2 Sweat the carrots and onions in butter, add the beans and sweat for a further 2 or 3 minutes.
3 Moisten with the wine and stew for about 15 minutes; add the white stock and bouquet garni and continue to cook until purée-d.
4 Rub through a fine sieve; re-boil and check for consistency (adjust with stock as necessary); season.
5 Blend in the cream and 30 g (1 oz) butter; serve with sippets.

269 Purée or Crème crécy – Cream of carrot soup [to yield 1 litre (1 quart)]

750 g (1½ lb) thinly-sliced carrots	2·5 ml spoon [½ tea-spoon] sugar	60 g (2 oz) rice, Carolina
90 g (3 oz) finely-chopped onions	1·5 l (1½ qt) white stock (Recipe 6)	125 ml (1 gill) fresh cream
90 g (3 oz) butter	1 sprig thyme	1 bay-leaf

1 Place the onions, carrots, thyme, bay-leaf, sugar, in a small saucepan with the butter and stew until tender.
2 Add the white stock; boil, skim and add the rice.
3 Cook gently till a purée.
4 Rub through a tammy; season and finish with cream and 30 g (1 oz) butter.

270 Crème or Purée cressonnière – Cress and potato purée (to yield 1 quart)

750 g (1½ lb) diced, peeled potatoes	125 ml (¼ pt) cream	bouquet garni
60 g (2 oz) onions	2 egg yolks liaison	seasoning
60 g (2 oz) leeks	2 watercress bunches	90 g (3 oz) butter
	1·5 l (1½ qt) white stock (Recipe 6)	

1 Pluck the leaves from 1 bunch of watercress, blanch and refresh.
2 Blanch the other bunch and the stalks; chop finely.
3 Sweat off the onions, leeks, and potatoes in 60 g (2 oz) butter under cover.
4 Moisten with stock, add the chopped cress, boil and skim.
5 Add bouquet garni and simmer until a complete purée.
6 Rub through a sieve, re-boil; finish with the liaison.
7 Blend in the remaining butter.

8 Garnish with the watercress leaves.
9 Check consistency and if required dilute with a little boiled milk.

Note. The soup may be prepared as a velouté (Recipe 296).

271 Crème d'orge – Cream of barley soup (to yield 1 litre (1 quart)]

    30 g (1 oz) white celery   1·5 l (1½ qt) chicken stock   30 g (1 oz) butter
    240 g (½ lb) pearl barley   (Recipe 11)   seasoning
    125 ml (¼ pt) cream

1 Wash barley and soak in lukewarm water for 2 hours.
2 Drain and add 750 ml (1½ pint) of chicken stock and celery. Cook gently under cover until a purée for approximately 2½ hours.
3 Rub the purée through a fine sieve and dilute with the other 750 ml (1½ pint) of chicken stock.
4 Reheat, season, blend in the cream and butter.
5 Adjust consistency with boiled milk.

272 Crème Dubarry – Cream of cauliflower soup [to yield 1 litre (1 quart)]

    1 l (1 qt) white stock   125 ml (1 gill) cream   60 g (2 oz) onions
      (Recipe 6)   (warm)   (diced)
    375 ml (¾ pt) milk   60 g (2 oz) flour   60 g (2 oz) white of leek
    500 g (1 lb) cauliflower   75 g (2½ oz) butter   (diced)
                        seasoning   bouquet garni

1 Wash cauliflower and remove faded leaves.
2 Break into small sections (retaining some small pieces for garnish which should be cooked separately).
3 Blanch the remainder of the cauliflower.
4 Sweat the leeks and onions in the butter and make a white roux with the flour.
5 Moisten with the stock and milk; add the blanched cauliflower, boil and skim; add bouquet garni.
6 Simmer until the cauliflower falls into a purée.
7 Rub through a fine sieve; re-boil, correcting consistency with boiled milk, adjust seasoning and add the small pieces of cauliflower; blend in the cream with 15 g (½ oz) butter.

273 Purée or Crème Esau [to yield 1 litre (1 quart)]
Prepare as Cream of Lentil (Recipe 278), garnished with 60 g (2 oz) boiled rice.

274 Purée or Crème flamande – Brussels sprouts and potato purée [to yield 1 litre (1 quart)]

    1·5 l (1½ qt) white stock   120 g (4 oz) diced   1 egg yolk
      (Recipe 6)   white of leek   125 ml (1 gill)
    500 g (1 lb) Brussels sprouts 90 g (3 oz) onions   cream
    500 g (1 lb) diced potatoes (net) bouquet garni   90 g (3 oz) butter

1 Trim and blanch the sprouts.
2 Stew them in 60 g (2 oz) butter until tender.

3 Sweat the onions and leeks and moisten with the stock.
4 Add the stewed sprouts, boil and skim; add the bouquet garni.
5 Simmer until all the ingredients are in a purée and rub through a sieve.
6 Re-boil, adjust the seasoning and add liaison of egg yolks and cream.
7 Blend in 30 g (1 oz) butter.
8 Serve soup sippets separately.
  If the consistency is too thick, adjust with boiled milk.

275 Crème florentine – Cream of spinach soup [to yield 1 litre (1 quart)]

500 g (1 *lb*) *shredded spinach*	250 ml (½ *pt*) *fond de*	30 g (1 *oz*)
750 ml (1½ *pt*) *Béchamel*	*volaille* (*Recipe* 11)	*butter*
(*Recipe* 51)	125 ml (¼ *pt*) *fresh cream*	*seasoning*

1 Wash spinach well.
2 Boil in salt water 10 minutes; squeeze out all moisture.
3 Add the spinach to the Béchamel and correct consistency with stock.
4 Simmer for about 25 minutes.
5 Rub through a sieve.
6 Re-boil; season and blend in the butter and the cream.

276 Purée or Crème freneuse – Turnip and potato purée [to yield 1 litre (1 quart)]

250 g (½ *lb*) *finely-chopped*	1·5 *l* (1½ *qt*) *white stock*	125 ml (1 *gill*)
onions	(*Recipe* 6)	*cream*
500 g (1 *lb*) *diced turnips*	250 ml (½ *pt*) *milk*	*bouquet garni*
375 g (¾ *lb*) *diced potatoes*	120 g (4 *oz*) *butter*	*seasoning*

1 Sweat the onions in 90 g (3 oz) butter but do not colour.
2 Add the diced turnips and potatoes and sweat under cover for 10 minutes.
3 Moisten with stock, boil and skim; add bouquet garni and cook until purée-d.
4 Rub through sieve and adjust consistency with boiled milk.
5 Re-boil, season, blend in the cream and 30 g (1 oz) butter.
6 Serve with sippets.

277 Crème Judic [to yield 1 litre (1 quart)]

2 *medium lettuce*	250 ml (½ *pt*) *white*	250 ml (½ *pt*) *cream*
750 ml (1½ *pt*) *Béchamel*	*stock*	60 g (2 *oz*) *butter*
(*Recipe* 51)	(*Recipe* 6)	

Garnish: *Roundels of lettuce leaves spread with poached quenelle forcemeat* (Recipe 194), *using chicken.*

1 Wash lettuce, remove faded leaves.
2 Shred lettuce into coarse julienne.
3 Stew the lettuce until tender in 30 g (1 oz) butter.
4 Rub the lettuce through a fine sieve and add the Béchamel; simmer for 5 minutes.
5 Add the stock and simmer for a further 20 minutes.
6 Adjust the seasoning; blend in the cream and butter.
7 Add the garnish.

278 Crème de lentilles – Cream of lentils [to yield 1 litre (1 quart)]

300 g (10 oz) lentils	1·5 l (1½ qt) white	bouquet garni
60 g (2 oz) diced onions	stock (Recipe 6)	125 ml (¼ pt) fresh cream
60 g (2 oz) diced carrots	60 g (2 oz) bacon bones	60 g (2 oz) butter seasoning

1 Wash the lentils and drain.
2 Sweat the onions and carrots in 30 g (1 oz) butter, add the lentils and allow to sweat under cover for 5 minutes.
3 Add the stock, boil and skim.
4 Add the bouquet garni and cook the lentils until purée-d.
5 Rub the whole through a fine sieve.
6 Re-boil, adjust the consistency and seasoning.
7 Blend in the cream and the remaining butter.
8 Serve with sippets.

279 Potage or Crème Longchamps [to yield 1 litre (1 quart)]

1 l (1 qt) purée St Germain (Recipe 285)	30 g (1 oz) vermicelli	15 g (½ oz) chervil leaves

1 Poach vermicelli in stock.
2 Blanch chervil leaves.
3 Add the above garnish to 1 l (1 qt) purée St Germain.

280 Crème de mais – Cream of corn soup (or Indian corn soup) [to yield 1 litre (1 quart)]

180 g (6 oz) corn on the cob	125 ml (¼ pt) cream	125 ml (¼ pt) chicken
750 ml (1½ pt) Béchamel (Recipe 51)	250 ml (½ pt) milk seasoning	stock (Recipe 11) 30 g (1 oz) butter

1 Boil the corn in salted water for 20 minutes.
2 Scrape off the corn and stew in milk until tender and rub through a fine sieve.
3 Add the purée to the Béchamel and simmer for 20 minutes.
4 Correct the consistency with chicken stock.
5 Strain, adjust seasoning, blend in the cream and butter.

281 Purée or Crème Palestine – Jerusalem artichoke purée [to yield 1 litre (1 quart)]

500 g (1 lb) Jerusalem artichokes	500 ml (1 pt) milk	bouquet garni
5 shelled, crushed filberts	10 ml spoon [2 tea- spoons] fécule	125 ml (¼ pt) cream (warm)
500 ml (1 pt) white stock (Recipe 6)	90 g (3 oz) butter	seasoning

1 Wash and scrape artichokes and mince very finely.
2 Stew them with 30 g (1 oz) butter.
3 Add the filberts, moisten with stock; add bouquet garni and cook gently until purée-d.
4 Rub through fine sieve and replace in pan.

5 Dilute with fécule in the milk, add to the purée and re-boil.
6 Adjust the seasoning, blend in the cream and remainder of the butter.

282 Purée or Crème Parmentier – Potato soup or cream of potato soup [to yield 1 litre (1 quart)]

750 g (1½ *lb*) (*net*) peeled potatoes	*bouquet garni*	*pinch chopped parsley*
60 g (2 *oz*) *diced onions*	1·5 *l* (1½ *qt*) *white stock* (*Recipe* 6)	90 g (3 *oz*) *butter* *seasoning*
60 g (2 *oz*) *diced leeks*	125 *ml* (1 *gill*) *cream*	

1 Dice the potatoes.
2 Sweat the onions and leeks in 60 g (2 oz) butter under cover.
3 When soft add and sweat the potatoes.
4 Add the stock, boil, skim; put in the bouquet garni.
5 Simmer until the potatoes are purée-d.
6 Rub through a sieve, re-boil, season and blend in the cream and remaining butter.
7 Sprinkle a pinch of parsley on top before service.
8 Serve with croûtons.

283 Purée de pois – Pea soup [to yield 1 litre (1 quart)]

300 g (10 *oz*) *dried peas*	90 g (3 *oz*) *fine mire-poix* (*Recipe* 2)	*pinch of sugar*
1·5 *l* (1½ *qt*) *white stock* (*Recipe* 6)	1 *sprig of mint*	*seasoning* 90 g (3 *oz*) *butter*
250 g (½ *lb*) *raw ham or bones*	*bouquet garni*	

1 Soak the peas in cold water overnight and wash before use.
2 Sweat the mirepoix, add the peas and continue to sweat under cover.
3 Moisten with the stock, boil, skim, add bouquet garni and ham.
4 Simmer under cover till purée-d.
5 Rub through a sieve, re-boil, adjust consistency and season.
6 Blend in cream and butter.
7 Serve soup sippets.

Note. For fresh-pea purée see Recipe 285 (St Germain)

284 Purée or Crème soissonnaise – Haricot bean soup [to yield 1 litre (1 quart)]

500 g (1 *lb*) *haricot beans*	60 g (2 *oz*) *bacon bones*	*seasoning*
2 *whole carrots*	125 *ml* (¼ *pt*) *cream*	1·5 *l* (1½ *qt*) *fond blanc* (*Recipe* 6)
1 *onion clouté*	250 *ml* (½ *pt*) *milk*	
	30 g (1 *oz*) *butter*	

1 Soak beans and wash off.
2 Cook the beans with the stock and vegetables until purée stage.
3 Rub through a sieve.

4 Rectify the consistency with boiled milk.
5 Adjust seasoning; blend in the cream and 30 g (1 oz) butter.
6 Serve soup sippets separately.

285 Crème St Germain – Cream of fresh pea-soup [to yield 1 litre (1 quart)]

500 g (1 *lb*) *shelled peas*	250 ml (½ *pt*) *water*	*pinch salt*
30 g (1 *oz*) *green of leek*	500 ml (1 *pt*) *white*	60 g (2 *oz*) *shredded*
1 *sprig mint*	*stock* (*Recipe* 6)	*lettuce*
125 ml (¼ *pt*) *cream*	*pinch of sugar*	90 g (3 *oz*) *butter*

Garnish: 30 g (1 *oz*) *cooked peas*

1 Sweat the leeks and lettuce in 60 g (2 oz) butter.
2 Add the peas, mint, water and stew until tender.
3 Rub through a fine sieve.
4 Adjust the consistency with white stock and season.
5 Blend in the cream and butter.
6 Serve with soup sippets.

Note. i Quick-frozen peas are suitable in making this soup.
   ii Variants of St Germain by adding further garnish are:
      Crème Lamballe with cooked tapioca;
      Crème Longchamps with cooked vermicelli and chiffonade of sorrel.
  iii *Crème St Germain* may be made by replacing stock with an equal
      quantity of Béchamel; adjust consistency, when finishing, with white
      stock.

Further Thick Cream Soups. The following are not typical vegetable purées or
cream soups nor may they be readily classified among the conventional
veloutés.

286 Crème Germiny [to yield 1 litre (1 quart)]

1 *l* (1 *qt*) *white chicken stock* (*Recipe* 11)	4 *egg yolks*
125 ml (¼ *pt*) *cream*	30 g (1 *oz*) *cooked sorrel*
60 g (2 *oz*) *butter*	(*julienne*)
	cheese straws (*Recipe* 1188)

1 Sweat the sorrel in 30 g (1 oz) butter.
2 Boil with fond blanc.
3 Beat egg yolks and cream (liaison).
4 Add the liaison to fond blanc and mix well; draw to side of fire or reduce heat.
5 Blend in the remaining butter and season.
6 Serve cheese straws separately.

287 Crème portugaise [to yield 1 litre (1 quart)]

   1 *l* (1 *qt*) *cream of tomato* (*Recipe* 288)   30 g (1 *oz*) *plain boiled rice*

1 Basic Cream of Tomato soup garnished with plain boiled rice.
2 Serve a sauce-boat of soup sippets.

288 Crème de tomate – Cream of tomato soup [to yield 1 litre (1 quart)]

1 *or* 1·5 *l* (1 *or* 1½ *qt*) *white*
stock* (Recipe 6)
30 *g* (1 *oz*) *bacon rind*⎤
60 *g* (2 *oz*) *carrots*   ⎬*mirepoix*
60 *g* (2 *oz*) *onions*   ⎦
bouquet garni

750 *g* (1½ *lb*) *fresh*
tomatoes or
190 *ml* (1½ *gills*)
of tomato purée
60 *g* (2 *oz*) *flour*
60 *g* (2 *oz*) *butter*

10 *ml spoon* [1 *des-*
sertspoon] *sugar*
125 *ml* (1 *gill*)
cream seasoning
sippets

1 Sweat off the diced bacon-rind in 30 g (1 oz) butter.
2 Add the mirepoix and colour slightly.
3 Add the flour and make a blond roux.
4 Mix the tomatoes with the roux.
5 Add the stock and mix well, boil and skim.
6 Add the bouquet garni and simmer 1 hour at the side of the stove or over low heat.
7 Add the sugar and strain through a fine chinois.
8 Adjust the seasoning, add the cream, blend in the butter.

Note.   i Check for colour and consistency and if using fresh tomatoes add 15 ml spoon (1 tablespoon) of tomato purée.

      ii Tomato soup, as distinct from Cream of Tomato soup is simply the foregoing without cream-finish.

     *iii When using fresh tomatoes (as against canned purée) the lesser quantity of stock will be required.

CHICKEN VELOUTÉS AND CREAMS

Note. Among the following cream-soup examples, the first soup (Crème Derby) is not typical and may be regarded as a speciality soup.

289 Crème Derby [to yield 1 litre (1 quart)]

1·5 *l* (1½ *qt*) *chicken stock*
  (*Recipe* 11)
60 *g* (2 *oz*) *rice*
15 *g* (½ *oz*) *curry powder*
125 *ml* (¼ *pt*) *cream*

120 *g* (4 *oz*) *butter*
120 *g* (4 *oz*) *flour*
bouquet garni
60 *g* (2 *oz*) *diced*
  truffle

15 *g* (½ *oz*) *boiled rice*
18 *small chicken-*
  quenelles (*Recipe* 194
  using chicken meat)
30 *g* (1 *oz*) *butter*

1 Make a blond roux.
2 Blend the curry powder with the roux.
3 Moisten with stock and mix well.
4 Boil, skim then add bouquet garni.
5 Wash the rice and add to the velouté.
6 Simmer until the rice is well cooked.
7 Strain, re-boil, blend in the butter and cream. Season.
8 Garnish with the quenelles, boiled rice and truffles.

Note. Soak the rice in cold water for about 1 hour before adding.

290 Crème de volaille – Cream of chicken soup [to yield 1 litre (1 quart)]

750 *ml* (1½ *pt*) *thin Béchamel* (*Recipe* 51)	125 *ml* (1 *gill*) *cream*	60 *g* (2 *oz*) *cooked julienne of*
250 *g* (½ *lb*) *chicken purée*	30 *g* (1 *oz*) *butter*	*chicken*
500 *ml* (1 *pt*) *white stock* (*Recipe* 6)	*seasoning*	

1 Prepare chicken purée by using the cooked flesh of boiled fowl and rubbing through a fine sieve.
2 Add the chicken purée to Béchamel; simmer for a few minutes.
3 Add the white stock and simmer until the total liquid is 1 litre (1 quart).
4 Rub through sieve, adjust consistency with a little boiled milk.
5 Season; blend in the cream and butter; garnish with cooked julienne of chicken.

291 Crème de volaille princesse [to yield 1 litre (1 quart)]

As Recipe 290 with the addition of 60 g (2 oz) cooked, diced, asparagus tips as the garnish.

292 Velouté de volaille (basic recipe) – Chicken velouté soup [to yield 1 litre (1 quart)]

1·5 *l* (1½ *qt*) *white chicken stock* (*Recipe* 11)	125 *ml* (¼ *pt*) *cream* ⎫	120 *g* (4 *oz*) *flour*
60 *g* (2 *oz*) *julienne cooked chicken*	3 *egg yolks* ⎬ *for liaison*	*bouquet garni* *seasoning*
	150 *g* (5 *oz*) *butter* ⎭	

1 Make a blond roux with 120 g (4 oz) butter and the flour.
2 Moisten with chicken stock.
3 Boil, skim, add bouquet garni.
4 Simmer, reducing to 1 litre (1 quart).
5 Strain, season; blend in remaining butter, egg yolks and cream.
6 Garnish with the julienne of chicken.

293 Velouté Agnès Sorel [to yield 1 litre (1 quart)]

1 *l* (1 *qt*) *chicken velouté* (*Recipe* 292)	75 *g* (2½ *oz*) *butter*	3 *egg yolks*
240 *g* (8 *oz*) *fresh mushrooms*	125 *ml* (¼ *pt*) *cream*	*seasoning*

Garnish: 30 *g* (1 *oz*) *cooked white meat of chicken*
30 *g* (1 *oz*) *cooked fresh tongue*
30 *g* (1 *oz*) *julienne mushrooms*

1 Peel mushrooms, pound in mortar and pass through a sieve.
2 Add mushrooms to velouté.
3 Boil and simmer for 20 minutes; rub through a tammy.
4 Make a liaison with the cream and yolks and add to the velouté.
5 Season, blend in the butter.
6 Cut the tongue and chicken into julienne.
7 Fry off the julienne of mushrooms in butter.
8 Garnish the soup with mushrooms, tongue, and chicken.

294 Velouté Artois [to yield 1 litre (1 quart)]

| 250 ml (½ pt) purée haricot beans | 250 ml (½ pt) white stock (Recipe 6) | 30 g (1 oz) butter 125 ml (1 gill) cream |
| 500 ml (1 pt) chicken velouté (Recipe 292) | 5 ml spoon [1 tea-spoon] blanched chervil leaves | 30 g (1 oz) julienne of vegetables seasoning |

1 Mix haricot bean purée with the chicken velouté.
2 Simmer until the velouté is well flavoured with the beans.
3 Adjust consistency with the white stock.
4 Strain; blend in butter and cream.
5 Season, garnish with the cooked julienne and chervil leaves.

Note. To make haricot-bean purée, soak overnight in cold water 180 g (6 oz) haricot beans. Wash off and cook in a little stock until purée-d. Rub through a sieve.

295 Velouté Crécy [to yield 1 litre (1 quart)]

| 1·5 l (1½ qt) chicken velouté (Recipe 292) | bouquet garni 90 g (3 oz) | 750 g (1½ lb) thinly-sliced carrots |
| 125 ml (1 gill) cream | butter | pinch sugar |

1 Stew the carrots in 60 g (2 oz) butter and sugar until tender.
2 Melt the butter and add the flour to make a white roux.
3 Moisten with the chicken stock, add the sliced carrots and bouquet garni; boil, skim and simmer for 1 hour.
4 Strain through tammy, adjust the seasoning, blend in the remaining butter, garnish with 30 g (1 oz) brunoise of cooked carrots and finish with cream.

Note. All the vegetables must be rubbed through a sieve to obtain correct consistency.

296 Velouté cressonnière [to yield 1 litre (1 quart)]

| 2 bunches of watercress | 1·5 l (1½ qt) chicken velouté |
| 125 ml (1 gill) cream | (Recipe 292) |

1 Prepare the cress as for Crème cressonnière (Recipe 270).
2 Cook the cress in velouté; strain.
3 Garnish with blanched leaves of cress; finish with cream.

297 Velouté dame blanche [to yield 1 litre (1 quart)]

| 1 l (1 qt) basic velouté de volaille (Recipe 292) | 60 g (2 oz) butter 15 g (½ oz) pearl, | 18 chicken quenelles (Recipe 194) |
| 15 g (½ oz) diced, cooked chicken | Japanese sago or tapioca | 125 ml (1 gill) cream |

1 Cook the pearls in a little consommé.
2 Add the pearls, diced, cooked chicken and quenelles to basic velouté.
3. Finish with cream and butter.

COLD THICKENED SOUPS

298 Velouté de volaille glacé [to yield 1 litre (1 quart)]

60 g (2 *oz*) *flour*	2 *l* (2 *qt*) *chicken stock*	250 *ml* ($\frac{1}{2}$ *pt*)
60 g (2 *oz*) *butter*	(*Recipe* 11)	*cream*

1 Make a white roux from the flour and butter.
2 Moisten with chicken stock.
3 Reduce to 1 litre (1 quart).
4 Cool and stir in the cream.
5 Serve cold in cups.

Note. If too thick add a little cold chicken consommé (Recipe 235) to give the consistency of slightly-thickened consommé.

299 Vichyssoise or Crème Vichyssoise [to yield 1 litre (1 quart)]

white of 3 *leeks*	250 *g diced potatoes*	*salt*
60 *g* (2 *oz*) *finely-diced onion*	30 *g* (1 *oz*) *butter*	*cayenne pepper*
30 *g* (1 *oz*) *chopped chives*	875 *ml* (1$\frac{3}{4}$ *pt*) *chicken stock* (*Recipe* 11)	125 *ml* ($\frac{1}{4}$ *pt*) *chilled cream*

1 Dice the leeks into brunoise.
2 Sweat the onions, potatoes and leeks in butter; do not colour.
3 Add the stock and simmer till all the ingredients are soft.
4 Season and rub through a fine sieve.
5 Chill in the refrigerator.
6 Just before service stir in the chopped chives and chilled cream.

299a Crème Vichyssoise à la Ritz

This is a variant achieved with fine tomato concassé and strained juice to replace the 250 ml ($\frac{1}{2}$ pt) of chicken stock.

4. Eggs, Pastas, and Rice

THE items of this section (Eggs, Pastas or pâtes italiennes, and Rice) are linked together because they are all prepared by the chef entremettier (vegetable cook) and generally occupy a similar position on the menu as a preliminary course.

Pâtes italienne and rice are, alternatively used as garnish, part of a garnish or to accompany main dishes as a vegetable.

EGGS

Egg dishes prepared by the entremettier are used as a preliminary course (like pâtes and rice) at luncheons, with the exception of omelettes. These are sometimes additionally chosen by guests as main-course items for light luncheons and, of course, sweet omelettes (listed among the sweets in Chapter 8), are also prepared by the entremettier in kitchens with large brigades. For easy reference, the styles in this section are listed alphabetically, and examples of cold egg dishes, normally prepared in the larder, are also included here. Eggs prepared for breakfast service are also referred to briefly in Chapter 9.

300 Œufs brouillés – Scrambled eggs

1 Use a thick-bottomed copper saucepan.
2 For 3 eggs, melt 15 g ($\frac{1}{2}$ oz) butter in the pan.
3 Beat the eggs and season.
4 With the pan on the stove or over moderate-heat, add eggs and stir constantly with a wooden spoon.
5 Avoid fierce heat as this tends to coagulate the egg too much and too rapidly thus forming lumps in the mixture.
6 Finish with 30 g (1 oz) butter and a 15 ml spoon [1 tablespoon] of cream.
7 The eggs, when cooked, should have a soft, creamy consistency.

301 Œufs brouillés aux cannelons

8 *eggs*	60 g (2 oz) butter	parsley
4 *puff paste (Recipe 994) cornets*	62 ml ($\frac{1}{2}$ gill) cream	

1 Make eggs as Recipe 300.
2 Fill cornets with the egg.
3 Arrange cornets on dish points inwards.
4 Garnish with parsley.

302 Œufs brouillés Aumale

8 *eggs*	120 *g* (¼ *lb*) *diced kidney, sautéd*	60 *g* (2 *oz*) *butter*
120 *g* (¼ *lb*) *diced*	*and lié with Madeira sauce*	62 *ml* (½ *gill*) *cream*
tomatoes	(*Recipe* 44)	

1 Cook eggs as for Recipe 300.
2 Mix tomatoes and kidney and use as garnish to top the mounded egg.

303 Œufs brouillés Yvette

8 *eggs*	4 *tartlet cases*	4 *slices truffle*
62 *ml* (½ *gill*) *cream*	8 *asparagus tips* (*diced*)	62 *ml* (½ *gill*) *Nantau*
60 *g* (2 *oz*) *butter*	8 *crayfish tails* (*diced*)	*sauce* (*Recipe* 391)

1 Cook eggs as for Recipe 300.
2 Mix in asparagus and crayfish.
3 Place eggs in tartlet cases.
4 Top with slice of truffle.
5 Cordon of sauce round the egg.

304 Œufs durs – Hard-boiled eggs

Cook as for œufs mollets (Recipe 313) but for 10 minutes cooking time. It is not necessary to specify œufs durs on menu, as the garnish denotes this fact.

305 Œufs à la tripe

4 *hard-boiled eggs*	60 *g* (2 *oz*) *sliced onions*	*chopped parsley*
250 *ml* (½ *pt*) *cream*	30 *g* (1 *oz*) *butter*	
sauce (*Recipe* 65)		

1 Cook onions in butter without colouring.
2 Add onions to the sauce.
3 Heat eggs and slice into rounds.
4 Coat bottom of china dish with sauce.
5 Place eggs on top.
6 Coat eggs with sauce, sprinkle with chopped parsley and serve.

306 Œufs farcis Chimay

4 *hard-boiled eggs*	120 *g* (¼ *lb*) *duxelles*	250 *ml* (½ *pt*) *mornay*
30 *g* (1 *oz*) *grated cheese*	(*Recipe* 101)	*sauce*
		(*Recipe* 58)

1 Halve each egg lengthwise.
2 Sieve yolks.
3 Mix yolks with duxelles and pipe into each half-egg.
4 Coat with mornay sauce.
5 Sprinkle with cheese and glaze in hot oven.

307 Scotch eggs

4 *hard-boiled eggs*	250 g ($\frac{1}{2}$ *lb*) *breadcrumbs*	1 *egg for*
500 g (1 *lb*) *savoury*	60 g (2 *oz*) *flour*	*egg-wash*
minced meat (or sausage-meat)	*(seasoned)*	

1 Divide the meat into 4 portions.
2 Wrap meat round the floured egg.
3 Flour, egg-wash, and crumb each egg.
4 Fry in deep fat for 8 minutes.
5 Serve with fried parsley and tomato sauce (Recipe 34).

308 Œufs en cocotte – Eggs en cocotte (basic method)

Note. A special glazed earthenware cocotte is used, normally white inside, green or brown outside.

1 Heat and butter the cocotte.
2 Have ready a flat saucepan of hot water.
3 Break the egg into cocotte and season.
4 Lay cocotte in saucepan of hot water which should come only half-way up the cocotte.
5 Place saucepan on the stove and bring water to the boil.
6 Cover with a lid and draw to side of the stove.
7 Allow to simmer until the white of the egg is set and creamy and the yolk glossy.
8 Owing to condensation it may be necessary to pour off water which may gather on top of the egg.

309 Œufs en cocotte bergère

1 *tablespoon melted*	30 g (1 *oz*) *butter*	60 g (2 *oz*) *minced,*
meat glaze	60 g (2 *oz*) *sliced*	*cooked mutton*
(*Recipe* 13)	*mushrooms cooked in*	*Lié with demi-glace*
4 *eggs*	*butter*	(*Recipe* 29)

1 Place garnish in bottom of cocotte.
2 Break eggs on top of garnish.
3 Cook eggs as Recipe 308.
4 Serve with cordon of meat glaze round the egg.

310 Œuf en cocotte à la reine

4 *eggs*	60 g (2 *oz*) *butter*
60 g (2 *oz*) *creamed, minced chicken*	62 ml ($\frac{1}{2}$ *gill*) *fresh cream*

1 Place chicken in bottom of cocotte.
2 Break eggs on top of chicken.
3 Cook eggs as described in Recipe 308.
4 Serve with cordon of cream on top of eggs.

311 Œuf en cocotte bordelaise

4 *eggs*	4 *slices poached beef-marrow*
30 g (1 *oz*) *butter*	125 ml ($\frac{1}{4}$ *pt*) *sauce bordelaise* (*Recipe* 35)

1 Place slices of marrow in bottom of cocotte.
2 Break eggs on top of the marrow.
3 Cook eggs as Recipe 308.
4 Serve with cordon of sauce on top of eggs.

312 Œuf en cocotte petit duc

4 *eggs*	8 *asparagus tips cut in half crosswise*
45 g (1$\frac{1}{2}$ *oz*) *butter*	125 ml ($\frac{1}{4}$ *pt*) *sauce périgueux* (*Recipe* 45)

1 Heat the asparagus in butter.
2 Garnish the bottom of cocotte with the asparagus.
3 Break eggs on top of the garnish and cook as Recipe 308.
4 Serve with cordon of sauce on top of the eggs.

313 Œufs mollets – Soft-boiled eggs

General points:

1 For mollet, the eggs are boiled sufficiently long (3$\frac{1}{2}$ to 4$\frac{1}{2}$ minutes according to size) to set the whites leaving the yolks soft and creamy. The shell can thus be removed without breaking the egg.
2 Allow plenty of boiling water, roughly 750 ml (1$\frac{1}{2}$ pints) to two eggs, so that the water-temperature is only slightly lowered when the eggs are inserted. This allows quick return to boiling point and thus more accurate timing.
3 For large quantities of eggs use a wire basket in the boiling water. Convenient for insertion, this also ensures even cooking-time as they may be lifted out simultaneously.
4 When cooked, place the eggs immediately in a basin of cold running water until thoroughly cold. Shell the eggs carefully taking care not to break them.
5 When required for use, reheat in salted hot water.

314 Œufs mollets Halévy

4 *eggs*	2 *tomatoes concassé, hot*	15 *ml spoon* [1 *tablespoon*] *minced, creamed chicken*
4 *tartlet cases*	10 *ml spoon* [$\frac{1}{2}$ *tablespoon*] *melted meat glaze* (*Recipe* 13)	
125 *ml* ($\frac{1}{4}$ *pt*) *tomato sauce* (*Recipe* 34)		125 *ml* ($\frac{1}{4}$ *pt*) *suprême sauce* (*Recipe* 63)

1 Heat shelled, mollet eggs in hot water.
2 Garnish one half of the bottom of tartlet case with tomato and the other half with chicken-mix.
3 Place eggs on top of the garnish.
4 Coat one half of egg with tomato sauce.
5 Coat the other half with suprême sauce.
6 Divide the colours by means of a cordon of meat glaze.

315 Œufs mollets Argenteuil

250 *ml* (½ *pt*) *cream sauce* (*Recipe* 65) *with purée of green asparagus tips*	4 *eggs* 4 *tartlet cases*	12 *asparagus tips* 30 *g* (1 *oz*) *butter*

1 Heat eggs in salted, hot water.
2 Place asparagus tips in buttered dish and heat in oven.
3 Garnish bottom of tartlets with asparagus tips.
4 Place eggs on top of garnish.·
5 Coat eggs with cream sauce and serve very hot.

316 Œufs mollets florentine

4 *eggs* 4 *tartlet cases*	120 *g* (¼ *lb*) *cooked leaf spinach* 30 *g* (1 *oz*) *butter*	250 *ml* (½ *pt*) *mornay sauce* (*Recipe* 58) 15 *g* (½ *oz*) *grated cheese*

1 Heat eggs in salted, hot water.
2 Melt butter in pan and heat seasoned spinach.
3 Place spinach in bottom of tartlet cases.
4 Place eggs on top of spinach.
5 Coat eggs with sauce.
6 Sprinkle cheese on sauce and glaze under salamander.

317 Œufs mollets Mornay

Ingredients and method are the same as florentine but without the spinach.

318 Œufs mollets indienne

4 *eggs* 4 *tartlet cases*	250 *ml* (½ *pt*) *sauce kari* (*Recipe* 32 *but strained*)	30 *g* (1 *oz*) *boiled rice*

1 Heat eggs in hot, salted water.
2 Heat rice and dry.
3 Place rice in bottom of tartlets.
4 Place egg on top of rice.
5 Coat egg with sauce kari.

319 Œufs pochés – Poached eggs

General points:
1 Have ready a sauté-pan, containing salted water, acidulated with vinegar [1 teaspoon vinegar per 250 ml (½ pint) water.]
2 Bring water to the boil and break eggs, one at a time, over the water when it is boiling.
3 Allow to simmer. The white should envelop the yolk completely taking the shape of the raw egg.
4 Cook for three minutes.
5 Trim ragged edges before serving.
6 To remove taste of vinegar, place eggs in a separate pan of hot, salted water.
Garnishes for œufs mollets may be applied to œufs pochés.

320 Œufs sur le plat – Oven-baked buttered eggs

General points:
1 For this a special china fireproof dish is used. There are two sizes. The smaller for one egg (table d'hôte service), the larger to hold two eggs (à la carte service).
2 Place dish on top of stove and add a piece of butter.
3 Allow to melt, just simmer slightly. Use enough butter just to cover the bottom of the dish.
4 Add the egg carefully, seasoned with salt and pepper and allow to set slightly on the bottom. Then place in the oven to finish cooking.
5 The white should be just set and the yolk glossy.
6 Garnish is placed on the white part of the egg and if sauce is required, a cordon is placed round the egg. In some cases the garnish is placed directly in the dish, then the egg is added on top. Cook in the usual manner.

321 Œufs sur le plat Berçy

4 *eggs*	125 *ml* ($\frac{1}{4}$ *pt*) *tomato*	30 *g* (1 *oz*) *butter*
4 *grilled chipolata sausages*	*sauce* (*Recipe* 34)	

1 Cook the eggs as Recipe 320.
2 Garnish with sausage.
3 Cordon with tomato sauce.

322 Œufs sur le plat chasseur

4 *eggs*	62 *ml* ($\frac{1}{2}$ *gill*) *chasseur*	30 *g* (1 *oz*) *butter*
60 *g* (2 *oz*) *chicken's liver*	*sauce* (*Recipe* 38)	

1 Cook eggs as Recipe 320.
2 Sauté livers and cohere with chasseur sauce.
3 Garnish egg with livers and cordon of sauce.

323 Œufs sur le plat Cluny

4 *eggs*	4 *small* 3 *cm* (1$\frac{1}{2}$ *in*) *long chicken-croquettes*
125 *ml* ($\frac{1}{4}$ *pt*) *tomato sauce*	(*Recipe* 726 *using chicken instead of*
(*Recipe* 34)	*beef*)

1 Cook eggs as Recipe 320.
2 Garnish with chicken croquettes.
3 Finish with cordon of tomato sauce.

324 Œufs sur le plat Omar Pasha

4 *eggs*	30 *g* (1 *oz*) *grated*	60 *g* (2 *oz*) *finely-chopped*
30 *g* (1 *oz*) *butter*	*Parmesan cheese*	*onions*

1 Sweat the onions in butter and place in buttered egg-dish.
2 Break eggs over the onions.
3 Sprinkle cheese on the eggs.
4 Cook in hot oven until slight gratin forms.

325 Œufs sur le plat Meyerbeer

4 *eggs*   125 *ml* ($\frac{1}{4}$ *pt*) *sauce périgueux*   30 *g* (1 *oz*) *butter*
4 *lambs' kidneys*   (*Recipe 45*)

1 Cooks eggs as Recipe 320.
2 Garnish with grilled kidney.
3 Coat kidney with sauce and cordon of sauce round the egg.

326 Œufs sur le plat miroir

4 *eggs*   30 *g* (1 *oz*) *butter*   62 *ml* ($\frac{1}{2}$ *gill*) *cream*

1 Place eggs in dish and cover with cream.
2 Then cook as Recipe 320.

OMELETTES

General points:
i To be successful, use the omelet pan only for the making of omelettes.
ii A new pan may be 'seasoned' by half-filling it with oil. Heat on the stove, and allow it to lie warm for two hours.
iii After use, wipe the pan with a dry cloth or paper. On no account should water be used for cleaning.

Omelettes fourrées
These are omelettes with a filling or an interior garnish. Otherwise the garnish or flavouring is added to the egg (e.g. fines herbes).

Sweet Omelettes
In a large kitchen brigade, sweet omelettes are made (as are all omelettes) by the chef entremétier. (For sweet omelettes see Chapter 10.)

Flat Omelettes
Most omelettes are oval plump shapes (see Recipe 335) but Spanish omelette and similar kinds are prepared flat and round to cover the plate.

327 Omelette nature – Plain omelet

1 For each à la carte omelette, place 3 eggs (2 for table d'hôte service) in a bowl; season with salt and pepper.
2 Place pan on stove with oil or butter and heat. Pour off any surplus before adding the eggs.
3 Beat eggs in the bowl with a fork just sufficiently to incorporate yolks with the white.
4 Pour eggs into pan and shake briskly using a rotary movement. The fork may be used to loosen any egg which may stick to the sides of the pan.
5 Now loosen all round edges and fold side nearest into centre. Tap the handle sharply and the further side will come over the edge of the pan. Fold this into the centre.
6 Tilt the pan and turn out the completed omelette.

7 The degree of cooking depends on customer's requirements; 'baveuse' means very soft and sloppy inside.
8 When dished, omelettes may be brushed with melted butter to enhance appearance.

328 Omelette aux fines herbes

Prepare as plain omelette with the addition of chopped parsley.

329 Omelette à la turque

8 *eggs* 250 *g* ($\frac{1}{2}$ *lb*) *chicken's liver sauté and lié with*
60 *g* (2 *oz*).*butter* *sauce madère* (*Recipe* 44)

Make omelette as Recipe 325, slit and fill with chicken-liver mix.

330 Omelette andalouse (fourrée)

8 *eggs* 60 *g* (2 *oz*) *butter* 250 *g* ($\frac{1}{2}$ *lb*) *onions sliced*
125 *g* ($\frac{1}{4}$ *lb*) *diced* 125 *g* ($\frac{1}{4}$ *lb*) *diced* *in rings*
  pimentoes *tomatoes*

1 Heat tomatoes and pimentoes in butter.
2 Divide garnish into four.
3 Make separate omelettes and fill with garnish.
4 Dish and surround omelette with fried onion rings (oignons frits à la française, Recipe 871).

331 Omelette aux champignons – Mushroom omelet

8 *eggs* 250 *g* ($\frac{1}{2}$ *lb*) *sliced mushrooms cooked in*
60 *g* (2 *oz*) *butter* *butter*

1 Heat mushrooms in pan.
2 Pour in eggs and make omelette.
3 May be decorated with turned mushroom on top.

332 Omelette aux rognons (fourrée)

4 *sheep's kidneys, sliced, sauté and lié* 8 *eggs* 60 *g* (2 *oz*) *butter*
  with sauce madère (*Recipe* 44)

Prepare as Recipe 329.

333 Omelette au parmesan – Parmesan-cheese Omelet

8 *eggs* 60 *g* (2 *oz*) *butter* 60*g* (2 *oz*) *grated Parmesan cheese*

1 Add Parmesan cheese to eggs; cook omelet.
2 Sprinkle cheese on top.

Note. Cheese omelettes using other varieties of cheese may be similarly prepared.

334 Omelette aux pointes d'asperges (fourrée) – Asparagus-tip omelet

8 *eggs*   12 *asparagus tips heated in*   60 *g (2 oz) butter*
6 *diced asparagus-tips*   *butter*

1 Mix diced tips with eggs.
2 Make omelette in usual manner.
3 Cut omelette lengthwise.
4 Fill cavity with tips.

335 Omelette Clamart (fourrée)

250 *g* ($\frac{1}{2}$ *lb*) *petits pois à la française*   8 *eggs*   60 *g (2 oz) butter*
  (*Recipe* 882)

1 Make omelette as described in Recipe 327.
2 Before folding fill with some peas.
3 Dish and make a cavity lengthwise in omelette.
4 Fill cavity with remaining peas.

336 Omelette espagnole

8 *eggs*   4 *anchovies*   125 *g* ($\frac{1}{4}$ *lb*) *sliced onion*
125 *g* ($\frac{1}{4}$ *lb*) *julienne of*   125 *g* ($\frac{1}{4}$ *lb*) *tomato*   *cooked in butter*
  pimentoes   *concassé*   4 *olives*
60 *g (2 oz) butter*   *chopped parsley*

1 Mix garnish with eggs.
2 Make omelette but serve flat.
3 Top with criss-crossed anchovy fillets and stoned olives (halved).

Note. Some chefs include peas and garlic in garnish and use oil instead of butter.

337 Omelette lyonnaise – Onion omelet

8 *eggs*   125 *g* ($\frac{1}{4}$ *lb*) *sauté onions*   *seasoning*
60 *g (2 oz) butter*

Heat onions in pan and add beaten eggs and make omelette as Recipe 327.

338 Omelette parmentier – Potato omelet

8 *eggs*   180 *g (6 oz) diced potatoes,*   *chopped parsley*
60 *g (2 oz) butter*   0·5 *cm cubes, cooked in*
             butter

1 Add parsley to eggs.
2 Add potatoes to eggs in pan.
3 Finish and dish in usual fashion (Recipe 327).

339 Omelette paysanne

8 *eggs*   250 *g* ($\frac{1}{2}$ *lb*) *breast of bacon diced and*
180 *g (6 oz) diced*   *cooked*
  potatoes cooked in butter   60 *g (2 oz) shredded sorrel stewed in butter*

Prepare as flat omelette (Recipe 336).

COLD EGGS

These are normally prepared by the garde manger (larder). Examples of dishes are listed below but note the following general points for preparing cold eggs, particularly poached eggs:

  i Drain eggs well and trim.
 ii Coat well with sauce.
iii Decorate finely.
 iv Have aspic nearly at setting point when glazing.
  v Use the appropriate type of aspic.

340 Œufs à la russe

4 *hard-boiled eggs*	30 *g* (1 *oz*) *butter*	62 *ml* ($\frac{1}{8}$ *pt*) *mayonnaise*
250 *ml* ($\frac{1}{2}$ *pt*) *aspic*	125 *g* ($\frac{1}{4}$ *lb*) *Russian*	(*Recipe* 110)
(*Recipe* 122)	*salad* (*Recipe* 183)	

1 Slit the eggs lengthwise.
2 Remove and pass yolks through sieve, mix with the butter, and season.
3 Pipe (using star tube) the yolk mixture into the egg whites.
4 Decorate and glaze with aspic.
5 Cohere some Russian salad with aspic and mayonnaise and set in a fancy mould.
6 When the mould is set, place on a round flat dish and garnish with the stuffed eggs.

341 Œufs froids Alexandra

4 *cold poached eggs*	4 *slices truffle*	250 *mi* ($\frac{1}{2}$ *pt*) *chicken aspic*
250 *ml* ($\frac{1}{2}$ *pt*) *white*	4 *croustades*	(*Recipe* 122)
chaud-froid sauce	(*Recipe* 188)	15 *g* ($\frac{1}{2}$ *oz*) *caviar* [*or* 15 *g* ($\frac{1}{2}$
(*Recipe* 134)		*oz*) *lump fish-roe*]

1 Trim and dry the poached eggs.
2 Place on draining-wire and coat with chaud-froid sauce.
3 Place a slice of truffle on top of each coated egg when set.
4 Coat with aspic.
5 Trim eggs and place each in a croustade.
6 Pipe or arrange a border of caviar round each egg.
Note. Lump fish-roe may be used in place of caviar.

342 Œufs pochés niçoises

4 *poached eggs*	310 *ml* (2$\frac{1}{2}$ *gills*)	90 *g* (3 *oz*) *cooked, diced*
185 *ml* (1$\frac{1}{2}$ *gills*) *mayon-*	*aspic*	*French beans*
naise (*Recipe* 110)	(*Recipe* 122)	90 *g* (3 *oz*) *small, diced*
62 *ml* ($\frac{1}{8}$ *pt*) *cold tomato*	4 *croustades*	*potatoes* 0·5 *cm cubes*
sauce (*Recipe* 34)	(*Recipe* 188)	

1 Mix the tomato sauce and mayonnaise.
2 Cohere sauce with 62 ml ($\frac{1}{2}$ gill) aspic jelly at setting point.

3 Mix the French beans and potatoes with the sauce and leave a spoonful at the bottom of each croustade.
4 Coat each egg with the sauce and decorate and coat with aspic.
5 Place each egg on a garnished croustade.

343 Œufs moscovites

    4 *hard-boiled eggs*   250 *ml* ($\frac{1}{2}$ *pt*) *aspic*   30 *g* (1 *oz*) *caviar* [*or*
    8 *anchovy fillets*   (*Recipe* 123)   30 *g* (1 *oz*) *lump fish-*
    4 *artichoke bottoms*   *roe*]

1 Cut both ends off the eggs to imitate barrels.
2 Remove the centre with a round cutter.
3 Surround the top and base with anchovy fillets to resemble iron hoops.
4 Fill the centre with caviar.
5 Place each egg on artichoke bottoms and glaze with aspic.

PÂTES ITALIENNES AND NOODLES

Dry pâtes.
Pastas, from past'asciutta – dry pasta, are used in Italy, their country of origin as a preliminary course to a meal, normally luncheon; they are also used for the same course on hotel and restaurant menus.

    Besides the familiar spaghetti and macaroni there are many shapes and sizes, from the thread-like spaghettini (even finer than vermicelli) to zite – the fatter hollow tube which is larger than macaroni. Some of the tubes are grooved like millerighe, or grooved and curved like maniche. For fettucini, a strip pasta similar to nouille is used. Lasagne is a broader, crinkle-edged flat, ribbon pasta; lasagne matassa has a bundle shape. These are but a few; there are many more pastas including shell, ribbon, bow, and wheel shapes, and so on.

    Basically, all these varieties are prepared in a similar way – in boiling water – followed by the appropriate dressing of sauce, grated cheese, butter, and so on.

Fresh pâtes.
In addition there are fresh pastas (nouille types as distinct from dry) of which canneloni, ravioli, tagliatelle, tortellini are familiar examples. Lasagne and similar varieties are also made fresh.

Noodles – nouilles.
Nouilles, the French term for noodles, are long fresh pâte strips. These and other pâtes were used in Chinese cuisine before they were introduced to the western world.

General rules for cooking pâtes Italiennes.
  i Have a large pan with plenty of fast-boiling salted water.
  ii Add pâtes only when water boils rapidly and stir immediately to prevent cohesion.
 iii While cooking may be hastened by covering the pan, adjust heat to avoid boiling over.

iv Strain immediately after cooking.

Modes for preparing spaghetti, macaroni and other Italian pastes are inter-changeable. In addition to the sauces for dressing pâtes referred to in the recipes below, include Chasseur (Recipe 38), Lyonnaise (Recipe 43), and meat and chicken sauces generally.

MACARONI, NOODLES, AND SPAGHETTI

344 Macaroni au gratin

180 ml (1½ gills) mornay   180 g (6 oz) macaroni   21 g (¾ oz) butter
  sauce (Recipe 58)   30 g (1 oz) grated   seasoning
  little grated nutmeg   Parmesan cheese

1 Boil macaroni for 20 minutes in plenty of fast-boiling salted water and drain.
2 Toss in butter and season.
3 Mix with mornay sauce.
4 Sprinkle with cheese and gratin.

345 Macaroni italienne

180 g (6 oz) macaroni   a little crushed and chopped   21 g (¾ oz) butter
62 ml (½ gill) cream   garlic   salt
30 g (1 oz) Parmesan cheese

1 Boil macaroni for 20 minutes in plenty of fast-boiling salted water.
2 Drain and toss in butter with a little garlic, and season.
3 Stir in the cream and add a little cheese.
4 Serve the remainder of the cheese separately.

346 Macaroni napolitaine

125 ml (¼ pt) tomato sauce a little garlic, crushed 62 ml (½ gill) cream
  (Recipe 34)   and chopped   120 g (¼ lb) tomato
30 g (1 oz) grated   seasoning   concassé
Parmesan cheese   180 g (6 oz) macaroni

1 Boil macaroni as Recipe 344.
2 Drain and toss in butter with garlic and seasoning.
3 Add tomato concassé, half the cheese, and mix in the cream and seasoning.
4 Serve with a cordon of tomato sauce, but serve cheese separately.
Note. For à la carte service, plain macaroni is often sent to the dining-room with tomato concassé, tomato sauce and grated cheese served separately and placed before the guest.

347 Nouilles au beurre – Noodles with butter

250 g (½ lb) sifted flour   4 yolks   1·25 ml spoon [¼ tea-
1 whole egg   30 g (1 oz) milk   spoon] salt
15 ml spoon [1 dessert-
  spoonful] oil

1 Sift flour and salt.
2 Make a bay and add all remaining ingredients.
3 Mix to a smooth dough.
4 Roll out in 2 thin pieces of 6 × 25 cm (3 by 12 inches) and let paste rest for 3 hours.
5 To cook cut into thin strips of 3 mm (⅛-inch) wide.
6 Cook in plenty of boiling salted water for 18 minutes.
7 Drain, toss in butter.

Note. Noodles may also be served like pastas in styles such as Milanaise, Napolitaine, Niçoise, etc., or as a garnish (with, for example, Hungarian goulash).

348 Nouilles niçoises

180 g (6 oz) *nouilles*   *a little crushed*   15 g (½ oz) *grated*
   (*Recipe* 347)   *chopped garlic*   *Parmesan cheese*
30 g (1 oz) *thinly-sliced*   125 g (¼ lb) *tomato*   *seasoning*
   onion   *concassé*
30 ml (¼ gill) *oil*

1 Boil and drain nouilles (Recipe 347).
2 Fry off the onions in oil. Add tomato concassé and garlic.
3 Add the nouilles, season, and add cheese.

349 Spaghetti au parmesan

180 g (6 oz) *spaghetti*   30 g (1 oz) *grated*   60 g (2 oz) *butter*
   (*unbroken*)   *Parmesan cheese*   *seasoning*

1 Cook spaghetti in plenty of fast-boiling water for 18 minutes.
2 Drain well and toss in butter; season and mix in Parmesan cheese.

350 Spaghetti bolognaise   Sauce

30 g (1 oz) *finely-chopped*   125 g (¼ lb) *finely-*   62 ml (½ gill) *tomato*
   shallots   *chopped fillet-beef*   *sauce* (*Recipe* 34)
1 *clove chopped garlic*   62 ml (½ gill) *demi-*   30 g (1 oz) *butter*
62 ml (½ gill) *tomato*   *glace*   *seasoning*
   concassé   (*Recipe* 29)

1 Fry off the shallots in butter.
2 Add the meat and brown.
3 Add the tomato concassé and garlic.
4 Moisten with the tomato sauce and demi-glace.
5 Simmer until the meat is cooked, and season.

Note. The sauce is served separately in some hotels. A sauce-boat of tomato sauce and another of tomato concassé, are blended by the waiter in the dining-room. Macaroni, ravioli and noodles can be served in the same way.

351 Spaghetti milanaise

180 g (6 oz) *long spaghetti*   15 g (½ oz) *julienne*   15 g (½ oz) *julienne*
15 g (½ oz) *julienne ham*   *tongue*   *cooked mushrooms*
7 g (¼ oz) *julienne truffles*

Prepare as napolitaine (Recipe 346) plus the julienne of ham, tongue, mushroom and truffles.

CANNELONI AND RAVIOLI

352 Canneloni italienne

ravioli paste (*Recipe* 353)   125 ml (1 gill) jus lié 30 g (1 oz) butter
filling italienne (*Recipe* 355)   (*Recipe* 30)   30 g (1 oz) Parmesan

1 Cut the ravioli paste in squares 6 cm × 6 cm (3 by 3 inches).
2 Cook the paste for 18 minutes.
3 Drain – spread on the stuffing and roll.
4 Butter a dish well, place the canneloni on it and pour on the jus lié; sprinkle with cheese.
5 Bake in moderate oven for 10 minutes.

353 Pâte à ravioli – Ravioli paste

250 g (½ lb) flour   1·25 ml spoon [¼ teaspoon] salt
37 g (1¼ oz) oil   95 ml (3¾ fluid oz) water

1 Sift flour and salt.
2 Make pliable dough with the oil and water.
3 Divide into halves and roll out into 2 very thin oblongs of paste.

FILLINGS FOR RAVIOLI AND CANNELONI

354 Florentine filling

30 g (1 oz) finely-chopped   250 g (½ lb) chopped   1 crushed clove of
 shallots   spinach   garlic
1 egg yolk   seasoning

Mix all the ingredients and season.

355 Italienne filling

90 g (3 oz) braised beef   125 g (¼ lb) chopped   1 chopped garlic clove
pinch of mixed herbs   cooked spinach   1 egg yolk
30 g (1 oz) cooked brains   seasoning

Mix all the ingredients and season.

RAVIOLIS

356 Ravioli florentine

Paste and filling as Recipes 353 and 354   30 g (1 oz) butter
250 ml (½ pt) thin Mornay sauce   30 g (1 oz) grated Parmesan
 (*Recipe* 58)   cheese

1 Cook, drain, toss in butter.
2 Coat with mornay sauce.
3 Sprinkle with cheese and brown.

357 Ravioli italienne

    125 *ml* (1 *gill*) *tomato sauce*   30 *g* (1 *oz*) *butter*
    30 *g* (1 *oz*) *Parmesan cheese*   *Paste and filling* (*Recipes* 353 *and* 355)

1 Having prepared the paste, lay one thin sheet of paste on marble slab.
2 Use a plain tube and pipe the garnish 2 cm (1 inch) apart in rows.
3 Egg-wash in between each piece and garnish.
4 Lay the other sheet of paste evenly on top.
5 Cut between each piece of garnish with the rotella or small round cutter.
6 Cook in boiling, salted water for 15 minutes; drain, toss in butter, coat with
   tomato sauce, sprinkle with Parmesan cheese and brown.

GNOCCHI AND POLENTA

Gnocchi (noques, the French term, is sometimes used) are, in effect, tiny
dumplings and come from the Italian cuisine. In that country they are usually
made either from semolina (the hard grains of wheat remaining in the sieve
after milling) or from a potato and flour mix. French chefs make a pasta from
a paste that is virtually the same as choux paste (Gnocchi Parisienne, Recipe
358). Egg is normally the binding agent for all types though potato gnocchi
may be made without it. These basic gnocchi are known as Romaine (semolina); Piedmontaise (potatoes and flour); Parisienne (water and flour and
eggs – a choux paste).

    Polenta is similar to semolina (Romaine) gnocchi but made with water
instead of milk. Let it harden, cut into wedges and fry with garlic and onions.
In some parts maize or buckwheat flour or semolina is boiled in saffron water
and served in wedges from the plainly-boiled mass. In Corsica, a kind of
Polenta is made with chestnut flour.

358 Gnocchi parisienne – Paris style (basic choux type)

    75 *g* (2½ *oz*) *flour*   2 *eggs*   125 *ml* (1 *gill*) *water*
    15 *g* (½ *oz*) *grated*   190 *ml* (1½ *gills*) *thin*   60 *g* (2 *oz*) *butter*
       Parmesan cheese   *Mornay sauce* (*Recipe* 58)   *pinch salt*

1 Melt butter in water.
2 Boil – rain in flour with salt and mix to a smooth paste.
3 Cool; blend in eggs one at a time.
4 Place paste in savoy bag with plain tube.
5 Pipe into boiling salted water using a wet knife to cut into small pieces
   during the piping process.
6 Poach gently for 10 minutes; drain, sauté lightly in butter and season.
7 Cover with Mornay sauce; sprinkle with cheese and gratinate.

Note. Spatzelli, a Swiss species, is prepared in the same way as Gnocchi
Parisienne except that a small plain tube is used. Spatzelli is used as a garnish
for Hungarian goulash.

359 Gnocchi piedmontaise – Piedmont style (basic potato gnocchi)

250 g (½ *lb*) *potato*	30 g (1 *oz*) *butter*	1 *egg yolk*
125 g (¼ *lb*) *cooked chicken purée*	15 g (½ *oz*) *flour seasoning*	15 g (½ *oz*) *Parmesan cheese*

1 Dry-mash the potatoes.
2 Mix with chicken purée and flour.
3 Bind with egg yolks and season.
4 Roll on a fork.
5 Poach in boiling salted water for 5 minutes.
6 Toss in butter, sprinkle with Parmesan cheese.
Tomato sauce (Recipe 34) may be served.

360 Gnocchi romaine – Roman style (basic semolina gnocchi)

500 *ml* (1 *pt*) *milk*	1 *clove crushed garlic*	15 g (½ *oz*) *grated cheese*
45 g (1½ *oz*) *butter*	*a little grated nutmeg*	(*Parmesan and Gruyère*)
190 *ml* (1½ *gills*) *Mornay sauce* (*Recipe 58*)	180 g (6 *oz*) *semolina*	1·25 *ml spoon* [¼ *tea-spoon*] *salt*
	1 *egg yolk*	

1 Boil milk with the garlic, salt and nutmeg.
2 Rain in the semolina and mix smoothly.
3 Cook on the side of stove for about 12 minutes.
4 Cool slightly and beat in egg yolks.
5 Turn out on a greased dish 1 cm (½ inch) thick.
6 Allow to go cold and cut into crescent shapes with a 3-inch cutter.
7 Sauté lightly in butter, cover with sauce, sprinkle with Parmesan cheese and brown. *Note*: Tomato sauce (Recipe 34) may be used in place of Mornay.

361 Gnocchi italienne

500 g (1 *lb*) *potatoes*	1 *egg yolk*	*seasoning*
15 g (½ *oz*) *flour*	30 g (1 *oz*) *Parmesan cheese*	

1 Dry-mash potatoes.
2 Season and bind with egg yolks and flour.
3 Allow to go cold, roll on a fork 2 cm (1 inch) long.
4 Poach gently in boiling salt water for 4 minutes.
5 Drain and sauté in butter; season and sprinkle with Parmesan cheese, and gratinate.

Note. Other well-known styles of gnocchi are Florentine (potato, egg, and flour gnocchi with spinach and cooked ham); and Valdostana (also a potato, egg, and flour type with butter and Parmesan cheese).

RICE

Rice, and rice dishes prepared by the chef entremettier (as distinct from sweet-rice cookery) belong to the same category on menus as Italian pastas.

General rules for cooking rice:
i Clean thoroughly without washing, picking out any impurities by hand.

 ii Cook in large, open saucepan with plenty of free boiling water.
iii Add rice gradually to the boiling water.
 iv Refresh and strain immediately the rice is cooked.

Types of rice. The types of rice most frequently used in the kitchen are:
  i Patna – Long-grained for Indian pilaffs.
 ii Piedmont – Italian rice for risotto dishes.
iii Carolina – Sweet dishes: very white, soft-cooked.
 iv Rice flour – Milled from broken grains.
    Patna and Piedmont rice are used for boiling (including pilaff and risotto
dishes) and served with savoury dishes; they are also used to garnish soup.
Carolina rice is largely confined to sweet cookery.
    The different types are judged by their origin, shape, size, colour, and the
shine of the grains of rice. A top-quality rice can be recognized by the large-
sized grains and their glossy and transparent appearance. Good grains should
not boil to pieces within 20 minutes but cheap kinds cook floury-white and
quickly boil away. Using the best and most suitable types, approximate
cooking times range from 12 minutes (for boiling 'al dente' or firm 'to the
teeth') to 15 minutes for soup garnish and risotto, and to 18 to 20 minutes for
pilaff. Sweet-milk rice is usually boiled softly (from 25 minutes to 30 minutes).

362 Riz nature – Plain boiled rice

> 180 g (6 oz) *Patna or Piedmont rice*   2·5 l (½ gallon) *water*   sal

1 Cook for 18 minutes in boiling salt water (according to general rules above).
2 Refresh and drain.

Note. See Riz indienne, Recipe 365.

363 Riz créole

> 45 g (1½ oz) *tomato concassé*   30 g (1 oz) *sliced cooked mushrooms*
> 15 g (½ oz) *diced pimentoes*

Add to the basic pilaff (Recipe 366) all the above as garnish.

364 Riz égyptienne

> 30 g (1 oz) *diced cooked mushrooms*   30 g (1 oz) *cooked ham*
> 30 g (1 oz) *diced fried chicken's liver*

Mix all the ingredients and add the basic rice pilaff (Recipe 366).

365 Riz indienne

> 180 g (6 oz) *patna rice*

1 Cook for 15 minutes in 2·5 l (½ gallon) of boiling salt water.
2 Strain and dry on a serviette.
3 Keep warm in the oven.

PILAFF AND RIZOTTO

The difference between a pilaff and risotto is that in the former grains are firmer and well separated whereas a risotto has softer grains and a denser mass.

366 Riz pilaff – Pilaff (alternative spellings: Pilau, Pillaw)

45 g (1½ oz) *finely-chopped onions*	60 g (2 oz) butter	(*Recipe* 6) *or fish*
fond blanc (*twice the volume of rice*)	1 *small bouquet garni*	*stock when pilaff accompanies fish*
180 g (6 oz) *Patna rice*	375 ml (3 gills) *white stock*	

1 Sweat the onions in 30 g (1 oz) butter.
2 Add the rice and sweat for 2 or 3 minutes.
3 Moisten with twice the volume of boiling stock, season lightly.
4 Add bouquet garni; boil and cover with greased paper.
5 Place lid on top and cook in moderate oven 150° C (300° F) for 18 to 20 minutes (when all stock will have been absorbed).
6 Remove bouquet garni, adjust seasoning and fork-in 30 g (1 oz) of butter.

Note. All grains of rice must be separate.

367 Rizotto – Riz italienne (Rice, Italian style)

180 g (6 oz) *Piedmont rice*	30 g (1 oz) *finely-chopped onions*	1 *small bouquet garni*
500 ml (1 pt) *fond blanc* (*Recipe* 6)	30 g (1 oz) *butter*	15 g (½ oz) *grated Parmesan cheese*

1 Sweat the onions in butter.
2 Wash the rice, and sweat for 2 or 3 minutes.
3 Add bouquet garni and 500 ml (1 pint stock).
4 Add a little salt, boil and draw to the side of the stove and simmer till very soft and all stock has evaporated; stir frequently with wooden spatula.
5 When cooked, fork in 15 g (½ oz) of grated Parmesan cheese.

368 Rizotto milanaise

180 g (6 oz) *Piedmont rice*	30 g (1 oz) *finely-chopped onions*	1 *small bouquet garni*
15 g (½ oz) *sliced raw mushrooms*	60 g (2 oz) *tomato concassé*	*pinch saffron*
500 ml (1 pt) *fond blanc* (*Recipe* 6)	30 g (1 oz) *butter*	15 g (½ oz) *grated Parmesan cheese*

Cook rice as Recipe 367 but infuse the saffron with a little boiling water and add the infused liquor during the cooking together with mushrooms and tomato concassé.

369 Rizotto piémontaise

15 g (½ oz) *diced pimentoes*	7 g (¼ oz) *diced truffle*	15 g (½ oz) *sliced, raw mushrooms*

As Recipe 367, garnished with the additional ingredients. If using fresh pimentoes stew in 30 g (1 oz) of butter till tender.

5. Fish

FISH cookery (apart from the fish preparation and cold dishes of the garde manger) is, in the traditional kitchen brigade, separated from other sections and under the control of the chef poissonnier, or fish cook. Fish dishes must also be created from culinary basics or fonds de cuisine and, in many instances, from sauces containing fish or sauces specially created to accompany fish. Therefore, this section begins with the fonds de cuisine, sauces, and mise-en-place for fish cookery.

BASIC PREPARATIONS

Court-bouillon. If the delicate flavours of fish are to be preserved and enhanced, the liquor in which they are poached should be prepared with care so as to match the fish to the sauce with which it will subsequently be dressed. This liquor is called a court-bouillon and is fundamentally a dilution of water with either vinegar, white or red wine with aromatics and flavouring. Also used as a fish poaching-liquor, bouillon au lait, or milk stock, is a simple dilution of milk and salted water in roughly, equal parts, particularly when white fish is prepared in 'light' style or for invalids.

When fish is actually presented 'au-court-bouillon' then care must be taken to ensure that vegetable ingredients are attractive and intact: for example, for onions use button onions, and carrots should appear in neatly sliced roundels.

370 Court-bouillon blanc – White court-bouillon

2 l (2 qt) water	1 sliced onion	250 ml (½ pt) milk
1 bay-leaf	juice of 1 lemon	1 teaspoon salt
30 g (1 oz) parsley stalk	6 peppercorns	

1 Boil and simmer ingredients together for 10 minutes.
2 Strain and use for plainly boiled white fish.

371 Court-bouillon ordinaire – Ordinary court-bouillon

5 l (5 qt) water	500 g (1 lb) onions	1 sprig thyme
375 ml (¾ pt) malt vinegar	60 g (2 oz) salt	2 bay-leaves
24 ground peppercorns	60 g (2 oz) parsley	
360 g (¾ lb) carrots	stalks	

1 Slice the onions and carrots thinly.
2 Place the vegetables and the rest of the ingredients in the water.
3 Simmer for 20 minutes.
4 Strain and use as required.

Used for lobster, shellfish, trout and salmon.

372 Court-bouillon au vin blanc – White wine court-bouillon

500 *ml* (1 *pt*) *dry, white wine*	1 *bouquet garni*	30 *g* (1 *oz*) *thinly-*
500 *ml* (1 *pt*) *boiled water*	7 *g* (¼ *oz*) *salt*	*sliced carrots*
60 *g* (2 *oz*) *minced onions*	6 *peppercorns*	

1 Allow the boiled water to cool before using.
2 Add ingredients, bring to the boil and simmer for ½ hour.
3 Strain through muslin.

Used for fresh-water fish and white fish.

373 Court-bouillon au vin rouge – Red wine court-bouillon

500 *ml* (1 *pt*) *red wine*	1 *bouquet garni*	6 *peppercorns*
500 *ml* (1 *pt*) *water*	15 *g* (½ *oz*) *parsley stalks*	60 *g* (2 *oz*) *thinly-*
60 *g* (2 *oz*) *minced onions*	7 *g* (¼ *oz*) *salt*	*sliced carrots*

1 Use boiled, cooled water.
2 Boil and simmer all ingredients for ½ hour.
3 Strain through muslin.

Used for fresh-water fish.

FISH STOCK AND BASICS

Stock, essence, glaze, and velouté are as essential for the preparation of fish dishes as are the fonds or basics listed in Chapter 1 for other types of dishes.

374 Fumet de poisson – Fish stock [to yield 10 litres (2 gallons)]

5 *kg* (10 *lb*) *white*	150 *g* (5 *oz*) *parsley*	1 *bouquet garni*
fish-bones	*including stalks*	240 *g* (½ *lb*) *butter*
and trimmings	750 *g* (1½ *lb*) *sliced*	10 *l* (10 *qt*) *cold water*
1 *lemon*	*onions*	

1 Butter the bottom of a saucepan.
2 Place in sliced onions and washed parsley.
3 Lay the fish-bones and trimmings (preferably of sole, whiting or turbot) on these aromatics and squeeze over the juice of 1 lemon.
4 Cover saucepan and allow to sweat.
5 Pour over the cold water.
6 Bring to the boil, skim, and simmer for 20 minutes.
7 Strain through muslin.

375 Essence de poisson – Fish essence

Reduce fumet de poisson (Recipe 374) by open boiling and evaporating by one-half.

376 Glace de poisson – Fish glaze

1 Reduce 8 litres (8 quarts) fumet de poisson or 4 litres (4 quarts) essence de poisson (Recipes 374 and 375) to 250 ml (½ pint).

2 Pour into jars when still hot; the fish glaze should be of a thick syrupy consistency.

377 Velouté de poisson – Fish velouté [for 1 litre (1 quart)]

120 *g* (4 *oz*) *flour*	1·5 *l* (1½ *qt*) *fish stock* (*Recipe* 374)
120 *g* (4 *oz*) *butter*	6 *crushed peppercorns*

1 Melt butter and add flour to make a blond roux (Recipe 24).
2 Allow roux to cool, add the boiling fish stock and mix smoothly with wooden spoon.
3 Boil; skim; add the peppercorns and continue to simmer slowly over moderate heat until reduced to 1 litre (1 quart).
4 Strain through muslin; butter the surface to prevent the formation of a skin.

SAUCES FOR FISH

For convenience the fish-sauce recipes which follow have been arranged alphabetically. Those, in addition to the fumet and fonds (basics) introducing this section, that are generally considered basic are sauces vin blanc, vin rouge, Nantua and normande.

Most frequently 'en-place' in the chef poissonnier's bain-marie or used by him are Béchamel derivatives (e.g., sauces mornay, anchois, and shrimp sauce prepared in the English style) together with other sauces from Chapter 1 such as hollandaise, and glace de viande (for meunière treatments). Butter, including beurre fondu, noir and noisette, is also required.

378 Sauce anchois – Anchovy sauce

500 *ml* (1 *pt*) *sauce normande* (*Recipe* 394)	90 *g* (3 *oz*) *anchovy butter* (*Recipe* 400)	30 *g* (1 *oz*) *filleted anchovy*

1 Blend the anchovy butter into the sauce normande.
2 Wash the anchovy fillets and cut into small dice.
3 Garnish the sauce with diced anchovy.

379 Anchovy sauce – English-style (Béchamel derivative)

500 *ml* (1 *pt*) *Béchamel* (*Recipe* 51)	30 *g* (1 *oz*) *butter*
15 *ml spoon* [1 *tablespoon*] *anchovy essence*	65 *ml* (½ *gill*) *cream* *seasoning*

1 Blend the anchovy essence into Béchamel.
2 Add the butter and cream and mix well.
3 Season and strain.

380 Sauce Bercy

30 *g* (1 *oz*) *finely-chopped shallots*	125 *ml* (1 *gill*) *cream*	90 *g* (3 *oz*) *butter*
375 *ml* (¾ *pt*) *fish velouté* (*Recipe* 377)	30 *g* (1 *oz*) *finely-chopped herbs*	125 *ml* (¼ *pt*) *fish stock* (*Recipe* 374)
125 *ml* (¼ *pt*) *white wine*	(*tarragon, chervil, parsley*)	*juice of* ½ *lemon*

1 Sweat off the shallots in a little butter.
2 Add the fish stock and white wine and reduce to one-third.
3 Pour on the fish velouté and reduce the total liquid to 250 ml ($\frac{1}{2}$ pint).
4 Blend in the cream and butter, season and garnish with the fine herbs.

Note. A Bercy reduction, a combination of shallots, parsley, white wine, and fish stock, is commonly required in fish-cookery. Bercy sauce is sometimes referred to as fines-herbes sauce. *N.B.* For large numbers add a little sabayon 2 eggs per litre (quart), also add a little whipped cream, this gives a quick glaze; a useful method for banquets.

381 Sauce bourguignonne

45 g (1$\frac{1}{2}$ oz) maniéd butter (Recipe 19)	30 g (1 oz) finely-chopped shallots	1 sprig thyme 12 crushed peppercorns
500 ml (1 pt) red wine	seasoning	5 ml spoon [1 teaspoon]
1 bay-leaf	60 g (2 oz) butter	meat glaze (Recipe 13)

1 Sweat off shallots and peppercorns in 30 g (1 oz) butter.
2 Add the aromatics, pour on the wine and reduce to 250 ml ($\frac{1}{2}$ pint).
3 Thicken the liquid with the maniéd butter and work in the meat glaze.
4 Season and strain, blend in the butter.

Note. It is trade practice to add a little half-glaze to this type of sauce when making the reduction. Use 250 to 500 ml ($\frac{1}{4}$ pt to 1 pt) of red wine.

Bourguignonne sauce can be used for egg dishes as well as fish.

382 Sauce Cardinal I

500 ml (1 pt) Béchamel (Recipe 51)	125 ml (1 gill) cream	2 × 15 ml spoon [2 tablespoons]
250 ml ($\frac{1}{2}$ pt) fish fumet (Recipe 374)	90 g (3 oz) lobster butter (Recipe 402)	brandy seasoning

1 Reduce Béchamel and fish fumet to 500 ml (1 pint).
2 Blend in the cream, lobster butter, brandy. Season.

383 Sauce Cardinal II

250 ml ($\frac{1}{2}$ pt) fish fumet (Recipe 374)	seasoning	125 ml (1 gill) cream
250 ml ($\frac{1}{2}$ pt) lobster sauce (Recipe 386)	250 ml ($\frac{1}{2}$ pt) Béchamel (Recipe 51) 60 g (2 oz) butter	2 × 15 ml spoon [2 tablespoons] brandy

1 Reduce fish fumet, Béchamel, lobster sauce to 500 ml (1 pint).
2 Blend in cream, butter and brandy; season.
3 If required for glazing, add 125 ml (1 gill) of sauce Hollandaise.

384 Sauce aux crevettes – Shrimp sauce (English style)

500 ml (1 pt) Béchamel (Recipe 51)	60 g (2 oz) shelled shrimps	125 ml ($\frac{1}{4}$ pt) cream
125 ml ($\frac{1}{4}$ pt) fish stock (Recipe 374)	60 g (2 oz) shrimp butter (Recipe 401)	seasoning

1 Add cream, fish stock to Béchamel and reduce to 500 ml (1 pint).
2 Blend in shrimp butter.

3 Garnish the sauce with the shelled shrimps tossed in butter.
4 Adjust the seasoning.

385 Sauce genevoise

240 g (½ lb) *fine mirepoix*	1 *bouquet garni*	180 g (6 oz) *butter*
(*Recipe* 4)	500 ml (1 pt) *fish stock*	1 *glass brandy*
½ *bottle red wine*	(*Recipe* 374)	2 × 15 ml *spoon* [2
500 ml (1 pt) *Espagnole*	500 g (1 lb) *salmon-head*	*tablespoons*] .
(*Recipe* 28)	*and bones*	*anchovy essence*

1 Sweat off the mirepoix in 60 g (2 oz) butter.
2 Add the salmon-head and bones and stew with lid on for 20 minutes.
3 Add the Espagnole, fish stock, and simmer.
4 Strain the liquid through a fine chinois.
5 Add the red wine to the strained sauce and reduce to 375 ml (¾ pint).
6 Add the anchovy essence, pass through a muslin, season and blend in the butter, add brandy.

386 Sauce homard – Lobster sauce

500 g (1 lb) *lobster, shell-*	12 *crushed peppercorns*	125 ml (1 gill)
cooked (*including coral*	1 *bouquet garni*	*brandy*
and spawn)	1·25 l (2½ pt) *fish stock*	90 g (3 oz)
180 g (6 oz) *fine mirepoix*	(*Recipe* 374)	*butter*
(*Recipe* 4)	125 ml (1 gill) *white*	200 ml (1½ gill)
½ *clove crushed garlic*	*wine*	*tomato purée*
240 g (½ lb) *tomato concassé*	90 g (3 oz) *flour*	*salt*

1 Pound the lobster shell, coral and spawn in the mortar.
2 Sweat off the shells in the butter.
3 Add the mirepoix and garlic and sweat on.
4 Add the flour to make a roux and continue to cook for a few minutes.
5 Now mix in thoroughly, the tomato purée and fresh tomatoes.
6 Blend in the stock and white wine, stirring to a smooth sauce.
7 Bring to the boil, skim, add crushed peppercorns and bouquet garni.
8 Simmer for 1 hour on side of stove.
9 Strain, add brandy, and season.

Note. The above sauce can be made by using the same proportion of raw lobster.

387 Sauce Joinville

500 ml (1 pt) *normande sauce*	60 g (2 oz) *shrimp butter*	15 g (½ oz) *diced,*
(*Recipe* 394)	(*Recipe* 401)	*cooked*
60 g (2 oz) *crayfish butter**	15 g (½ oz) *diced shrimp-*	*mushrooms*
15 ml *spoon* [1 *tablespoon*]	*tails*	22 g (¾ oz) *diced*
brandy		*truffles*

1 Blend in the butter to the finished normande sauce.
2 Heat in the shrimps, mushrooms and truffles in a 15 ml spoon (1 tablespoon) brandy and add to the sauce as a garnish.
3 Adjust the seasoning.

   * Crayfish butter is made in the same way as shrimp butter (Recipe 401).

388 Sauce marinière

30 g (1 oz) *finely-chopped*
shallots
30 g (1 oz) *fines herbes*
375 ml (¾ pt) *fish velouté*
(*Recipe* 377)
juice of ½ *lemon*
90 g (3 oz) *butter*

125 ml (¼ pt) *mussel stock*
or Recipe 374 *using*
mussels
125 ml (¼ pt) *white wine*
125 ml (1 gill) *cream*
2 egg yolks } *liaison*

24 *bearded cooked*
mussels
30 g (1 oz) *diced*
shrimp-tails

1 Sweat off the shallots in 30 g (1 oz) butter.
2 Add the mussel stock and wine and reduce to one-third.
3 Pour in the fish velouté and reduce to 250 ml (½ pint).
4 Draw to the side of the stove and blend in butter and liaison.
5 Add the fines herbes; season and garnish with the mussels and shrimps.

Note. This must not be confused with the classic recipe for moules (mussels) marinière.

389 Sauce matelote

500 *ml* (1 *pt*) *half-glaze*
(*Recipe* 29)
30 g (1 oz) *chopped shallots*
120 g (4 oz) *butter*
1 *sprig thyme*

cayenne pepper
120 g (4 oz) *mush-*
rooms
250 ml (½ pt) *fish stock*
(*Recipe* 374)

1 *bay-leaf*
6 *crushed pepper-*
corns
250 ml (½ pt) *red*
wine

1 Sweat off peppercorns and shallots in 30 g (1 oz) butter.
2 Add wine and bay-leaf, thyme, fish stock and make a reduction.
3 Pour on the demi-glace and simmer to 375 ml (¾ pint).
4 Season and strain through tammy-cloth.
5 Add a pinch of cayenne pepper and blend in butter.

390 Sauce matelote (white)

12 *cooked button-*
onions

12 *small turned*
mushrooms

125 *ml* (1 gill) *cream*
250 *ml* (½ pt) *white wine*

Same method as Recipe 389 using fish velouté (Recipe 377) instead of half-glaze and white wine instead of red wine.

Note. Garnish the sauce with button onions and mushrooms cooked (à blanc) and finish off sauce with a little cream.

391 Sauce Nantua I

500 *ml* (1 *pt*) *Béchamel*
(*Recipe* 51)
250 *ml* (½ pt) *cream*

1 *glass sherry*
30 g (1 oz) *diced*
prawns

90 g (3 oz) *crayfish*
butter (*as Recipe*
401, *using crayfish*)

1 Reduce Béchamel and cream by one-third to 500 ml (1 pint).
2 Pass through a fine chinois.
3 Blend in crayfish butter and sherry.
4 Season, garnish with diced prawns.

392 Sauce Nantua II

250 *ml* (½ *pt*) *Béchamel* (*Recipe* 51)	250 *ml* (½ *pt*) *cream*	30 *g* (1 *oz*)
250 *ml* (½ *pt*) *lobster sauce*	90 *g* (3 *oz*) *butter*	*diced*
(*Recipe* 386)	1 *glass sherry*	*prawns*

1 Reduce Béchamel, cream and lobster sauce by one-third to 500 ml (1 pint).
2 Strain through fine chinois.
3 Blend in butter and sherry.
4 Season, garnish with diced prawns.

393 Sauce Newburg

1 *kg* (2 *lb*) *raw lobster*	1 *glass Madeira*	240 *g* (½ *lb*) *tomato*
125 *ml* (1 *gill*) *oil*	1 *glass brandy*	*concassé*
120 *g* (¼ *lb*) *fine mirepoix*	240 *g* (8 *oz*) *butter*	500 *ml* (1 *pt*) *fish*
(*Recipe* 2)	250 *ml* (½ *pt*) *cream*	*stock*
125 *ml* (¼ *pt*) *white wine*	1 *bouquet garni*	(*Recipe* 374)

1 Divide the head of the lobster into two and remove the creamy parts and blend these well with 60 g (2 oz) butter.
2 Divide the tail into 4 thick slices.
3 Place the oil and 30 g (1 oz) butter into a thick saucepan and fry the head and tail to a fine red colour; flambé with brandy.
4 Add the mirepoix and tomato concassé and sweat under cover for a few minutes.
5 Moisten with the wine and fish stock; add the bouquet garni; cook with lid on for 20 minutes.
6 Remove the lobster, re-boil sauce, add the cream and finish off by adding the creamy parts of the lobster.
7 Strain through a fine chinois; add the Madeira; season and blend in the remainder of the butter.

Note. The sauce may be garnished with a small dice of cooked lobster-meat.

394 Sauce normande

1 *l* (2 *pt*) *fish velouté*	250 *ml* (½ *pt*) *fish stock*	*salt and pepper*
(*Recipe* 377)	(*Recipe* 374)	125 *ml* (1 *gill*) *oyster*
125 *ml* (1 *gill*)	5 *egg yolks*	*liquor*
mushroom liquor	250 *ml* (½ *pt*) *cream*	120 *g* (4 *oz*) *butter*
juice of ½ *lemon*	*cayenne pepper*	

1 Place in a thick-bottomed pan the following: fish velouté, mushroom liquor, fish stock, lemon juice, oyster liquor.
2 Reduce by one-third on a quick fire (brisk heat).
3 Beat up the egg yolks and cream and add to the sauce – draw to the side of the fire (reduce heat).
4 Blend in the butter, season and pass through muslin-cloth.

395 Sauce portugaise

120 g (4 oz) butter	7 g (¼ oz) chopped	60 g (2 oz) finely-
85 ml (⅙ pt) olive oil	parsley	chopped shallots
¼ clove crushed garlic	480 g (1 lb) tomato	375 ml (¾ pt) thin
15 ml spoon [1 tablespoon]	concassé	tomato-sauce
fish glaze (Recipe 376)	165 ml (⅓ pt) white wine	(Recipe 34)

1 Lightly colour the shallots in the oil and add the garlic.
2 Make a reduction of the wine.
3 Add tomato concassé and sweat for a few minutes.
4 Add the tomato sauce, simmer for a few minutes and draw to the side of the stove (reduce heat); add fish glaze.
5 Thicken with butter, adjust seasoning, and add parsley.

396 Sauce vin blanc I – White wine sauce

375 ml (¾ pt) fish velouté	lemon juice	30 g (1 oz) finely-
(Recipe 377)	salt	chopped shallots
125 ml (¼ pt) white wine	250 ml (½ pt) fish fumet	125 ml (¼ pt) cream
120 g (4 oz) butter	(Recipe 374)	cayenne pepper

1 Reduce the shallots, white wine and fish stock to one-third pt.
2 Add the fish velouté and cream, reduce the total sauce to 375 ml (¾ pt).
3 Blend in the butter and add the seasoning.

397 Sauce vin blanc II

375 ml (¾ pt) fish velouté	salt and pepper	3 egg yolks
(Recipe 377)	250 ml (½ pt) fish fumet	125 ml (¼ pt) } liaison
125 ml (¼ pt) white wine	(Recipe 374)	cream
120 g (4 oz) butter	30 g (1 oz) chopped	cayenne
lemon juice	shallots	

1 Reduce the shallots, white wine and fish stock to one-third pt.
2 Add the fish velouté and reduce to 250 ml (½ pt).
3 Draw to side of the fire, blend in butter, liaison, and season.

398 Sauce vin blanc III

4 egg yolks	15 ml spoon [1 tablespoon] fish fumet (Recipe 374)

Beat the egg yolk and fish stock to ribbon stage (forming a sabayon) in bain-marie.
Add this sabayon to Recipe 396.

Note. If this method is used, no hollandaise is required; but when Sauce vin blanc is required for large parties, use Recipe 396 with equal parts of sauce hollandaise (Recipe 72). This combination is recommended as the sauce does not relax and can stand until needed.

399 Sauce vin rouge – Red wine sauce

> 15 g (½ oz) *fine mirepoix*   5 ml *spoon* [1 *teaspoon*]   500 ml (1 *pt*) *demi-*
> (*Recipe* 4)   *anchovy essence*   *glace* (*Recipe* 29)
> 250 ml (½ *pt*) *red wine*   *pinch cayenne pepper*   120 g (4 *oz*) *butter*

1 Fry, to golden colour, mirepoix in 30 g (1 oz) butter.
2 Add wine and reduce by half.
3 Moisten with demi-glace and reduce total liquid to 375 ml (¾ pint).
4 Strain the sauce, season and finish with butter, anchovy essence and cayenne pepper.

Note. For a red wine sauce for meat, see Sauce Bordelaise (Recipe 35).

BUTTERS FOR FISH

The fish cook also makes use of melted and noisette butter. He uses beurre noir (particularly with raie [skate]); the compound butters such as beurre maître d'hôtel (Recipe 89); and beurre vert (tinted with spinach juice). Beurre manié is used to thicken a sauce that is too thin. The following are three examples of beurres composés (compound butters) with fish itself in their composition.

400 Beurre d'anchois – Anchovy butter

> 120 g (4 oz) *butter*   15 ml *spoon* [1 *table-*   *juice of* ½ *lemon*
> 4 *anchovies*   *spoon*] *anchovy essence*   *cayenne pepper*

1 Pound the butter and anchovies in a mortar.
2 Add the lemon juice and anchovy essence and cayenne pepper; mix well.
3 Roll in greased paper and keep in refrigerator till required.

401 Beurre de crevettes – Shrimp butter

> 120 g (4 oz) *shrimps*   120 g (4 oz) *butter*   *juice of* ½ *lemon*

1 Shell the shrimps.
2 Pound lemon juice, butter, and shrimps in mortar.
3 Rub through a medium sieve.
4 Roll in greaseproof paper and keep until required.

402 Beurre de homard – Lobster butter

> 1 *lobster shell, coral and spawn*   *pinch cayenne pepper*
> 180 g (6 oz) *butter*

1 Pound the lobster shell, coral and spawn in with the butter and cayenne.
2 Cook slowly in double boiler till all the butter rises to the top.
3 Strain and butter through a chinois.
4 Allow to cool and reserve for use.

Salpicons. As well as the salpicons listed in Chapter 1 (Recipes 103–9), there are those especially suited for use in fish dishes. Examples are the shrimp mushrooms, and truffle, sweated in butter and cohered with Sauce Suprême for fish dishes; e.g.; Joinville (see Recipe 387); and the salpicon used in Sole Otéro (Recipe 446).

TYPES OF FISH

A wide range of fish dishes may be prepared by using basic cooking methods (i.e. poaching, grilling, pan-frying and deep-frying) with the accompaniment of sauces in this and preceding chapters. The main types of fish are:

Fresh-Water Fish include those from river and lake such as fresh-water bream, carp, perch, pike, salmon, trout, sturgeon.

Sea-Water Fish may be further sub-divided into:
   Round oily fish – such as herrings and mackerel.
   White round – such as cod, haddock, whiting.
   Flat white – such as brill, lemon sole, plaice, sole, halibut, turbot.
   Shellfish – comprising (a) *Crustacea* such as: crab, crayfish, lobster, prawns, shrimps, scampis.
   (b) *Molluscs* such as: clams, oysters, mussels, scallops (in this category, snails, though not true fish, may conveniently be considered).
   Frogs (grenouilles) – although these do not belong to this category they are included.

CUTS OF FISH

Although small fish such as trout and lemon sole are often cooked whole, and large ones such as turbot and salmon may similarly be presented in their entirety, fish is frequently cut into steaks or filleted and cut into portions. These are named as follows:

Sole (with application to similar flat fish)
Filets – fillets: lightly flatten with bat and cook flat.
Goujons or en goujons – gudgeon cut: thin strips of fillet for deep-frying or meuniére.
Mignon: fillet folded as a cornet (triangular fold as for paper piping-bag).
Paupiette: flattened fillet, coated with fish farce and rolled; usually poached.
Plié – folded: flattened and folded in two.
Suprême: alternative name for fillet.

Salmon, turbot, and similar, larger fish
Côtelette: a fish cutlet or steak with bone. (Alternative name for tronçon).
Darne: a straight cut through the bone (and correctly from the middle) to yield the finest cut of round fish, such as salmon.
Médaillon: a medallion-shaped portion from larger fillets.
Suprême: a fillet (or portion of large fillet).
Tronçon: a steak cut with bone.

TREATMENT OF FROZEN FISH

Generally, portioned frozen fish should not be defrosted prior to cooking and especially not defrosted for poaching, boiling and grilling. But if portioned fish is to be deep fried *à l'anglaise* (pané, crumbed) it is advantageous to defrost partially to make the portion flexible enough to be crumb or batter treated.

Bulk-packed frozen fish of larger varieties, i.e. large cod or other white fillets, may require just sufficient defrosting to enable separation and cutting to take place.

In all cases where some defrosting is indicated, normal defrosting in room temperature and *never* by immersion in warm water should be employed.

All methods for fresh fish in the following recipes may be applied to frozen fish.

METHODS OF COOKING FISH

403 Poisson bouilli – Boiled fish

Fish can be boiled in salted water (or in salted and vinegared water) but it is preferable to use a court-bouillon (Recipes 370–73), which should be pre-prepared, and the ingredients boiled together for 10 minutes. Larger, whole fish are usually covered with cold court-bouillon (or cooking-liquor), brought to boil and simmered gently so that outer parts do not flake away. Small fish and small cuts of fish are, however, plunged into already boiling liquor. For plainly-boiled white fish use a court-bouillon (Recipe 370) for cooking-liquor. Soak the fish in a little cold, salted water before boiling.

Use the following general guide for boiling fish, but always test to check: when fish is cooked, a skewer or fork will easily detach flesh from bone cleanly.

Boiling for hot service.
  i Simmer large whole fish (e.g. turbot and brill) for 20 minutes (approximately).
 ii Simmer small cuts of fish for 10 to 15 minutes (approximately).
iii For whole salmon see Recipe 427.
 iv For cuts of salmon see Recipe 428.

Boiling for cold service.
  i Simmer whole large fish (e.g. turbot) and cuts for 5 minutes after coming to boil, then cover closely and cool in own liquor.
 ii For whole salmon see Recipe 489 and for cuts, Recipe 490.

404 Poisson poché – Poached fish

	Mis-en-place	
finely-chopped shallots	*lemon juice*	*butter*
fish stock	*greased kitchen-paper*	

1 Butter a shallow fish-dish.
2 Sprinkle on the shallots.
3 Lay fish flat on top.
4 Half cover with fish stock.
5 Cover with greased paper.
6 Poach in moderate oven.

405 Poisson braisé – Braised fish

Braising is generally applicable to whole or sliced salmon, sturgeon, turbot or trout.

Mis-en-place

| *aromatics* | *carrots* | *onions* |
| *wine* | *fish stock* | *seasoning* |

1 Place the seasoned fish on a bed of vegetables and aromates.
2 Moisten with red or white wine and fish stock.
3 The liquid should cover ¾ of the fish.
4 Cook under cover and baste frequently.
5 Drain well reserving the liquor as the sauce is made from its reduction.

406 Baked fish

Applicable to whole fish, plain or stuffed, and to cuts.
1 Butter a dish and place fish on top.
2 Cover with greased paper.
3 Baste frequently with butter.

407 Poisson frit á l'anglaise – Fried fish (English style)

Mis-en-place

| *flour* | *white breadcrumbs* | *parsley* |
| *egg-wash* | *lemon* | |

1 Pass prepared fish through flour, egg-wash, and breadcrumbs.
2 Deep fry, serve with lemon and fried parsley.
Frying temperature. Between 175° C (350° F) and 190°C (375° F) according to speed of heat recovery.
Time. About 3 minutes for fillets of average size.
Note. Add a little oil to egg-wash.

408 Poisson frit à la française – Fried fish (French style)

Mis-en-place

| *seasoned flour* | *lemon* | *parsley* |
| *milk* | | |

1 Marinate the fish in milk
2 Pass through seasoned flour.
3 Deep fry in oil.
4 Garnish with lemon and parsley.

409 Poisson à l'Orly

Mis-en-place

| *instant marinade (Recipe 125)* | *batter coating* |
| *tomato sauce (Recipe 34)* | *parsley* |

1 Marinate fish for 1 hour.
2 Dip in batter.

3 Fry in deep fat.
4 Garnish with fried parsley.
5 Serve tomato sauce separately.

Shallow- or pan-fried Fish. Shallow-frying is suitable for small round fish or slices of larger ones.

410 Poisson meunière

Mis-en-place

seasoned flour	*lemons*	*butter for beurre*
oil	*chopped parsley*	*noisette* (*Recipe* 82)

1 Pass fish through seasoned flour.
2 Shallow fry both sides in hot oil.
3 Garnish with slices of lemon.
4 Finish with beurre noisette, chopped parsley and lemon juice.

Note. All round fish must be ciselé first.

411 Poisson doré – gilded

Mis-en-place

seasoned flour   *clarified butter*

1 Pass fish through seasoned flour.
2 Shallow fry both sides in clarified butter.
3 Season and serve on hot dish.

412 Poisson grillé – Grilled fish

Mis-en-place

oil   *seasoned flour*   *butter*

1 If fish is whole, ciseler.
2 Pass through seasoned flour.
3 Brush both sides with oil.
4 Cook both sides under grill and baste with butter.
5 Serve on dish without d'oyley or paper; garnish with lemon and parsley.

Suitable sauces: *Parsley butter, devil, piquante, béarnaise.*

FISH DISHES FOR HOT SERVICE

The recipes selected and listed below are intended to act as examples of main treatments. With rare exceptions (such as au bleu, mostly confined to trout) dish names and methods may be applied to more than the fish chosen. For example, plaice (plie) may be prepared, like sole, en goujons or as Goujons de plie. Indeed most methods cited for sole may be used for turbot and other white fish, and recipes for cod (cabillaud) may equally be applied to fresh haddock (aiglefin or aigrefin).

Some cold-service recipes appear at the end of this chapter, but it should be noted that cold fish (including herrings and mackerel) are dealt with in

Chapter 2, 'Larder Preparations', and further fish dishes are contained, it is thought more appropriately, among breakfast dishes.

All recipes are for 4 covers except modes for large whole fish.

BLANCHAILLES – WHITEBAIT

413 Blanchailles diablées – Devilled whitebait

500 g (1 *lb*) *whitebait*	240 g (½ *lb*) *seasoned flour*	7 g (¼ *oz*) *cayenne pepper*
250 ml (½ *pt*) *milk*	60 g (2 *oz*) *salt*	*deep fat*

1 Soak whitebait in milk. Defrost frozen ones first.
2 Drain well and place a little at a time in the seasoned flour.
3 Sieve well on cane sieve.
4 Deep fry until golden brown and crisp.
5 Drain well and dust with a combination of salt and cayenne pepper.
6 Dress on serviette and garnish with quarters of lemon and fried parsley.

Note. Ample dredging-flour (used freshly each time) is essential if the whitebait are to remain separate and not stick together; therefore, also avoid cooking too many at one time. Strain fat after use.

414 Blanchailles frites or Blanchailles frites au citron – Fried whitebait with lemon

Basically as Recipe 413 but without the use of cayenne pepper.

CABILLAUD – COD

415 Cabillaud meunière

4, 180 g (6-*oz*) *darnes of cod*	190 ml (1½ *gills*) *oil*	125 g (¼ *lb*) *butter noisette*
8 *lemon slices*	7 g (¼ *oz*) *chopped parsley*	(*Recipe* 82)

1 Cook as Recipe 410.
2 Remove skin and centre bone.
3 Garnish with lemon slices.
4 Coat with beurre noisette and sprinkle with chopped parsley.

416 Cabillaud poché

4, 180 g (6-*oz*) *darnes of cod*	1 *l* (1 *qt*) *white court-bouillon* (*Recipe* 370)	4 *lemon slices*
12 *potatoes, medium size*		*sprigs of parsley*

1 Wash the cod steaks.
2 Place in boiling court-bouillon.
3 Simmer for approximately 10 minutes.
4 Drain, garnish with slices of lemon and boiled 'turned' potatoes.
5 Pour a little of the cooking-liquid over before service.
6 Decorate with sprigs of parsley.

417 Cod roe meunière

750 g (1½ lb) cod roe	120 g (¼ lb) butter	120 g (¼ lb) seasoned
750 ml (1½ pt) court-bouillon	chopped parsley	flour
(Recipe 371)		

1 Place roe in cold court-bouillon.
2 Bring slowly to the boil.
3 Allow to cool in its own liquor.
4 Cut in thick slices.
5 Pass through seasoned flour.
6 Cook à la meunière (Recipe 410).

Cod roe may also be sliced after boiling and served cold for hors d'œuvre in marinade or vinaigrette.

ÉPERLANS - SMELTS

418 Éperlans frits – Fried smelts

16 medium smelts	120 g (¼ lb) seasoned flour	2 beaten eggs
2 lemon halves	240 g (½ lb) white breadcrumbs	

1 Remove fins and eyes, and clean.
2 Pass through flour, egg, and crumbs.
3 Fry in deep fat to golden colour.
4 Drain, season with salt and cayenne pepper.
5 Serve with lemon and tartare sauce (Recipe 114).
6 Garnish with fried parsley.
Smelts may also be prepared as St Germain, meunière or à l'Orly (Recipes 421, 410, 409).

MERLAN - WHITING

419 Merlan frit en colère – Fried whiting en colère

4 medium whiting	2 beaten eggs	deep fat for frying
2 lemons	240 g (½ lb) white	120 g (¼ lb)
fried parsley	breadcrumbs	seasoned flour

1 Trim fins and remove eyes.
2 Skin both sides starting from head.
3 Place tail through eyes.
4 Flour, egg, and crumb.
5 Deep fry; drain and season; dress on dish-paper; garnish with lemon and fried parsley.

420 Merlan à l'anglaise – Whiting (English style)

4 medium whiting	240 g (½ lb) white breadcrumbs
120 g (¼ lb) clarified butter	120 g (¼ lb) parsley butter
(Recipe 84)	(Recipe 89)

1 Skin and fillet whiting.
2 Pass through butter and white breadcrumbs; season.

3 Brush with clarified butter and grill both sides.
4 Garnish with parsley butter.

421 Merlan St Germain

4, 180 g (6-oz) whole whiting
240 g (½ lb) white breadcrumbs
120 g (¼ lb) melted butter
240 g (1 lb) pommes noisette (Recipe 903)
125 ml (¼ pt) sauce béarnaise
(Recipe 73)
seasoning

1 Remove fins and scales, open down back, gut and remove backbone; leave head on and remove eyes.
2 Melt the butter; season fish lightly, dip fish in melted butter then in breadcrumbs.
3 Place on a buttered tray, sprinkle the fish with melted butter and grill gently until golden brown.
4 Dish (*no* paper or d'oyley) and surround with roasted noisette potatoes.
5 Garnish heads with sprigs of parsley and serve sauce béarnaise separately. (A thread of béarnaise may be piped down the centre of each fish.)

Note. This method can be applied to sole, smelts and fresh haddock. (Sole are kept whole with black skin removed, gutted and with head left on.)

422 Merlan farci – Stuffed whiting

4 medium whiting
120 g (¼ oz) chopped parsley
180 g (6 oz) white breadcrumbs
pinch of mixed herbs
180 g (6 oz) clarified butter (Recipe 84)
1 egg
30 g (1 oz) finely-chopped onions

1 Trim fins and eyes from fish.
2 Sweat the onions in butter to golden brown.
3 Mix onions, crumbs, parsley and herbs and bind with egg; season.
4 Place equal parts of stuffing into the flap of the fish.
5 Bake in a buttered dish approximately 15 minutes.
6 Garnish with lemon and sprigs of parsley.

Note. Haddock is frequently prepared in the same way.

RAIE – SKATE

423 Raie au beurre noir – Skate with black butter

1 kg (2 lb) skate
30 g (1 oz) capers
2 × 15 ml spoon [2 tablespoons] vinegar
120 g (¼ lb) butter
juice of 1 lemon
7 g (¼ oz) parsley
500 ml (1 pt) court-bouillon (Recipe 370)

1 Soak skate overnight.
2 Cut into 4 equal portions.
3 Cook in court-bouillon for 10 minutes.
4 Skin both sides when cooked.
5 Sprinkle on capers, lemon juice, and parsley.
6 Make a beurre noisette (Recipe 82) very brown and add the vinegar.
7 Pour over the skate.

Note. Skate is also deep-fried or meunière. In such cases, skin before cooking.

ROUGET – RED MULLET

Red Mullet is normally cooked without being gutted or 'drawn'; hence its popular designation 'woodcock of the sea'.

424 Rouget en papillote – Red mullet in paper

4, 250 g (8-oz) red mullet	4 sheets greaseproof	125 ml (1 gill) demi-
60 g (2 oz) finely-chopped	paper	glace (Recipe 29)
mushrooms	250 ml (½ pt) oil	8 slices of boiled ham
15 g (½ oz) butter	seasoning	

1 Prepare by cleaning, scaling, and removing the eyes; then grill the mullet.
2 Sweat mushrooms in butter, mix with the demi-glace and season.
3 Cut the paper into large heart-shapes using full sheet for each one.
4 Oil both sides of the paper.
5 Place 1 slice of ham on one side of each heart then lay the mullet on top and coat each with sauce; lay another slice of ham on each one.
6 Seal both sides of the paper together.
7 Set the paper containing the fish on silver dishes containing hot oil and place in oven to rise.

425 Rouget grillé – Grilled red mullet

4, 250 g (8-oz) red mullet	120 g (¼ lb) seasoned	125 ml (1 gill) oil
120 g (¼ lb) shrimp butter	flour	4 lemons
(Recipe 401)	fried parsley	

1 Clean and remove scales and eyes.
2 Ciseler, flour, and brush with oil and season.
3 Grill both sides and baste during cooking process.
4 Garnish with shrimp butter, lemons, and fried parsley.

426 Rouget livournaise

4, 250 g (½-lb) red mullet	4 g (⅛ oz) julienne truffle	salt
240 g (½ lb) tomato concassé	15 g (½ oz) finely-chopped	seasoning
125 ml (¼ pt) fish stock	shallots	peppermill
(Recipe 374)	120 g (¼ lb) butter	cayenne

1 Remove scales, eyes, and gut.
2 Butter oval fish-plaque.
3 Sprinkle with chopped shallots.
4 Place the melted butter on top.
5 Cover the fish with tomato concassé.
6 Pour over the fish stock and add a little seasoning.
7 Cover with greased paper, bring to boil.
8 Oven-bake for approximately 15 minutes.
9 When cooked, remove from liquid and keep warm.
10 Reduce the cooking-liquor to one-third and enrich with butter and truffles and adjust seasoning.
11 Coat the sauce over the well-drained fish and glaze.

SAUMON – SALMON

427 Boiled Salmon (for hot service)

To cook whole 5 kg (10-lb) Salmon:

1 Fill the salmon-kettle three-quarters full with cold court-bouillon (Recipe 371).
2 Gut, scale, and clean the salmon, making sure that eyes are removed and all blood washed away.
3 Place the cleaned salmon on the perforated rack and lower gently into the liquid and add a 15 ml spoon (1 tablespoon) of salt.
4 Bring slowly to the boil with lid on and simmer on the side of the stove for 30 minutes.
5 When cooked, drain and remove skin from both sides.
6 Place on a serviette and garnish with turned, boiled potatoes and sprig of parsley.
7 Serve melted butter and sauce hollandaise (Recipe 72) separately.

428 Darne de saumon poché – Poached salmon middle-cut steak

1 *l* (1 *qt*) *court-bouillon* (*Recipe* 371)	360 *g* (¾ *lb*) *potatoes*
salt	¾ *sliced cucumber*

1 Cut 4, 180 g (6-oz) slices of salmon.
2 Wash and remove all blood.
3 Place in boiling court-bouillon.
4 Simmer for 10 minutes.
5 Before service remove skin and bone in the centre.
6 Garnish with boiled, turned potatoes and sprigs of parsley.
7 Serve hollandaise sauce (Recipe 72) and slices of cucumber.

429 Darne de saumon grillé, sauce béarnaise

4, 180 *g* (6-*oz*) *slice*	120 *g* (¼ *lb*) *parsley butter*	4 *lemon slices*
salmon	(*Recipe* 89)	125 *ml* (¼ *pt*) *sauce*
sprigs parsley	120 *g* (¼ *lb*) *seasoned flour*	*béarnaise*
125 *ml* (1 *gill*) *oil*	¼ *sliced cucumber*	(*Recipe* 73)

1 Wash salmon of all blood.
2 Pass through seasoned flour.
3 Brush both sides with oil, season.
4 Grill both sides slowly and baste.
5 Remove skin and centre bone.
6 Garnish with parsley butter and lemon slices.
7 Dress on silver dish without d'oyley and garnish with sprigs of parsley.
8 Serve béarnaise sauce and sliced cucumber separately.

430 Darne de saumon Chambord

4, 180 *g* (6-*oz*) *darnes of salmon*	4 *slices of truffles*	4 *fried soft roes*
250 *ml* (½ *pt*) *red wine*	4 *turned mushrooms*	60 *g* (2 *oz*) *butter*
16 *glazed button onions*	15 *g* (½ *oz*) *beurre*	*seasoning*
4 *fish quenelles* (*Recipe* 461)	*manié* (*Recipe* 19)	

1 Braise salmon in red wine (Recipe 405).
2 When cooked, drain, remove skin and centre bone.
3 Reduce cooking-liquor by half and thicken with beurre manié.
4 Blend in butter and seasoning.
5 Garnish the salmon with the mushrooms and coat with sauce.
6 Set to glaze.
7 Garnish with the soft roes meunière, quenelles and glazed onions.
8 Garnish each darne with a slice of truffle.

431 Côtelette de saumon Pojarski – Salmon cutlets

375 g (¾ lb) raw fillet salmon	120 g (¼ lb) seasoned flour	125 ml (¼ pt) milk
salt and pepper	120 g (¼ lb) white breadcrumbs	breadcrumbs
2 beaten eggs	120 g (¼ lb) clarified butter (Recipe 84)	for coating

1 Mince the salmon finely.
2 Soak the 125 g (½ lb) breadcrumbs in milk and squeeze out all the moisture.
3 Mix the bread with the salmon and season.
4 Shape into cutlets.
5 Flour, egg, and crumb.
6 Sauté in clarified butter.

431a Salmon Fishcakes – See Recipes 1204 and 1205.

SOLE

Treatment and recipes for sole may be applied to other white fish, even the small cuts of larger fish such as brill and turbot. Especially may lemon sole (limande) be prepared as Dover sole. Plaice (plie) is generally grilled, deep-fried or meunière. Except in obvious cases (such as Colbert) the following methods may be used for fillets (filets) as well as whole sole. When fillet of sole is required, remove black and white skin before filleting.

432 Sole Bercy

4, 360 g (¾ lb) Dover soles	125 ml (¼ pt) fish stock (Recipe 374)	120 g (¼ lb) butter juice of 1 lemon
15 g (½ oz) chopped parsley	125 ml (¼ pt) white wine	125 ml (¼ pt) cream ⎱ liaison
30 g (1 oz) finely-chopped shallots	125 ml (¼ pt) fish velouté (Recipe 377)	2 egg yolks ⎰ (optional)

1 Prepare soles for poaching.
2 Grease tray with butter and shallots.
3 Place sole on top, white side up.
4 Add wine, fish stock, lemon juice and parsley.
5 Cover with greased paper, bring to boil, then cook in moderate oven for 15 minutes.
6 Drain, remove side bones and keep warm.
7 Reduce cooking-liquor by half and add fish velouté; reduce further until it will coat back of spoon; add parsley.

8 Draw to side of fire, thicken with butter. Glaze.
9 Alternative to 8, a liaison may be used prior to glazing.

433 Sole bonne femme

4, 360 g (¾ lb) Dover soles   salt   125 ml (¼ pt) fish stock
30 g (1 oz) finely-chopped   cayenne pepper   (Recipe 374)
   shallots   15 g (½ oz)   120 g (¼ lb) butter
180 g (6 oz) sliced mushrooms   chopped parsley   125 ml (¼ pt) ⎱ liaison
125 ml (¼ pt) white wine   juice of 1 lemon   cream ⎰ (optional)
125 ml (¼ pt) fish velouté   1 egg yolk
   (Recipe 377)

1 Trim fins, remove eyes, gut and remove black skin, scrape white skin.
2 Grease fish-pan, sprinkle with shallots and sliced mushrooms.
3 Lay sole on the top, sprinkle with parsley.
4 Moisten with fish stock, white wine and lemon juice; season.
5 Cover with greased paper.
6 Boil and cook in moderate oven for 15 minutes.
7 Drain and trim off side bones.
8 Reduce cooking-liquid by half.
9 Add fish velouté and reduce. (If liaison is used, add now.)
10 Thicken with butter.
11 Coat the fish with the sauce and glaze.

434 Sole Boistelle (or Sole aux champignons)

1 As for Bonne femme (Recipe 433); do not glaze.
2 Garnish with fleurons (puff paste, Recipe 1024).

435 Sole Colbert

4, 360 g (¾ lb) Dover soles   480 g (1 lb) white bread-   drainers
120 g (¼ lb) parsley butter   crumbs   fried parsley
   (Recipe 89)   2 lemons   deep fat
120 g (¼ lb) seasoned flour   2 eggs for egg-wash

1 Trim fins, remove eyes and gut.
2 Remove black skin and scrape white skin.
3 Make incision along back-bone (or spine) on the skinned side; with filleting knife partially detach on that side the two fillets from the centre; fold back in 2 flaps to form a 'purse'.
4 Break centre bone, thus exposed, in 3 places.
5 Paner and place between 2 spikers taking care to keep flaps open.
6 Fry in deep fat; when cooked, remove centre bone.
7 Fill with sliced parsley butter.
8 Present on a dish-paper, flap side uppermost; garnish with fresh parsley and half lemon.

436 Sole dieppoise

4, 360 g (¾ lb) Dover   30 g (1 oz) finely-   62 ml (⅛ pt) white wine
   soles   chopped shallots   15 g (½ oz) shrimp tails
125 ml (¼ pt) fish velouté   30 g (1 oz) bearded,   120 g (¼ lb) butter
   (Recipe 377)   cooked mussels   62 ml (⅛ pt) cream

8 *turned mushrooms*   *juice of* 1 *lemon*   125 *ml* ($\frac{1}{4}$ *pt*) *fish*
4 *g* ($\frac{1}{8}$ *oz*) *chopped*   8 *fleurons Puff paste*   *stock* (*Recipe* 374)
    parsley   (*Recipe* 1024)

1 Trim fins, remove eyes, gut and remove black skin, scrape white skin.
2 Grease fish-pan with butter, sprinkle with shallots; lay sole on top, white skin uppermost.
3 Moisten with fish stock, wine and lemon juice; cover with greased paper, boil and cook in moderate oven for 15 minutes.
4 Drain sole, remove side fins, and keep warm.
5 Reduce cooking-liquid by half, add the fish velouté and shrimp tails and mussels; reduce further till the sauce coats the back of a spoon.
6 Add the cream and the chopped parsley.
7 Thicken with butter and season.
8 Place a little sauce on bottom of serving dish; place the soles on top, white side uppermost.
9 Do *not* glaze; garnish each sole with turned mushrooms and cover completely with the sauce.
10 Garnish with fleurons.

437 Sole Doria

4, 360 *g* ($\frac{3}{4}$ *lb*) *Dover soles*   12 *slices peeled lemon*   125 *ml* ($\frac{1}{4}$ *pt*) *oil*
120 *g* ($\frac{1}{4}$ *lb*) *seasoned flour*   15 *g* ($\frac{1}{2}$ *oz*) *chopped*   *cucumber*
60 *g* (2 *oz*) *butter*   *parsley*

1 Remove fins, eyes, gut, remove black skin and scrape white skin.
2 Peel cucumber and cut into small sections and turn like small olives.
3 Cook the turned cucumber in a little salted water and butter.
4 Pass the sole through the seasoned flour and shallow fry in oil, white-skinned side first.
5 Place the sole on a silver dish and garnish each one with a row of turned cucumbers down the centre; complete the garnish with slices of lemon and a little chopped parsley.
6 Coat with beurre noisette (Recipe 82).

438 Filet de sole Dugléré

2, 750 *g* (1$\frac{1}{2}$ *lb*) *Dover*   1 *finely-chopped shallot*   *juice of* $\frac{1}{2}$ *lemon*
    soles   240 *g* ($\frac{1}{2}$ *lb*) (*net*) *tomato*   90 *g* (3 *oz*) *butter*
125 *ml* ($\frac{1}{4}$ *pt*) *fish velouté*   *concassé*   62 *ml* ($\frac{1}{8}$ *pt*) *white*
    (*Recipe* 377)   125 *ml* ($\frac{1}{4}$ *pt*) *fish stock*   *wine*
$\frac{1}{2}$ *oz chopped parsley*   (*Recipe* 374)   62 *ml* ($\frac{1}{8}$ *pt*) *cream*

1 Remove both skins and fillet.
2 Wash bones and make 250 ml ($\frac{1}{2}$ pt) fish stock; reserve 125 ml ($\frac{1}{4}$ pt) and make the other 125 ml ($\frac{1}{4}$ pt) into fish velouté.
3 Grease tray with butter and sprinkle with shallots and lay on the sole.
4 Sprinkle the tomato concassé on top, add the fish stock, wine and lemon juice, and parsley.

5 Cover with greased paper and place in the oven approximately 15 minutes.
6 Drain sole and keep warm.
7 Reduce cooking-liquid by half and add the strained fish velouté.
8 Add the cream; thicken with butter; season and add a little chopped parsley.
9 Place a little of the sauce in the bottom of the dish; place the sole on top and cover completely with the remainder of the sauce; do *not* glaze.

Note. For whole sole method see Sole vin blanc (Recipe 448).

439 Goujons de sole frits

500 *g* (1 *lb*) *filleted sole*	500 *g* (1 *lb*) *white breadcrumbs*	2 *lemons*
240 *g* (½ *lb*) *seasoned flour*	2 *eggs for egg-wash*	

1 Cut each fillet into 4 or 5 strips, 6 cm (3 inches) long.
2 **Flour, egg-wash, and crumb and roll each strip.**
3 **Fry in deep fat.**
4 **Drain and season.**
5 **Serve on a dish-paper, garnish with lemon and fried parsley.**

440 Sole au gratin

4, 360 *g* (¾ *lb*) *Dover soles*	120 *g* (¼ *lb*) *white*	1 *lemon*
30 *g* (1 *oz*) *finely-chopped shallots*	*breadcrumbs*	120 *g* (¼ *lb*) *butter*
16 *cooked mushrooms*	120 *g* (4 *oz*) *sliced, raw mushrooms*	375 *ml* (¾ *pt*) *gratin sauce* (*Recipe* 441)
7 *g* (¼ *oz*) *chopped parsley*	125 *ml* (¼ *pt*) *white wine*	

1 Prepare the soles as for Colbert (Recipe 425).
2 Place a walnut-size piece of butter under each fillet.
3 Place the sole on a well-greased china dish with some finely-chopped shallots and a little gratin sauce.
4 Garnish each sole with 4 cooked mushrooms and surround with 15 g (½ oz) sliced mushrooms.
5 **Pour over each sole the white wine and coat with gratin sauce (Recipe 441).**
6 **Pour a little melted butter over the sole and sprinkle with breadcrumbs and bake in a moderate oven.**
7 Serve the sole on the same dish and before service squeeze a little lemon juice on top and sprinkle with chopped parsley.

441 Gratin sauce (for fish au gratin)

30 *g* (1 *oz*) *finely-chopped shallots*	240 *g* (½ *lb*) *finely-chopped mushrooms*
250 *ml* (½ *pt*) *demi-glace* (*Recipe* 29)	15 *g* (½ *oz*) *butter*

1 Sweat the shallots in butter.
2 Wash and squeeze the mushrooms and chop finely.
3 Add the mushrooms to the butter and cook for a few minutes.
4 Moisten with the demi-glace and simmer for approximately 10 minutes.
5 Add a little chopped parsley and season.

442 Sole grenobloise

Prepare as Sole Doria (Recipe 437) using 60 g (2 oz) capers in place of cucumbers.

443 Sole grillée

4, 360 g (¾ lb) Dover soles	120 g (¼ lb) seasoned flour	2 lemons
120 g (¼ lb) parsley butter	125 ml (1 gill) oil	

1 Trim fins, remove eyes and gut.
2 Remove black skin and scrape white skin.
3 Pass through seasoned flour and brush both sides with oil.
4 Grill black-skin side first and turn over and grill the other side slowly.
5 Garnish with parsley butter and half lemons; do *not* serve on dish-paper or d'oyley.

444 Sole Marguery

4, 360 g (¾-lb) Dover soles	125 ml (¼ pt) fish	4 fleurons (Recipe 1024)
125 ml (¼ pt) white wine	stock (Recipe 374)	125 ml (¼ pt) ⎱ liaison
125 ml (¼ pt) fish velouté	16 bearded, cooked	cream ⎰ (optional)
(Recipe 377)	mussels	2 egg yolks
30 g (1 oz) shelled	30 g (1 oz) finely-	120 g (¼ lb) butter
shrimps	chopped shallots	juice of ½ lemon

1 Trim fins, remove eyes and gut.
2 Remove black skin, scrape white skin.
3 Grease tray with butter, add shallots.
4 Place sole on top, white side uppermost.
5 Add wine, lemon juice, and fish stock.
6 Cover with greased paper, bring to boil, then cook in moderate oven for 15 minutes.
7 Drain and remove side-bones; keep warm.
8 Reduce cooking-liquid by half and add fish velouté; reduce further until the sauce covers the back of a spoon.
9 Draw to side of fire, (add liaison if used) and thicken with butter, and season.
10 Garnish the centre of each sole with shrimps and mussels tossed in butter.
11 Cover with sauce and glaze.
12 Garnish with fleurons.

445 Goujons de sole Murat

12 pieces fillet sole	120 g (¼ lb) seasoned flour	juice of ½ lemon
4 artichoke bottoms	480 g (1 lb) diced potatoes	125 ml (¼ pt) oil
60 g (2 oz) butter	7 g (¼ oz) chopped parsley	

1 Cut the sole into goujons (Recipe 439).
2 Roll in seasoned flour.
3 Toss in hot oil à la meunière (Recipe 410).
4 Sauter the diced potatoes and artichoke bottoms in butter.
5 Mix the sole, artichoke bottoms and potatoes together and toss in butter.
6 Season, add lemon juice.
7 Sprinkle with chopped parsley.

446 Paupiette de sole Otéro

4 *large baked potatoes*	8 *paupiettes of sole*	½ *glass brandy*
30 g (1 oz) *diced, cooked lobster*	4 *slices of truffle*	125 ml (¼ pt) *lobster sauce (Recipe 386)*
250 ml (½ pt) *fish stock (Recipe 374)*	30 g (1 oz) *shelled shrimps*	
250 ml (½ pt) *Mornay sauce (Recipe 58)*	120 g (¼ lb) *diced, cooked mushrooms*	15 g (½ oz) *grated Parmesan cheese*
	60 g (2 oz) *butter*	62 ml (½ gill) *cream*

1 Bake the potatoes on a bed of salt, remove the tops and make the interior into pommes duchesse (Recipe 909).
2 Pipe the edge of each potato with a star tube and brown lightly.
3 Toss the lobster, mushrooms and shrimps in a little butter and mix with the brandy and lobster sauce.
4 Place a little of this mixture into the bottom of each potato.
5 Poach the sole in fish stock, covered with greased paper, in a moderate oven for 15 minutes.
6 Drain the sole well and keep warm.
7 Reduce the cooking-liquor to a glaze and combine it with Mornay sauce; finish the sauce with cream and butter.
8 Place the sole into potato and cover with the sauce.
9 Sprinkle with cheese, and brown.
10 Garnish with a slice of truffle.
11 Serve on a serviette with sprig of parsley.

447 Sole Véronique

4, 360 g (¾ lb) *Dover soles*	30 g (1 oz) *finely-chopped shallots*
125 ml (¼ pt) *fish stock (Recipe 374)*	125 ml (¼ pt) *cream* } *liaison*
½ *glass curaçao*	2 *egg yolks* } *(optional)*
120 g (¼ lb) *white grapes*	120 g (¼ lb) *butter*
125 ml (¼ pt) *fish velouté (Recipe 377)*	*juice of* ½ *lemon*

1 Prepare soles for poaching.
2 Grease tray with butter; add shallots.
3 Place sole on top, white side up.
4 Add wine, fish stock, and lemon juice.
5 Cover with greased paper, bring to boil, then cook in moderate oven for 15 minutes.
6 Drain, remove side-bones and keep warm.
7 Reduce cooking liquor by half, add fish velouté and reduce further until it coats the back of spoon; draw to side of fire, (add liaison, if used) thicken with butter and season.
8 Garnish centre of sole with blanched, de-pipped grapes.
9 Cover with sauce and glaze.

448 Sole vin blanc

4, 360 g (¾-lb) *Dover soles*	30 g (1 oz) *finely-chopped shallots*
125 ml (¼ pt) *white wine*	8 *fleurons (Recipe 1024)*

125 ml (¼ pt) fish stock (Recipe 374)   120 g (¼ lb) butter
125 ml (¼ pt) fish velouté   125 ml (¼ pt) cream ⎱ liaison
   (Recipe 377)   2 egg yolks   ⎰ (optional)
juice of ¼ lemon   15 g (½ oz) meat glaze (Recipe 13)

1 Trim fins, remove eyes, gut.
2 Remove black skin, scrape white skin.
3 Grease tray with butter, sprinkle with shallots.
4 Place sole, white skin uppermost, on top.
5 Pour on wine, fish stock and lemon juice, cover with greased paper and place in moderate oven for 15 minutes.
6 Remove sole, trim side-bones and keep warm.
7 Reduce cooking-liquid by half, add fish velouté and reduce until it coats a wooden spoon.
8 Remove from fire and add the liaison (if used).
9 Thicken with butter and season.
10 Place a little sauce on bottom of dish.
11 Coat remainder of sauce over fish.
12 Place a pattern of mosaic over sole with the meat glaze.
13 Garnish with fleurons.

Note. Method also applies to Filet de sole (Sole fillets).

449 Sole Waleska

4, 360 g (¾-lb) Dover soles   250 ml (½ pt) fish stock   62 ml (⅛ pt) cream
300 ml (12 fl oz) Mornay   (Recipe 374)   60 g (2 oz) butter
  sauce (Recipe 58)   15 g (½ oz) grated   4 slices truffle
juice of ½ lemon   Parmesan cheese
8 slices cooked lobster

1 Prepare sole for poaching.
2 Grease tray with butter.
3 Place on sole, white side up.
4 Add fish stock and lemon juice.
5 Cover with greased paper. Bring to boil, and then cook in moderate oven for 15 minutes.
6 Drain, remove side-bones and keep warm.
7 Reduce cooking-liquid to a glaze and add to Mornay sauce.
8 Garnish each sole with sliced lobster.
9 Finish sauce with cream and butter; season.
10 Coat the sole, sprinkle with cheese, and brown under the grill.
11 Garnish with slices of truffle.

TRUITE – TROUT

450 Truite au bleu

4 live, blue trout   240 g (½ lb) potatoes   500 ml (1 pt) water
60 g (2 oz) vegetable (onion,   1 bay leaf   1 sprig thyme
  carrot sliced)*   125 ml (¼ pt) vinegar   ¼ teaspoon salt
62 ml (½ gill) white wine

* Cut à la russe in decoratively-channelled roundels.

1 Simmer the vegetables in the water and white wine with thyme, bay-leaf and salt to make a court-bouillon.
2 Take the trout from the tank and stun; gut, and plunge into the vinegar for about 5 minutes.
3 Remove the trout from the vinegar and plunge into boiling court-bouillon; simmer for 5 minutes.
4 Leave the liquid with the trout and garnish with boiled potatoes cut Parisienne size.
5 Serve melted butter and sauce hollandaise (Recipe 72) separately.

451 Truite grillée – Grilled trout

4, 240 g (8-oz) trout	120 g (4 oz) parsley butter (Recipe 89)	15 g (½ oz) seasoned flour
125 ml (1 gill) oil	4 slices lemon	sprig parsley

1 Clean and ciseler trout.
2 Pass through seasoned flour.
3 Brush both sides with oil and season.
4 Grill both sides (approximately 6 minutes).
5 Garnish with lemon slices and sprig of parsley.
6 Serve parsley butter separately.

452 Truite Cléopatra

4, 240 g (8-oz) trout	120 g (¼ lb) butter	4 soft roes
15 g (½ oz) chopped parsley	4 slices lemon	15 g (½ oz) capers
30 g (1 oz) shelled shrimps	juice of ¼ lemon	

1 Cook trout as for meunière (Recipe 410).
2 Garnish with shrimps, capers, and soft roes (cooked as meunière).
3 Finish with beurre noisette (Recipe 82), lemon juice, and parsley.

453 Truite belle meunière

4, 240 g (8-oz) trout	120 g (¼ lb) butter	4 soft roes
15 g (½ oz) chopped parsley	4 turned mushrooms	juice of ¼ lemon
4 blanched tomatoes	8 slices lemon	flour
125 ml (1 gill) oil		

1 Clean and ciseler trout.
2 Cook as for meunière (Recipe 410).
3 Garnish with cooked mushrooms and soft roes, meunière, and quartered, skinned tomatoes with pips removed.
4 Finish off with slices of lemon on top of trout, beurre noisette (Recipe 82), lemon juice and parsley.

Note. Garnish should be arranged neatly on top of each trout.

453a Truite saumonée – Salmon trout

Salmon trout may be prepared as above recipes or as for salmon.

TURBOT AND OTHER WHITE FISH

Other of the larger white fish include: Turbotin – Baby turbot (known as chicken turbot); Barbue – Brill; Flétan – Halibut. For the cuts commonly used for such larger, flat fish proceed as follows:

Tronçon (steak cut) – divide fish down the middle (through bone) and cut into 180 g (6 oz) steaks (with bone).

Filet or Suprême (fillet) – fillet then skin fish on *both* sides and cut into 120 to 180 g (4 to 6 oz) protions.

Note. Many of the treatments given for sole may be applied.

454 Turbot poché hollandaise

4, 180 g (6-oz) tronçons of turbot	sprigs parsley	190 ml (1½ gills)
360 g (¾ lb) small, turned potatoes	500 ml (1 qt) white court-bouillon (Recipe 370)	sauce
	4 slices lemon	hollandaise (Recipe 72)

1 Cut turbot into tronçons.
2 Soak in water for 2 hours.
3 Wash off and cook in boiling, white court-bouillon and simmer 10 minutes.
4 Remove skin and centre bone.
5 Garnish with boiled potatoes, lemon slices, and sprig of parsley.
6 Serve with a little of the cooking-liquor.
7 Hollandaise sauce is served separately.

FISH SOUPS OR STEWS

455 Bouillabaisse

1 sliced French loaf	120 g (¼ lb) Frédas (squid)	2 cloves crushed garlic
120 g (¼ lb) conger eels	16 crayfish	120 g (¼ lb)
120 g (¼ lb) rascasses (hog-fish)	24 mussels in shell	tomato concassé
240 g (½ lb) John Dory	240 g (½ lb) julienne of leek and onions	good pinch saffron
240 g (½ lb) whiting	2 bay-leaves	250 ml (2 gills) oil
120 g (¼ lb) red mullet	pinch of fennel	250 ml (½ pt) white wine

1 Cut large fish leaving small fish whole.
2 Cook the leek and onions in oil; add the garlic, fennel, bay-leaves.
3 Add the fish and sweat under cover for a few minutes.
4 Add the tomato and moisten with the wine and a little fish stock.
5 Bring to the boil, add the mussels and saffron; cook approximately 15 minutes; season, using the peppermill liberally.
6 Serve in a large tureen with toasted slices of bread which have been piquéd with garlic.

Note. This soup/stew is so identified with the Marseilles region and dependent upon Mediterranean fish of that region that its suitability for menus and culinary repertoires elsewhere is dubious.

456 Matelote d'anguilles – Eel matelote

750 g (1½ lb) eels	*15 g (½ oz) butter* } *for beurre*	*1 bouquet garni*
20 glazed button onions	*15 g (½ oz) flour* } *manié*	*1 clove garlic*
8 heart-shaped croûtons	*60 g (2 oz) butter*	*62 ml (½ gill) cream*
250 ml (½ pt) red wine	*8 whole, cooked mushrooms*	
8 cooked crayfish	*30 g (1 oz) finely-chopped shallots*	

1 Sweat the shallots.
2 Section the eels and sweat under cover with the shallots for a few minutes.
3 Add a clove of crushed garlic.
4 Moisten with the red wine, add the bouquet garni and braise in the oven until tender.
5 Reduce the cooking-liquor and thicken with beurre manié. Season, add a little cream and blend in the butter.
6 Mix the eels with the sauce and garnish with mushrooms, onions, and crayfish.
7 Dip the end of the croûtons in chopped parsley.

457 Matelote normande

240 g (½ lb) conger eel	*4 poached oysters*	*125 ml (¼ pt) fish velouté (Recipe 377)*
120 g (¼ lb) turbot	*8 mushrooms*	*125 ml (¼ pt) cream*
60 g (2 oz) carp	*60 g (2 oz) butter*	*30 g (1 oz) chopped shallots*
120 g (¼ lb) pike	*250 ml (½ pt) red wine*	*bouquet garni*
6 crayfish	*125 ml (1 gill) cider*	*8 croûtons*

1 Cut the fish into sections and sweat under cover with the shallots.
2 Moisten with wine and cider, add bouquet garni, simmer until tender.
3 Remove fish and place in large tureen.
4 Reduce cooking-liquor by half, add the fish velouté and cream and reduce further until the sauce coats a spoon.
5 Enrich with butter and season.
6 Pour sauce over fish and garnish with mushrooms, poached oysters, and cooked crayfish.
7 Finish off with heart-shaped croûtons.

458 Waterzoi

240 g (½ lb) carp	*125 ml (¼ pt) white wine*	*pinch sage*
240 g (½ lb) pike	*125 ml (¼ pt) fish stock (Recipe 374)*	*60 g (2 oz) butter*
240 g (½ lb) eel	*bouquet garni*	*salt and pepper*
60 g (2 oz) thinly-sliced carrots		*8 slices buttered French bread*
120 g (¼ lb) small onion rings		

1 Cook the vegetables in the fish stock and white wine with the herbs until tender; season.
2 Cut the fish into sections in the bone and sweat under cover for a few minutes.
3 Pour over the liquid and cook.
4 Serve in a large soup-tureen and garnish the top with the bread.

MOUSSES, MOUSSELINES, AND QUENELLES OF FISH

These are made from a variety of fish (including shellfish) and commonly from pike and whiting.

459 Mousse de sole (or Mousse de merlan) – Sole (or whiting) mousse

> 240 g (½ lb) raw fillet-sole (or whiting)   250 ml (½ pt) fresh cream
> 1 egg white   seasoning

1 Mince the fish finely.
2 Pound in the mortar; gradually add the beaten egg whites; season and pound until well bound.
3 Rub through fine sieve.
4 Place the mixture in a bowl on ice and gradually add the cream.
5 Place in a buttered mould and cook in bain-marie.

460 Mousselines de poisson

1 Prepare as for mousse (Recipe 459) but shape with a 30 ml spoon (2 tablespoons) and poach.
2 Mousellines are served, with the appropriate sauce, as a dish in themselves.

461 Quenelles (of fish)

Preparation as for mousses or moussellines (Recipes 459 and 460) but either (i) shape with teaspoons into smaller balls or ovals or (ii) pipe into small balls. Quenelles are used as component of or garnish to a dish.

SHELLFISH

General Points. Because shellfish begin to decompose swiftly after death, they are brought alive into the kitchen. For many dishes, particularly for cold service, shellfish are simply placed into boiling, salted water (or court bouillon) and cooked, in the case of lobster, crab, langoustine, for approximately 20 minutes per 500 g (lb). Scampi, crayfish, prawns and shrimps take only up to 10 minutes, according to size. It is important not to over-cook for this toughens the flesh. As in the case of white fish, methods and recipes for shellfish are interchangeable particularly where similar types are concerned. Crustaceans may be accorded similar treatment in cooking and dressing, i.e. many methods are interchangeable.

Main crustaceans used in the kitchen are:

Shrimps – crevettes grises (often abbreviated to crevettes). Prawns – crevettes roses. Dublin Bay Prawns or Scampi – langoustine. Crayfish – écrevisses. Crayfish – langoustes. Lobsters – homards. Crabs – crabes.

Other shellfish treated in this chapter are:

> Oysters (huitres) – Mussels (moules) – Scallops (coquilles St Jacques)

Similar methods may be applied to others such as cockles (coques).

462 Crevettes roses frites – Fried prawns

> 500 *ml* (1 *pt*) *shelled prawns*   2 *eggs*   *deep fat*
> 120 *g* (¼ *lb*) *flour*   *seasoning*

1 Flour, egg and crumb.
2 Fry in deep fat.
3 Serve with Sauce tartare (Recipe 114).

463 Curried Prawns

1 Toss shelled prawns in butter, mix with curry sauce (Recipe 32).
2 Serve with plain boiled rice.

464 Écrevisses – Crayfish

1 These are frequently cooked in court-bouillon (Recipe 370) for 15 minutes and are used for garnish.
2 They may also be prepared as Newburg or Américaine (Recipes 471 and 468).

COQUILLES ST JACQUES – SCALLOPS

465 Coquilles St Jacques Mornay – Scallops mornay

> 4 *coquilles St Jacques*   250 *ml* (½ *pt*) *mornay sauce*
> 240 *g* (½ *lb*) *duchesse potatoes*   (*Recipe* 58)
> (*Recipe* 909)   30 *g* (1 *oz*) *grated Parmesan cheese*

1 Apply gentle heat to open coquille.
2 Remove fish and deep shell.
3 Cook the fish in court-bouillon (Recipe 371) approximately 5 to 10 minutes.
4 Surround each deep shell with duchesse potatoes.
5 Place a little sauce in the bottom of each shell, slice and lay fish on top.
6 Cover fish with sauce, sprinkle with Parmesan cheese.
7 Brown under grill.

466 Coquilles St Jacques parisienne

> 4 *coquilles St Jacques*   4 *slices truffle*   250 *ml* (½ *pt*) *white wine*
>   *sauce* (*Recipe* 396)

Prepare as for Mornay (Recipe 465) but substitute white wine sauce for Mornay.
Glaze and garnish with slices of truffle.

467 Coquilles St Jacques au lard – Scallops with bacon

> 8 *rolls bacon*   15 *g* (½ *oz*) *chopped*   120 *g* (4 *oz*) *flour*
> 4 *coquilles St Jacques*   *parsley*   62 *ml* (½ *gill*) *oil*
> 120 *g* (¼ *lb*) *butter*   4 *lemon slices*

Blanch and cook the coquilles St Jacques à la meunière (Recipe 410).
Garnish with roll of cooked bacon.
Finish off with chopped parsley, lemon slices and beurre noisette (Recipe 82).

HOMARD – LOBSTER

468 Homard américaine – Lobster Américaine

1·5 kg (3 lb) raw lobster
250 ml (½ pt) fish stock
    (Recipe 374)
120 g (¼ lb) brunoise
    vegetable (Recipe 752)
1·25 ml spoon [¼ teaspoon]
    chopped tarragon
240 g (½ lb) tomato concassé

10 ml spoon [½ tablespoon]
    tomato purée
125 ml (¼ pt) white wine
60 g (2 oz) butter
62 ml (½ gill) oil
1·25 ml spoon [¼ teaspoon]
    chopped parsley

½ bouquet garni
240 g (½ lb) rice
    for rice pilaff
    (Recipe 366)
½ glass brandy

1 Cut the raw lobster as explained for Newburg (Recipe 471) but do not remove meat.
2 Remove the brain from the head and mix well with equal parts of butter (pound in the mortar).
3 Fry the lobster in a sauté pan in the oil.
4 Add the brandy and flamber.
5 Add the brunoise and half the parsley and tarragon and sweat under cover for 5 minutes.
6 Add the tomato concassé, fish stock and tomato purée; bring to the boil add bouquet garni and cook under cover for 20 minutes.
7 Remove meat from the shells and keep warm. (On the Continent the fish may be left in shell.)
8 Reduce the sauce and thicken with the lobster butter and season.
9 Dress the lobster in a timbale; decorate with the heads and strain sauce over with a coarse chinois. Sprinkle with remainder of parsley and tarragon.
10 Serve with rice pilaff.

469 Homard Cardinal

4 half-lobsters
1 egg yolk
62 ml (⅛ pt) cream   } liaison
60 g (2 oz) cooked, diced mushrooms

250 ml (½ pt) lobster
    sauce (Recipe 386)
15 g (½ oz) diced
    truffles
1 glass brandy

30 g (1 oz) grated
    Parmesan
    cheese
30 g (1 oz) butter
4 sliced truffles

1 Remove meat from shells.
2 Leave the meat from the claws whole but dice the remainder.
3 Sweat the lobster in butter and flamber with brandy.
4 Mix the diced truffles and mushrooms with a little of the lobster sauce form a salpicon.
5 Heat the shells and place the salpicon in the bottom.
6 Place the lobster inside the shell with the claws in the head part.
7 Add the egg yolks and cream to the remainder of the lobster sauce and coat each lobster.
8 Sprinkle with cheese and brown under grill.
9 Garnish each lobster with slice of truffle.
10 Serve on d'oyley-covered dish with sprigs of parsley.

470 Homard Mornay

4 *half-lobsters*	30 *g* (1 *oz*) *Parmesan cheese*	1 *egg yolk* ⎫
375 *ml* (3 *gills*) *Mornay*	30 *g* (1 *oz*) *butter*	62 *ml* ($\frac{1}{8}$ *pt*) ⎬ *liaison*
sauce (*Recipe* 58)	*seasoning*	*cream* ⎭

1 Remove meat from shells and leave the claw meat whole.
2 Cut the lobster into scallops and sweat the lobster in butter with the claws.
3 Add the egg yolks and cream into the mornay sauce.
4 Line the bottom of each shell with a little sauce.
5 Mix a little sauce with the lobster meat and fill in each shell, placing the claw part in the head.
6 Cover with the remainder of sauce.
7 Sprinkle with cheese and brown under grill.
8 Serve on d'oyley-covered silver dish and garnish with parsley.

471 Homard Newburg

1 *kg* (2 *lb*) *cooked lobster*	$\frac{1}{2}$ *glass sherry*	180 *g* (6 *oz*) *rice*
1 *egg yolk* ⎫	250 *ml* ($\frac{1}{2}$ *pt*) *lobster*	*for pilaff*
62 *ml* ($\frac{1}{8}$ *pt*) ⎬ *liaison*	*sauce* (*Recipe* 386)	(*Recipe* 366)
cream ⎭	4 *slices truffle*	
62 *mi* ($\frac{1}{2}$ *gill*) *brandy*	45 *g* (1$\frac{1}{2}$ *oz*) *butter*	

1 Cut the lobster head in half and the tail section in tronçons.
2 Remove meat from claws and tail sections.
3 Toss the lobster in butter and flamber in the brandy, then add the sherry.
4 Add the lobster sauce and cook for about 5 minutes.
5 Add the liaison of egg yolks and cream; draw to side of stove (reduce heat).
6 Season and thicken with butter.
7 Serve the lobster in a timbale and garnish with slices of truffle; serve also a timbale of rice pilaff.
8 Lobster Newburg may also be prepared by simply adding a liaison and omitting lobster sauce.

472 Homard Thermidor

4 *half-lobsters*	62 *ml* ($\frac{1}{8}$ *pt*) *fish stock*	1 *egg yolk* ⎫
375 *ml* (3 *gills*) *Mornay*	(*Recipe* 374)	62 *ml* ($\frac{1}{8}$ *pt*) ⎬ *liaison*
sauce (*Recipe* 58)	2·5 *ml spoon* [$\frac{1}{2}$ *teaspoon*]	*cream* ⎭
30 *g* (1 *oz*) *shallots*	*diluted mustard*	15 *g* ($\frac{1}{2}$ *oz*) *parsley*
(*chopped*)	30 *g* (1 *oz*) *Parmesan*	30 *g* (1 *oz*) *butter*
62 *ml* ($\frac{1}{8}$ *pt*) *white wine*	*cheese*	

1 Prepare lobster as for mornay (Recipe 470).
2 Sweat the shallots in butter and make a reduction with the parsley, wine and fish stock; add to the Mornay sauce and blend in the diluted mustard; effect a liaison with the egg yolks and cream.
3 Pour a little sauce in bottom of each shell.
4 Sweat the lobster in butter and mix with a little of the sauce and fill in each half.
5 Coat with sauce; sprinkle with cheese and brown under the grill.
6 Serve as for mornay.

HUITRES – OYSTERS

473 Huitres Mornay

| 24 *oysters* | 250 *ml* ($\frac{1}{2}$ *pt*) *Mornay sauce (Recipe* 58) | 30 *g* (1 *oz*) *Parmesan cheese* |

1 Beard and cook the oysters for 3 minutes in a little fish stock (Recipe 374) and drain.
2 Wash the deep shells, place a little mornay sauce on the bottom of each one; place the oysters on top and coat with mornay sauce.
3 Sprinkle with cheese and brown.
4 Serve on silver with d'oyley and parsley.

474 Huitres florentine

Prepare as for huitres mornay (Recipe 473) but place a little cooked leaf-spinach on the bottom of each shell.

MOULES – MUSSELS

475 Moules marinière

1 *kg* (2 *lb*) *mussels*	15 *g* ($\frac{1}{2}$ *oz*) *flour* ⎱ *beurre*	*juice of* $\frac{1}{4}$ *lemon*
30 *g* (1 *oz*) *finely-chopped shallots*	15 *g* ($\frac{1}{2}$ *oz*) *butter* ⎰ *manié*	*cayenne pepper*
30 *g* (1 *oz*) *butter*	62 *ml* ($\frac{1}{8}$ *pt*) *fish stock* (*Recipe* 374)	62 *ml* ($\frac{1}{8}$ *pt*) *white wine*
62 *ml* ($\frac{1}{2}$ *gill*) *cream*		

1 Wash and scrape the mussels well.
2 Place in a pan with the shallots, herbs, wine and fish stock.
3 Cook quickly under cover for 5 minutes.
4 Remove mussels; take off the beards and half the shell.
5 Place in a casserole to keep warm.
6 Decant the cooking-liquor to clean pan and reduce by half with a little cream.
7 Thicken slightly with the beurre manié and enrich the sauce with a little butter: season, add lemon juice and cayenne pepper.
8 Pour the sauce over.

SCAMPI (LANGOUSTINES) – DUBLIN BAY PRAWNS

476 Scampi frits – Fried scampi

| 500 *g* (1 *lb*) *scampi tails* | 375 *g* ($\frac{3}{4}$ *lb*) *white breadcrumbs* | 2 *eggs* |
| 120 *g* ($\frac{1}{4}$ *lb*) *flour* | | |

1 Cook the scampi in court-bouillon (Recipe 371) for a few minutes.
2 Allow to cool; drain.
3 Flour, egg, and crumb.
4 Fry crisp in hot fat; season and drain.
5 Serve with fried parsley, lemon, and sauce tartare (Recipe 114).

477 Scampi Germaine

500 g (1 *lb*) *scampi*	250 *ml* ($\frac{1}{2}$ *pt*) *sauce béarnaise*
240 g ($\frac{1}{2}$ *lb*) *riz pilaff* (*Recipe* 366)	(*Recipe* 73)
62 *ml* ($\frac{1}{2}$ *gill*) *cream*	

1 Cook the scampi in court-bouillon (Recipe 372).
2 Drain and mix with sauce béarnaise, add a little cream.
3 Serve with a border of rice pilaff.
4 Glaze under grill.

478 Scampi créole

500 g (1 *lb*) *scampis*	240 g ($\frac{1}{2}$ *lb*) *riz pilaff* (*Recipe* 366)	2 *eggs*
15 g ($\frac{1}{2}$ *oz*) *curry powder*	375 g ($\frac{3}{4}$ *lb*) *white crumbs*	120 g ($\frac{1}{4}$ *lb*) *flour*

1 Cook scampi in court-bouillon (Recipe 371) and then cool.
2 Mix 7 g ($\frac{1}{4}$ oz) curry powder with the crumbs.
3 Flour, egg, and crumb.
4 Mix the remainder of curry powder with rice pilaff.
5 Fry the scampi in deep fat.
6 Serve with a surround of rice with scampi in the middle.
7 Serve separately curry sauce in sauce-boat.

478a Brochette de scampi – Skewered scampis

4 *rashers streaky bacon*	3 *mushroom caps*	1 *tomato*
4 *scampis*	2 *bay-leaves* (*blanched*)	125 *ml* ($\frac{1}{2}$ *gill*)
2 *thick slices cucumber*	*pinch chopped chervil*	*tomato sauce*
120 g ($\frac{1}{4}$ *lb*) *riz pilaff*	7 g ($\frac{1}{4}$ *oz*) *sultanas*	(*Recipe* 34)
(*Recipe* 366)	7 g ($\frac{1}{4}$ *oz*) *pimentoes*	30 g (1 *oz*) *peas*
15 g ($\frac{1}{4}$ *oz*) *currants*	120 g ($\frac{1}{4}$ *lb*) *white breadcrumbs*	

1 Blanch the scampis and refresh.
2 Roll the scampis in bacon.
3 Cut the cucumber into rounds about 1 cm ($\frac{1}{2}$ inch) thick and blanch.
4 Alternate the scampis, cucumber, bay leaves, tomato, mushrooms on a silver skewer, and brush with butter.
5 Roll the brochette in white-crumbs with chervil.
6 Brush with oil, and grill gently.
7 Serve on a bed of pilaff rice garnished with fruit, peas and pimentoes, with a cordon of tomato sauce.

EDIBLE SNAILS

479 Escargots – Snails

1 Allow to 'desgorge' for 12 hours by soaking in water.
2 Marinate in wine and aromatics for 3 hours.
3 Gently simmer them in their own juice.
4 Remove from shells and trim.
5 Boil the shells with bicarbonate of soda for 30 minutes.
6 Return to shells.
7 Fill with beurre d'escargots (as for other beurres composés (compound butters)) using fines herbes, garlic and butter.

GRENOUILLES – FROGS

An alternative name for grenouilles in the kitchen is nymphes, therefore, 'Cuisses de nymphes' is often used instead of Cuisses de grenouilles (frogs' legs). These, specially bred for table use, are prepared in many ways of which the following are examples:

480 Cuisses de nymphes aux fines herbes

1 Season; toss in butter with chopped shallots, chopped parsley and lemon juice.
2 Add·beurre noisette (Recipe 82).

481 Cuisses de nymphes frites

1 Dip in batter.
2 Fry in deep fat.
3 Serve with green parsley and lemon.

482 Cuisses de nymphes au gratin

Poach and serve with Italienne Sauce (Recipe 42) and grated Parmesan cheese. (Remove feet).

483 Cuisses de nymphes à la meunière

1 Pass in milk and flour.
2 Fry in butter, lemon juice, and chopped parsley.

484 Cuisses de nymphes poulette

1 Poach in white wine and fish stock (Recipe 374) and mushrooms.
2 Add fish velouté (Recipe 377).
3 Thicken with egg yolks and cream.

485 Cuisses de nymphes à la mode paysanne

Sauté in butter with garlic, concassé tomatoes, and chopped parsley.

486 Cuisses de nymphes en brochette

1 Thread on silver skewer with mushrooms.
2 When cooked, roll in white breadcrumbs containing chopped parsley and garlic.
3 Brown under grill.

FISH FOR COLD SERVICE

487 Salade de poisson – Fish salad

As main course

360 g (¾ lb) cooked white fish free from skin and bone	1 blanched tomato 4 anchovy fillets	7 g (¼ oz) capers 4 stoned olives

| 1 *lettuce* | 62 *ml* (½ *gill*) *vinaigrette* | *seasoning* |
| 1 *hard-boiled egg* | (*Recipe* 118) | |

1 Flake the fish and marinate with the vinaigrette and season.
2 Finely shred the outside leaves of lettuce retaining the heart.
3 Place the lettuce on the bottom of a large salad bowl; season.
4 Pile the fish neatly on top of the lettuce.
5 Decorate with criss-cross anchovies and capers.
6 Garnish with hearts of lettuce cut into quarters, quarters of egg and tomato in between the lettuce hearts.
7 Place the stoned olives neatly on top of the fish and sprinkle a little pepper.
8 Serve vinaigrette separately.

488 Mayonnaise de poisson – Mayonnaise of fish

Prepare as above, using same ingredients but coat the fish with mayonnaise sauce (Recipe 110). See also Recipe 492.

SALMON

489 Boiled Salmon
For Cold Service
1 Using a 5 kg (10-lb) salmon proceed as for hot salmon (Recipe 427) but simmer only for 10 minutes.
2 Then remove from the fire and allow to cool in its cooking-liquor under cover.
3 When cold, skin, and decorate.

490 Saumon poché en belle vue

| 500 *ml* (1 *pt*) *white chaud-*
froid (*Recipe* 134) | 500 *ml* (1 *pt*) *fish aspic*
(*Recipe* 123) | 4, 180 *g* (6-*oz*) *slices*
of salmon |

1 Poach salmon in court-bouillon.
2 Allow to become cold and drain.
3 Remove skin and bone.
4 Coat with chaud-froid.
5 Allow to set and decorate.
6 Coat with fish aspic.
7 Garnish with small darioles of Russian salad and cucumber.

SALMON WITH MAYONNAISE

Salmon mayonnaise (or Darne de saumon mayonnaise) differs from Mayonnaise de saumon which is shown in the two recipes for Salmon mayonnaise and Mayonnaise of salmon which follow. The difference applies when other fish are prepared in the same way.

491 Darne de saumon mayonnaise – Salmon mayonnaise

4, 180 g (6-oz) darnes of cold salmon	125 ml (¼ pt) mayonnaise sauce (Recipe 110)	120 g (4 oz) finely-sliced cucumber
1 lettuce	62 ml (⅛ gill) vinaigrette (Recipe 118)	750 ml (1½ pt) court-bouillon
1 hard-boiled egg		(Recipe 371)
1 blanched tomato		

1 Place the salmon in simmering court-bouillon (Recipe 371) for 5 minutes. Allow to cool in the liquor under tight cover.
2 Remove the skin and centre bone.
3 Dress neatly on a large flat oval dish.
4 Garnish round the sides with quarter-hearts of lettuce, well drained, egg and tomato (firm).
5 Garnish the top of the salmon with a few slices of cucumber marinated with vinaigrette and dress on a ravier with a little chopped parsley sprinkled on top.
6 Serve the mayonnaise sauce (which should be of stiff consistency) in sauce-boat with the ravier of cucumber separately.

492 Mayonnaise de saumon – Mayonnaise of salmon

750 g (¾ lb) cooked salmon, free of skin and bone	1 hard-boiled egg	62 ml (⅛ gill) vinaigrette (Recipe 118)
1 large lettuce	1 blanched tomato	7 g (¼ oz) capers
90 g (3 oz) thinly-sliced skinned cucumber	4 anchovy fillets	125 ml (¼ pt) mayon-
	4 stoned olives	naise (Recipe 110)
	seasoning	

1 Flake the salmon and marinate in vinaigrette; season.
2 Finely shred the outer leaves of lettuce retaining the hearts.
3 Place the shredded lettuce on the bottom of a large salad-bowl, season lightly.
4 Pile the salmon neatly on top of the lettuce.
5 Coat the salmon evenly with 125 ml (¼ pt) sauce mayonnaise and place the remainder in a sauce-boat.
6 Decorate the top of the salmon with criss-crosses of anchovies, capers and the stoned olives.
7 Garnish the sides of the bowl with quarters of lettuce hearts, cucumber slices, hard-boiled egg and stoned olives.
8 Final presentation, dust the top of salmon with a little paprika or chopped lobster-coral: do *not* sprinkle with chopped parsley.

SHELLFISH

CRABE – CRAB

493 Dressed Crab

4, 500 g (1-lb) crabs	1 lettuce	2 blanched
4 hard-boiled eggs	125 ml (¼ pt) mayonnaise (Recipe 110)	tomatoes

1 Cook crab in court-bouillon (Recipe 371) for 20 minutes and allow to cool.
2 Remove purse and claws and shred meat finely.
3 Mix the soft part with a little mayonnaise and breadcrumbs; season.
4 Dress each side of crab with this mixture and place meat in the centre.
5 Decorate with chopped hard-boiled egg.
6 Serve with French salad and sauce-boat of mayonnaise.

CREVETTES GRISES – SHRIMPS AND PRAWNS

494 Potted Shrimps (or Prawns)

375 g (¾ lb) butter
nutmeg

250 g (½ lb) shelled shrimps (or prawns)
seasoning

1 Melt the butter, add shrimps and season.
2 Fill into small pots and cover with clarified butter.

COCKTAIL DE CREVETTES

495 Shrimp Cocktail

240 g (½ lb) peeled shrimps
62 ml (½ gill) whipped
   cream
15 ml spoon [1 dessert-
   spoon] tomato ketchup
2·5 ml spoon [½ teaspoon]
   chopped parsley

5 ml spoon [½ dessert-
   spoon] Worcester
   sauce
4 slices lemon
500 ml (1 pt) mayon-
   naise (Recipe 110)
4 stoned olives

4 blanched tomatoes
1 large lettuce
   (julienne)
7 g (¼ oz) finely-
   chopped onions

1 Mix mayonnaise, onions, cream.
2 Add Worcester sauce, parsley and tomato ketchup.
3 Remove pips from tomatoes and rub through fine sieve.
4 Mix with sauce.
5 Add shrimps and season.
6 Place a little lettuce in the bottom of each glass. Serve in suitable goblets, which, if desired, may be rimmed with a little chopped parsley.
7 Place the shrimp mixture on top.
8 Garnish with olive and a little shredded lettuce, and slice of lemon dipped in parsley.

496 Crevettes roses – Prawns

Shell the tails of the prawns and hang over a goblet containing crushed ice.

HOMARD – LOBSTER

497 Demi-homard froid, Sauce mayonnaise – Cold half-lobster, sauce mayonnaise

4 half lobsters
½ sauce-boat mayonnaise
   (Recipe 110)

2 blanched tomatoes
4 hard-boiled eggs

1 lettuce
15 g (½ oz) capers

1 Cut the whole lobster in half.
2 Remove the brain and intestines.
3 Fill the head part with capers and place the shelled claw on top.
4 Garnish with quarters of lettuce, tomatoes, and hard-boiled eggs.
5 Serve a sauce-boat of mayonnaise.

498 Mayonnaise de homard – Mayonnaise of lobster

> 1 *kg* (2 *lb*) *cooked lobster*   250 *ml* (½ *pt*) *mayonnaise*   2 *hard-boiled eggs*
> 8 *anchovy fillets*   (*Recipe* 110)   2 *blanched tomatoes*
> 4 *stoned olives*   12 *capers*   1½ *lettuce*

1 Cut the lobster in two and the tail in sections. Break the claws and remove meat whole; also remove meat from the tail section.
2 Wash the lettuce well and shred one and cut the other two into quarters.
3 Place the shredded lettuce in a large glass salad-bowl and season.
4 Place the lobster meat on top and coat with mayonnaise.
5 Decorate with the anchovies, olives, and capers.
6 Garnish the bowl with lettuce hearts, quarters of egg, tomato, and lobster claws.

499 Salade de homard – Lobster salad

1 Proceed as for Lobster Mayonnaise but do not coat the meat with mayonnaise sauce.
2 Serve vinaigrette (Recipe 118) separately from sauce-boat.

Mayonnaise and Salads of Shellfish:
Other shellfish such as langouste, langoustine, may be prepared as for lobster.

500 Cocktail de homard

Prepare as Recipe 495 but substitute lobster for shrimp; cut lobster into small dice.

HUITRES – OYSTERS

501 Huitres nature

Allow 6 oysters per person.

1 Serve on deep shell.
2 Present on a bed of crushed ice with lemon and parsley; and thinly-cut brown bread and butter.

502 Langouste – Crayfish

1 Cook in court-bouillon (Recipe 371) for 20 minutes, allow to cool in its cooking-liquor.
2 May be used for cold dishes as for lobster.

6. Meat, Poultry, and Game

THE arrangement of the contents of this section has been determined by the modes of cookery involved in the recipes rather than by the main items of meat (or bird) that are used. Such meat foods are, in a kitchen, organized in the classic French manner, prepared either by the roast cook (including the subordinate grillardin or grill cook), the saucier (sauce cook), or, in the case of cold dishes, the garde manger (larder chef). The last-named, of course, has an important part in preparing a mise-en-place, or items of mise-en-place, for many hot dishes. Similarly, the vegetable cook (chef entremettier) customarily supplies vegetable garnishes to, for example, the saucier when he is preparing a dish with, for example, a jardinière garnish. This makes it difficult if not impossible to arrange professional recipes strictly according to section or partie responsibility. It was, nevertheless, thought that such responsibilities linked with the basic cookery-methods employed should help to determine arrangement rather than that the sequence should be merely alphabetical in terms of the main ingredients.

In this section, the roast course is largely covered by the recipes for roasting and grilling and it is normally apparent which items are suitable for dinner (e.g. the finer roasts of beef such as fillets, poultry, and game with fine garnishes) and which for lunch. In the entrée course, items appear which may be prepared by the grill cook and the saucier. This course normally follows the fish and precedes roasts on full dinner menus, but may also be featured as the principal course in shorter dinner menus or in a luncheon. Some of the finer dishes such as those of small cuts sauté (e.g. tournedos, noisettes) are appropriate for dinner or evening service while braises, stews, and so on, are suitable only for luncheon or midday meals.

The relevée or remove is not featured as an additional, separate course on modern menus. Relevées today consist of the larger joints of meat and birds, treated by a mode such as poêlé, and with a good garnish act as a substitute for an entrée or roast on menus.

It will be apparent that the range of possibilities for items in this section may be expanded by the use of the sauces listed in Chapter 1, and in applying vegetable garnishes from Chapter 7.

Dividing recipes for meat (including offal), poultry, and game, according to the chief modes of cooking, i.e. whether for roasting or boiling, etc., permits dishes to be grouped as they are allocated to the appropriate parties or sections of the professional kitchen. An attempt to build a logical sequence has not, however, meant a slavish adherence to these considerations. Ease of reference has been a further factor in determining the arrangement.

Although large establishments may have a separate grill cook (grillardin) this work together with deep-frying, particularly fried potatoes and the cooking of savouries is linked with the duties of the chef rôtisseur (roast chef).

ROASTS

True roasting is exposing food to the radiant heat of a fire; traditionally on a spit (therefore, à la broche is used as an alternative term for rôti – roasted) or by hanging in a Dutch oven. For 'spitted' roasts: all red meats should be properly 'set' by fierce heat and then, according to their size, exposed to the penetrating heat from a fire that has a little or no flame. For small game the fire should, however, have more flame than glowing embers. But for white meats, regulate the fire to allow the joint to cook and colour at the same time.

When roasting, aim at retaining all the juice. Today, this is usually done in the oven, by putting meat in a hot oven 200° C (400° F) for 10 minutes and then reducing the temperature to 180° C (360° F). The meat is basted frequently with fat. The joint should be raised out of the fat to prevent the meat from 'frying' and becoming hard. This may be done by using a trivet or by resting the joint on a bed of roughly-cut vegetables. Take care not to over-brown the vegetables otherwise a singed or acrid flavour will be given to the jus rôti (gravy), which is made later by déglacé-ing the roasting-tray.

Amount of Roasting. Beef, particularly, and also game and mutton are generally preferred rather underdone (saignant).
Lamb, pork, veal and poultry are usually well cooked (bien cuit).

Testing when done. Very underdone red meat remains resilient to pressure; when it is cooked adequately the meat should not resist finger pressure.
In the case of white meats (including poultry), juice-flow when cooked should be clear or 'white'.

SUITABLE JOINTS FOR ROASTING

Beef	Pork	Veal	Lamb and Mutton
Fillet	Leg	Leg (Cuisse or	Best end
(Filet de bœuf)	(Cuisse de	Cuissot de veau)	(Carré)
Foreribs	porc	Loin (Longe)	Leg (Gigot)
(Premier côte	Loin	Shoulder	Saddle (Selle)
de bœuf)	(Longe de	(Épaule)	Shoulder (Épaule)
Middle ribs	porc		
(Côte de bœuf)	Shoulder		
Sirloin	(Épaule de		
(Aloyau)	porc)		
Topside (Tranche			
tendre)			
Rump (Culotte de			
bœuf)			
Wing end (Côte de			
bœuf)			

APPROXIMATE ROASTING TIMES FOR MEAT, GAME, AND POULTRY

Beef:	15 to 20 minutes per 500 g (lb) and 20 minutes over
Mutton:	25 minutes per 500 g (lb) and 20 minutes over
Lamb:	20 minutes per 500 g (lb) and 20 minutes over
Veal:	25 minutes per 500 g (lb) and 20 minutes over
Venison:	25 minutes per 500 g (lb) and 20 minutes over
Pork:	25 minutes per 500 g (lb) and 25 minutes over
Black game:	Total time $\frac{3}{4}$ hour
Hazel hen:	Total time $\frac{3}{4}$ hour
Quails:	Total time 10 minutes
Guinea fowl:	Total time $\frac{3}{4}$ hour
Hare:	Total time 1 hour
Rabbit:	Total time $\frac{3}{4}$ hour
Chicken:	15 minutes per 500 g (lb) (or 2·5 kg (5-lb) chicken: 1 hour)
Duck:	20 minutes per 500 g (lb) (or 2 kg (4-lb) duck: 1 hour)
Duckling:	15 minutes per 500 g (lb) (or 1·5 kg (3-lb) duckling: $\frac{3}{4}$ hour)
Turkey:	20 minutes per 500 g (lb)
Goose:	20 minutes per 500 g (lb)
Grouse:	Total time 20 to 25 minutes
Pheasant:	Total time $\frac{3}{4}$ hour
Partridge (young):	Total time 15 to 25 minutes
Woodcock (young):	Total time 15 to 20 minutes
Snipe:	Total time 10 to 15 minutes
Lark:	Total time 10 to 15 minutes
Wild Duck:	Total time 20 minutes to $\frac{3}{4}$ hour (roasted for à la presse, 12 minutes)

The above cooking times *are approximate*. Times must be adjusted according to the size, shape, thickness, and age of joints and birds. When roasting in metal foil higher temperatures may be used.

Meats that are normally preferred underdone (beef and, sometimes, lamb) are roasted in a hot oven; small birds (particularly game) in a very hot oven; while well-roasted (bien cuit) meats and poultry are finished in a moderate temperature. To facilitate carving, allow underdone meat to 'rest' in a warm place for a few minutes.

As it is particularly relevant here, we are repeating the table of 'Oven Temperatures' that appears on page xii at the front of the *Compendium*.

OVEN TEMPERATURES

	Gas Mark	Degrees Celsius	Degrees Fahrenheit
Very cool	¼	115	240
	½	120	250
Cool	1	135	275
	2	150	300
Warm	2	150	300
	3	160	325
Moderate	3	160	325
	4	175	350
Moderately hot	5	190	375
	6	200	400
Hot	7	215	425
	8	230	450
Very hot	9	245	475

GARNISHES FOR ROASTS

Accompaniments and stuffings for roasts. In addition to the modes of presentation outlined in the recipes of this section, the following are customary accompaniments for roasts.

503 Meat garnishes

Beef: Yorkshire pudding, horse-radish sauce, unthickened gravy, watercress.
Lamb: Mint sauce or mint jelly, unthickened gravy, watercress.
Mutton: Onion sauce, red-currant jelly, unthickened gravy, watercress.
Pork: Sage and onion stuffing, apple sauce, unthickened gravy.
Veal: Lemon stuffing, baked or grilled bacon, jus lié (slightly-thickened gravy).

504 Poultry garnishes

Capon: As for chicken (or turkey).
Chicken and poussin: Grilled bacon, bread sauce, pommes chips (game chips), unthickened gravy, watercress.
Duck, duckling or goose: Sage and onion stuffing, apple sauce, unthickened gravy, watercress.

Guinea fowl: Croûtons, bread sauce, thin gravy, game chips, grilled bacon.
Pigeon: As for chicken.
Turkey: Bread sauce, Cranberry sauce, sausages, gravy, chestnut stuffing (or alternative stuffing).

505 Game garnishes

Venison: Red-currant jelly, sour cream, jus or jus lié (slightly thickened gravy).
Hare: Red-currant jelly, gravy, stuffiing-balls.
Rabbit: Stuffing (sage and onion or lemon stuffing), bacon, jus lié or piquante sauce.

506 Game-bird garnishes

Grouse	
Partridge	
Pheasant	Croûtons, gravy, game chips, fried breadcrumbs (and/or
Plover	bread sauce), watercress.
Ptarmigan	
Woodock	

Widgeon	Orange salad, gravy, game chips, watercress, also fried
Wild duck	breadcrumbs (and/or bread sauce).

507 Yorkshire pudding

120 g (¼ lb) flour	salt	62 ml (⅛ pt) water
2 eggs	62 ml (⅛ pt) milk	

1 Gradually mix the eggs into the sifted flour and salt.
2 Add sufficient liquid until a beating consistency (that of cream) is achieved then beat well.
3 Allow the mixture to stand for at least half an hour before using.
4 Give a final beating before pouring into a roasting-tray of smoking fat. Cook in a hot oven for 25 minutes.

508 Farce au gratin – Poultry and game stuffing.

240 g (½ lb) chicken livers	1 bay-leaf	60 g (2 oz) butter
120 g (¼ lb) fat bacon	1 sprig thyme	seasoning
30 g (1 oz) chopped onions		

1 Cut the bacon into small pieces and fry gently in butter; add herbs.
2 Add the onions and cook until golden brown.
3 Add the chicken livers, fry quickly and season.
4 Pass through a fine sieve then place in basin covered with buttered paper. (A little chopped truffle may be added to this farce.)

Note.
i Farce au gratin is sometimes referred to as farce polonaise.
ii Also used for spreading on croûtons.

509 Chestnut stuffing

360 g (¾ lb) chestnuts   30 g (1 oz) breadcrumbs   salt, pepper
60 g (2 oz) finely-chopped suet   brown stock (Recipe 8)   grated nutmeg

1 Slit, bake, peel, and coarsely-chop the chestnuts.
2 Add the finely-chopped suet and mix well with the crumbs, add sufficient stock to moisten and season with salt, pepper, and nutmeg.

Used for turkey and other fowls. (Often with addition of 60 g (2 oz) pork sausage-meat.)

510 Forcemeat balls

Ingredients as Recipe 512.

1 Shape into the desired size of ball.
2 Flour, egg and crumb and deep-fry.

511 Oyster forcemeat

6 large oysters   pinch ground mace   salt, pepper
60 g (2 oz) white breadcrumbs 7 g (¼ oz) chopped parsley 1 small egg
62 ml (½ gill) white stock   grated zest of lemon   21 g (¾ oz) butter
  (Recipe 6)

1 Beard and poach the oysters (with the beards) in stock.
2 Drain, remove the beards and chop the oysters.
3 Mix the oysters with the breadcrumbs, lemon, mace, parsley, and butter; add the oyster stock and season and bind with beaten egg.

Use for poultry (and fish).

512 Plain forcemeat

60 g (2 oz) finely-chopped   62 ml (½ gill) milk   salt, pepper
  beef suet   2·5 ml spoon [½ teaspoon]   1 small egg
120 g (4 oz) breadcrumbs   mixed herbs
7 g (¼ oz) chopped parsley

1 Mix all the ingredients.
2 Bind with beaten egg; milk and season.

Used for veal, mutton, rabbit. If used for poultry, e.g. turkey, incorporate 240 g (½ lb) pork sausagemeat.

513 Sage and Onion stuffing

2 large onions   62 ml (¼ pt) brown stock (Recipe 8) 3 g (⅛ oz) salt and
7 g (¼ oz) sage   60 g (2 oz) breadcrumbs   pepper
21 g (¾ oz) fat

1 Chop the onions finely and cook to golden colour in fat.
2 Add the brown stock and cook the onions.
3 Add the sage and white breadcrumbs, season and allow to cook for a few minutes at side of the stove.

Used for pork, duck, goose and rabbit.

514 Veal stuffing

60 g (2 oz) *chopped beef suet*	7 g ($\frac{1}{4}$ oz) *chopped parsley*	*salt, pepper*
30 g (1 oz) *finely-chopped*	2·5 *ml spoon* [$\frac{1}{2}$ *teaspoon*]	1 *egg for*
cooked ham	*mixed herbs*	*binding*
60 g (2 oz) *breadcrumbs*	$\frac{1}{2}$ *grated lemon zest*	

1 Mix all the ingredients.
2 Bind with the beaten eggs and season.

Used for chicken, turkey, rabbit, veal.

ROASTS OF BEEF

515 Contrefilet de bœuf rôti – Roast boned-sirloin of beef

1 This rather flat joint (the boned-sirloin without the fillet) is cooked quickly [15 minutes per 500 g (lb)] in a hot oven.
2 It is generally larded. (For beef roasting see page 141.)

516 Filet de bœuf piqué bouquetière – Larded beef-fillet bouquetière

750 g (1$\frac{1}{2}$ lb) *long-fillet*	60 g (2 oz) *butter*	125 *ml* ($\frac{1}{4}$ *pt*) *sauce*
beef	*seasoning*	*Madère* (*Recipe* 44)
90 g (3 oz) *peas*	$\frac{1}{2}$ *wine-glass Madeira*	60 g (2 oz) *sliced*
120 g ($\frac{1}{4}$ lb) *carrots*	12 *glazed button onions*	*vegetables* (*carrots*
120 g ($\frac{1}{4}$ lb) *turnips*	4 *blanched tomatoes*	*and onions*)
4 *turned mushrooms*	120 g ($\frac{1}{4}$ lb) *bacon fat*	

1 Turn and glaze all vegetables (except those to be minced).
2 Trim the fillet (i.e. remove all nerves).
3 Cut the fat bacon into strips and insert these into the fillet with the larding needle and tie up, and season.
4 Melt the butter in a suitable roasting tray and colour the fillet well on both sides.
5 Add the sliced vegetables and cook in a hot oven 190° C (375° F) for $\frac{1}{2}$ hour, basting frequently.
6 When cooked, déglacer the pan with a little Madeira and add the sauce.
7 Garnish a silver dish with bouquets of the prepared vegetable, place the fillet in the centre; strain the sauce and serve it separately.
8 Brush a little meat glaze over the fillet.

517 Roast forerib or sirloin of beef, and Yorkshire pudding

1 Remove surplus fat.
2 Remove the nerve and chine the vertebræ.
3 Tie up and place on roasting tray.
4 Cover with liquid fat and season.
5 Place in hot oven 200° C (400° F) to seal; reduce heat to 190° C (375° F) and baste frequently (see cooking time).
6 When cooked pour away surplus fat from tray and retain residue, add brown stock, boil and season; remove all fat and strain for roast gravy.
7 Serve Yorkshire pudding (Recipe 507) as garnish.

ROASTS OF LAMB OR MUTTON

518 Carré d'agneau rôti, sauce menthe – Roast best end of lamb and mint sauce

4 *pairs of cutlets, best end lamb*   125 *ml* (¼ *pt*) *mint sauce* (*Recipe* 100)
1 *bunch watercress*   60 *g* (2 *oz*) *dripping*
250 *ml* (½ *pt*) *brown stock*   8 *cutlet frills*
  (*Recipe* 7 *or* 8)

1 Prepare the carré by removing the vertebræ bone; trim off each cutlet end.
2 Roast by placing on a bed of vegetables and coating with fat and seasoning.
3 Roast in hot oven basting frequently; reduce oven temperature when meat is sealed.
4 When cooked, place cutlet-frill on each cutlet and serve mint sauce and gravy separately.
5 Garnish with watercress.

519 Couronne d'agneau bouquetière – Crown of lamb bouquetière

750 *g* (1½ *lb*) *best end of lamb*   4 *turned mushrooms*   120 *g* (4 *oz*) *butter*
12 *turned carrots*   90 *g* (3 *oz*) *cooked peas* *seasoning*
12 *turned turnips*   90 *g* (3 *oz*) *cooked*   12 *button onions*
120 *g* (¼ *lb*) *matignon* (*Recipe* 3)   *French beans*

1 Prepare best end of lamb as for roast carré of lamb.
2 Arrange the carrés in the shape of a crown and sew into position.
3 Place the crown on the matignon and also place a few potatoes in the centre of the crown in order to keep its shape when roasting.
4 Carefully baste during the roasting process; when cooked, garnish each cutlet end with a frill.
5 Glaze the carrots, turnips and onions and garnish the dish with bouquets of each vegetable.
6 Serve gravy separately.

520 Épaule d'agneau farcie – Roast stuffed shoulder of lamb

1·25 *kg* (2½ *lb*) *shoulder of*   60 *g* (2 *oz*) *white bread-*   1 *small egg*
  lamb   *crumbs*   *little milk*
250 *ml* (½ *pt*) *brown stock*   30 *g* (1 *oz*) *chopped suet*   1·25 *ml spoon*
  (*Recipe* 7 *or* 8)   1·25 *ml spoon* [¼ *teaspoon*]   [¼ *teaspoon*]
60 *g* (2 *oz*) *carrots* ⎫ *mire-*   *mixed herbs*   *lemon rind*
60 *g* (2 *oz*) *onions*   ⎭ *poix* 7 *g* (¼ *oz*) *chopped parsley*   *seasoning*

1 To make stuffing, mix breadcrumbs, suet, mixed herbs, lemon rind and parsley together, bind with the egg, milk and season.
2 Bone out the scapula and humerus-bone in the shoulder.
3 Place the stuffing in the centre and roll and tie.
4 Place the shoulder on the mirepoix in a roasting tray, cover with fat and season.
5 For the first 10 minutes the oven temperature should be 200° C (400° F); then reduce to 180° C (360° F); baste frequently.

6 When cooked, pour away surplus fat from roasting tray and add the brown stock to make the gravy; season and strain and remove all fat.
7 Garnish the shoulder with watercress; serve mint sauce and gravy separately.

521 Gigot d'agneau rôti boulangère – Roast leg of lamb boulangère

1·25 *kg* (2½-*lb*) *leg of lamb*	240 *g* (½ *lb*) *sliced onions*	250 *ml* (½ *pt*) *white stock*
500 *g* (1 *lb*) *sliced potatoes*	45 *g* (1½ *oz*) *butter*	*seasoning*

1 Prepare the leg of lamb as for roasting and season.
2 Seal the lamb in a hot oven and then finish cooking by placing it on a bed of boulangère potatoes (Recipe 937).
3 Serve lamb with the boulangère garnish.

522 Selle d'agneau rôtie – Roast saddle of lamb.

1 Skin the saddle and remove surplus fat and kidneys.
2 Trim and tie into shape and lightly score with a small knife.
3 Roast in the usual manner.
4 May be carved: (a) English style – cut as for noisettes; (b) French style – lengthwise.
N.B. Short saddles are best for banquets.

ROASTS OF PORK, VEAL, AND VENISON

523 Roasts of pork

Cuisse de porc rôtie – Roast leg of pork
Longe de porc – Roast loin of pork

1 For cuisse (leg): remove pelvic bone. For longe (loin): score the skin and tie the meat.
2 Place in roasting tray and cover with a little good dripping, seal in hot oven; reduce heat and cook slowly, basting frequently.
3 Serve with crackling, sage and onion stuffing, apple sauce, and gravy.

Note. Épaule de porc – Shoulder of pork; though not a prime joint is also sometimes roasted.

524 Roasts of Veal

1 Joints of veal may be piqué, with strips of fat.
2 They are in any case normally covered with slices of back-fat and roasted on a bed of root vegetables with frequent basting. An example is:

524a Longe de veau rôtie chasseur – Roast loin of veal and sauce chasseur

1 Piqué the loin with fat bacon.
2 Roast on a bed of aromatics and serve sauce chasseur (Recipe 38) separately.

525 Hanche de venaison rôtie – Roast haunch of venison

1 Trim off a haunch of venison by removing chine-bone and the end of the knuckle.
2 Wrap well in greased paper to prevent fat from burning.
3 Roast for 2½ to 3 hours basting frequently.
4 Remove the paper, brush with butter to colour a good brown.
5 Dredge lightly with flour and continue to baste until it is well coloured.
6 Make a gravy with the residue from the pan plus any trimmings.
7 Serve red-currant jelly separately.
8 May also be served with chestnut purée.

Note. Venison should be well hung for at least 6 days before use.

526 Cuissot de chevreuil, sauce cassis

½ *leg venison*	30 *g* (1 *oz*) *meat glaze*	125 *ml* (¼ *pt*) *sauce*
240 *g* (½ *lb*) *fat bacon*	(*Recipe* 13)	*poivrade* (*Recipe* 47)
1 *l* (1 *qt*) *red wine*	15 *ml spoon* [1 *table-*	62 *ml* (½ *gill*) *port wine*
marinade (*Recipe* 126)	*spoon*] *black-currant jelly*	

1 Carefully skin the leg of venison.
2 Piqué it evenly with the fat bacon.
3 Cover with the marinade and allow to marinate for 10 hours.
4 Roast it as for roast haunch and when cooked, brush with meat glaze; garnish with watercress.
5 Remove all fat from the roasting tray and put the marinade liquid in the pan; reduce to 500 ml (1 pint), add the sauce poivrade, port, and black-currant jelly; reduce to correct consistency, season and strain.
6 Pour some of the sauce around the joint and serve remainder separately.

ROASTS OF POULTRY

527 Trussing Poultry and Game

1 Remove winglets and feet.
2 Insert needle and string through winglets.
3 Press legs back and continue insertion of needle through the middle of leg at joint.
4 Pass needle diagonally towards the parson's nose and pull the string right through.
5 Pass the needle through a small piece of skin on the legs, and insert needle on the opposite side towards the middle of the other leg.
6 Pull string through and tie.

528 Poulet rôti au lard – Roast chicken with bacon

1, 2 *kg* (4-*lb*) *chicken*	8 *slices bacon*	240 *g* (½ *lb*) *game chips*
120 *g* (¼ *lb*) *mirepoix*	125 *ml* (¼ *pt*) *bread*	1 *bunch watercress*
(*Recipe* 3)	*sauce* (*Recipe* 96)	30 *g* (1 *oz*) *dripping*
125 *ml* (¼ *pt*) *brown*	125 *ml* (¼ *pt*) *gravy*	*salt, pepper*
stock (*Recipe* 8)	(*Recipe* 18)	

1 Clean and truss the bird.
2 Place the fat in roasting tray and heat.
3 Season the chicken inside and outside and roll them in the hot fat.
4 Place it leg-side down first and add the mirepoix and place in oven
   190° C (375° F); baste frequently.
5 Turn over on the other leg and continue basting.
6 Turn the chicken on its back and cook until golden brown.
7 Allow approximately 20 minutes per 500 g (lb) plus 20 minutes extra.
8 When cooked, remove string and keep hot.
9 Pour away surplus fat from roasting tray and rinse with brown stock;
   season, strain, and skim off fat.
10 Garnish the chicken with game chips, grilled bacon, and watercress.
11 Serve gravy and bread sauce separately.

529 Chapon rôti – Roast capon

Prepare and cook as chicken; garnish as chicken (or also with turkey
accompaniments).

530 Dinde rôti – Roast turkey (young turkey is designated Dindonneau)

1, 2·5 kg (5-*lb*) *turkey*	*fat bacon*	*bacon rolls*
480 g (1 *lb*) *turkey stuffing* (*Recipe* 509)	250 *ml* (½ *pt*) *bread*	240 g (½ *lb*)
190 *ml* (1½ *gills*) *brown stock* (*Recipe* 8)	*sauce* (*Recipe* 96)	*chipolatas*

1 Stuff the crop and sew the apron to carriage.
2 Pull sinews from legs and truss as Recipe 527.
3 Cover with fat bacon and place in roasting tray with hot fat.
4 Roast on the leg sides first then the back. Baste frequently.
5 Present with grilled chipolatas, bacon rolls and watercress.
6 Serve bread sauce and gravy separately.

531 Oie rôtie farcie – Roast stuffed goose

1, 2 *to* 2·5 *kg* (4 *lb to* 5 *lb*)	30 g (1 *oz*) *chopped suet*	30 g (1 *oz*)
goose	60 g (2 *oz*) *breadcrumbs*	*chopped onions*
15 g (½ *oz*) *dripping*	1 *small egg*	*pepper, salt*
9 *sage leaves*		

1 Pick, draw, and singe the goose.
2 Blanch the sage and onions together, strain, chop and mix with the crumbs,
   suet, and seasoning; bind with egg.
3 Stuff the inside and truss.
4 Roast in the usual way and baste frequently.
5 Serve with cress, gravy, and apple sauce.

531a Oie rôtie – Roast goose

May be prepared without interior stuffing but with separately-served stuffing,
apple sauce, and gravy.

532 Caneton rôti – Roast duck

Prepare, cook, and serve as for roast goose (Recipe 531).

ROAST GAME BIRDS

Note. Roast game birds are presented en croûtons prepared as follows:

533 Croûtons for game

1 Take bread slice of approximately 1·5 cm (¾-inch) thickness.
2 Cut to the size of the bird to be served.
3 Hollow out the top-centre slightly to form a 'bed'.
4 Fry to golden brown in clarified butter.
5 Spread the hollow part with farce au gratin (Recipe 508).

534 Bécasse flambée – Flamed woodcock

1 *whole bird*	2 *oblong croûtons*	*juice of ½ lemon*
¼ *glass brandy*	(*Recipe 533*)	*pinch cayenne*
125 *ml* (¼ *pt*) *estouffade*	62 *ml* (½ *gill*) *cream*	*farce au gratin*
(*Recipe 8*)	30 *g* (1 *oz*) *butter*	(*Recipe 508*)
15 *g* (½ *oz*) *foie gras*		

1 Skewer with beak and do not clean.
2 Roast for 8 minutes.
3 Skin, remove legs, and breast.
4 Withdraw entrails.
5 Chop the carcass, entrails, and legs.
6 Sweat with butter under cover.
7 Add brandy and flambé.
8 Add the estouffade and reduce.
9 Work in the cream, foie gras, and butter.
10 Strain, place the suprêmes on croûtons (as Recipe 533); napper with the sauce.
11 Serve salade Japonnaise (Recipe 221).

535 Bécasse rôtie – Roast woodcock

4 *slices fat bacon*	240 *g* (½ *lb*) *game chips*	10 *ml spoon* [½
4 *oblong croûtons*	(*Recipe 927*)	*tablespoon*]
120 *g* (¼ *lb*) *white bread-*	1 *bunch watercress*	*brandy*
crumbs	250 *ml* (½ *pt*) *game*	60 *g* (2 *oz*) *farce*
125 *ml* (¼ *pt*) *bread sauce*	*stock* (*Recipe 12*)	*au gratin*
(*Recipe 96*)	4 *woodcock*	(*Recipe 508*)

1 Remove the gizzard and eyes.
2 Truss by piercing the legs with the beak.
3 Cover with the fat bacon and roast quickly in hot fat for 18 minutes.
4 Remove from pan, pour away any surplus fat and rinse with game gravy and brandy; season and strain.
5 Fry the croûtons in butter and spread with farce au gratin.

6 Dress on croûtons (Recipe 533).
7 Garnish with game chips and watercress.
8 Serve with the breadcrumbs tossed in butter, but serve gravy and bread sauce separately.

535a Bécassine rôtie – Roast snipe
Prepare as woodcock.

536 Caille rôtie – Roast quail.
Factors in selection and cooking:
1 Select quails white and very fat.
2 Remove gizzard only just before cooking.
3 Wrap them in buttered vine leaves and thin slices of bacon.
4 Roast in fast oven for 10 to 12 minutes.
5 Serve on toasted croûtons with half-lemon.
6 Serve their own gravy.

536a Caille rôtie aux raisins – Roast quail with grapes

4 *quails*	120 g (¼ lb) farce au gratin	120 g (¼ lb) white
4 *slices bacon*	(*Recipe* 508)	*grapes*
4 *large vine leaves*	125 ml (¼ pt) game stock (Recipe 12)	

1 Clean the quails but draw only the gizzard and entrails, leaving heart and liver.
2 Blanch, peel, and stone the grapes, and stuff the quails with a mixture of farce au gratin and grapes.
3 Truss the quails and wrap in slices of bacon then in vine leaves.
4 Brush them with butter and roast in very hot oven for 10 to 12 minutes.
5 Remove the vine leaves and bacon from quails and place quails on croûtons (as Recipe 533).
6 Serve lemon and roast gravy.

537 Caneton sauvage rôti – Roast wild duck

1 Roast quickly and keep underdone.
2 Allow 20 minutes full cooking time.
3 Garnish with lemon slices and watercress. Serve on croûtons (Recipe 533) with game gravy (Recipe 18)

537a Caneton sauvage à l'Anglaise
This is prepared similarly but served with apple sauce.

538 Faisan rôti – Roast pheasant

1 *pheasant*	125 ml (¼ pt) game stock	1 croûton (as
120 g (¼ lb) fine mirepoix	(*Recipe* 12)	*Recipe* 533)
(*Recipe* 2)	1 *bunch watercress*	240 g (½ lb) farce au
125 ml (¼ pt) bread sauce	8 *slices lean bacon*	gratin (Recipe
(*Recipe* 96)	240 g (½ lb) game	508)
1 *large slice fat bacon*	*chips*	

1 Clean, truss, and stuff birds with the farce au gratin; tie fat bacon over and around the pheasants.
2 Proceed to roast in the same manner as roast chicken (Recipe 528) until moderately underdone.
3 When cooked, remove string and fat bacon; pour away surplus fat from roasting tin and rinse with game stock; season and strain.
4 Dress the pheasants on the croûtons (spread with farce).
5 Garnish the birds with grilled bacon, game chips, and watercress.

539 Roast grouse

4 *young grouse*	120 g (¼ *lb*) *white bread-*	240 g (½ *lb*) *game chips*
4 *croûtons*	*crumbs*	120 g (¼ *lb*) *farce au*
4 *slices fat bacon*	125 ml (¼ *pt*) *game stock*	*gratin* (*Recipe* 508)
4 *slices lean bacon*	(*Recipe* 12)	125 ml (¼ *pt*) *bread*
1 *bunch watercress*		*sauce* (*Recipe* 96)

1 Clean and truss; wrap with fat bacon, tie up and stuff with farce au gratin.
2 Roast quickly until moderately underdone – approximately 25 minutes.
3 Remove bacon and string; pour away surplus fat from roasting tray and rinse with game stock; season and strain.
4 Sauté the croûtons in butter and spread with farce (Recipe 533).
5 Dress the grouse on each croûton with grilled bacon on top.
6 Garnish with game chips and watercress, and serve breadcrumbs tossed in butter, gravy, and bread sauce.

539a Perdreau rôti – Roast partridge

To prepare, use the same method as for roast grouse.

540 Pluvier rôti – Roast plover.

1 Proceed as for roast grouse but do not cover with fat bacon.
2 Cook in rapid oven until moderately underdone.
3 Serve only gravy and a little watercress.

541 Pintade rôtie – Roast guinea fowl

Prepare as for roast pheasant. (Guinea fowl being domestically reared is therefore not truly game but is prepared in a similar style.)

GRILLS

Grilling or broiling. Traditionally, grills are prepared on hot grids above a bright well-ventilated fire, preferably charcoal for cleanliness and flavour. But there are satisfactory modern substitutes such as gas- or electrically heated radiants. Grilling is used for small cuts of meat, poultry, and fish: meat and poultry cuts are brushed with oil and seasoned; fish is also passed through seasoned flour. Meat is trimmed and also slightly flattened with a bat. Grilling times depend on meat thickness and guest's requirements.

Terms for degrees of grilling:
bient cuit – well cooked.
à point – medium (literally, 'to the point', i.e. just done).
saignant – underdone (literally 'bleeding', i.e. flows with red juice when cut).
au bleu – very underdone or rare (literally, 'blue' inside).
flared – burnt on the outside and raw inside.
   Beef cuts are normally preferred underdone rather than well-cooked through, lamb and mutton are generally liked à point or well cooked, and pork, well cooked.

BEEF GRILLS

Entrecôte (sirloin steak)	300 g (10 oz)	– A cut from the boned sirloin.
Entrecôte double	600 g (20 oz)	– A double-sized entrecôte.
Entrecôte minute	300 g (10 oz)	– An entrecôte batted flat.
Rumpsteak	240 g (8 oz)	– A steak from the boned rump.
Point steak	270 g (9 oz)	– Steak from the triangular piece of rump.
Porterhouse (T bone steak)	900 g (1¾ lb)	– A cut through sirloin, bone and fillet.
Châteaubriand	600 g (20 oz)	– A cut from head fillet (for 2 or more persons).
Filet (fillet)*	300 g (10 oz)	– A cut from middle fillet.
Tournedos	240 g (8 oz)	– A cut from middle fillet, the fat removed, circled with string (and sometimes, back fat) to keep round shape.
Côte à l'os	750 g (1½ lb)	– Cut from the wing-end with bone (equivalent to a large cutlet – for 2 or more).
Carpet-bag steak	600 g (20 oz)	– Double entrecôte, incised for six oysters as stuffing and sewn (piqué) with back-fat strips (for 2 or more).

LAMB GRILLS

Chop	300 g (10 oz)	– Cut from loin (half-saddle).
English chop	500 g (16 oz)	– Complete cut across saddle, including kidney skewered-in.
Cutlet	90 to 120 g (3 to 4 oz)	– From the best end.
Double cutlet	240 g (8 oz)	– 2 cutlets joined from best end.
Chump chop	300 g (10 oz)	– Cut from leg-end of loin.
Filet mignon	120 g (4 oz)	– Small fillet from inside saddle.
Kidneys		– 2 per portion, split open and skewered.
Noisette	90 g (3 oz)	– Cut from saddle.

 * An English-style fillet steak is not trimmed but grilled with its own surrounding fat.

PORK GRILLS

Chop	240 g (8 oz) – Cut from saddle.
Cutlet	200 to 240 g (7 to 8 oz) – Cut from best end.
Fillets	180 g (6 oz) – Under-cut from saddle.
Steak (gammon)	300 g (10 oz) – Cut from gammon-slice.

MIXED GRILLS

A standard mixed grill is likely to consist of:

1 *lamb cutlet* 90 g (3 oz)	1 *pork sausage* 60 g (2 oz)
1 *lamb's kidney*	1 *bacon rasher* (*back*)

together with mushroom, tomato, pommes paille (straw potatoes) and watercress, but substitutions and/or additions may include lambs' or calves' liver, small tournedos, and parsley butter.

VEAL

Except for veal kidneys, similar veal cuts to those of other meats listed above are normally sautéd, not grilled.

POULTRY GRILLS

Poussins and small chickens may be grilled (Recipes 553-7). Legs of chicken are also grilled from raw and, on occasion, cooked chicken-legs are coated with devilled mixture and grilled.

GRILLED BONES

Beef rib-bones, if sufficient meat is attached, may also be grilled. Bones from cooked rib-roasts may similarly be devilled for grilling.

DRESSING AND GARNISHING OF GRILLS

Accompaniments which may be served with grills include:

i Sauces: Béarnaise, choron, châteaubriand, etc.
ii Butters: Montpelier, garlic, hongroise, mustard, mâitre d'hotel (parsley butter), etc.
iii Watercress (vert pré): and straw potatoes.

The use of these accompaniments determines the dish's menu title: e.g., Tournedos grillé béarnaise or Filet de boeuf grillé mâitre d'hotel.

542 Other garnishes for grills:

Américaine: Grilled bacon, tomatoes with pommes paille.
Bouquetière: (Particularly for tournedos, châteaubriand), glazed mixed olive-turned vegetables with sherry-flavoured demi-glace as a separate sauce.
Continentale: Grilled mushrooms, tomatoes with pommes soufflées.
Garni: Grilled tomatoes, mushrooms, pommes paille, French fried onions (usually also sauce béarnaise).

Mirabeau: Spanish black olives within rolled anchovy-fillet, beurre d'anchois, pommes paille and watercress.

Tyrolienne: Grilled tomatoes, French fried (deep) onions, pommes paille, mâitre d'hotel butter.

BEEF GRILLS

543 Entrecôte grillé vert pré – Grilled sirloin steak

4, 300 g (10-oz) entrecôte steaks	240 g (½ lb) straw potatoes	62 ml (½ gill)
120 g (¼ lb) parsley butter	(Recipe 929)	oil
(Recipe 89)	1 bunch watercress	seasoning

1 Brush with oil and season.
2 Place on hot grill and cook both sides, basting frequently.
3 Garnish with straw potatoes, watercress and parsley butter.

Note. Double and minute entrecôtes, tournedos, rump, and point steaks are similarly prepared.

543a Filet de bœuf grillé

In addition, this is accompanied by a piece of grilled suet. Cuts from the filet (including châteaubriand) are lightly batted before oiling and seasoning.

543b Châteaubriand

1 Originally and traditionally, a large fillet steak grilled between a sandwich of two, thin, inferior steaks later discarded, the châteaubriand is today plainly grilled as Recipe 543, accompanied by a piece of grilled suet and other appropriate grill garnishes.
2 It is 'finished' by carving at the guéridon (side-table service) by the waiter.

543c Porterhouse steak

This may be prepared and served (without grilled suet) as châteaubriand.

LAMB OR MUTTON GRILLS

544 Mixed grill

4, 90 g (3-oz) trimmed lamb cutlets	4 slices back bacon	4 cutlet frills
	4 small pieces lamb's liver	1 bunch watercress
4 sheep's kidneys	4 sausages	62 ml (½ gill) oil
4 whole tomatoes	straw potatoes	seasoning
parsley butter	(Recipe 929)	
(Recipe 89)	4 medium mushrooms	

1 Remove skin from kidney, slit open and skewer; brush with oil, and season.
2 Similarly prepare the mushrooms and tomatoes for grilling (cultivated mushrooms need not be peeled).

3 Prick the sausage with a fork.
4 Dust the liver with a little seasoned flour.
5 Place each commodity on separate trays if grilling under salamander or direct on to an underfired or charcoal grill; season while cooking.

Presentation. Place the grilled mushrooms on top of the tomatoes, and arrange the cutlets (with frills on), sausages, liver, bacon, neatly on a silver dish. The kidney should be filled with parsley butter (Recipe 89) and served underdone. Garnish with watercress and straw potatoes. Brush with oil.

545 Chop d'agneau grillé – Grilled lamb chop

120 g (¼ *lb*) *parsley butter* (*Recipe* 89)	4, 300 g (10-*oz*)	62 *ml* (½
240 g (½ *lb*) *straw potatoes* (*Recipe* 929)	*chops*	*gill*) *oil*
1 *bunch watercress*		*seasoning*

1 Remove from the saddle the skin, kidneys and surplus fat.
2 Divide into two parts by cutting right through the vertebræ lengthwise.
3 Cut the saddle into chops 300 g (10-*oz*) each.
4 Brush both sides with oil, season and grill; approximate full cooking time 20 minutes.
5 Serve with parsley butter separately; garnish with straw potatoes and watercress.

546 Côtelette d'agneau grillée – Grilled lamb cutlet

120 g (¼ *lb*) *parsley butter* (*Recipe* 89)	8, 120 g (4-*oz*)	62 *ml* (½
240 g (½ *lb*) *straw potatoes* (*Recipe* 929)	*cutlets*	*gill*) *oil*
1 *bunch watercress*		*seasoning*

1 Remove cutlets from the carré (best end) and well trim the cutlet bones.
2 Brush with oil, season and grill both sides.
3 Garnish each cutlet with a frill and the dish with straw potatoes and watercress.
4 Serve parsley butter separately.

547 Rognons de mouton grillés

240 g (½ *lb*) *straw potatoes* (*Recipe* 929)	8 *sheep's kidneys*	62 *ml* (½
120 g (¼ *lb*) *parsley butter* (*Recipe* 89)	1 *bunch watercress*	*gill*) *oil*
seasoning		

1 Skin the kidney and cut lengthwise but not completely in half.
2 Skewer each one to remain open and to retain *their* shape.
3 Brush with oil and grill both sides and season; (kidneys are normally served underdone).
4 Garnish each one with parsley butter.
5 Serve watercress and straw potatoes.

PORK AND GAMMON GRILLS

548 Côtelettes de porc grillées, sauce Robert

Grill the cutlets and serve with sauce Robert (Recipe 49).

549 Grilled gammon steak

4, 180 g (6-oz) gammon steaks   straw potatoes (Recipe 929)   watercress

1 Cut the fat with little slits all round.
2 Brush with oil and grill both sides.
3 Garnish with cress and straw potatoes.
4 Serve sauce diable (Recipe 40) separately.

550 Barbecued gammon

1 Dust a thick gammon rasher with mixed spice, sprinkle with brown sugar and grill.
2 Serve with grilled pineapple and piquante sauce (Recipe 46).

VEAL GRILLS

551 Rognon de veau grillé – Grilled veal kidney

4 kidneys   straw potatoes   watercress
120 g ($\frac{1}{4}$ lb) parsley butter (Recipe 89)   (Recipe 929)   seasoning

1 Trim the kidneys leaving a slight layer of fat.
2 Cut in half, lengthwise, without separating the two halves.
3 Impale on a small skewer to keep shape.
4 Season with salt and pepper, brush with butter, and grill both sides; remove skewer before serving.
5 Garnish with parsley butter, watercress, and straw potatoes.

552 Rognon de veau grillé américaine

4 veal kidneys   4 rashers streaky bacon
4 tomato halves   60 g (2 oz) butter

1 Remove skin and cut lengthwise in half, but not in two.
2 Skewer to keep open, season, brush with oil and grill both sides.
3 Wrap the streaky bacon round the tomatoes and grill.
4 Dress the kidney and tomato on a serving dish and finish with beurre noisette (Recipe 82).

POULTRY GRILLS

553 Preparation of chicken, poussin, and pigeon for grilling

1 Cut open from the back, spread out and flatten with the bat.
2 Remove the rib-bones and insert 2 skewers through the wings to keep flat.
3 Rub both sides with lemon juice and season with salt and pepper.
4 Immerse the bird in oil for about 10 minutes.

554 Chicken spatchcock

1, 2 *kg* (4-*lb*) *chicken*	9 *gherkins*	1 *bunch watercress*
120 *g* (¼ *lb*) *white breadcrumbs*	240 *g* (½ *lb*) *straw*	125 *ml* (¼ *pt*) *diable*
120 *g* (¼ *lb*) *melted butter*	*potatoes*	*or piquante sauce*
seasoning	(*Recipe* 929)	(*Recipes* 40 *or* 46)
125 *ml* (1 *gill*) *oil*		

1 Prepare the chicken for grilling (Recipe 553).
2 Brush with melted butter and half-cook in oven.
3 Sprinkle both sides with white breadcrumbs, pour over melted butter and complete by grilling; baste frequently.
4 Serve on a silver flat and garnish with fanned gherkins, watercress and straw potatoes.
5 Serve sauce diable or piquante separately.

555 Poulet grillé américaine

1, 2 *kg* (4-*lb*) *chicken*	8 *bacon rashers*	125 *ml* (¼ *pt*) *devil sauce*
4 *tomatoes*	240 *g* (½ *lb*) *straw*	(*Recipe* 40)
1 *bunch watercress*	*potatoes* (*Recipe* 929)	4 *mushrooms*

1 Prepare as for chicken diable (Recipe 556) and garnish with grilled tomatoes, mushrooms, bacon, cress and straw poatoes.
2 Devil sauce is served separately.

556 Poulet grillé diable

1, 2 *kg* (4-*lb*) *chicken*	120 *g* (¼ *lb*) *white bread-*	1 *bunch watercress*
8 *slices bacon*	*crumbs*	125 *ml* (1 *gill*) *oil*
½ *tablespoon mustard*	240 *g* (½ *lb*) *straw potatoes*	125 *ml* (¼ *pt*) *devil*
seasoning	(*Recipe* 929)	*sauce* (*Recipe* 40)
120 *g* (¼ *lb*) *melted*		
butter		

1 Prepare the chicken for grilling (Recipe 553).
2 Brush with diluted mustard and melted butter and half-cook in the oven.
3 Sprinkle both sides with white breadcrumbs, pour over the melted butter and complete by grilling, basting frequently.
4 Serve on a silver flat, garnish the chicken with grilled bacon, watercress and straw potatoes.
5 Serve devil sauce separately.

557 Poulet grille crapaudine

1, 2 *kg* (4-*lb*) *chicken*	4 *grilled tomatoes*	125 *ml* (¼ *pt*) *sauce*
120 *g* (¼ *lb*) *pommes paille*	1 *bunch watercress*	*diable* (*Recipe* 40)
(*Recipe* 929)	4 *grilled mushrooms*	

1 Singe and clean chicken.
2 Do not remove winglets or feet.
3 Cut from the breast-top through rib-cage to the joint of the wing.
4 Pull the breast-bone up in the form of a hinge until the chicken lies flat in the shape of a frog or toad.
5 Bat the cut side to facilitate cooking and removal of bone when cooked.

6 Cook as for Chicken Spatchcock (Recipe 554).

7 When cooked, decorate the tip of the breast with roundels of cooked egg and slices of truffle to form two eyes.

8 Garnish the dish with grilled tomatoes and mushrooms, pommes pailles and watercress.

9 Serve sauce diable separately.

Note. Poussins may be treated in the same way.

BRAISING

Braising combines baking (or oven roasting) with stewing. Joints or pieces of meat are browned quickly in fat in the oven and then moistened with stock and cooked slowly under cover. In the traditional brigade this cooking is undertaken by the chef saucier (sauce cook).

While many of the less costly cuts, if suitably prepared, may be braised the following are generally considered the most suitable joints for braising in the piece:

Beef – Rump, silverside, topside, thick flank, aitch bone

Mutton (or Lamb), Pork, and Veal – Leg, shoulder, breast

Poultry may be braised and the method is particularly suitable for game birds when they are older such as older partridge, pheasant or grouse. Offal including liver, heart, sweetbreads, and so on, are all used in braising.

GARNISHES

558 Garnishes for all braised joints

Examples of types of garnish and accompaniments used with braised joints of meat include:

Nemours: Noodles and Duchesse potatoes.

Badoise: Braised red cabbage, lean bacon, Duchesse potatoes.

Bourgeoise: Turned carrots, button onions, lardons.

Charollaise: Cauliflower villeroy, croustades of turnip purée.

Clamart: Artichoke bottoms filled with purée of fresh peas, château potatoes.

Mercédes: Braised lettuce, grilled tomatoes and mushrooms, croquette potatoes.

Moderne: Cauliflower Mornay, stuffed tomato, Duchesse potatoes.

Richelieu: Braised lettuce, stuffed tomatoes, mushrooms, pommes château.

St Florentin: Cèpes bordelaise, pommes St Florentin.

Samaritaine: Timbales of rice, braised lettuce, Dauphine potatoes.

Soissonnaise: With braised haricots blancs.

559 Braised joints (red meat)

1 When meat cuts for braising are very lean, they may be piquéd, i.e., threaded by larding needle or daube needle with strips of fat placed regularly.

2 Meat is then placed in a marinade (Recipe 126) usually for 24 hours and turned at regular intervals: the acid action of the wine helps to tenderize while the mirepoix and aromatics impart flavour.

3 Place the joint in a braising-pan on the thickly-sliced vegetables and aromatics (taken from the mirepoix); baste with a little fat and roast with the lid off until the meat and vegetables are lightly coloured. This seals the meat fibres for juice and flavour retention. Pour over the marinade liquor and reduce it to a syrupy consistency (glaze); sprinkle the meat with flour and place in the oven.

4 When brown (singé), remove from the oven and three-quarters cover the meat with brown stock; add concassé tomatoes, cover with tight lid and place to cook in a moderate oven; (if tomato purée is used instead of fresh tomatoes, add before the stock).

5 During cooking, baste and turn the meat in the sauce to prevent skin formation; when the meat is cooked, remove from the pan.

Sauce and garnish

Reduce the liquor until it is a sauce of the required consistency, skimming frequently to ensure a glossy finish. Strain and add the appropriate garnish. If the joint is to be served whole, it is glazed. This is done after it is cooked by placing the meat on a tray in the oven and sprinkling with the sauce until the joint is glossy. If the meat is to be presented carved, this process serves no purpose.

Alternative thickenings:

1 Demi-glace: Moistening may also be done with demi-glace (Recipe 29) instead of stock in which case omit the flour before adding the sauce.

2 Fécule or Arrowroot: Another method is to use brown stock but omit the flour and thicken the sauce with fécule or arrowroot after the meat is cooked.

560 Culotte de bœuf braisé jardinière – Braised beef jardinière

1 *kg* (2 *lb*) *beef*	*jardinière garnish* (*Recipe* 755)
500 *ml* (1 *pt*) *brown stock*	500 *ml* (1 *pt*) *marinade*
(*Recipe* 7 *or* 8)	(*Recipe* 126)

Note. Culotte is the top of rump cut. Other suitable joints are topside, silverside, and thick flank.

1 Lard the beef and place in marinade for 12 hours, turning frequently.

2 Remove the beef from the marinade and place in braising-pan to seal off.

3 Add the vegetables from the marinade and dust meat with flour (singer) and place in the oven so that flour will brown.

4 Half-cover with brown stock and the marinade liquor and add a little tomato purée and bouquet garni; cover with lid and baste frequently.

5 When the meat is cooked remove from the pan, reduce the sauce to the required consistency and strain through a fine chinois being careful to remove all fat.

6 Slice thickly and serve with jardinière of vegetables tossed in butter.

561 Bœuf braisé à la mode

1 Proceed as for braising with the addition of 1 calf's foot.

2 Garnish with diced calf's-feet meat and turned, glazed vegetables (bouquetière as Recipe 755)

562 Bœuf braisé bourguignonne

1 *kg* (2 *lb*) *topside beef*	500 *ml* (1 *pt*) *red-wine*	120 *g* (¼ *lb*) *diced*
240 *g* (½ *lb*) *button*	*marinade* (*Recipe* 126)	*bacon*
onions	240 *g* (½ *lb*) *button*	4 *heart-shaped*
seasoning	*mushrooms*	*croûtons*

1 Lard the beef and place in a red-wine marinade for 12 hours.
2 Remove, drain and brown the meat in hot fat; dredge with flour and with the vegetable from the marinade place in the oven to brown.
3 Add the liquid from the marinade and sufficient brown stock to half cover the meat.
4 When cooked, remove meat and reduce the sauce to the required consistency; remove all fat and strain through a fine chinois; season.
5 May be served whole or sliced; garnish with glazed onions, mushrooms, fried diced bacon and heart-shaped croûtons.

563 Bœuf braisé bourgeoise

As Recipe 560 but with vegetable-garnish bourgeoise, Recipe 754.

564 Langue de bœuf braisée – Braised ox-tongue

½ *ox-tongue*	240 *g* (½ *lb*) *button onions*	360–500 *g* (¾–1 *lb*) *carrots* (*to yield* 16 *pieces carrots*)

Braise the tongue as for ordinary braising.
When two-thirds cooked surround with the carrots also two-thirds cooked, and the small onions browned in butter.
Simmer gently until cooked and remove all grease before service.

565 Braised pieces (white meat)

White meat for braising include not only joints of veal but also poultry (including turkey) and sweetbreads. Sweetbreads are first soaked in cold salted water to withdraw the blood (dégorger). Except for sweetbreads which must be blanched first, the joint or bird must be stiffened in butter.
Place the joint in a suitable braising-pan, lay it on the roots and aromatics, moisten with a little veal stock and reduce. Continue this process until a glaze is obtained. Then add enough veal stock to half-cover the joint and place in a moderate oven with a tight lid.
The meat requires constant basting while it cooks to prevent drying. As the stock is gelatinous it forms a coating on the surface and so prevents the juices escaping. It is for that reason the first stock must be reduced to a glaze before the final addition of the stock. The meat is known to be cooked when a clear liquid escapes if pricked with a needle.
White meats that are braised are always larded and glazed.

Sauce: The accompanying sauce is made by reducing the cooking-liquor and adding the appropriate wine and either demi-glace for a brown sauce or velouté and cream for a white sauce.

566 Fricandeau de veau briarde – Leg fillet of veal briarde

    1 *kg* (2 *lb*) *leg fillet of veal*   2 *lettuce*   360 *g* (¾ *lb*) *carrots*

1 Cook as for noix de veau florentine (Recipe 567).
2 Garnish with braised lettuce and new carrots à la crème.
3 Serve with the reduced cooking-liquor strained and all fat removed.

567 Noix de veau florentine – Cushion of veal with spinach

    1 *kg* (2 *lb*) *veal*   500 *g* (1 *lb*) *spinach* (*in leaf*)

1 Piqué the cushion of veal with fat bacon.
2 Proceed to braise as for white braising (see notes on white braising).
3 Garnish with leaf spinach tossed in butter.
4 Serve with the reduced cooking-liquor, strained and free from fat.

568 Poitrine de veau farcie – Stuffed breast of veal

    1 *kg* (2 *lb*) *veal*

Stuffing:

240 *g* (½ *lb*) *fine sausage-meat*	*tarragon and chives*	30 *g* (1 *oz*)
30 *g* (1 *oz*) *dry duxelles*	*grated zest of* ½ *lemon*	*butter*
(*Recipe* 101)	*salt and pepper*	1 *small egg*
7 *g* (¼ *oz*) *chopped parsley*		

1 For the stuffing mix all ingredients.
2 Bone the thickest part of the veal-breast to form a pocket.
3 Place the stuffing in the pocket and sew up, taking care to remove string
  when cooked.
4 Braise the veal as for white braising; approximate time 3 hours.
5 Garnish with spinach (Florentine) or Jardinière or Bourgeoise.
6 Serve the reduced cooking-liquor as a sauce.

569 Rognonnade de veau braisée – Braised saddle, best end and kidneys of vea

1 Bone the loin and best end of veal in one piece.
2 Insert the veal kidneys along the length and tie with plenty of fat bacon t
  cover the outside.
3 Stiffen the veal in butter and colour lightly on both sides.
4 Now prepare a fine mirepoix (Recipe 2) and place the veal on top and add
  little veal stock; cover and reduce this stock to a glaze, then half-cover wit
  veal stock; baste well and frequently.
5 When cooked, reduce liquor, add a little cream and strain; season.
6 Garnish with turned mushrooms, and serve with a sauce-boat of cooking
  liquid, and the sauce.
7 This dish can be presented whole or sliced.

570 Selle de veau braisée Metternich

1 Trim the saddle and remove the kidneys.
2 Cut sufficient slices of fat bacon to cover the top of the saddle and secur
  firmly with string.

3 Slightly stiffen the saddle both sides in butter.
4 Now place the meat on a bed of aromatics and root vegetables in a pan just big enough to hold it. Moisten with a little stock and reduce to form a glaze; half-cover the meat with the veal stock and cook with lid on in a moderate oven and baste frequently.
5 When cooked, remove the fillets from the joints with care and cut into regular-sized collops.
6 Spread over the saddle bone a few 15 ml spoons (tablespoons) of Béchamel (Recipe 51) flavoured with paprika.
7 Reconstruct the fillets on the saddle bone in such a way as to make them appear untouched and between each collop insert a 5 ml spoon (teaspoon) of Béchamel and 2 slices of truffle.
8 Cover the saddle completely with thin Béchamel sauce flavoured with paprika and set to glaze.
9 Serve separately: rice pilaff (Recipe 366) and a sauce-boat of the braising liquid.

BRAISING HAM

571 Jambon braisé au madère – Braised ham and Madeira sauce

1 Parboil the ham for ½ hour in boiling water.
2 Remove rind and trim off excess fat for an even appearance.
3 Stud with cloves.
4 Place the ham on a matignon (Recipe 4) in a suitable braising-pan.
5 Add 500 ml (1 pt) Madeira and cover two-thirds with brown stock and sprinkle a layer of brown sugar on top of the ham.
6 Set to cook in a moderate oven, basting frequently to give an even glaze.
7 When the ham is cooked and evenly glazed dé-glacer the pan with demi-glace (Recipe 29), remove all grease and strain.
8 Finish off the sauce with 60 g (2 oz) butter per pint.
9 Suitable garnishes for ham include, spinach, braised lettuce, endives and vegetable purées.

572 Jambon braisé alsacienne

Prepare with braised sauerkraut and Madeira sauce (Recipe 44).

573 Jambon braisé florentine

Prepare with purée of spinach and sauce Madère (Recipe 44).

574 Jambon sous la cendre

1 Bone and remove skin.
2 Stuff with veal forcemeat (Recipe 514) and truffles; tie up.
3 Envelop with short paste (Recipe 995) and decorate.
4 Cook gently in the oven.
5 Serve with sauce Périgueux (Recipe 45) and purée of spinach.

BRAISING OF POULTRY

575 Caneton braisé aux petits pois – Braised duckling and green peas

1, 2 kg (4-*lb*) *duckling*	480 g (1 *lb*) *fresh peas*	*bouquet garni*
240 g (½ *lb*) *button onions*	120 g (¼ *lb*) *brown stock*	30 g (1 *oz*)
180 g (6 *oz*) *breast pork*	(*Recipe* 7 *or* 8)	*butter*
500 *ml* (1 *pt*) *demi-glace*		*seasoning*
(*Recipe* 29)		

1 Dice the pork into lardons and blanch.
2 Place butter in a braising-pan and brown the lardons and onions.
3 When browned, remove from the braising-pan and brown the trussed ducks in the residue fat.
4 Drain off the fat, add the half-glaze and stock; boil and add the bouquet garni.
5 Cook under cover, basting frequently.
6 When half-cooked, add the onions, lardons and peas and continue cooking.
7 Skim all the fat from the sauce, check for seasoning and consistency.
8 Coat the ducks in the sauce and garnish.
9 Cooking should be in a moderate oven for 1 hour or according to quality of duck.

576 Canard braisé à l'orange – Braised duck with orange

1, 2 kg (4-*lb*) *duck*	120 *ml* (¼ *pt*) *brown*	30 g (1 *oz*)
500 *ml* (1 *pt*) *demi-glace* (*Recipe* 29)	*stock* (*Recipe* 7 *or* 8)	*butter*
1 *bouquet garni*	½ *lemon*	*seasoning*
2 *oranges*		

1 Brown the ducks in the braising-pan.
2 Cover the ducks with the demi-glace and stock; boil and add bouquet garni.
3 Cook under cover in a moderate oven, basting frequently.
4 Cut into fine julienne the zest of 1 orange and ½ lemon, and blanch.
5 Extract the juice from the lemon and all the oranges.
6 When the ducks are cooked, remove all fat from sauce and reduce to a stiff consistency; strain through a tammy, add the orange and lemon juice; check for seasoning and consistency.
7 Add the julienne of orange and lemon at the last moment.
8 Glaze the ducks and coat with the sauce.
9 Surround the dish with orange sections.
10 Serve a sauce-boat of sauce.

577 Caneton braisé aux navets – Braised duckling with turnips

1, 2 kg (4-*lb*) *duckling*	125 *ml* (¼ *pt*) *brown stock*	90 g (3 *oz*) *butter*
240 g (½ *lb*) *button onions*	(*Recipe* 7 *or* 8)	125 *ml* (¼ *pt*)
500 *ml* (1 *pt*) *demi-glace*	2·5 *ml* spoon [½ *teaspoon*] *sugar*	*white wine*
(*Recipe* 29)	360 g (¾ *lb*) *turned turnips*	*seasoning*

1 Clean and truss the duckling.
2 Brown the duckling in 45 g (1½ oz) butter in braising-pan.

3 Drain away the butter and rinse with white wine; add the demi-glace and brown stock.
4 Return the ducklings to this sauce, boil, skim and add bouquet garni.
5 Cover and braise gently in moderate oven, basting frequently.
6 Sprinkle the turnips with sugar and glaze to a light brown.
7 Cook the onions and glaze in butter.
8 When the ducklings are half-cooked transfer to a clean pan and add the garnish of turnips and onions.
9 Re-boil the sauce, remove all fat and strain over the ducklings and complete the cooking.
10 Present with the garnish of onions and turnips arranged round the birds.

POÊLER

The process of poêler resembles that of pot-roasting. The cooking vessel, the poêle, is a deep fireproof one in which the joint or bird to be cooked is placed on a bed of mirepoix (the size of the cut varying according to the size of the piece). Joints and birds for roasting may be cooked in this manner and, even, some of the superior pieces may be poêlé.

A cocotte is, in effect, a poêle so that when cooking (as distinct from simply dishing up) is 'en cocotte' then the method of cooking is poêler. These dishes are the responsibility of the chef saucier (sauce cook) in a traditional kitchen brigade.

578 Method of poêler

1 Butter a large pan or casserole and place a layer of raw mirepoix (Recipe 2) of vegetables on the bottom.
2 Place the meat or poultry on top of the vegetables and cover meat with plenty of butter.
3 Place a lid on top and cook in a moderate oven, basting frequently with butter.
4 When the meat or poultry is cooked remove the lid to colour the meat.
5 Remove meat, add some good veal stock (Recipe 10) to the pan and simmer for 10 minutes.
6 Remove all grease and strain the sauce through a muslin.
7 Add the appropriate garnish.

579 Noix de veau poêlée – Cushion of veal poêlée

625 g (1¼ lb) veal cushion	30 g (1 oz) carrots	30 g (1 oz) celery
250 ml (½ pt) brown veal stock (Recipe 10)	30 g (1 oz) onions	1 small sprig thyme
	90 g (3 oz) butter	seasoning
1 bay-leaf		

1 Bard the veal with fine slices of back fat and tie lightly with string.
2 Melt the butter in a casserole or small braising-pan and lay the aromatics and thick, sliced vegetables on the bottom.
3 Season the meat well, place on the bed of roots and baste well with melted butter.

4 Cover with a tight-fitting lid and place in a moderate oven to cook.
5 Baste often with butter, taking care not to brown the vegetables.
6 When veal is almost cooked, remove lid so that the joint may colour lightly.
7 Remove joint when cooked and remove string.
8 Add the brown stock to vegetables and simmer gently for 10 minutes.
9 Adjust seasoning, strain gravy through muslin, and remove all excess fat.
10 This joint is normally served with a vegetable garnish, i.e., florentine, bouquetière.
11 Gravy is served separately.

Note.
i The veal may be piqué or larded. Larding is to be preferred as this helps to retain juice in the joint.
ii Other joints such as Longe de veau (loin), épaule (shoulder) may, of course, be poêlé.

580 Caneton poêlé bigarade – Duck bigarade

1, 2 kg (4-lb) duck   ½ lemon   3 cubes of sugar
3 oranges   15 ml spoon [1 tablespoon] vinegar

1 Clean and truss the duck.
2 Poêlé the duck (Recipe 578).
3 Cut into fine julienne the zest of 1½ oranges and ½ lemon, blanch.
4 Squeeze the juice from the oranges and lemon, reduce the braising-sauce until it is dense; strain.
5 Add the lemon and orange juice to bring the sauce to its normal consistency; add the vinegar and the dissolved sugar.
6 Garnish with the julienne of orange and lemon zest; check the sauce for seasoning and consistency; if the sauce is too thin, cohere with a little arrowroot.
7 Serve the duck in thin slices and garnish the duck with orange fillets and the sauce poured over.

581 Pigeon poêlé à l'anglaise

4 pigeons   120 g (¼ lb) breadcrumbs   9 slices lean
120 g (¼ lb) chicken livers   15 g (½ oz) chopped onions   bacon

1 Toss the onions, breadcrumbs and chicken's liver in butter and season.
2 Stuff the pigeons and truss.
3 Poêlé (as Recipe 578).
4 Serve with grilled bacon and gravy.

582 Poularde poêlé Chimay – Chicken (young fowl) poêlé
For poêlé:

240 g (½ lb) noodles	60 g (2 oz) minced carrots	1 bay-leaf
1, 2 kg (4-lb) chicken	120 g (¼ lb) minced onions	125 ml (¼ pt)
15 g (½ oz) foie gras	30 g (1 oz) raw ham	brown veal
62 ml (½ gill) cream	60 g (2 oz) butter	stock (Recipe 10)
½ glass sherry		

1 Par-cook half the quantity of noodles and toss in butter, mix with cream and diced foie gras and season.
2 Stuff the chicken with this mixture.
3 Sweat off the ham and vegetables in butter and de-glacer with sherry.
4 Truss the chicken and colour in butter; poêlé as in Recipe 578 adding the herbs and stock; cook under cover, basting frequently; when cooked remove the chicken; skim all fat from the sauce and thicken with a little arrowroot; season, and strain some over the chicken.
5 Sauté the remainder of the raw noodles and garnish.
6 Serve in a large casserole with some of the sauce, serving the remainder separately.

583 Poularde Souvaroff

1, 2 kg (4-lb) chicken	150 g (5 oz) diced truffles	flour and water paste
240 g (½ lb) foie gras	½ glass Madeira	5 small white truffles

1 Stuff the chicken with the foie gras and diced truffles.
2 Poêler the chicken (Recipe 578) but when three-quarters cooked, place in a large cocotte.
3 Deglacer the poêlé pan and reduce this liquor; season and strain over the chicken.
4 Cook the whole truffles in the sherry for 2 or 3 minutes and add these to the chicken.
5 Seal the lid well down with flour and water paste and continue cooking in the oven for 30 minutes approximately.
6 Serve the birds in the cocotte and do not break the seal until at the table.

Note. Pheasant, Faisan Souvaroff, may be similarly prepared.

584 Poulet en cocotte bonne femme – Chicken bonne femme

1, 2 kg (4-lb) chicken	18 button onions	480 g (1 lb) potatoes
240 g (½ lb) lardons	120 g (¼ lb) butter	chopped parsley

1 Truss the chicken and season.
2 Colour the chicken in butter in a large cocotte and continue cooking.
3 Add a garnish of cocotte potatoes (large olive-shape, château-cooked as Recipe 902), lardons and button onions fried in butter.
4 Sprinkle with a little chopped parsley before service.

585 Poulet en cocotte champeaux

1, 2 kg (4-lb) chicken	360 g (¾ lb) button onions	120 g (¼ lb) butter
200 ml (1½ gills) demi-glace	500 g (1 lb) potatoes	seasoning
(Recipe 29)	125 ml (¼ pt) white wine	

Truss the chicken and season.
2 Colour the chicken in butter, add the white wine and demi-glace and continue cooking.

3 Glaze the onions and fry the potatoes cut to large olive-size (cocotte) to
golden brown; remove all fat from the sauce and season.
4 Garnish with the potatoes and onions.
5 Sprinkle a little chopped parsley before service.

586 Poussin polonaise

4 *single poussin*	120 g (¼ lb) white breadcrumbs	juice of ½ lemon
240 g (½ lb) farce au	7 g (¼ oz) chopped parsley	2 small hard-
gratin (Recipe 508)	120 g (¼ lb) butter	boiled eggs

1 Stuff the birds with farce.
2 Poêler as Recipe 578.
3 Toss the breadcrumbs in butter until golden colour.
4 Pass the eggs through medium sieve and add to the crumbs.
5 Dress the poussin in a large cocotte and pour over the poêlé gravy.
6 Garnish with the egg and crumbs. Add beurre noisette (Recipe 82) and
sprinkle with chopped parsley.

SAUTER AND FRYING

Deep-frying is applied to meat chiefly when it is compounded into croquette
and similar composite items. Calf's liver is sometimes thinly sliced, floured
egged and crumbed for deep-frying accompanied by fried parsley (foie de
veau frit) and corned beef or cooked meat may be made into fritters.

Shallow-frying or sauté is, however, a common and important method of
cooking meat, particularly the better small cuts which may be cooked either
plain, or pané (breadcrumbed). Meat cuts, poultry and game dishes involving
shallow-frying or sauté-ing are assigned to the chef saucier (sauce cook) in a
large professional brigade.

Cuts for Sauter.
  i Beef cuts used for sauter include: tournedos, entrecôte, rump and point
steaks.
 ii Lamb cuts so used are: noisettes, filet mignon and côtelettes. *Noisette* is
literally a hazel-nut but in cookery it also means a small round piece of
lean meat. A slice of boned loin of lamb about 2 cm (1 inch) thick, nicely
trimmed and cut wedge-shape is a noisette.
iii Veal cuts for sauter include: escalope, grenadin, médaillon, côtelette.
Grenadins de veau are thick escalopes from the noix studded with truffles and
fat. *Médaillons* are also cut from the noix, shaped as tournedos and can
also be studded with truffles or back fat.
iv Pork cuts such as escalope and côte may be treated similarly to veal in
sauté-ing.
 v Chicken, particularly suprêmes are also dealt with by sauté-ing, plain, and
pané (breadcrumbed).

GARNISHES FOR SAUTER

587 Garnishes for small cuts

These are largely interchangeable and include (particularly for tournedos sauté au beurre and dished on croûtons):

Arenberg – Tartlettes filled with carrots and spinach, slices of truffles, béarnaise sauce or sauce madère.

Baron Brisse – Sauce demi-glace, tomato concassé, artichoke bottoms, souffléd potatoes, small balls of truffle.

Catherine – Sauce bordelaise, small pommes macaire, marrow.

Chanteclère – Sauce au porto (as Recipe 44 substituting port for madeira), julienne of truffles, lamb's kidneys, cockscomb tartelettes filled with asparagus heads.

Dauphine – Sauce madère, dauphine potatoes.

Duroc – Sauce chasseur, noisette potatoes.

588 Garnishes for entrecôtes

Also for other steaks sauté au beurre:

Cecilia – Sauce béarnaise, large-grilled mushrooms, asparagus tips souffléd potatoes.

Champignons – Mushroom sauce, grilled mushrooms.

Hongroise – Sauce hongroise, plain-turned boiled potatoes.

Lyonnaise – Sauce lyonnaise.

589 Garnishes for noisettes

Also for filet mignon, and cutlets of lamb sautéd au beurre; (for noisettes, serve on croûtons cut to size):

Marseillaise – Half-glaze sauce, small tomatoes filled with olives, garlic, anchovy fillets, copeaux potatoes.

Massena – Sauce Périgueux, artichoke bottoms filled with sauce, slice of bone marrow on top.

Dubarry – Sauce madère, small cauliflower covered with mornay sauce.

Creçy – Sauce madère, glazed carrots.

Clamart – Sauce madère, artichoke bottoms filled with green peas.

Fleuriste – Demi-glace sauce, halves of tomato filled with jardinière of vegetables.

Method of Sauter. Sauter literally means 'to jump', and describes the method of tossing meat in shallow, hot fat for frying. A jumping or tossing process is also used in some forms of shallow-frying such as vegetables: for example, pommes sautées. The same technique is used in meat cookery for dishes such as sauté de bœuf Strogonoff, or foie de volaille, rognons, etc.

Generally, however, in sauté-ing small cuts such as tournedos, escalopes, noisettes, and similar cuts, the pieces are simply laid in hot butter or oil (or a mixture of both) in a sauté-pan (plat à sauter or sautoir). For small thin pieces, rapid heat may be continued; for larger ones a moderate, steady heat is preferable. The correct plat à sauter has a handled cover used when larger pieces are slowly finished or when sauce or deglazing liquor has been added. Additionally, when several pieces, such as noisettes, are required together, they may be assembled on the cover's flat surface and slid simultaneously into the hot fat.

BEEF SAUTÉS

590 Bitok à la russe

300 g (10 oz) minced, raw veal (or topside of beef)	200 ml (1½ gills) milk	125 ml (¼ pt) sauce Smitane (Recipe
60 g (2 oz) finely-chopped onions	480 g (1 lb) white breadcrumbs seasoning	591) 1 egg yolk

1 Cook the onions to golden brown in a little butter.
2 Soak the breadcrumbs in milk and squeeze to remove all liquid.
3 Mix the meat, onions, breadcrumbs together and season; bind with egg yolks.
4 Scale into 90 g (3-oz) pieces, and shape like tournedos; dip in flour and sauté in clarified butter.
5 Coat with sauce Smitane.

591 Sauce Smitane

30 g (1 oz) finely-chopped onions	30 g (1 oz) butter juice of ¼ lemon	15 ml spoon [1 tablespoon] mushroom ketchup or
250 ml (½ pt) sour cream		essence

1 Fry the onions to golden colour in butter.
2 Add the cream and reduce by half.
3 Add the mushroom ketchup and lemon juice.
4 Garnish with a little butter, season; do not strain.

592 Filet de bœuf sauté Strogonoff

30 g (1 lb) fillet beef	juice of ½ lemon	120 g (¼ lb)
30 g (1 oz) finely-chopped shallots	pinch of tarragon	butter
¼ clove crushed garlic	125 ml (¼ pt) double cream	seasoning

1 Cut the fillet into rough julienne or small escalopes.
2 Cook the shallots to golden colour in butter in sauté pan.
3 Quickly sauté the escalopes in butter; drain and add to shallots.
4 Reduce the cream with the meat and shallots; add the tarragon, a squeeze of lemon juice, thicken with butter; and season.

593 Filet de bœuf sauté à la minute hongroise

As Recipe 592 but dust meat with 7 g (¼ oz) paprika before sauté-ing.

594 Hamburger or Hamburg steak

500 g (1 lb) minced rump or
topside of beef
60 g (2 oz) finely-chopped
onions
5 eggs

2 large onions
7 g (¼ oz) chopped
parsley
120 g (¼ lb) flour
seasoning

125 ml (¼ pt) sauce
piquante
(Recipe 46)
125 ml (1 gill) milk

1 Cook the chopped onions to golden colour.
2 Mix the meat, onions and parsley together.
3 Bind with 1 whole egg and season.
4 Shape into rounds and scale at 90 g (3 oz) each.
5 Flour and sauté in clarified butter.
6 Place a fried egg on top of each hamburger and garnish the dish with French-fried onions.
7 Serve separately sauce piquante.

595 Tournedos Rossini

4, 180 g (6-oz) tournedos
4 round croûtons
120 g (¼ lb) butter

4 medallions of foie gras
4 slices truffle
125 ml (¼ pt) Madeira

125 ml (¼ pt)
demi-glace
(Recipe 29)

1 Cook the tournedos in clarified butter (Recipe 84).
2 When nearly cooked add the croûtons and cook to golden brown.
3 Remove the string and dress the tournedos on the buttered croûtons.
4 Déglacer the pan with Madeira, add the demi-glace and simmer.
5 Gently heat the foie gras and place on top of the tournedos.
6 Butter and adjust seasoning of sauce, strain over the tournedos and finish off with slice of truffle.

LAMB AND MUTTON SAUTÉS

596 Côtelette d'agneau Reform – Lamb cutlet Reform

8, 90 g (3-oz) cutlets
125 ml (¼ pt) sauce
Reform (Recipe 48)
240 g (½ lb) white bread-
crumbs
7 g (¼ oz) chopped ham

7 g (¼ oz) chopped tongue
7 g (¼ oz) chopped parsley

Garnish: 15 g (½ oz) of cooked and julienne-cut:
ham, tongue, gherkins, egg white, beetroot,
truffles

62 ml (½ gill) oil
60 g (2 oz) butter

1 Add the chopped ham, tongue, and parsley to white breadcrumbs.
2 Trim and flatten the cutlets with the batte.
3 Pané the cutlets in flour, egg and prepared crumbs.
4 Sauté both sides of cutlet to golden brown gently in oil.
5 Toss the garnish in a little butter and dress the cutlets in the form of a crown.
6 Finish with beurre noisette (Recipe 82) and place a frill on each cutlet.
7 Serve the sauce Reform separately in sauce-boat.

597 Epigramme d'agneau provençale

500 g (1 *lb*) *breast of lamb*	120 g (¼ *lb*) *duxelle*	1 *small carrot*
4 *lamb cutlets*	(*Recipe* 101)	1 *small onion clouté*
4 *small tomatoes*	125 *ml* (¼ *pt*) *tomato*	62 *ml* (½ *gill*) *oil*
240 g (½ *lb*) *white bread-*	*sauce* (*Recipe* 34)	*seasoning*
crumbs		

1 Cook the breast of lamb in water with a carrot and onion clouté.
2 When cooked, remove the bones and press; when cold, cut into diamond shapes, 4 cm by 4 cm (2 inches by 2 inches).
3 Pané the diamonds and cutlets and sauter gently in oil until golden brown.
4 Blanch the tomatoes and remove the seeds; stuff with the duxelle.
5 Arrange the cutlets and epigrammes neatly on a dish, garnish with the stuffed tomatoes, and finish with a beurre noisette (Recipe 82).
6 Serve tomato sauce (Recipe 34) separately.

598 Noisette d'agneau niçoise

8 *noisettes* [90 g (3 *oz*) *each*]	8 *croûtons*	360 g (¾ *lb*) *château*
4 *small tomatoes*	180 g (6 *oz*) *French*	*potatoes*
125 *ml* (¼ *pt*) *sauce Madère*	*beans*	(*Recipe* 902)
(*Recipe* 44)	*seasoning*	

1 Cook château potatoes in butter and drain.
2 Cook the French beans and arrange in small bouquets in serving dish.
3 Blanch the tomatoes and cook whole in butter.
4 Sauté the noisettes quickly in butter; season.
5 Shallow fry the croûtons in oil.
6 Déglacer the noisette pan with sauce Madère.
7 Arrange the noisettes on the croûtons and arrange on the serving dish in the form of a crown.
8 Add the tomatoes and potatoes to dish.
9 Strain the sauce on the noisettes.
10 Sprinkle a little chopped parsley over the potatoes.

VEAL SAUTÉS

599 Côte de veau en cocotte – Veal cutlet in cocotte

4, 300 g (10-*oz*) *veal cutlets*	240 g (½ *lb*) *diced mush-*	120 g (¼ *lb*) *butter*
500 g (1 *lb*) *potatoes*	*rooms*	*seasoning*
12 *glazed onions*		

1 Dust cutlets with flour and season.
2 Sauté in clarified butter.
3 Toss the mushrooms in butter and cook the cocotte potatoes (cut to olive size) to golden brown.
4 Mix the onions, potatoes and mushrooms, sprinkling over cutlets when cooked.
5 Dress them in a large casserole and finish off with a beurre noisette (Recipe 82) and chopped parsley.

600 Côte de veau bonne femme

Prepare as Recipe 599 omitting mushrooms.
Veal cutlets may, of course, be prepared in similar style to veal escalopes.

601 Côtelette de veau Pojarski

500 g (1 *lb*) *veal fillet*	1 *egg white*	125 *ml* (1 *gill*) *milk*
120 g ($\frac{1}{4}$ *lb*) *white breadcrumbs*	62 *ml* ($\frac{1}{2}$ *gill*) *cream*	*seasoning*
15 g ($\frac{1}{2}$ *oz*) *butter*	*clarified butter*	

1 Remove all nerves from the veal, mince finely and pass through a sieve.
2 Pound the veal in a mortar and bind with the egg whites and beat in the cream.
3 Soak the crumbs in milk, squeeze out all moisture (panada).
4 Mix the veal and panada together and season and add 30 g (1 oz) butter.
5 Shape as cutlets, flour, egg and crumb.
6 Sauté both sides in clarified butter (Recipe 84).

602 Fricadelles de veau

360 g ($\frac{3}{4}$ *lb*) *lean veal*	1 *egg*	*grated nutmeg*
180 g (6 *oz*) *butter*	7 g ($\frac{1}{4}$ *oz*) *salt*	
75 g (2$\frac{1}{2}$ *oz*) *milk-soaked breadcrumbs*	30 g (1 *oz*) *chopped, cooked onions*	

1 Remove all fat and gristle from veal and mince very finely.
2 Squeeze all moisture from breadcrumbs and mix the veal, eggs, onions and breadcrumbs together with the butter; season.
3 Divide into portions approximately 100 g (3$\frac{1}{2}$ oz) each and shape into quoits.
4 Dust with flour and cook both sides in clarified butter.
5 Serve with sauce Robert (Recipe 49) separately.

603 Escalope de veau Holstein

4, 180 g (6-*oz*) *escalopes*	5 *eggs*	12 *anchovy fillets*
240 g ($\frac{1}{2}$ *lb*) *white breadcrumbs*	240 g ($\frac{1}{4}$ *lb*) *butter*	4 *slices lemon*

1 Flatten escalopes with the batte, flour, egg and crumb.
2 Sauté and garnish with lemon slices, fried eggs topped with a criss-cross of anchovies.
3 Finish with beurre noisette (Recipe 82).

604 Escalope de veau milanaise

4, 180 g (6-*oz*) *escalopes*	180 g (6 *oz*) *spaghetti*	15 g ($\frac{1}{2}$ *oz*)
120 g ($\frac{1}{4}$ *lb*) *butter*	62 *ml* ($\frac{1}{2}$ *gill*) *tomato*	*Parmesan cheese*
4 *lemon slices*	*sauce* (*Recipe* 34)	*seasoning*
360 g ($\frac{3}{4}$ *lb*) *white bread-crumbs*	60 g (2 *oz*) *tomato concassé*	1 *egg*

7 g ($\frac{1}{4}$ *oz*) *each, julienne cooked: ham, tongue, mushroom, truffles*

1 Soak the ham, tongue, and truffles in a little sherry.
2 Flour, egg, and crumb the escalopes.

3 Sauté in clarified butter and oil.
4 Cook spaghetti 18 minutes in boiling water and drain.
5 Toss in butter with the garnish, mix in tomato concassé and sauce, sprinkle in cheese; season.
6 Dress the garnish alongside of escalopes and garnish each escalope with lemon slices and finish with beurre noisette (Recipe 82).

605 Escalope de veau napolitaine

Garnish napolitaine:

4, 180 g (6-oz) escalopes	125 ml (1 gill) tomato	15 g (½ oz)
180 g (6 oz) spaghetti	sauce	Parmesan cheese
	(Recipe 34)	120 g (¼ lb) butter
		3 tomato concassé

1 Prepare and cook escalopes as Recipe 604.
2 Cook spaghetti 18 minutes in boiling water and drain.
3 Toss in butter, mix with tomato concassé and tomato sauce; season and sprinkle with cheese.
4 Dress the garnish alongside the escalopes with a slice of lemon on each escalope.
5 Place a thread of tomato sauce (cordon) around the dish; finish with beurre noisette (Recipe 82).

606 Escalope de veau suédoise

4, 180 g (6-oz) escalopes	30 g (1 oz) finely-	½ glass brandy
200 ml (1½ gills) double cream	chopped shallots	juice of ¼ lemon
240 g (½ lb) sliced mushrooms	180 g (6 oz) butter	

1 Dust the escalopes with flour and season.
2 Sauté in butter and remove from pan.
3 Sweat the shallots, add the mushrooms, and sweat until cooked under cover, then add brandy.
4 Add the cream and reduce to half its quantity, draw to side of stove, add lemon juice and monter au beurre (as defined in glossary).
5 Season and coat sauce over the escalopes.

PORK SAUTÉS

607 Côtelette de porc charcutière – Pork cutlet charcutière

4, 240 g (8-oz) pork cutlets	82 ml (⅛ pt) white wine	30 g (1 oz) butter
30 g (1 oz) finely-chopped onions	2·5 ml spoon [½ teaspoon] mustard	15 g (½ oz) julienne of gherkins
250 ml (½ pt) demi-glace (Recipe 29)	15 g (½ oz) meat glaze (Recipe 13)	seasoning

1 Trim and sauté the cutlets.
For the sauce:
2 Fry the onions gently without colouring in the sauté pan.

3 Add white wine and reduce.
4 Add demi-glace and further reduce.
5 Add diluted mustard; season and garnish with gherkin julienne, and finish with meat glaze and butter.
6 Serve sauce separately in sauce-boat.

608 Côtelette de porc flamande

> 4, 240 g (8 oz) cutlets   *seasoning*   60 g (2 oz) butter
> 4 apple rings

1 Dust the cutlets with flour and season.
2 Partly fry both sides, place the apple rings on top and finish cooking in the oven.
3 Add a beurre noisette (Recipe 82) before serving.

609 Escalope de porc Zingara

> 4 pork escalopes   125 ml (¼ pt) demi-glace (Recipe 29)
> 4 slices cooked ham   62 ml (⅛ pt) tomato sauce (Recipe 34)
> 62 ml (⅛ pt) white wine   30 g (1 oz) julienne of cooked ham, tongue,
> 60 g (2 oz) butter   mushroom and truffle

1 Remove all nerves and sinews from the pork fillet and flatten with the batte.
2 Flour the escalopes and sauté in butter; cut the ham the size of the escalope.
3 Place the previously-heated ham on top of the escalope.
4 Déglacér the pan with the wine and add the half-glaze, tomato sauce and mushroom liquor (resulting from mushroom cooking); reduce for a few minutes.
5 Add the julienne of ham, tongue, mushrooms, and truffles; season and finish with butter.
6 Surround the escalopes with the sauce.

610 Escalope de porc viennoise

> 4 escalopes   7 g (¼ oz) capers   12 anchovy fillets
> 1 hard-boiled egg   62 ml (½ gill) oil   4 g (⅛ oz) chopped parsley
> 4 stoned olives   4 slices lemon   120 g (¼ lb) butter

1 Prepare the escalopes, flour, egg, and crumb.
2 Sauté to golden colour in oil and butter.
3 Pass the egg yolks and the whites separately through a medium sieve.
4 Arrange the eggs, parsley, and capers rainbow fashion on each side of the centre of escalopes.
5 Garnish each escalope with a criss-cross of anchovy fillets, olives, and slice of lemon.
6 Finish with beurre noisette (Recipe 82).

Note. Veal escalopes are similarly prepared.

OFFAL SAUTÉS

611 Brochettes de rognons – Skewered kidneys

8 *sheep's kidneys*	120 g (¼ lb) breadcrumbs	120 g (¼ lb) straw
120 g (¼ lb) lean bacon	seasoning	potatoes
240 g (½ lb) small	30 g (1 oz) melted butter	(Recipe 929)
mushrooms		1 bunch watercress

1 Remove the skin from kidneys.
2 Cut into roundels 1 cm (one-third inch) thick.
3 Season kidneys and sauté quickly in butter.
4 Impalé them on skewers alternating them with 2 cm (1-inch) squares of blanched lean bacon and slices of sauté mushrooms.
5 Brush with melted butter, sprinkle with breadcrumbs and grill.
6 Serve on the skewer and garnish with straw potatoes and watercress.

612 Cervelles au beurre noir – Brains with black butter

4 *sheep's or calf's brains*	1 *bay-leaf*	2·5 *ml spoon* [½ *teaspoon*]
30 g (1 oz) sliced carrots	1 sprig thyme	salt
15 g (½ oz) thinly-sliced	1 sprig (or stalk)	7 g (¼ oz) chopped parsley
onions	parsley	30 g (1 oz) butter
10 ml spoon [½ table-	seasoning	lemon juice
spoon] vinegar		

1 Soak the brains in cold salted water.
2 Remove the membrane.
3 Boil 500 ml (1 pt) water with the onions, parsley stalk, carrots, thyme, bay-leaf and salt till the vegetables are cooked; then add the brains and simmer for 5 minutes and drain.
4 Sauté the brains gently in clarified butter (Recipe 84) and season.
5 Cook the 30 g (1 oz) butter to dark noisette stage and then add the vinegar, pour over the brains and garnish with chopped parsley.

613 Escalope de ris de veau maréchale – Escalope of sweetbread maréchale

4 *calves' sweetbreads*	16 *asparagus tips*	120 g (¼ lb) butter
4 *slices truffle*		

1 Blanch the sweetbreads, skin and press.
2 Cut into escalopes and season.
3 Flour, egg, and crumb and sauté to a golden colour in clarified butter (Recipe 84).
4 Garnish with asparagus tips and slices of truffle.
5 Finish with beurre noisette (Recipe 82).

614 Foie de veau au lard – Liver and bacon

500 g (1 lb) calves' liver	30 g (1 oz) flour	seasoning
8 slices back bacon	30 g (1 oz) butter	

1 Skin the liver and cut into medium slices.
2 Dip in seasoned flour and fry both sides quickly in clarified butter.
3 Garnish with grilled bacon.
4 Finish with beurre noisette (Recipe 82).

615 Foie de veau lyonnaise – Calves' liver lyonnaise

500 g (1 lb) calves' liver   190 ml (1½ gills) lyonnaise sauce (Recipe 43)

Prepare and cook as for foie de veau au lard (Recipe 614), but omit the bacon and coat with Lyonnaise sauce.

616 Foie de veau aux fines herbes

Prepare as Recipe 615 but coat with the following sauce:

616a Sauce fines herbes or Sauce Bercy (for meat)

30 g (1 oz) finely-chopped shallots   500 ml (1 pt) demi-glace   120 g (¼ lb)
125 ml (¼ pt) wine (white)   (Recipe 29)   butter
15 g (½ oz) meat glaze (Recipe 13)   15 g (½ oz) fine herbs   seasoning

1 Sweat the shallots in 30 g (1 oz) of butter.
2 Make a reduction of white wine.
3 Add the demi-glacé and simmer for 10 minutes.
4 Add meat glaze and herbs.
5 Blend in the butter, adjust seasoning; do not strain.

617 Ris de veau sauté St Germain – Calves' sweetbreads St Germain

1 kg (2 lb) calves' sweet-   250 g (½ lb) fresh-pea   120 g (¼ lb) butter
  breads   purée   7 g (¼ oz) cooked peas
500 g (1 lb) pommes   250 ml (½ pt) sauce béar-   500 g (1 lb) glazed
  parisiennes (Recipe 904)   naise (Recipe 73)   carrots

1 Blanch, trim, and sauté sweetbreads, basting frequently with butter.
2 Garnish bouquets of potatoes and carrots.
3 Serve sauce béarnaise and pea purée separately.
4 Finish with beurre noisette (Recipe 82) and fried parsley.

618 Rognon de veau bordelaise

4 kidneys   120 g (¼ lb) sliced cepes   4 heart-shaped
190 ml (1½ gills) sauce   15 g (½ oz) diced bone   croûtons
  bordelaise (Recipe 35)   marrow

1 Skin and cut the kidney into small escalopes.
2 Sauté quickly in clarified butter and drain.
3 Mix the kidney with the sauce, marrow and cepes.
4 Garnish with the croûtons, the ends dipped in parsley.

619 Rognons sautés chasseur

8 sheep's kidneys   62 ml (⅛ pt) tomato   7 g (¼ oz) chopped onions
125 ml (¼ pt) demi-   sauce (Recipe 34)   30 g (1 oz) butter
  glace (Recipe 29)   180 g (6 oz) mushrooms   125 ml (¼ pt) white wine
7 g (¼ oz) meat glaze   7 g (¼ oz) fines herbes   120 g (¼ lb) tomato
  (Recipe 13)   concassé

1 Skin and cut the kidneys into small escalopes.
2 Fry the kidneys quickly in butter, drain and keep warm.

3 Sweat the onions in a sauté pan in butter, add the sliced mushrooms and make a reduction of the white wine.

4 Add the tomato concassé, moisten with the demi-glace and tomato sauce and simmer for 10 minutes; skim, add the meat glaze and blend in the butter, add the fines herbes and season.

5 Mix the kidneys with the sauce and garnish with heart-shaped croûtons.

620 Rognons sautés Turbigo – Kidneys sautés Turbigo

8 *sheep's kidneys*	30 g (1 oz) *finely-chopped shallots*	*seasoning*
½ *glass sherry*	250 ml (½ pt) *demi-glace (Recipe 29)*	7 g (¼ oz) *chopped*
9 *heart-shaped*	60 g (2 oz) *butter*	*parsley*
croûtons	120 g (¼ lb) *mushrooms*	9 *chipolatas*

1 Blanch and grill the chipolatas.

2 Remove the skin from kidney and cut into half lengthwise.

3 Peel (optional if cultivated), remove stalks and wash the mushrooms. Cut into quarters and toss in butter.

4 Sauté the kidney quickly in butter and drain.

5 Fry shallots in a little butter until golden brown.

6 Deglaze the pan with the sherry.

7 Add demi-glacé and reduce by half; seaon and enrich with butter.

8 Add the kidney and mushrooms to sauce.

9 Garnish with chipolatas, heart shaped croûtons (croûton ends dipped in parsley).

CHICKEN SAUTÉS

621 Sauté of chicken

1 Thoroughly clean the bird.

2 Cut off the legs, pull gently from the bird and cut each leg in two pieces at the join.

3 Cut off the wings (pinch up a piece of flesh between the thumb and forefinger before cutting).

4 Cut the body in half, cutting through rib cage.

5 Cut the breast diagonally across in two pieces.

6 Cut the base or undercarriage in three pieces.

7 This yields 8 pieces. The undercarriage pieces are cooked and used to build up the centre of the dish when serving, although not served as portions.

8 Place the pieces in a sauté pan with oil or clarified butter (Recipe 84).

9 Colour quickly and finish the cooking under cover. (White meat will cook before dark meat).

Note. Alternatively the wing, with trimmed wing-bone only, may be used as a suprême and legs may be boned and prepared as a separate dish. Pieces may be sautéd, plain, or panéd. Game birds may be similarly prepared.

622 Typical Chicken Sauté Garnishes

Poulet sauté Beaulieu: Deglacér with white wine, add demi-glacé garnish of artichoke bottoms, tomatoes, stoned olives, and cocotte potatoes.

Poulet sauté Bordelaise: Deglacér with red wine, add demi-glacé garnish of shallots, quarters of artichokes ,French fried onions, and sautéd potatoes.

623 Typical Suprêmes Sautées Garnishes

Suprême de volaille Maréchale: Egg and crumb; garnish of asparagus tips, slice of truffle, beurre noisette.
Suprême de volaille Richelieu: Egg and crumb; garnish top with parsley butter and slice of truffle.
Suprême de volaille Maryland: Egg and crumb; add garnish Maryland.

624 Ballotine de volaille chasseur – Chicken ballotine chasseur

250 ml ($\frac{1}{2}$ pt) sauce chasseur   125 g ($\frac{1}{4}$ lb) fine force-   4 raw chicken-legs
    (Recipe 38)   ment (Recipe 195)

1 Bone the legs neatly without cutting the drumstick.
2 Stuff with the forcemeat and sew up.
3 Sauté in butter, remove the string and coat with sauce chasseur.

625 Poulet sauté archiduc – Chicken sauté archiduc

1, 2 kg (4-lb) chicken   90 g (3 oz) finely-chopped   juice of $\frac{1}{4}$ lemon
5 slices truffle   onions   120 g ($\frac{1}{4}$ lb) butter
200 ml (1$\frac{1}{2}$ gills) fresh cream 125 ml ($\frac{1}{4}$ pt) chicken   15 ml ($\frac{1}{8}$ gill)
seasoning   velouté (Recipe 37)   Madeira
$\frac{1}{2}$ glass brandy

1 Joint the bird as for sauté (Recipe 621).
2 Fry in butter without colouring.
3 Add the onions, previously cooked in butter, and complete the cooking of the chicken under cover.
4 When cooked, withdraw the pieces and keep hot.
5 Moisten the onions with brandy and reduce; add the cream and velouté and rub through fine chinois.
6 Finish the sauce with butter, Madeira, and lemon juice; pour sauce over chicken.
7 Decorate with slices of truffle.

626 Poulet sauté arlésienne

1, 2 kg (4-lb) chicken   190 ml (1$\frac{1}{2}$ gills) demi-   9 heart-shaped
125 ml ($\frac{1}{4}$ pt) white wine   glace (Recipe 29)   croûtons
240 g ($\frac{1}{2}$ lb) concassé   190 ml (1$\frac{1}{2}$ gills) tomato 7 g ($\frac{1}{4}$ oz) chopped
tomatoes   sauce (Recipe 34)   parsley
1 egg-plant   1 clove chopped
1 large onion   garlic

1 Cut the chicken as for sauté (Recipe 621), sauté in butter and remove from the pan when cooked.
2 Rinse the pan with the white wine and reduce; add garlic, tomato sauce, demi-glace and reduce by one-third.
3 Peel the egg-plant, cut into roundels, dip in flour, and deep-fry.
4 Slice the onions into rings and French-fry.
5 Toss the tomato concassé in butter.
6 Season the sauce and finish with butter.

7 Arrange the chicken neatly on a dish and coat with the sauce.
8 Garnish with alternate bouquets of tomato, onions, egg-plant, and croûtons.
9 Sprinkle a little chopped parsley on the chicken.

627 Poulet sauté chasseur

1, 2 kg (4-lb) chicken	240 g (½ lb) tomato	90 g (3 oz) butter
190 ml (1½ gills) demi-	concassé	½ glass brandy
glace (Recipe 29)	7 g (¼ oz) finely-	125 ml (¼ pt) white wine
62 ml (⅛ pt) tomato sauce	chopped onions	15 g (½ oz) meat glaze
(Recipe 34)	7 g (¼ oz) fines herbes	(Recipe 13)
9 heart-shaped croûtons	6 sliced mushrooms	
chopped parsley		

1 Cut the chicken as for sauté (Recipe 621); season, and dust with flour.
2 Sauter in butter until cooked; (the white meat will cook quicker than the darker flesh).
3 Sauté the chopped onions in the residue and rinse the pan with the white wine.
4 Add the sliced mushrooms and cook for a few minutes; then add the tomato concassé.
5 Add the 2 sauces, brandy, herbs, and meat glaze and reduce to 190 ml (1½ gills); check the sauce for seasoning and consistency; enrich with a little butter.
6 Arrange the chicken neatly on the serving dish and coat with the sauce.
7 Garnish with the croûtons fried in butter – the ends dipped in parsley. (Though not 'classic', these enhance the dish.)

628 Poulet sauté hongroise

1, 2 kg (4-lb) chicken	180 g (6 oz) tomato concassé	125 ml (¼ pt)
30 g (1 oz) finely-	120 g (¼ lb) rice (rice pilaff	cream
chopped onions	Recipe 366)	120 g (¼ lb)
15 g (½ oz) paprika		butter

1 Cut the chicken as for sauté (Recipe 621), sauté in butter without colouring.
2 Withdraw from the sauté pan, sweat the onions, add the paprika and tomato concassé; replace the chicken and finish cooking under cover.
3 When the chicken is cooked, withdraw; add the cream to the sauce, enrich with butter, and season.
4 Mix a little cooked tomato concassé with the rice and arrange as a border.
5 Dress the chicken to the centre and coat with the sauce.

629 Poulet sauté Marengo

1, 2 kg (4-lb) chicken	125 ml (¼ pt) white wine	1 clove bruised garlic
4 heart-shaped croûtons	4 crayfish cooked in	4 stoned olives
4 French-fried eggs	court-bouillon	250 ml (½ pt) half-glaze
(deep fried)	(Recipe 371)	(Recipe 29)
4 slices truffle	8 turned mushrooms	62 ml (⅛ pt) tomato
62 ml (⅛ pt) oil	240 g (½ lb) tomato	sauce (Recipe 34)
30 g (1 oz) butter	concassé	chopped parsley

1 Cut as for sauté (621); colour the pieces in oil and finish cooking under cover.
2 When cooked, pour away the oil; déglacé the pan with the white wine; add garlic, tomato concassé, half-glaze, tomato sauce, and reduce to correct consistency; season, add the chicken, and simmer for a few minutes at the side of the stove.
3 Dress the chicken in crown-shape, cover with the sauce.
4 Garnish with the cooked mushrooms, crayfish, olives, and French-fried eggs.
5 Complete the garnish with croûtons fried in butter – the ends dipped in parsley.

630 Poulet sauté Maryland

1, 2 *kg* (4-*lb*) *chicken*	4 *slices bacon*	125 *ml* (¼ *pt*) *sauce*
1 *tin sweetcorn*	120 *g* (¼ *lb*) *butter*	*Raifort* (*Recipe* 99)
1 *egg yolk*	4 *small croquette potatoes*	*fried parsley*
2 *bananas* .	(*Recipe* 913)	*white breadcrumbs*
4 *small grilled tomatoes*		

1 Cut the chicken as for sauté (Recipe 621).
2 Flour, egg, and crumb; and sauté in clarified butter (Recipe 84).
3 Drain the liquid from the sweetcorn; bind with egg yolks and a little flour; 8 small pancakes 0·5 cm (¼-inch) thick, 4 cm (2 inches) in diameter and fry.
4 Grill the bacon, bananas, and tomatoes.
5 Arrange the chicken on the centre of dish; garnish around neatly and finish with beurre noisette.
6 Decorate with fried parsley.
7 Serve hot horse-radish sauce (Raifort) separately.

631 Suprême de volaille Maryland

Prepare as Recipe 630.

632 Suprême de volaille en papillote – Wing fillet of chicken en papillote

2, 1·5 *kg* (3-*lb*) *chickens*	4 *sheets grease-*	*oil*
125 *ml* (¼ *pt*) *sauce.italienne* (*Recipe* 42)	*proof paper*	120 *g* (¼ *lb*)
4 *slices cooked ham*	*seasoning*	*butter*
30 *g* (1 *oz*) *flour*		

1 Cut the greaseproof paper into large heart-shapes and oil both sides.
2 Flour and season the suprêmes and sauter in butter to a golden colour.
3 Place a slice of ham on each side of the prepared paper; lay the suprême on top of the ham and a tablespoon of the sauce on top of each.
4 Fold the paper over and seal securely.
5 Place in a hot dish containing oil and soufflé them for 2 or 3 minutes in a hot oven; serve in the papers.

633 Suprême de volaille maréchale

2, 1·5 *kg* (3-*lb*) *chickens*	120 *g* (¼ *lb*) *butter*	125 *ml* (¼ *pt*) *jus lié*
16 *asparagus tips*	4 *slices truffle*	(*Recipe* 30)

1 Remove the suprême from chicken.
2 Season, flour, egg and crumb; fry both sides in butter.
3 Garnish with asparagus tips, thread of jus lié and beurre noisette (Recipe 82).
4 Decorate with slices of truffle.

SAUTÉS OF POULTRY OFFAL

634 Désirs de Mascotte – Cock's kidneys Mascotte

45 g (1½ oz) butter   2 whole truffles   seasoning
12 fresh cocks' kidneys   125 ml (¼ pt) demi-glace (Recipe 29)   glass sherry
6 round croûtons   ¼ lemon juice

1 Season the kidneys with salt, pepper, and cayenne.
2 Sauté them in butter for a few minutes and drain – keep warm.
3 Rinse the pan with the sherry, add the demi-glacé, season and enrich the sauce with butter; add the kidneys and sliced truffle.
4 Fry the croûtons in butter and dress the kidneys on them.
5 Sprinkle with a little parsley.

635 Brochettes de foies de volaille – Skewered chicken livers

240 g (½ lb) chicken livers   120 g (¼ lb) white bread-   1 bunch watercress
120 g (¼ lb) mushrooms   crumbs   4 silver skewers
4 bay-leaves   240 g (½ lb) straw potatoes   120 g (¼ lb) bacon
60 g (2 oz) butter   (Recipe 929)

1 Sauté the livers quickly in butter.
2 Cut the bacon in pieces 2 cm (1 inch) square, 0·5 cm (¼ inch) thick, and blanch.
3 Cut the mushrooms into pieces of 2 cm (1 inch) and sauté in butter.
4 Impale the liver, bacon, and mushrooms alternately on each skewer with a bay-leaf.
5 Brush over with melted butter, sprinkle with crumbs, grill and baste.
6 Serve on the skewers and garnish with straw potatoes.

636 Foies de volaille sautés au vin rouge – Sauté of chicken livers in red wine

360 g (¾ lb) chicken livers   45 g (1½ oz) finely-chopped   90 g (3 oz) butter
125 ml (¼ pt) red wine   shallots   7 g (¼ oz) meat
190 ml (1½ gills) demi-   1 sprig thyme   glaze (Recipe 13)
glace (Recipe 29)   1 bay-leaf

1 Remove gall bladder and cut into 2 cm (1-inch) pieces.
2 Quickly fry in butter and drain.
3 Sweat the shallots in sauté pan and déglacer with red wine; add the demi-glace and herbs and reduce by half; add the meat glaze.
4 Season, strain, and enrich with butter; strain over the livers.

HARE SAUTÉ

637 Râble de lièvre à l'allemande – Saddle of hare à l'allemande

2 *saddles of hare*	120 g (¼ *lb*) *butter*	120 g (¼ *lb*) *fat bacon*
250 *ml* (½ *pt*) *fresh cream*	15 g (½ *oz*) *meat glaze*	*seasoning*
500 *ml* (1 *pt*) *red-wine*	(*Recipe* 13)	*juice of* ¼ *lemon*
marinade (*Recipe* 124)		

1 Remove the skin and nerves from the saddles and piqué with fat bacon.
2 Place in the red-wine marinade for 2 days, turning frequently.
3 Remove the saddles and vegetables from the marinade and dry well.
4 Brown the saddles in butter and set to cook with the vegetables from the marinade.
5 When nearly cooked, remove the vegetables, pour in the cream and complete the cooking, basting with cream frequently.
6 When cooked, remove the saddles, dress on a large entrée dish, and keep warm.
7 Reduce the cooking-liquor, add meat glaze, lemon juice and enrich with butter; season.
8 Strain the sauce over the saddles.

BOILING AND POACHING

638 Boiling of meats

1 Boiling is cooking by immersion in boiling liquid; usually water or stock in the case of meats.
2 The boiling temperature of water, 100° C (212° F) is raised to 104° C (220° F) when salted.
3 Once the boiling process is well started it is normal to reduce the heat so that meat is simmered (boiled very gently).
4 Most boiled meats and poultry dishes are the responsibility of the chef saucier (sauce cook) in a large kitchen brigade.

Cooking times. Boiling time varies according to the thickness of joints and is generally 20 minutes per 500 g (lb). Large joints of salt beef may take up to 25 or 30 minutes per 500 g (lb). For fowls allow 15 to 20 minutes per 500 g (lb) according to age; 2 kg (4-lb) to 2·5 kg (5-lb) birds will take from 1 to 1½ hours.

Quantities. As the cooking-loss when boiling meat may vary between 15 per cent to 20 per cent, this should be taken into account when estimating recipe quantities. Thus, for 8, 90 g (3-oz) portions of boiled silverside, 750 g (1½-lb) boneless meat will not suffice and at least 1 kg (2 lb) should be allowed. For larger joints the percentage-loss will be less and the net amount required will be nearer the portion's total weight.

639 Suitable boiling joints

While most of the cheaper cuts of meat and also older fowls and game may be boiled, the most suitable for plainer, boiled dishes are:

Beef	*Mutton*	*Pork*	*Bacon*	*Veal*
Silverside	Leg	Hand and spring	Gammon	Head
Brisket	Head	Head and feet	Forehock	
Plate		(for brawn)	Collar	

Note. Lamb and veal (except for heads) are seldom plainly boiled. Beef and pork joints are frequently pickled in brine.

640 Poaching

The method of poaching is used for fish and eggs and also for white meat, particularly poultry. In practice, poached poultry does not materially differ from boiled poultry; though, traditionally, flesh (for example fish-flesh) is actually half-steamed when poached as the piece is only partially covered with liquor and, once boiling is well started, it is covered by a lid (or, usually for fish, buttered paper) and finished in a moderate oven.

641 Garnishes

Garnishes and accompaniments for boiled pieces include:
Alsacienne: Sauerkraut (choucroute) with bacon and pommes vapeur.
Anglaise: Plainly-boiled vegetable garnish e.g., cabbage, carrot, turnip and boiled potato.
Flamande: Bacon, cabbage, carrot, turnip and potato.

642 Boiling fresh meat

1 Wipe the meat and remove any surplus fat.
2 Tie the meat in shape and place in sufficient boiling water or stock to cover.
3 Add whole vegetables to flavour the cooking liquor or stock.
4 Boil quickly for the first 10 minutes to seal and retain the meat juices.
5 Simmer until tender.

643 Boiling salt beef

1 Wash the salt beef in cold water to draw out salt.
2 Place in cold water, bring slowly to boiling-point and skim thoroughly.
3 Simmer gently; add mixed root-vegetables to flavour the cooking-liquor.

644 Boiled silverside of beef and dumplings

1 Silverside to be pickled (Recipe 132) at least 5 days.
2 Wash and cook as Recipe 643.
3 When cooked, garnish with turned carrots and turnips and some peas for colour.
4 Cook the dumplings (Recipe 645) in the cooking-liquor.

645 Paste for dumplings

240 g (½ lb) flour	90 g (3 oz) suet	salt
7 g (¼ oz) baking powder	water to mix	

1 Skin and chop the suet finely using a little of the measured flour to prevent sticking.
2 Sift flour, baking powder and salt; mix all ingredients with cold water to form a slack dough.
3 Prepare in 60 g (2-oz) portions; cook for 20 minutes in the stock.

646 Boiled leg of mutton and caper sauce

1 For whole leg [approx. 3·5 kg (7 lb)] remove pelvic bone and tie up.
2 Soak in cold water overnight and wipe.
3 Place in cold water, bring to the boil removing scum; add a little salt and bouquet garni, onion clouté, and some whole vegetables.
4 Turn some carrots and turnips, and cook in some of the stock.
5 When the meat is cooked, garnish with the vegetables and a few fresh peas for colour and serve a little stock.

Note. Caper sauce, Recipe 64, should be made from the cooking-liquor. Parsley sauce is also suitable.

647 Boiled salt pork

1 Cook as for boiled, pickled beef.
2 Garnish with cabbage, butter beans, or pease pudding.

648 Boiled ham

1 For whole gammon [approx. 7 kg (14 lb)] soak overnight in cold water.
2 Saw a small piece off the knuckle-end.
3 Place in cold water with 2 apples clouté with cloves.
4 Simmer approximately 4 hours and allow to become cold in the cooking liquor.
5 Remove skin and trim.

Note. Cider, up to half the total quantity, may be added to the water for cooking.

BOILED OFFAL DISHES

649 Tête de veau vinaigrette – Calf's head vinaigrette

1 *calf's head*	15 *ml spoon* [1 *tablespoon*] *vinegar*	1 *bay-leaf*
30 *g* (1 *oz*) *flour*	15 *g* (½ *oz*) *thinly-sliced carrots*	1 *sprig thyme*
1 *lemon juice*	15 *g* (½ *oz*) *thinly-sliced onions*	*seasoning*

1 Scald the calf's head before boning.
2 Begin boning the head down the centre towards the nose and remove the ears.
3 Remove the brains and tongue, and place the brains to soak in cold salted water.
4 Prepare a blanc thus: Mix the flour in 2 litres (2 quarts) of water, add the lemon juice, bring to the boil and add 15 ml spoon [1 tablespoon] salt.

5 Cut the calf's head in 4 cm (2-inch) squares and place to cook in the blanc.
6 Cook the tongue in a separate pan and skin when cooked.
7 Remove all the membranes from the brain and cook for 2 to 4 minutes in 500 ml (1 pint) of water with the onions, carrots, thyme, bay-leaf and a little salt; then sauter the brains in butter.
8 Place the calf's head in a large cocotte with a little of the cooking-liquor and garnish with slices of tongue and brains; serve hot.

Note. The ears may be cooked and sliced for hors d'œuvre.

650 Sauce vinaigrette for calf's head

250 *ml* ($\frac{1}{2}$ *pt*) *olive oil*   30 *g* (1 *oz*) *chopped capers*   15 *g* ($\frac{1}{2}$ *oz*) *finely-*
125 *ml* ($\frac{1}{4}$ *pt*) *vinegar*   15 *g* ($\frac{1}{2}$ *oz*) *chopped parsley*   *chopped onions*
salt, pepper   *pinch of mustard*

1 Place the seasoning in a bowl and gradually add the oil and vinegar.
2 Garnish with the parsley, onions, and capers.

651 Tête de veau poulette

1 *calf's head*   250 *g* ($\frac{1}{2}$ *lb*) *white mushrooms*
500 *g* (1 *lb*) *button onions*   *sauce poulette* (*as Recipe* 59)

1 Prepare and cook calf's head as Recipe 649.
2 Serve with button onions, white mushrooms, and sauce poulette.

Note. Other suitable garnishes for calf's head include Financière, Godard, Ravigote, Tortue and Toulousaine.

652 Pieds de veau – Calves' feet

Cook in a blanc and serve as calf's head (Recipes 649–651).

653 Pieds de veau tyrolienne

4 *calves' feet*   240 *g* ($\frac{1}{2}$ *lb*) *tomato concassé*   1 *clove crushed garlic*
60 *g* (2 *oz*) *chopped*   250 *ml* ($\frac{1}{2}$ *pt*) *sauce poivrade*   15 *g* ($\frac{1}{2}$ *oz*) *chopped*
onions   (*Recipe* 47)   *parsley*

1 Cook the calves' feet 'à blanc' (see Recipe 649) and remove bones.
2 Simmer for 10 minutes with the tomatoes, garlic, parsley, and poivrade sauce.
3 Dress in a timbale.

654 Pieds de veau vinaigrette

4 *calves' feet*   62 *ml* ($\frac{1}{8}$ *pt*) *sauce vinaigrette* (*Recipe* 650)

1 Cook 'à blanc', remove bones.
2 Serve hot with some of the cooking liquor.
3 Serve vinaigrette sauce separately.

655 Pieds de porc – Pigs' trotters

1 Plainly boil without blanc but with thyme, bay-leaf, onion, carrot.
2 Bone and dress in cocotte, otherwise as for calf's head (Recipe 651).
3 Similar sauces and garnishes, e.g. poulette (Recipe 59) and vinaigrette (Recipe 650) are used.

656 Pieds de porc Sainte Menehould

4 *pig's feet*	1 *bay-leaf*	5 *ml spoon* [½ *dessertspoon*] *salt*
120 *g* (¼ *lb*) *carrots*	1 *sprig thyme*	*French mustard*
1 *onion clouté*	2 *l* (2 *qt*) *water*	120 *g* (¼ *lb*) *parsley butter* (*Recipe* 89)

1 Scald the feet and scrape to remove all hairs; split down the middle.
2 Cook the feet with the water, onions, whole carrots, bay-leaf, thyme, a little lemon juice and salt.
3 When cooked, remove the bones being careful not to destroy the shape of the feet; allow to cool and press lightly.
4 Brush lightly with French mustard, flour; then brush with melted butter and crumb with white breadcrumbs.
5 Brush again with melted butter and grill both sides gently; baste frequently.
6 Serve with parsley butter.

BOILED AND POACHED POULTRY

657 Poularde bouillie à l'anglaise – Boiled chicken (English style)

1, 2 *kg* (4-*lb*) *chicken*	240 *g* (½ *lb*) *turned turnips*	240 *g* (½ *lb*) *button onions*
240 *g* (½ *lb*) *raw ham*	1 *white leek*	125 *ml* (¼ *pt*) *parsley sauce*
240 *g* (½ *lb*) *turned carrots*	120 *g* (¼ *lb*) *white celery*	(*Recipe* 70)
		seasoning

1 Clean and truss chicken.
2 Cover the chicken with salted water; bring to boil and skim.
3 Add the ham and vegetables; simmer until tender.
4 When cooked, serve with a garnish of sliced ham and vegetables.
5 Serve the parsley sauce and cooking-liquor separately.

658 Poularde pochée à l'écossaise – Poached chicken (Scottish style)

1, 2 *kg* (4-*lb*) *chicken*	1 *bay-leaf*	90 *g* (3 *oz*) *fine*
120 *g* (¼ *lb*) *pearl barley*	1 *sprig thyme*	*brunoise of carrots,*
120 *g* (¼ *lb*) *pork sausage-meat*	*juice of* ¼ *lemon*	*onions, white of*
	3 *egg yolks*	*leek, celery*
30 *g* (1 *oz*) *chopped onion*	62 *ml* (⅛ *pt*) *mushroom*	180 *g* (6 *oz*) *French*
190 *ml* (1½ *gills*) *cream*	*liquor*	*beans*
1 *onion piqué*	30 *g* (1 *oz*) *flour*	*seasoning*
1 *carrot*	30 *g* (1 *oz*) *butter*	

1 Cook the pearl barley, drain well and combine with the sausage-meat and the onion cooked in butter. Mix with 2 × 15 ml spoon [2 tablespoons] of cream, season and stuff the birds.
2 Poach the chicken with the carrot, onions and herbs.

3 Make a white roux with the flour and butter; add $\frac{1}{2}$ l (1 pt) of the cooking-liquor, mushroom liquor and reduce to 250 ml ($\frac{1}{2}$ pt); add lemon juice.
4 Make a liaison of the egg yolks and 125 ml ($\frac{1}{4}$ pt) of cream; season and strain.
5 Garnish with brunoise of vegetables (Recipe 755) cooked in chicken stock.
6 Skin the chicken and pour the sauce over.
7 Serve separately the French beans, cooked and mixed with a little cream.

659 Poularde pochée au riz and sauce suprême

Fowls may be poached and served with pilaff rice (Recipe 366) and with sauce suprême (Recipe 63) made with the cooking-liquor.

660 Poularde pochée Stanley

1, 2 kg (4-*lb*) chicken	2·5 ml spoon [$\frac{1}{2}$ teaspoon] curry powder	125 ml ($\frac{1}{4}$ pt) chicken velouté (Recipe 27)
500 g (1 *lb*) onions	62 ml ($\frac{1}{6}$ pt) cream	120 g ($\frac{1}{4}$ lb) rice
45 g (1$\frac{1}{2}$ oz) julienne truffle	45 g (1$\frac{1}{2}$ oz) cooked julienne mushrooms	

1 Clean the chicken from the crop and remove the wish-bone.
2 Partly cook the rice as for pilaff (Recipe 366) and mix with the mushrooms and truffles.
3 Stuff the chicken (crop end) and truss.
4 Slice the onions, blanch, and add the curry powder.
5 Poach the birds with onions under cover; add a little stock.
6 When the chicken is cooked rub the onions and liquid through the tammy or fine sieve and add the chicken velouté.
7 Add cream and reduce to a good coating sauce.
8 Pass through a fine chinois, add a little cream and adjust seasoning.

For service:
 i Remove the skin but leave the rice inside the birds.
 ii Wings may be removed, breast-bone cut out and the wings replaced on top
 iii Napper with sauce.
 iv Garnish top with a little julienne of truffles.

661 Poularde pochée Derby

1, 2 kg (4-*lb*) pullet	45 g (1$\frac{1}{2}$ oz) diced truffles	4 whole truffles
120 g ($\frac{1}{4}$ lb) rice	125 ml ($\frac{1}{4}$ pt) cream	4 round croûtons
60 g (2 oz) diced foie gras	4 slices foie gras	$\frac{1}{2}$ glass champagne
125 ml ($\frac{1}{4}$ pt) veal stock (Recipe 9)	7 g ($\frac{1}{4}$ oz) arrowroot seasoning	60 g ($\frac{1}{8}$ lb) butter

1 Clean the chickens from the crop end and remove the wish-bone.
2 Partly cook the rice as for pilaff (Recipe 366) and mix with the diced foie gras and truffles.
3 Stuff the birds and truss.
4 Poêler the chickens in a large casserole, basting frequently.
5 When the chickens are cooked, place on a suitable dish.

Toss the sliced foie gras in butter and set on the round croûtons which have been cooked to a golden colour in butter.

7 Cook the truffles in champagne and place these in between the foie gras.
8 Remove all fat from the cooking-liquid; add the veal stock and truffle liquid.
9 Reduce approximately to 125 ml ($\frac{1}{4}$ pt) and lié with diluted arrowroot, adjust seasoning; strain a little sauce over the birds and serve the remainder separately.

STEWING – ÉTUVER

662 Stewing of meats

Stewing is the process of simmering meat in liquor; the term is normally applied to the preparation of small cuts of meat, or poultry, when the resulting product may be a stew, goulash, ragoût, braised steak, curry, or even, a sauté de bœuf.

Using terms like braised and sauté in such circumstances may be confusing but it should be noted that there are two main types of stewing:
 i when the meat is first browned and,
 ii when the meat is stewed either plain or blanched.

The first method, when the meat is browned, so resembles braising that the term, braised steak, may reasonably be used. For beef dishes, when the browning stage is one of sauter in hot fat, the term sauté is sometimes retained in the title despite the fact that the subsequent (and principal) form of cooking is stewing as, for example, in sauté de bœuf bourguignonne.

663 Étuver

Étuver virtually means to cook in the food's own juice using butter (possibly a little stock or other cooking-liquor) only to start the slow, oven-cooking which must be sealed under cover to prevent liquor from evaporating.

Almost all meats, game, and poultry can be stewed: if cuts are selected, it is so that the finest pieces can be reserved for roasting, grilling, and the quicker cookery processes.

664 En daube

Cooking 'en daube' is akin to braising, and involves cooking in a daubière, a lidded cooking-vessel that is usually a large earthenware stew-pan which is used for oven-to-table service. Mutton or beef can be treated en daube. In the case of beef:

1 Cut the topside of beef into squares of 6 cm by 2 cm (3 by 1 inch) thick.
2 Lard each piece with pieces of back-fat and roll in chopped parsley and crushed garlic.
3 Pickle for 1 hour in a mixture of brandy, white wine, and oil.
4 Place the meat with alternate layers of belly pork, sliced carrots, chopped

onions, thyme, bay-leaves, tomatoes, stoned, black olives, bunch herbs; season as you go and then cover with pickle.

5 Seal the lid of the daubière with paste and set to cook in the oven for approximately 2 hours.

665 En casserole and en cocotte

Meats may, of course, be oven-stewed or braised, 'en cocotte' and 'en casserole'. There is sometimes confusion because sauté dishes can be presented or finished en cocotte without having been completely cooked in that vessel.

666 Blanquette

This is a stew or ragoût without colour and is made of white meats such as poultry, veal, or rabbit. For blanquettes the meat is blanched and the sauce is made from the stock in which the meat is cooked; the garnish is cooked separately.

667 Fricassé

The result is similar to a blanquette. The meat is cooked without colour, but in this case both the garnish and the meat are cooked in the sauce.

STEWED BEEF

668 Bifteck braisé bourgeoise – Braised steak bourgeoise

4, 180 g (6-oz) *rump or topside*	*bouquet garni*	12 *turned carrots*
30 g (1 oz) *flour*	500 ml (1 pt) *estouffade*	12 *turned turnips*
30 g (1 oz) *dripping*	*(Recipe 8)*	12 *button onions*
30 g (1 oz) *boiled French beans*	120 g (¼ lb) *mirepoix*	21 g (¾ oz) *tomato*
cut into diamonds	*(Recipe 2)*	*purée*

1 Fry off the steaks in fat.
2 Fry off mirepoix and add to meat; place all in braising-pan.
3 Singé the meat with flour and brown in the oven.
4 Add the tomato purée and brown stock; mix well.
5 Boil and skim; add bouquet garni and cook under cover in moderate oven.
6 When cooked, remove meat, reduce and strain sauce, adjust seasoning, and pour over meat.
7 Cook and glaze the vegetables and garnish.

669 Carbonnade de bœuf

750 g (1½ lb) *topside*	250 ml (½ pt) *beer*	250 ml (½ pt) *brown*
360 g (¾ lb) *thinly-sliced onions*	30 g (1 oz) *flour*	*stock (Recipe 8)*
30 g (1 oz) *butter*		*seasoning*

1 Cut the meat free from fat and into small escalopes.
2 Roll in flour and sauté in butter.
3 Sweat the onions.

4 Prepare alternate layers of onions and meat in a casserole, seasoning each layer.
5 Pour over beer and brown stock.
6 Braise under cover in the oven.
7 Adjust the seasoning and remove all fat before serving; sprinkle with chopped parsley.

670 Goulash de bœuf hongroise – Hungarian goulash (of beef)

750 g (1½ lb) topside of beef	20 g (¾ oz) tomato purée	20 g (¾ oz) flour
360 g (¾ lb) diced onions	20 g (¾ oz) parisienne	bouquet garni
15 ml spoon [1 table-	potatoes (Recipe 904)	500 ml (1 pt) white
spoon] paprika	120 g (¼ lb) gnocchis	stock (Recipe 6)
62 ml (½ gill) oil	parisienne	seasoning
15 g (½ oz) butter	(Recipe 358)	

1 Remove fat from meat and cut into 2 cm (1-inch) cubes.
2 Roll in paprika and fry in oil.
3 Sweat the onions in butter in braising-pan.
4 Add the meat to onions, dust with flour, and brown in oven.
5 Blend in the tomato purée, pour on stock, and mix well.
6 Boil, skim, add bouquet garni and cook under cover in moderate oven.
7 Skim frequently during cooking, and 10 minutes before completion; add blanched parisienne potatoes and allow them to finish cooking in the sauce.
8 Adjust seasoning and remove all fat.
9 Garnish with gnocchis parisienne; do not strain sauce.

Note. Hungarian goulash is also commonly made with veal.

671 Kari de bœuf – Curried beef

750 g (1½ lb) topside or	60 g (2 oz) chopped apples	7 g (¼ oz) currants
thick flank	15 g (½ oz) chutney	7 g (¼ oz) sultanas
30 g (1 oz) flour	500 ml (1 pt) estouffade	15 g (½ oz) desic-
bouquet garni	(Recipe 8)	cated coconut
20 g (⅝ oz) curry powder	30 g (1 oz) dripping	125 ml (¼ pt) milk
60 g (4 oz) chopped onion	15 g (½ oz) tomato purée	
120 g (¼ lb) rice	seasoning	

1 Remove fat from meat and cut into 2 cm (1-inch) cubes and fry off.
2 Sweat onions in a braising-pan, add meat and curry powder.
3 Singé with flour, and brown in oven.
4 Blend in the tomato purée, add stock, and mix well.
5 Boil, skim, add bouquet garni, and cook under cover in moderate oven.
6 Cook for approximately 1 hour; add chopped apple and chutney.
7 Soak the sultanas and currants in warm water for a few minutes; drain, and add these to the meat just before cooking is completed.
8 Soak the coconut in milk for a few minutes, squeeze out and add resulting liquid to the curry.
9 Adjust seasoning (including hot mango-kasundi) and remove surplus fat.
10 Serve with plainly-boiled rice, separately.

Accompaniments.

i Bombay Duck: This may be deep-fried or grilled (1 per portion).
ii Poppadums: These may be deep-fried or grilled (1 per portion).
iii Mango Chutney and/or
iv Lime Pickle (or similar Indian conserves).
v French-fried onion rings.
vi Sambals or Raviers: Diced apples, onion and tomato salad, bananas, sliced or diced, cucumber, yoghourt sprinkled with nutmeg, grated coconut, lemon quarters (in lieu of limes).

Note. This is an anglicized type of curry dish derived also from adaptations evolved in British kitchens by French chefs or in the French kitchen and is given because of the possible demand for this version of 'curry'. See also Recipe 677 for curried lamb and Recipe 678 for a more traditional Indian method.

672 Paupiettes de bœuf farcies – Beef olives

750 g (1½ lb) topside of beef · 7 g (¼ oz) chopped parsley · 15 g (½ oz) chopped onions
4 stoned olives · 120 g (¼ lb) finely-minced steak · 1 bouquet garni
1·25 ml spoon [¼ teaspoon] mixed herbs · 1 small egg · 15 g (½ oz) breadcrumbs
500 ml (1 pt) demi-glace (Recipe 29) · 60 g (2 oz) fine mirepoix (Recipe 4) · 30 g (1 oz) dripping

1 Remove fat from meat and cut into 4 thin escalopes.
2 Beat them flat with the cutlet bat.
3 Mince the trimmings finely and combine with the 120 g (¼ lb) of minced steak and sweated onions.
4 Add the herbs and breadcrumbs; bind the mixture together with the egg; season.
5 Divide the stuffing equally; place in centre of each escalope with the stoned olive in the middle; roll and tie; shallow-fry briskly to colour.
6 Fry the mirepoix and place the olives and mirepoix in a suitable braising-pan.
7 Cover with demi-glace; add bouquet garni, and braise in moderate oven.
8 When cooked, remove string and reduce sauce; adjust seasoning and strain over the olives.
9 Garnish: jardiniére (Recipe 755) or rice pilaff (Recipe 366).

673 Sauté de bœuf bourguignonne – Beef sauté bourguignonne

750 g (1½ lb) topside of beef · 15 g (½ oz) tomato purée · 18 glazed button onions
90 g (3 oz) diced onions · 1 clove chopped garlic · 8 heart-shaped croûtons
500 ml (1 pt) brown stock (Recipe 8) · 1 bouquet garni · 21 g (¾ oz) fat
190 ml (1½ gills) red wine · 9 small mushrooms · 15 g (½ oz) chopped parsley
21 g (¾ oz) flour · 120 g (¼ lb) lardons

1 Remove fat from meat and cut into 2 cm (1-inch) cubes.
2 Fry off meat in the fat, add the onions and garlic and place in braising-pan

3 Singé with flour and brown in oven.
4 Add tomato purée and mix well; add wine and stock.
5 Boil, skim, add bouquet garni and cook under cover in moderate oven.
6 When cooked, remove meat, re-boil sauce and reduce; skim, season, and pour over meat.
7 Blanch the lardons and fry off.
8 Garnish meat with glazed onions and the cooked mushrooms.
9 Present with heart-shaped croûtons dipped in parsley.

674 Sauté de bœuf jardinière

750 g (1½ lb) topside of beef	750 ml (¾ qt) brown stock	1 bouquet garni
30 g (1 oz) flour	(Recipe 7 or 8)	45 g (1½ oz) mire-
30 g (1 oz) dripping	30 g (1 oz) tomato purée	poix (Recipe 2)
seasoning		

Garnish jardinière:

15 g (½ oz) French beans cut in
    diamond shape
15 g (½ oz) peas

30 g (1 oz) carrots ⎞ cut into
30 g (1 oz) turnips ⎠ bâtons

Remove fat from meat and cut into 2 cm (1-inch) cubes; fry off in dripping.
Fry off mirepoix, drain, add to meat and place in braising-pan.
Dust with flour (singer), and brown in oven.
Add tomato purée and blend in stock.
Bring to boil and skim; add bouquet garni and season lightly; cover with lid.
Cook in moderate oven for 1½ hours; skim frequently.
When cooked remove meat from sauce.
Re-boil sauce, season, and strain over meat; garnish with jardinière of vegetables.

75 Scotch beef mince

500 g (1 lb) topside of beef	15 g (½ oz) dripping	4 baked onions
240 g (½ lb) finely-chopped	250 ml (½ pt) (approx.) white	seasoning
onions	stock (Recipe 6)	
4 heart-shaped croûtons		

Remove fat and mince beef finely through medium cutter.
Sweat the onions in the dripping.
Add the minced beef and sweat under cover.
Moisten with sufficient white stock or water to cover and slightly season.
Simmer until cooked, adjust seasoning.
Garnish with baked onions and heart-shaped croûtons having previously dipped the ends in chopped parsley.

The dish may be further garnished with dumplings (Recipe 645) or with a jardinière of vegetables (as in Recipe 674).

STEWS OF LAMB AND MUTTON

676 Irish stew

750 g (1½ lb) stewing lamb   120 g (¼ lb) cabbage (sliced)   8 turned potatoes
240 g (½ lb) sliced celery   240 g (½ lb) sliced leek   seasoning
240 g (½ lb) sliced onions   500 g (1 lb) sliced potatoes

1 Prepare 4 neck cutlets and 8 pieces of breast of lamb or mutton.
2 Blanch and refresh the meat.
3 Mix the onions, leeks, celery, and cabbage together; and season.
4 Cut the potatoes into roundels; divide into 2 equal portions and place on
  the bottom of a braising-pan, sprinkle half of the mixed vegetables on top
  and season.
5 Lay the meat neatly on top of the vegetables and season (some chefs add
  bouquet garni).
6 Cover the meat with the remainder of the vegetables and arrange the
  remainder of the sliced potatoes on top; season.
7 Cover with water, bring to the boil, cover and cook for approximately 1½
  hours.
8 Arrange the turned potatoes on top and finish off the cooking under cover.
9 Remove all fat and sprinkle with chopped parsley before service.

Note. Some prefer to garnish with button onions and to pass the liquid with its
softened potato content through a strainer to yield a very thin purée.

677 Kari d'agneau – Curry of lamb

650 g (1¼ lb) lean lamb   22 g (¾ oz) flour   seasoning
90 g (3 oz) finely-chopped onion   30 g (1 oz) lard   500 ml (1 pt) brown
20 g (⅝ oz) curry powder   bouquet garni   stock (Recipe 7)

1 Remove all fat from the lamb and cut into cubes.
2 Fry the lamb and onions to a golden brown in the lard.
3 Dredge the meat with the curry powder and mix well; dredge with the flour
  and cook in the oven for a few minutes.
4 Moisten with the stock and stir well; bring to boil, skim, and add the
  bouquet garni.
5 Cook in a moderate oven with lid on for approximately 1½ hours.
6 When cooked, remove all grease, check sauce for seasoning and consistency.
7 Serve plainly-boiled rice separately with mango chutney, Bombay duck and
  poppadums (see Recipe 671 for other accompaniments).

678 Lamb or mutton curry (Indian style)

750 g (1½ lb) stewing lamb   30 g (1 oz) tomato   30 g (1 oz) curry
  (or mutton)   purée   powder (or to
2 small Spanish onions   1 clove garlic   taste)
60 g (2 oz) butter   0·5 cm (¼ inch) cinnamon   2–3 cloves
1 crushed bay-leaf   stick   2–3 cardamom
62 ml (2½ fl. oz) yoghourt   salt, cayenne pepper   seeds

1 Finely slice the onions and sweat in butter for 10 minutes to a golden brown.
2 Add crushed garlic, curry powder, salt and cayenne pepper; continue to sweat for further 3 minutes.
3 Add tomato purée, mix well, then add yoghourt.
4 Trim the meat of fat, cut into fairly small pieces and brown rapidly in sauté-pan.
5 Add the meat to the curry sauce, déglacer the pan with brown stock and add this liquor to the sauce.
6 Tie the cinnamon stick, cloves, cardamom seeds and bay-leaves in a muslin bag for easy removal before service.
7 Cover tightly and simmer on top of stove or cook in oven until meat is tender.
8 Serve plainly-boiled rice separately; for accompaniments see Recipe 671.
Note.
i Curry is improved by preparation 24 hours in advance of service. Surplus fat may be removed before re-heating, although correctly in Indian style this is a fatty dish.
ii Chicken, rabbit, raw mince, and cooked meats can be curried in similar style.

679 Navarin d'agneau aux primeurs – Brown-lamb stew with spring vegetables

750 g (1½ lb) stewing lamb	bouquet garni	22 g (¾ oz) tomato
240 g (½ lb) button onions	500 ml (1 pt) brown	purée
240 g (½ lb) turned	stock (Recipe 7)	seasoning
carrots	30 g (1 oz) flour	120 g (¼ lb) mirepoix
240 g (½ lb) turned turnips	1 clove crushed	(Recipe 2)
240 g (½ lb) turned potatoes	garlic	30 g (1 oz) dripping

1 Cut 4 neck cutlets and 8 pieces of breast of lamb 5 cm × 5 cm (2½ by 2½ inches), free from fat.
2 Put the dripping in a braising-pan and sauter the lamb to a golden brown.
3 Add the mirepoix to the meat and colour.
4 Pour off the fat and dust with the flour; place in oven to brown.
5 Remove from the oven, add the tomato purée and mix well; add the chopped garlic and moisten with the stock.
6 Bring to the boil and skim; add bouquet garni.
7 Simmer under cover in a moderate oven for approximately 1½ hours.
8 Sauter the button onions, carrots, turnips in butter to a golden brown and blanch the potatoes.
9 Remove the meat from the pan and place in a clean pan; add the sauté vegetables and turned potatoes.
10 Strain the sauce, correct the seasoning, consistency and colouring; dilute with a little stock, if necessary.
11 Add the sauce to the meat and vegetables; bring to the boil and simmer until the meat and vegetables are tender.
12 Remove all fat; dress on an entrée dish and arrange the garnish neatly; sprinkle with chopped parsley.

Note. Navarin d'agneau, similarly prepared, may be garnished jardinière or bouquetière.

680 Ragoût de mouton aux haricots blancs – Haricot mutton

750 g (1½ lb) neck of lamb	500 ml (1 pt) brown stock (Recipe 7)	Garnish: 120 g (¼ lb) haricot beans
120 g (¼ lb) diced onions	15 g (½ oz) tomato purée	120 g (¼ lb) bacon bones
120 g (¼ lb) diced carrots	seasoning	1 whole carrot
30 g (1 oz) flour	½ clove garlic	1 onion clouté
30 g (1 oz) dripping		

1 Soak the beans overnight in water and rinse.
2 Cover with cold water, bring to boil and skim.
3 Add the bacon bones, carrot and onion clouté, simmer until tender.
4 Strain off the stock and keep the beans hot until required.
5 Cut the lamb in pieces of 4 cm × 4 cm (2 by 2 inches) and remove surplus fat.
6 Put the dripping in a braising-pan and fry the meat and vegetables until golden brown; drain off surplus fat.
7 Dust the meat and vegetables with flour and brown in the oven.
8 Remove from oven, add the crushed clove of garlic, tomato purée, and mix well.
9 Mix the brown stock and liquor from cooking the beans 500 ml (about 1 pint).
10 Boil and skim; add bouquet garni and cook under cover for approximately 2 hours in moderate oven.
11 When cooked, remove meat and place in clean pan.
12 Strain the sauce, correct for colour, seasoning and consistency, pour over the meat and garnish with cooked beans.

Note. Fried lardons may be included in the garnish.

VEAL

681 Blanquette de veau à l'ancienne

750 g (1½ lb) tendron of veal	1 onion clouté	30 g (1 oz) butter
500 ml (1 pt) white stock (Recipe 6)	1 small carrot	62 ml (⅛ pt) cream ⎫
	bouquet garni	⎬ liaison
12 button mushrooms	30 g (1 oz) flour	1 egg yolk ⎭
12 button onions	seasoning	heart-shaped croûtons

1 Cut the veal tendron into approximately 90 g (3-oz) pieces.
2 Blanch and refresh.
3 Cover with stock, boil and skim; add onion clouté, carrot, bouquet garni and simmer gently for 1½ hours.
4 Prepare a white roux with the flour and butter; strain the stock from the veal over roux and mix well; cook for 20 minutes.
5 Transfer the veal to a large casserole and add the onions and mushrooms which have been cooked à blanc.
6 Finish off the sauce with the liaison; add a few drops of lemon juice; adjust the seasoning and strain over the veal.
7 Garnish with croûtons.

Note. Having added the liaison do not re-boil. In the case of blanquette fillet of veal may be used.

682 Fricassé de veau à l'ancienne

750 g (1½ lb) *fillet of veal or boned shoulder*
180 g (6 oz) *button onions*
60 g (2 oz) *button mushrooms*

bouquet garni
500 ml (1 pt) *white veal stock (Recipe 9)*
90 g (3 oz) *butter*
30 g (1 oz) *flour*

125 ml (¼ pt) *cream*
1 *egg yolk* } *liaison*
heart-shaped croûtons
seasoning

1 Cut the veal into 60 g (2-oz) pieces.
2 Place the butter in a braising-pan and stiffen the veal without colouring.
3 Sprinkle the veal with flour and allow to cook for a few minutes.
4 Moisten with white stock and mix well; boil, skim, add bouquet garni and cook under cover in moderate oven.
5 Meanwhile turn the mushrooms and cook the onions à blanc (Recipe 759).
6 When the veal is cooked, transfer it to another pan and add the garnish.
7 Reduce the sauce and draw to side of stove; add the liaison of cream and egg yolks; season and strain over the veal.
8 Garnish with croûtons fried in oil; dip ends in parsley.

683 Goulash de veau hongroise

Prepare as Recipe 670 but using veal.

684 Jarret de veau (Osso Bucco) milanaise – Veal knuckles (Milan style)

1 kg (2 lb) *veal knuckle*
240 g (½ lb) *tomato concassé*
500 ml (1 pt) *thin tomato sauce (Recipe 34)*

1 *clove crushed garlic*
bouquet garni
125 ml (1 gill) *white wine*
seasoning

62 ml (½ gill) *oil*
120 g (¼ lb) *finely-chopped onions*

1 With a saw cut the knuckles of veal in 8 slices, approximately 4 oz each.
2 Dust with flour and fry to golden brown in oil.
3 Remove veal from pan; sweat the onions and garlic in the remaining oil; swill with the white wine, and reduce.
4 Add the tomatoes and sweat for a few minutes; place the veal on top and moisten with the tomato sauce; bring to the boil and add the bouquet garni.
5 Cook under cover in a moderate oven and when cooked, degrease and adjust seasoning.
6 Serve a risotto milanaise (Recipe 368), separately.

685 Paupiette de veau financière

4, 280 g (7-oz) *veal escalopes*
180 g (6 oz) *fine forcemeat (Recipe 195)*
4 *slices of truffle*

8 *chicken quenelles (Recipe 194 or 717)*
4 *turned mushrooms*
4 *chicken's kidneys*

4 *stoned olives*
4 *cockscombs (Recipe 750)*

1 Prepare 4 escalopes 8 cm (4 inches) long by 4 cm (2 inches) wide, and season.
2 Cover each with forcemeat and roll into scrolls; tie to keep shape.

3 Braise in manner of beef olives (Recipe 672).
4 Strain the sauce when cooked; garnish with mushrooms, olives, quenelles, cockscombs, and chicken's kidneys; pour over sauce and finish with slices of truffle.

686 Sauté de veau marengo

750 g (1½ lb) breast of veal	125 ml (1 gill) white wine	Garnish:
30 g (1 oz) chopped onions	bouquet garni	12 glazed button onions
360 g (¾ lb) tomato concassé	1 clove crushed garlic	240 g (½ lb) diced mushrooms
500 ml (1 pt) demi-glace (Recipe 29)	250 ml (½ pt) oil	8 heart-shaped croûtons chopped parsley

1 Cut the veal into 60 g (2-oz) pieces.
2 Fry in oil until golden.
3 Add the onions and garlic and fry for a few minutes.
4 Drain away all the oil and moisten with the wine and reduce; add the tomato concassé and the demi-glace.
5 Bring to the boil, skim, add bouquet garni.
6 Cover and cook in moderate oven for 1½ hours.
7 Transfer the veal to another pan; add the mushrooms and onions, and cover with the strained sauce.
8 Cook for a further 15 minutes; remove all fat, and adjust seasoning.
9 Garnish with croûtons fried in oil and the ends dipped in parsley.

687 Tendrons de veau

1 Tendrons are cut from the breast of veal and are the extreme end of the ribs including cartilage of the sternum.
2 They are cut crosswise into pieces approximately 90 g (3 oz) each for use in dishes such as sauté de veau (Recipe 686 as above).
3 Breast of veal can be braised whole (see notes on white braising) as well as in smaller pieces.

CASSEROLE OR OVEN-STEWS OF LAMB, MUTTON, AND PORK

688 Chump chop Champvallon

4, 300 g (10-oz) chump chops	120 g (¼ lb) sliced tomatoes	240 g (½ lb) sliced onion
500 g (1 lb) sliced potatoes	250 ml (½ pt) white stock (Recipe 6)	60 g (2 oz) lard seasoning
4 slices bacon	bouquet garni	

1 Trim the chump chops well and fry to golden colour in lard.
2 Place a slice of tomato and bacon on the top of each chop.
3 Butter an earthenware dish and place on the bottom a layer of sliced potato, then another layer of onions.

4 Place the chops on this bed and another layer of onions and potatoes, seasoning each layer; add the bouquet garni.
5 Moisten well with seasoned stock and add a few knobs of butter.
6 Cook in a moderate oven.
7 Remove all grease before service and sprinkle with chopped parsley.

Note. There are alternative presentations of this dish, but this preparation has proved acceptable.

689 Lancashire hot-pot

500 g (1 *lb*) *stewing lamb*   625 g (1¼ *lb*) *sliced potatoes*   *seasoning*
120 g (¼ *lb*) *kidney*   500 g (1 *lb*) *sliced onions*

1 Prepare 4 pieces of neck cutlets and 4 pieces of breast cut into 4 cm × 4 cm (2 by 2-inch) squares, and the kidney into smaller pieces.
2 Fry off the meat and kidney to a golden colour in a little fat and drain.
3 Slice the potatoes into thin roundels.
4 Layer potatoes liberally on the bottom of a braising-pan and sprinkle with a layer of the sliced onions, and season.
5 Place the meat neatly on top of this layer and repeat layering to fill dish.
6 Finish by placing the remaining sliced potatoes neatly, in overlapping rows on top.
7 Add water or white stock to just below surface, and scatter a few knobs of butter or brush surface with melted butter, and season.
8 Put in a moderate oven; when the potatoes are brown, cover with grease-proof paper and allow to finish cooking – approximately 2½ hours.
9 Before service, remove all grease and sprinkle with chopped parsley.
10 Serve a bowl of pickled cabbage as a garnish.

Note. Oysters and other variants are added in some areas of Lancashire. Some do not fry off the meat, some do not include kidney.

690 Cassoulet de porc

750 g (1¼ *lb*) *breast of pork*   240 g (½ *lb*) *pork rind*   120 g (¼ *lb*) *garlic*
240 g (½ *lb*) *haricot beans*   120 g (¼ *lb*) *bread-*   *sausage*
1 *small carrot*   *crumbs*   360 g (¾ *lb*) *sliced*
1 *onion clouté*   120 g (¼ *lb*) *lardons*   *bacon*
4 *casseroles*

1 Soak the beans and cook until tender with the carrot, onion clouté, and pork rind.
2 Dice the pork into 2 cm (1-inch) squares, fry to golden colour in lard.
3 Blanch the lardons.
4 Line each casserole with sliced bacon and fill with alternate layers of beans, pork and bacon and the garlic sausage cut into thick slices.
5 Moisten each casserole with the haricot bean cooking-liquor.
6 Cover with breadcrumbs, baste frequently with some of the reserved haricot-bean liquor.
7 Approximate cooking-time, 1 hour in moderate oven.

691 Choucroûte garnie – Sauerkraut garnish

360 g (¾ lb) sauerkraut	1 onion clouté	250 ml (½ pt) fond blanc
4 frankfurters	240 g (½ lb) garlic	(Recipe 6)
240 g (½ lb) shoulder	ham-sausage	240 g (½ lb) turned
bacon	120 g (¼ lb) lard	potatoes
120 g (¼ lb) bacon rind	2 peeled carrots	bouquet garni

1 Line a thick-bottomed braising-pan with bacon rind.
2 Place the choucroûte on top and insert the onions and carrots in the middle with the piece of bacon.
3 Cut the lard into small pieces and place on top.
4 Add the stock and bouquet garni; cover with a tight-fitting lid and braise for approximately 1 hour in the oven.
5 Remove lid, place garlic sausage and the frankfurters on top.
6 Replace lid and continue to cook for a further 15 minutes.
7 Serve with plain boiled potatoes.

STEWS OF OFFAL

692 Foie de bœuf braisé bourgeoise – Braised ox-liver bourgeoise

500 g (1 lb) ox-liver	120 g (¼ lb) glazed carrots	120 g (¼ lb) lardons
250 ml (½ pt) demi-glace	500 g (1 lb) glazed onions	chopped parsley
(Recipe 29)	60 g (2 oz) flour	22 g (¾ oz) dripping

1 Remove all skin from liver and cut into 8 equal slices.
2 Dip each piece in flour and shallow-fry each piece in smoking fat.
3 Drain and cover with demi-glace and cook under cover in the oven until tender.
4 Remove from pan and arrange the pieces neatly in an entrée dish.
5 Check the sauce for seasoning and consistency and strain over the liver
6 Blanch and fry off the lardons in butter and strain.
7 Garnish the liver with bouquets of glazed vegetables and the lardons sprinkle with chopped parsley.

693 Queue de bœuf braisé printanière – Braised oxtail printanière

1 kg (2 lb) oxtail	30 g (1 oz) tomato purée	180 g (6 oz) glazed
bouquet garni	30 g (1 oz) dripping	turnips
240 g (½ lb) mirepoix	500 ml (1 pt) brown stock	180 g (6 oz) glazed
(Recipe 2)	(Recipe 7 or 8)	onions
30 g (1 oz) flour	180 g (6 oz) glazed carrots	seasoning

1 Remove all fat from oxtail and cut the thicker part into 4 cm (2-inch) sections.
2 Melt the dripping in a large braising-pan and fry the tail sections to golden brown; fry the mirepoix in a frying-pan; drain and add to the tail
3 Sprinkle in the flour, and cook for a few minutes in the oven.
4 Add the tomato purée; mix well, and moisten with the stock.
5 Boil, skim, add bouquet garni, and cook under cover in a moderate oven until tender (usually not less than 3 hours).

6 When cooked remove the sections and place in clean pan.
7 Reduce the sauce; check for seasoning and consistency; strain over the tails.
8 Garnish with glazed vegetables.

694 Ris de veau – Calves' sweetbreads

1 Stews, or braisings, of sweetbreads may be prepared by applying white-braising principles (Recipe 565): before braising, soak the sweetbreads in cold water overnight to remove blood.
2 Blanch and refresh; trim and remove skin.
3 Piqué with fat bacon or truffles.

Garnish examples include:

695 Ris de veau bonne maman

Garnish with large vegetable julienne and the reduced cooking-liquor.

696 Ris de veau aux champignons

Garnish with mushrooms and mushroom sauce.

697 Ris de veau financière

Garnish with salpicon financière (Recipe 103).

698 Ris de veau braisé Demidoff

1 *kg* (2 *lb*) *calves' sweetbreads*	60 *g* (2 *oz*) *carrots*	6 *small onions*
15 *g* ($\frac{1}{2}$ *oz*) *truffles*	60 *g* (2 *oz*) *turnips*	30 *g* (1 *oz*) *celery*
30 *g* (1 *oz*) *bacon*		

1 Cut the vegetables with the demidoff knife into half-moon shapes and the onions into roundels and stew in butter.
2 Piqué the prepared sweetbreads with the bacon and truffles and white braise.
3 Add 25 ml (1 fluid oz) of truffle essence to the braising sauce and also the garnish.
4 Serve in a cocotte coated with the garnish and sauce.

699 Rognons de veau en cocotte

4 *veal kidneys*	120 *g* ($\frac{1}{4}$ *lb*)	10 *ml spoon* [$\frac{1}{2}$ *table-*
120 *g* ($\frac{1}{4}$ *lb*) *lardons*	*quartered mush-*	*spoon*] *sherry*
360 *g* ($\frac{3}{4}$ *lb*) *potatoes*	*rooms*	62 *ml* ($\frac{1}{2}$ *gill*) *veal gravy*
120 *g* ($\frac{1}{4}$ *lb*) *glazed*	120 *g* ($\frac{1}{4}$ *lb*) *butter*	(*Recipe* 10)
button onions		

1 Trim the kidney leaving a slight layer of fat round it.
2 Fry in butter in a large casserole; cook gently for 30 minutes, turning the kidneys frequently.
3 Blanch and fry lardons and place in the casserole with the cooked mushrooms and fried cocotte (turned to olive shape) potatoes.
4 Complete cooking for another 10 minutes, and at the last minute add veal gravy and sherry.

700 Tripe and onions

> 500 g (1 *lb*) ox-tripe   bouquet garni   500 g (1 *lb*) onions
> (*prepared, i.e. dressed*)   62 *ml* (½ *gill*) cream   22 g (¾ *oz*) *flour*
> 500 *ml* (1 *pt*) milk   22 g (¾ *oz*) butter   seasoning

1 Cut the prepared tripe into pieces 4 cm × 4 cm (2 by 2 inches).
2 Peel the onions, cut in half, slice thinly and blanch.
3 Add the onions to the tripe and pour over the milk; simmer gently with the bouquet garni.
4 Make a white roux with the flour and butter and when tripe is cooked make a sauce with the strained cooking-liquor.
5 Mix the tripe with the sauce and simmer for a few minutes at the side of the stove.
6 Season and finish with the cream.
7 If the sauce is too thick, dilute with a little boiled milk.

701 Tripes à la mode de Caen

> 1 *kg* (2 *lb*) fresh ox-tripe   125 *ml* (¼ *pt*) white   120 g (¼ *lb*) beef suet
> (*i.e. not prepared by*   wine   2 *whole carrots*
> *tripe dresser*)   250 *ml* (½ *pt*) cider   2 *whole onions*
> 30 g (1 *oz*) ox-feet   ½ *glass brandy*   cloutés
> (*boned*)   240 g (½ *lb*) tomato   1 *clove garlic*
> bouquet garni   concassé

1 Lay on the bottom of a braising-pan the whole carrots and onions cloutés.
2 Cut the ox-feet into four pieces and add this to the vegetables.
3 Add the tripe in large pieces which should consist of the honeycomb, manyplies, and the reed.
4 Place the tomatoes and crushed garlic on top with the bouquet garni.
5 Moisten with wine, cider, brandy, and lay the bones of the feet on top with layers of suet; season.
6 Place a lid on top and seal with flour and water-paste.
7 Cook slowly in oven for 10 hours.

STEWS OF POULTRY AND GAME

702 Coq au vin

> 2 *kg* (4 *lb*) chicken   250 *ml* (½ *pt*)   1 *bay leaf*
> 120 g (¼ *lb*) lardons   red wine   1 *sprig thyme*
> 120 g (¼ *lb*) turned mushrooms ⎱garnish   60 g (2 *oz*)   garlic
> 120 g (¼ *lb*) button onions ⎰   butter
> 15 g (½ *oz*) meat glacé   heart-shaped
> 30 g (1 *oz*) (*approx.*) beurre-manié   croûtons
> seasoning   chicken blood

Note. This dish is ideally made from a freshly-slaughtered bird as the blood should be utilized in the sauce.

1 Clean the chicken, retain blood and liver.
2 Cut as for sauté. (Chop the carcass.)

3 Colour chicken pieces and carcass in butter – withdraw from pan.
4 Cook off the garnish in the residue and reserve.
5 Replace the chicken and carcass pieces in the pan.
6 Add the garlic and herbs.
7 Cover with red wine and simmer until cooked.
8 Reduce the cooking liquid to half. Add the meat glacé.
9 Thicken with beurre-manié and the blood. Strain and season.
10 Dress the chicken in a cocotte, add the garnish and cover with sauce.
11 Chop and sauté the chicken liver in butter. Spread on croûtons and add to decorate dish.

703 Fricassée de volaille à l'ancienne

1, 2 *kg* (4-*lb*) chicken	*seasoning*	22 *g* (¾ *oz*) *flour*
	bouquet garni	120 *g* (¼ *lb*) *butter*
240 *g* (½ *lb*) *button onions*	120 *ml* (¼ *pt*) *cream*⎫ *liaison*	375 *ml* (¾ *pt*) *chicken stock* (*Recipe* 11)
	2 *egg yolks* ⎭	
120 *g* (¼ *lb*) *turned mushrooms*	8 *fleurons* (*Recipe* 1024)	*pinch chopped parsley*
		pinch chives

1 Cut the chicken (Recipe 621) as for sauté and the carcass into 3 equal parts.
2 Gently sauter in butter in a large sauteuse. Do not colour.
3 Dust the chicken with flour and cook a little.
4 Moisten with stock; mix well; add bouquet garni, and bring to boil and simmer under cover in moderate oven until half-cooked.
5 Cook the mushrooms and onions in a little stock and butter.
6 Remove the chicken and place in a clean pan; add the mushrooms and onions, strain the liquor over, and continue the cooking.
7 When the chicken is cooked, add the liaison and season.
8 Dress the chicken neatly on a silver dish with the garnish around; decorate with fleurons and sprinkle with chopped parsley and chives.

704 Pigeon en compôte – Stewed pigeon

2 *young pigeons*	240 *g* (½ *lb*) *breast of pork*	60 *g* (2 *oz*) *butter*
125 *ml* (¼ *pt*) *tomato sauce* (*Recipe* 34)	240 *g* (½ *lb*) *mushrooms*	*bouquet garni*
	375 *ml* (¾ *pt*) *demi-glace* (*Recipe* 29)	62 *ml* (⅛ *pt*) *white wine*
12 *button onions*		

1 Truss the pigeon; peel and quarter the mushrooms; cut the pork into lardons and blanch.
2 Fry the onions, mushrooms, and pork, in butter in the braising-pan; remove and set the pigeons to brown in same butter.
3 When the pigeons are brown take them out and drain the fat from the pan; make a reduction of the white wine, add the demi-glace and tomato sauce and return the birds.
4 Boil, skim, add bouquet garni and cook under cover, basting frequently.
5 When cooked, remove birds and garnish with onions, mushrooms, and pork.
6 Reduce the sauce to correct consistency, season, enrich with butter and strain.

7 Place the birds in a large cocotte and pour over the sauce; sprinkle with chopped parsley.

705 Salmis de faisan – Salmis of pheasant

1 *pheasant*	45 g (1½ oz) *chopped shallots*	1 *slice truffle*
125 ml (¼ pt) red wine	190 ml (1½ gills) *demi-glace*	60 g (2 oz) *butter*
6 *ground peppercorns*	(*Recipe* 29)	15 g (½ oz) *meat*
1 *bay-leaf*	9 *turned mushrooms*	*glaze* (*Recipe* 13)
½ *glass brandy*	*heart-shaped croûtons*	*chopped parsley*

1 Truss and roast the pheasant, keeping it underdone; cut as for sauté chicken (Recipe 621) and chop the carcass in small pieces.
2 Skin the jointed pheasant and place in a buttered pan with the meat glaze and brandy; keep on the side of the stove to keep warm.
3 Pound the carcass and any trimmings and place them in a sauté-pan with the peppercorns, herbs, red wine, and shallots; and reduce the wine by half.
4 Add the demi-glacé; simmer until it coats a wooden spoon; strain through a fine strainer; season and enrich with butter.
5 Cook the mushrooms in butter.
6 Pour the sauce over the pheasant; dress it neatly on a silver serving-dish.
7 Garnish the dish with the mushrooms, truffle slices, and croutons. (The carcass is not served.)

706 Salmis de caneton Montreuil – Salmis of duck

1, 2 *kg* (4-*lb*) *duck*	60 g (2 oz) *fine mirepoix*	9 *turned mushrooms*
45 g (1½ oz) *butter*	(*Recipe* 2)	4 *heart-shaped*
190 ml (1½ gills) *demi-*	125 ml (1 gill) *sherry*	*croûtons*
glace (*Recipe* 29)	30 g (1 oz) *diced cooked*	*seasoning*
62 ml (⅛ pt) *tomato*	*ox-tongue*	*chopped parsley*
sauce (*Recipe* 34)	2 *large truffles*	1 *bouquet garni*

1 Truss the ducks and partly roast.
2 Cut into joints and chop the carcass.
3 Butter a sauté-pan, cover the bottom with the vegetables and bouquet garni and place on top the pieces of duck and chopped carcass; season and place in the oven for 10 minutes.
4 Drain off the butter and pour in the sherry and add the two sauces; cook under cover until tender.
5 When cooked, place the duck in a large cocotte; remove all fat from the sauce; season and strain.
6 Cut the truffles and tongue into julienne; cook the mushrooms in butter and garnish the duck; pour over the sauce.
7 Garnish with the croûtons fried in butter with the ends dipped in parsley. (The carcass is not served.)

Salmis, General Note. All cooked game may be used in preparing salmis.

RABBIT AND HARE STEWS

707 Stewed rabbit

1 Rabbits should be drawn immediately they are dead.
2 Loosen the skin along the slit edges.

3 Pull the skin over the hind legs, cutting the tail away with the skin and first joint of each leg; the skin is then pulled right over the head.

4 The ears may be skinned or cut off the skin.

5 Take out the·eyes; steep the rabbit in cold salt-water for 2 hours.

Note. This method of preparation applies to all rabbit stews. These are similar to poultry and meat stews. A basic example is given in the next recipe.

708 Ragoût de lapin jardinière – Stewed rabbit jardinière

1 *rabbit*	*bouquet garni*	*chopped parsley*
120 g (¼ *lb*) *mirepoix*	15 g (½ *oz*) *tomato*	*jardinière of vegetables*
(*Recipe 2*)	*purée*	(*Recipe 755*)
750 *ml* (1½ *pt*) *brown*	30 g (1 *oz*) *dripping*	30 g (1 *oz*) *flour*
stock (*Recipe 7*)	*seasoning*	

1 Joint the rabbit, fry in hot fat in a braising-pan. Add the mirepoix which has been previously fried; drain off all fat.

2 Dredge with flour and cook in the oven for 3 or 4 minutes.

3 Add the tomato purée and mix well; moisten with the brown stock.

4 Bring to boil, skim, add bouquet garni.

5 Cook under cover for approximately 1 hour.

6 When cooked, remove the rabbit and place in large entrée-dish.

7 Reduce the sauce to the correct consistency; remove all fat; season and strain over the rabbit.

8 Garnish with jardinière of vegetables and sprinkle with a little chopped parsley.

709 Stewed hare

1 If it is desired to develop the game-flavour, do not remove the insides for 2 to 4 days.

2 Hares should be hung by their forelegs.

3 Skin the same way as a rabbit (Recipe 707).

4 Slit the thin membrane at the end of the breast and take out the blood, heart, and liver; these offals are saved for the making of the sauce and for soups.

5 A young hare should weigh about 3 kg (6 lb) and the age may be determined by grasping an ear with both hands at the tip and pulling it in opposite directions. If the ear tears easily, it is young; if it resists, the hare is old and should be set aside for soup and pâtés.

710 Civet de lièvre bourguignonne – Jugged hare bourguignonne

1 *hare* 3 *kg* (6 *lb*)	45 g (1½ *oz*) *flour*	15 g (½ *oz*) *parsley stalk*
500 g (1 *lb*) *button*	60 g (2 *oz*) *dripping*	120 g (¼ *lb*) *sliced carrots*
onions	*bouquet garni*	*onions, celery*
240 g (½ *lb*) *small*	30 g (1 *oz*) *tomato*	1 *clove crushed garlic*
mushrooms	*purée*	12 *peppercorns*
240 g (½ *lb*) *lardons*	Red-wine marinade:	1·25 *ml spoon* [¼ *teaspoon*]
16 *heart-shaped*	500 *ml* (1 *pt*) *red wine*	*salt*
croûtons	62 *ml* (½ *gill*) *oil*	
1 *l* (1 *qt*) *brown stock*	1 *sprig thyme*	
(*Recipe 7*)		

1 Joint the hare, retaining the blood and liver.
2 Place the hare in the marinade for at least 8 hours, frequently turning.
3 Remove the hare and vegetables from the marinade and fry in the dripping.
4 Singer with flour and brown in the oven for 5 or 6 minutes.
5 Mix in the tomato purée and the liquor from the marinade and stock; boil, skim, and add the bouquet garni; cover and cook in a moderate oven.
6 When cooked, remove hare and place in a clean pan; re-boil sauce and thicken with the hare's blood; season and strain over the hare.
7 Blanch the lardons and fry off; glaze the onions; fry the mushrooms and garnish the hare.
8 Fry the croûtons in butter; dip the ends in parsley and decorate.

Accompaniments:
 i Chop the liver and mix with a little sausage-meat and red-currant jelly; roll in balls, dip in egg and crumbs and deep-fry.
ii Serve also red-currant jelly.

FURTHER DISHES OF MEAT, POULTRY, AND GAME

KEBABS AND MEAT PILAFFS

711 Kebab orientale

2 *fillet mignon*	120 g (¼ lb) lean pork	seasoning
4 *lamb's kidneys*	4 large mushrooms	7 g (¼ oz) chopped parsley
8 *bay-leaves*	7 g (¼ oz) powdered	15 g (½ oz) honey
60 g (2 oz) melted butter	thyme	120 g (4 oz) breadcrumbs

1 Skin the kidney and cut into roundels, 0·7 cm (⅓-inch) thick; sauté quickly in butter.
2 Cut the lamb and pork into 2 cm (1-inch) squares, 0·5 cm (¼ inch) thick.
3 Sauté the mushrooms cut into thick slices.
4 Alternate kidney, mushrooms, bay-leaf, pork, lamb, on a silver skewer and season.
5 Melt the honey and brush over the kebab.
6 Mix the breadcrumbs with the powdered thyme and parsley.
7 Brush over with melted butter and grill all over.
8 Serve with pilaff or risotto (Recipes 362 to 369) and leave on the skewers.

712 Pilaff de mouton

625 g (1¼ lb) boned leg of mutton	240 g (½ lb) diced onions seasoning	bouquet garni 30 g (1 oz) flour
750 g (1½ lb) tomato concassé	750 ml (1½ pt) brown stock	15 g (½ oz) tomato purée
5 ml spoon [½ dessert-spoon] ground ginger	(Recipe 7 or 8)	30 g (1 oz) dripping

1 Remove all fat from mutton and cut into 3 cm (1½-inch) squares.
2 Cook the onions in butter.

3 Fry the meat to golden brown in a braising-pan; drain off all fat and add the ginger.
4 Sprinkle the meat with flour and cook for a few minutes in the oven.
5 Add the tomato purée and concassé and onions to the meat; mix well; boil, skim, and add bouquet garni.
6 Cover and simmer in moderate oven; when cooked, remove the meat and place in a clean pan.
7 Reduce cooking-liquor, check for seasoning and consistency and strain over meat.
8 Serve with rice pilaff (Recipe 366):

713 Pilaff de volaille à la King

1 *medium fowl*	250 *ml* ($\frac{1}{2}$ *pt*) *chicken*	60 *g* (2 *oz*)
45 *g* (1$\frac{1}{2}$ *oz*) *pimentoes*	*velouté* (*Recipe* 27)	*butter*
240 *g* ($\frac{1}{2}$ *lb*) *white*	2 *egg yolks* ⎫	*rice pilaff*
mushrooms	62 *ml* ($\frac{1}{8}$ *pt*) ⎬ *liaison*	(*Recipe* 366)
seasoning	*cream* ⎭	

1 Boil the fowl or chicken and carefully remove from the bone.
2 Cut the chicken into small pieces slantwise and toss in butter.
3 Cook the mushrooms in a little butter and stock; dice and heat the pimentoes in butter.
4 Add the garnish to the chicken and moisten with the chicken velouté and simmer for a few minutes.
5 Add the liaison and season; draw to the side of the stove.
6 Serve with a bordure of rice pilaff.

714 Émincé de volaille à la King

Prepare as Recipe 713 and serve within a bordure of pommes duchesse (Recipe 909).

HOT MOUSSES

715 Mousse de jambon – Hot mousse of ham

240 *g* ($\frac{1}{2}$ *lb*) *lean cooked*	15 *g* ($\frac{1}{2}$ *oz*) *frangipane*	*pepper*
ham	*panada*	*grated nutmeg*
1 *egg white*	(*Recipe* 192)	
pinch of paprika	250 *ml* ($\frac{1}{2}$ *pt*) *fresh cream*	

1 Pass the ham through a fine mincer then rub through sieve with the panada.
2 Pound in the mortar gradually adding the egg whites and season.
3 Place the mixture in a bowl on ice and slowly work in the cream.
4 Butter a charlotte mould and gently poach in a bain-marie covered with greaseproof paper.
5 Allow to cool slightly and take out of mould.
6 Serve a sauce-boat of sauce suprême (Recipe 63).

716 Basic recipe for hot mousse or mousseline de volaille

240 g (½ *lb*) *chicken*   1 *egg white*
salt, pepper   250 *ml* (½ *pt*) *fresh thick cream*

1 Remove all tendons and pass through a fine mincer.
2 Season with salt, pepper and little grated nutmeg and pound in the mortar with the egg whites.
3 Rub through a fine sieve into a bowl; place bowl on ice.
4 Gradually add the cream with care to form an even mixture.
5 Butter a charlotte mould and gently poach in a bain-marie.

717 Quenelles de volaille (with panada)

1, 1 *kg* (2 *lb*) *fowl*   30 g (1 *oz*) *butter* ⎫   *seasoning*
2 *egg whites*   60 g (2 *oz*) *flour*   ⎬ *panada*   125 *ml* (1 *gill*)
                            125 *ml* (1 *gill*) *white* ⎪   *cream*
                            stock (Recipe 6)   ⎭

1 Melt the butter in a saucepan; stir in the flour; cook slightly; add the stock and work until it becomes a smooth paste and leaves the side of the pan clean; allow it to cool on a plate.
2 Remove the sinews from the fowl and pass it through a fine mincer; place in the mortar and mix with the panada and egg whites; season.
3 Rub the mixture through a sieve; place in a bowl on ice and slowly work in the cream.
4 Mould with two spoons; gently poach.

Note:
i Quenelles may be made from pheasant, veal, lean pork, using the same recipe and method.
ii Similar considerations apply in shaping and sizing for mousse, mousseline, and quenelles of chicken and other meats as for fish (see Recipes 459–61).

CHARCUTERIE DISHES – PORK-BUTCHER AND SAUSAGE-MAKER DISHES

718 Boudin noir – Black pudding

4 *boudin*   120 g (¼ *lb*) *white crumbs*   8 *slices bacon*
French mustard

1 With a sharp knife, make little incisions on all sides of the boudin.
2 Brush with French mustard and roll in white crumbs; pour over melted butter and grill all sides gently.
3 Serve with grilled bacon.

719 Crépinettes de porc

500 g (1 *lb*) *fine pork*   250 *ml* (½ *pt*) *sauce*   *seasoning*
   sausage-meat   *Périgueux (Recipe 45)*   1 *egg yolk*
30 g (1 *oz*) *chopped truffles*   30 g (1 *oz*) *melted butter*   *pig's caul*

1 Soak the caul in tepid water to make it pliable.
2 Mix the pork sausage-meat and truffle together and bind with egg yolks; season.
3 Divide into 60 g (2-oz) portions and shape into flat rectangles.
4 Wrap a piece of caul round each crépinette; brush with melted butter and grill or sauter both sides gently.
5 Arrange in a circle and serve creamed potatoes (Recipe 896) and the sauce separately.

720 Saucisses au vin blanc

500 *g* (1 *lb*) *French or Cambridge sausage* (8 *to the lb*)	45 *g* (1½ *oz*) *butter*	250 *ml* (½ *pt*) *demi-glace*
125 *ml* (¼ *pt*) *white wine*	30 *g* (1 *oz*) *finely-chopped shallots*	(*Recipe* 29)
8 *oblong croûtons*		*seasoning*

1 Blanch and refresh sausages and sauté gently in butter.
2 Remove sausages and cook shallots to golden colour.
3 Déglacer with wine and reduce.
4 Add the demi-glace and reduce by half; enrich with butter, season.
5 Cook the croûtons in butter and dress the sausage on top; coat each with sauce.
6 Garnish with a little chopped parsley.

721 Frankfurters Strasbourg

500 *g* (1 *lb*) *sauerkraut*	120 *g* (¼ *lb*) *bacon*	¼ *bottle hock*
8 *frankfurter sausages*	120 *g* (¼ *lb*) *bacon rind*	1 *onion clouté*
120 *g* (¼ *lb*) *garlic sausage*		1 *whole carrot*
750 *g* (¾ *lb*) *boiled potatoes*	60 *g* (2 *oz*) *lard*	

1 Line a thick pan with bacon rind.
2 Divide the sauerkraut in equal parts and place one half on top of the bacon rind.
3 Lay on the carrots, onions, lard and bacon, and cover with the remainder of the sauerkraut; place the garlic sausage on top and cover with the bacon rind, moisten with the hock.
4 Put a lid on top and seal with flour and water-paste; braise for 2 hours.
5 When cooked, remove vegetables and garnish with sliced garlic-sausage, bacon, boiled frankfurters and boiled potatoes.

Note. Frankfurters should be placed in cold water and brought to the boil.

COMPOSITE OR MADE-UP DISHES

The following made-up dishes are of cooked meat, poultry, and game and, in most instances, are regarded as a means of using left-overs.

722 Chicken and ham cutlets

240 g (½ lb) *finely-diced cooked*   15 g (½ oz) *butter*   *seasoning*
   chicken   1 *egg yolk*   8 *cutlet-frills*
120 g (¼ lb) *finely-diced cooked*   125 ml (1 gill) *white* 8 *pieces of*
   ham   *stock*   *raw*
15 g (½ oz) *flour*   *(Recipe 6)*   *macaroni*

1 Melt the butter, add the flour and make a white roux.
2 Add the stock and mix to a smooth sauce.
3 Add the chicken and ham; mix well and cook for approximately 5 minutes
  at side of stove stirring frequently with the spatula.
4 Bind with the egg yolks; season, place on greased tray and leave to cool.
5 Shape into 8 cutlets; pass through flour, egg-wash and white breadcrumb;
  place a small piece of macaroni in each end to resemble cutlet-bone.
6 Fry in clarified butter and garnish with fried parsley.
7 Place a cutlet-frill on each piece of macaroni.

723 Cottage pie

500 g (1 lb) *finely-chopped cooked beef*   120 g (¼ lb) *finely-chopped*
125 ml (¼ pt) *demi-glace (Recipe 29)*   *onions*
360 g (¾ lb) *duchesse potatoes (Recipe*   *seasoning*
   909)   15 g (½ oz) *butter*

1 Sweat the onions in butter and add the cooked beef.
2 Add the demi-glace and simmer for approximately 15 minutes; season.
3 Place the meat in a pie-dish and pipe the duchesse potatoes on top.
4 Brush with egg-wash and brown in the oven.

Note. Shepherds pie is similarly made. Cooked lamb or mutton may also be
used in these dishes.

Cromesquis (Alternative spellings – Cromeskis, Kromeskis): These are small
rolls of savoury preparation composed of finely-chopped, cooked fowl, game,
or other meat rolled into cork shapes, wrapped in bacon, dipped in frying
batter, deep-fried in hot fat, and garnished with fried parsley. Tomato sauce
is served separately.

724 Cromesquis à la russe

150 g (5 oz) *diced cooked*   7 g (¼ oz) *diced*   125 ml (1
   chicken   *cooked mushrooms*   gill) *white*
60 g (2 oz) *diced cooked*   8 *slices bacon*   *stock*
   tongue   250 ml (½ pt) *frying*   *(Recipe 6)*
7 g (¼ oz) *truffles (diced)*   *batter*   15 g (½ oz)
1 *egg yolk*   *parsley sprigs*   *flour*
15 g (½ oz) *butter*   *seasoning*

1 Melt the butter, add the flour and make a white roux.
2 Add the stock and mix to a smooth paste.
3 Add the chicken, tongue, truffles, and mushrooms; cook for 5 minutes at
  the side of the stove, stirring frequently with a wooden spatula.
4 Bind with the egg yolks, and season.

5 Pour on to a greased tray and allow to cool.
6 Roll into 8 equal-sized corks; wrap a thin slice of bacon round each, dip in batter and fry in deep fat; drain and garnish with fried parsley.

Croquettes is the name given to oval, round ball- or cork-shapes of minced meats, fish, poultry, or game. These shapes are floured, egged, and crumbed and are deep-fried or shallow-fried.

725 Croquettes de gibier aux truffes – Game and truffle croquettes

240 g (8 oz) minced cooked game	1 egg yolk	125 ml (¼ pt) game stock
15 g (½ oz) finely-chopped truffle	15 g (½ oz) flour	(Recipe 12)
	15 g (½ oz) butter	
	seasoning	

1 Melt the butter, add the flour and make a blond roux.
2 Add the stock and mix to a smooth sauce.
3 Add the minced game and truffle; cook for a few minutes stirring frequently.
4 Bind with the egg yolks, and season.
5 Pour on to a greased tray and allow to cool.
6 Roll into 8 equal-sized corks; dip in flour, egg and crumb; fry in deep fat and garnish with fried parsley.

726 Croquettes de bœuf

360 g (12 oz) minced cooked beef	30 g (1 oz) finely-chopped onions	1 egg yolk
120 g (¼ lb) dry mashed potatoes	7 g (¼ oz) chopped parsley seasoning	125 ml (¼ pt) sauce piquante (Recipe 46)

1 Fry the onions to golden colour in butter.
2 Mix the meat, potatoes, parsley and onions together; bind with egg, and season.
3 Scale into approximately 90 g (3 oz) portions and shape into 5 cm (2½ inch) cylinders.
4 Dip in flour, eggwash and breadcrumbs and deepfry.
5 Garnish with a purée of fresh peas and serve sauce piquante separately.

727 Émincé de volaille
Though properly prepared from freshly-cooked fowl, émincés, such as émincé de volaille à la King, are sometimes adapted to make use of left-over cooked chicken.

728 Corned-beef hash

360 g (¾ lb) diced corned beef	90 g (3 oz) butter	chopped parsley
240 g (½ lb) finely-diced cooked potatoes	stock (Recipe 7 or 8) as necessary	seasoning

1 Combine the cooked potatoes with the corned beef, season; use stock as necessary to form.

2 Shallow-fry in butter and when beginning to colour shape as a large omelet, continue to cook to golden colour; sprinkle with chopped parsley for service.

729 Mazagran

500 g (1 lb) duchesse potatoes (Recipe 909)	500 g (1 lb) cooked lean ham	125 ml (¼ pt) demi-glace (Recipe 29)
240 g (½ lb) cooked lean beef seasoning	120 g (¼ lb) diced cooked mushrooms	60 g (2 oz) finely-chopped onions

1 Fry the onions to golden colour in butter.
2 Dice the beef and ham small, and mix with the onions.
3 Moisten with the sauce and cook for a few minutes.
4 Place a layer of duchesse potatoes on the bottom of the serving dish then a layer of meat, and neatly pipe a layer of potatoes on top.
5 Brown under grill.

730 Moussaka

2 large aubergines	½ tablespoon tomato purée	45 g (1½ oz) raw chopped mush-rooms
30 g (1 oz) finely-chopped onions	62 ml (½ gill) espagnole sauce (Recipe 28)	1 charlotte mould
½ clove chopped garlic	30 g (1 oz) butter	seasoning, chopped parsley
500 g (1 lb) cooked lean mutton		

1 Peel the aubergine (egg-plant) and cut into roundels; season, dip in flour, and fry in oil.
2 Cut the mutton into very fine dice.
3 Fry the onions to golden colour, in butter; add the garlic, meat, sauce, tomato purée, and the mushrooms; season well.
4 Butter the charlotte moulds and put a layer of the aubergine roundels on the bottom.
5 Cover with a layer of meat 2 cm (1-inch thick) and continue with alternate layers of meat and egg-plant, finishing with a layer of egg-plant; press down firmly.
6 Cook in a bain-marie for 1 hour with a greaseproof paper on top.
7 Let the mould stand for a few minutes before turning out and sprinkle the surface with chopped parsley before serving.

Alternative method:
1 Place the mixture in a pie-dish.
2 Garnish the top neatly with roundels of aubergine and sliced tomatoes, alternately.
3 Sprinkle with breadcrumbs and brown under grill.

PUDDINGS AND PIES OF MEAT, POULTRY, AND GAME

The recipes in this section are mostly in the British tradition.

731 A Hot Chicken pie

1, 2 *kg* (4-*lb*) *chicken*	240 *g* (½ *lb*) *button mush-*	*puff paste*
240 *g* (½ *lb*) *button*	*rooms*	(*Recipe* 994)
onions	250 *ml* (½ *pt*) *white stock*	4 *g* (⅛ *oz*) *parsley*
360 *g* (¾ *lb*) *parisienne*	(*Recipe* 6)	
potatoes (*Recipe* 904)		

1 Joint the chicken and gently fry in butter and place in pie dish.
2 Add the onions, button mushrooms, parsley, potatoes, and season; add the stock.
3 Proceed to cover and decorate as for steak pie.
4 Approximate cooking-time, 1½ hours.
Note. There are several versions of chicken pie, including diced chicken in cream sauce etc. as fillings.

732 Cornish pasty

360 *g* (¾ *lb*) *short pastry*	30 *g* (1 *oz*) *diced cooked*	*pinch mixed*
(*Recipe* 995)	*onions*	*herbs*
360 *g* (¾ *lb*) *cooked meat*	62 *ml* (½ *gill*) *demi-glace,*	*pinch parsley*
180 *g* (6 *oz*) *cooked*	*cold*	*salt, pepper*
potatoes	(*Recipe* 29)	

Cut the meat and potato into small dice; mix with the remainder of the ingredients, and season.
Roll out the pastry thinly and cut into rounds the size of a saucer.
Divide the meat mixture according to pastry.
Place a heap in the centre of each round and wet the edges.
Lift the edges of the pastry above the mixture and press the two together.
Flute the edges of the pastry with the fingers and prick each side to prevent bursting.
Brush over with milk and bake in a quick oven until browned, approximately 20 to 25 minutes.

733 Forfar Bridie

360 (¾ *lb*) *puff pastry*	*pinch mixed herbs*	7 *g* (¼ *oz*) *chopped*
(*Recipe* 994)	240 *g* (½ *lb*) *minced*	*parsley*
60 *g* (2 *oz*) *cooked diced onions*	*steak*	*seasoning*

1 Mix together the meat, onions, herbs and parsley; season and moisten with a little stock.
2 Roll out the paste thinly and cut into rounds the size of a saucer.
3 Place a heap of the meat mixture on one side of the round, wet the edges and turn over; make two small cuts on one side.
4 Egg-wash and bake in moderate oven for 20 to 25 minutes until browned.

734 Game pie (hot)

1 *pheasant*	500 *g* (1 *lb*) *diced mush-*	*pinch mixed herbs*
1 *partridge*	*rooms*	7 *g* (¼ *oz*) *parsley*
1 *grouse*	500 *ml* (1 *pt*) *thin brown*	*puff pastry*
500 *g* (1 *lb*) *rump steak*	*sauce*	(*Recipe* 994)
180 *g* (6 *oz*) *diced onions*	(*Recipe* 29)	

1 Joint the game and fry in butter until golden brown; cut the steak into small pieces.
2 Lay the game and other ingredients in alternate layers in the pie-dish and season.
3 Cover with the sauce.
4 Proceed to cover as for steak and kidney pie.
5 Cook for 1¾ hours, approximately.

735 Mutton pie

250 *ml* (½ *pt*) *white stock* (*Recipe* 6)	2 *raw potatoes*	2 *sheep's kidneys*
puff paste (*Recipe* 994)	30 *g* (1 *oz*) *chopped onions*	120 *g* (¼ *lb*) *tomato concassé*
4 *g* (⅛ *oz*) *chopped parsley*	500 *g* (1 *lb*) *fillet of mutton*	*salt, pepper*

1 Cut the mutton into thin slices.
2 Skin the kidney and slice into rounds.
3 Slice the potatoes as thick as a penny.
4 Fill the pie-dish with alternate layers of all the ingredients, seasoning each layer.
5 Cover with the stock.
5 Proceed to cover with the paste as for steak and kidney pie.
7 Cooking-time, 1½ hours.

736 Pigeon pie

2 *pigeons*	90 *g* (3 *oz*) *chopped onions*	*salt, pepper*
240 *g* (½ *lb*) *rump steak*	4 *g* (⅛ *oz*) *chopped parsley*	250 *ml* (½ *pt*) *brown stock* (*Recipe* 7)
120 *g* (¼ *lb*) *raw ham*	*pinch mixed herbs*	
puff paste		

1 Joint the pigeons and cut the steak into small escalopes.
2 Place the pigeons and other ingredients in alternate layers in the pie-dish, season and cover with brown stock.
3 Cover with puff paste as for steak and kidney pie and cook for 1¾ hours approximately.

737 Pork pie (cold)

(Pie filling)

360 *g* (¾ *lb*) *spare rib of pork*	3 *sheets gelatine*	240 *g* (½ *lb*) *hot-water paste*
120 *g* (¼ *lb*) *white bread-crumbs*	125 *ml* (1 *gill*) *white stock* (*Recipe* 6)	(*Recipe* 997)
	salt	*pepper*

1 Cut the lean and fat of the pork into 1 cm (½-inch) dice.
2 Add the breadcrumbs, stock, and seasoning.
3 Soak the gelatine in water.
4 Prepare hot-water paste and line the sides and bottom of a greased, oblong raised pie-mould, retaining sufficient paste to form a lid.
5 Place alternate layers of the meat-mixture and soaked, softened leaves of gelatine in the lined mould.

6 Moisten the edges of the mould, cover with paste, and decorate leaving a hole in the centre.
7 Cook for approximately 2 hours in a moderate oven.
8 When cold, fill with aspic jelly as necessary.

738 Rabbit pie

1 *young rabbit*	250 *ml* (½ *pt*) *brown stock*	*puff paste* (*Recipe*
120 *g* (¼ *lb*) *raw ham*	(*Recipe* 7)	994)
90 *g* (3 *oz*) *chopped onions*	7 *g* (¼ *oz*) *chopped parsley* salt, pepper	240 *g* (½ *lb*) *mushrooms*

1 Joint the rabbit and soak in cold salted water for 2 hours; rinse well.
2 Dice the mushrooms and cut the ham into small pieces.
3 Place the rabbit and other ingredients in alternate layers in the pie-dish; season and cover with brown stock.
4 Cover as for steak and kidney pie and cook for 1½ hours.

739 Sausage rolls

500 *g* (1 *lb*) *puff paste* (*Recipe* 994)   360 *g* (¾ *lb*) *sausage-meat*

1 Roll the puff paste into long strips 0·3 cm (⅛ inch) thick.
2 Roll the sausage-meat into long rolls using a little flour.
3 Place the sausage-meat along the centre of the paste.
4 Egg-wash the edges of the pastry and draw the bottom edge over the sausage, then turn over the egg-washed edge and seal carefully.
5 Cut through in slanting direction about 4 cm (2 inches) apart.
6 Make two slanting cuts on top of each and trim the ends.
7 Egg-wash, place on a damp tray, and bake in a hot oven for 20 to 30 minutes.

740 Sheep's head pie

2 *sheep's heads*	250 *ml* (½ *pt*) *sheep's head stock*	*short pastry*
120 *g* (¼ *lb*) *lean ham*	(*liquor from boiling heads*	(*Recipe* 995)
1 *hard-boiled egg*	*with stock ingredients from*	salt, pepper
4 *g* (⅛ *oz*) *parsley*	*Recipe* 6)	nutmeg

1 Boil the sheep's heads and remove all meat.
2 Cut the ham thinly and slice the eggs.
3 Fill the dish with layers of the various ingredients and season.
4 Add the stock and cover with short pastry.
5 Wash with milk and bake quickly for ¾ hour.

741 Steak and giblet pie

240 *g* (½ *lb*) *chicken's gizzards*	*pinch of herbs*	7 *g* (¼ *oz*) *flour*
240 *g* (½ *lb*) *rump steak*	250 *ml* (½ *pt*) *brown*	4 *g* (⅛ *oz*) *parsley*
240 *g* (½ *lb*) *button onions*	*stock* (*Recipe* 8)	*rough puff pastry*
240 *g* (½ *lb*) *mushrooms*	60 *g* (2 *oz*) *ox-*	(*Recipe* 993)
salt, pepper	*kidney*	

1 Cut the gizzards and steak into small escalopes.
2 Slice the mushrooms and kidney and toss with the gizzards and steak quickly in butter; drain, mix with the flour, and cook for a few minutes.
3 Add the onions, herbs, parsley, and season; cover with stock.
4 Cover with rough puff pastry, egg-wash, and bake in a moderate oven for approximately 1¾ hours.

742 Steak, kidney, and oyster pie

500 g (1 lb) rump steak	7 g (¼ oz) chopped	12 oysters
120 g (4 oz) ox-kidney	parsley	240 g (½ lb) puff
60 g (2 oz) mushrooms	190 ml (1½ gills) brown	paste
90 g (3 oz) diced onions	stock (Recipe 8) cold	(Recipe 994)

1 Remove fat from meat and cut into escalopes about 2 cm (1 inch) in length
2 Peel and slice mushrooms 0·5 cm (¼ inch) thick.
3 Beard the oysters.
4 Place meat, onions, parsley, and cold stock in a bowl and season; allow to stand for 1 hour.
5 Place a layer of meat, mushrooms, and oysters alternately in a 25 cm (10-inch) pie-dish.
6 Cover and decorate with puff paste, and egg-wash.
7 Bake in hot oven for approximately 1½ hours.

743 Steak and kidney pudding

		Paste for pudding:
500 g (1 lb) rump steak	250 ml (½ pt) brown	240 g (½ lb) sifted flour
120 g (4 oz) ox-kidney	stock (Recipe 8)	5 ml spoon [1 teaspoon]
7 g (¼ oz) chopped parsley	salt, pepper	baking-powder
	90 g (3 oz) diced	120 g (4 oz) beef suet
	onions	62 ml (1 gill) water
		(approx.)
		1·25 ml spoon [¼ teaspoon]
		salt

1 Cut the meat free from fat, into small pieces; skin the kidney and cut to same size.
2 Place the meat in a bowl with the kidneys, chopped parsley, and onions cover with cold stock, add a little Worcester sauce and season; allow to stand for 1 hour.
3 Prepare the paste by removing the skin from the suet and chopping finely with a little flour.
4 Sieve the flour, baking powder, and salt in a basin and mix it lightly with the suet and add water to form a soft paste.
5 Roll the paste to 0·5 cm (¼ inch) thickness and line a basin of suitable size reserving sufficient paste for a lid.
6 Fill the meat into the lined basin; wet the edges and cover, pressing the edges down firmly.
7 Damp a cloth in hot water, wring out and flour; tie on the cloth allowing sufficient room for the paste to expand.
8 Steam for 3½ hours.
9 Serve in the pudding-bowl or turn out.

744 Steak and oyster pudding

Prepare as Recipe 743 but allow 3 oysters (bearded) per person and place them in layers through the meat.

745 Steak pudding and mushrooms

Use the same method as for steak and kidney pudding (Recipe 743) but replace kidney by 250 g ($\frac{1}{2}$ lb) of sliced mushrooms.

746 Steak and cow-heel pie

1 *cow heel*	90 *g (3 oz) diced*	375 *ml ($\frac{3}{4}$ pt) brown*
240 *g ($\frac{1}{2}$ lb) puff*	*onions*	*stock, cold*
pastry	7 *g ($\frac{1}{4}$ oz) chopped parsley*	*(Recipe 7)*
(Recipe 994)	500 *g (1 lb) rump steak*	*salt, pepper*

1 Blanch the cow-heels and cook à blanc (Recipe 759).
2 When cooked, remove the bone and dice into 2 cm (1-inch) squares.
3 Remove all fat from the meat and cut into small escalopes about 2 cm (1 inch) in length.
4 Place the meat, cow-heels, onions, parsley in a bowl and cover with the cold brown stock; season with salt and pepper; allow to stand for 1 hour.
5 Place the meat in a pie-dish 25 cm (10-inch), cover with the puff paste, decorate, egg-wash, and cook for approximately 1$\frac{1}{2}$ hours.

747 Toad in the hole

8 *small sausages*   240 *ml ($\frac{1}{2}$ pt) batter (Recipe 507)*   30 *g (1 oz) dripping*

1 Skin the sausages and place in hot fat and cook in a baking-tin.
2 Pour the batter over the sausages and cook in hot oven for 15 minutes.

Note. The batter should be a little thicker than when used for plain Yorkshire pudding.

748 Veal and ham pie (cold)

500 *g (1 lb) lean fillet*	250 *ml ($\frac{1}{2}$ pt) white*	12 *slices streaky bacon*
of veal	*stock (Recipe 9)*	10 *ml spoon [$\frac{1}{2}$ table-*
120 *g ($\frac{1}{4}$ lb) raw ham*	*grated rind of $\frac{1}{2}$*	*spoon] chopped*
1 *hard-boiled egg*	*lemon*	*parsley*
125 *ml ($\frac{1}{4}$ pt) aspic*	240 *g ($\frac{1}{2}$ lb) puff paste*	30 *g (1 oz) chopped*
(Recipe 122)	*(Recipe 994)*	*onion*

1 Free the veal from sinews and cut into small, thin slices and treat the ham in a similar fashion.
2 Arrange the veal, ham, and bacon in layers in a pie-dish.
3 Cover each layer with a few slices of hard-boiled egg; sprinkle each layer with onions, lemon rind, parsley, salt, and pepper.
4 Add 125 ml ($\frac{1}{4}$ pt stock); line the rim of the pie-dish and cover with puff paste; leaving a hole in the centre; decorate.

5 Egg-wash, bake in a moderate oven for approximately 1¾ hours; add a little stock from time to time if required.
6 When cold fill with cool, but not set, aspic.

749 Bouchées and vol-au-vents

Note:
  i The method of making the circular puff-pastry cases for vol-au-vents and bouchées (similar but smaller) is given in Chapter 8.
  ii Vol-au-vents are used as hot entrées.
  iii Bouchées are used also for appetizers (hot or cold).

Examples of fillings for vol-au-vents and bouchées
Reine: quenelles, chicken, truffles, lié sauce suprême.
Montglas: tongue, quenelles, truffles, foie gras, sweetbread, chicken lié sauce Madère.
Financière: quenelles, cockscombs, sweetbreads, tongue, olives, mushrooms, truffles, lié sauce Madère.
Princesse: same as Reine, garnish asparagus tips, lié sauce suprême.
Diane: salpicon of game and truffles, blended with thickened salmis sauce.
Toulouse: chicken quenelles, mushrooms, sweetbreads, lié sauce suprême.

750 Crêtes et rognons de coq – Cockscombs and kidneys

Cockscombs and kidneys are included in garnishes such as financière (see Recipe 749).

To prepare and cook cockscombs:
  i Soak in salt water for 24 hours to remove blood.
  ii Place the cockscombs in cold water and heat to lukewarm.
  iii Drain and rub them in a cloth with a little gros sel (coarse salt) to remove the skins.
  iv Cook them à blanc (i.e. in flour-thickened, lemon-acidulated water).

To prepare and cook cock's kidneys: Soak in cold water for 3 hours, then cook à blanc.

COLD DISHES OF POULTRY AND HAM

751 Chapon en belle vue – Chaud-froid of capon

1 *large capon*	250 *ml* (½ *pt*) *white chaud-*	2 *slices cooked tongue*
500 *ml* (1 *pt*) *chicken*	*froid* (*Recipe* 134)	*aspic jelly*
stock (*Recipe* 11)	2 *large truffles*	(*Recipe* 122)

1 Truss and wrap the birds in buttered paper.
2 Gently simmer in a rich-flavoured chicken stock.
3 When cooked, cool and remove skins.
4 Reduce 250 ml (½ pt) of the cooking-liquor and stir into chaud-froid sauce
5 Stir this mixture until nearly set and pour quickly over the birds to coat them completely.

6 Allow the sauce to set and garnish with decorative pieces of truffle and tongue.
7 Mask with a coating of half-set aspic jelly.
8 Dress on a socle, neatly decorated, and garnish round the base with crescents of aspic jelly.
9 Place a garnished hâtelet in the centre.

752 Mayonnaise de volaille

500 g (1 *lb*) *cold boiled chicken*	4 *stoned olives*	4 *quarters lettuce*
30 *ml* (¼ *gill*) *vinaigrette*	125 *ml* (¼ *pt*)	*hearts*
(*Recipe* 118)	*mayonnaise*	4 *anchovy fillets*
2 *hard-boiled eggs*	(*Recipe* 110)	12 *capers*

1 Garnish the salad-bowl with shredded lettuce and season with salt and vinaigrette.
2 Skin the white meat of the chicken and cut into small collops.
3 Arrange the chicken, dome fashion, on top of the lettuce.
4 Cover chicken with mayonnaise sauce.
5 Decorate with olives, capers, and anchovy fillets.
6 Garnish with quarters of lettuce hearts and quarters of hard-boiled egg.

752a Salade de volaille – Chicken salad

1. Prepare as Recipe 752 with mayonnaise replaced by ordinary seasoning.

Pork pie
See Recipe 737.

753 Soufflé de jambon espagnole

120 g (¼ *lb*) *cooked lean ham*	125 *ml* (¼ *pt*)	62 *ml* (½ *gill*) *cream*
15 g (½ *oz*) *butter*	*espagnole sauce*	4 g (⅛ *oz*) *leaf*
7 g (¼ *oz*) *finely-chopped*	(*Recipe* 28)	*gelatine*
shallots	62 *ml* (½ *gill*) *aspic jelly*	*salt, pepper*
1 *egg white*	(*Recipe* 122)	*paprika*

Cut the ham into small dice and fry in butter with the shallots.
Pound the ham and sauce to a fine paste and rub through a fine sieve.
Place the mixture in a small pan and cook for a few minutes, season to taste, add aspic jelly and thoroughly dissolved leaf gelatine; allow to cool slightly.
Whip the egg white to a stiff froth, stir into the mixture, whip the cream and fold in gently.
Stir the mixture in a bowl on ice until it begins to set; pour into a prepared soufflé dish with a paper-band attached.
Keep in the refrigerator for 2 hours, remove paper-band and dust with a little paprika.

Veal and ham pie
See Recipe 748.

7. Vegetables

THE cooking of vegetables in a large professional kitchen operating on *partie* lines is allotted to the chef entremettier who also, as stated earlier, is responsible for the preparation and serving of eggs, pastas, and rice. A few exceptions amongst vegetables are the variety of deep-fried items, particularly potatoes, usually cooked under the supervision of the roast cook, and grilled vegetables such as tomatoes and mushrooms done by the grillardin. Vegetables for garnishes, when an integral part of the cooking, are normally done by the *partie* concerned, e.g. the saucier's preparation of the vegetables in bourgeoise. Otherwise, the chef entremettier not only prepares and cooks the vegetables for table d'hôte and à la carte service but also vegetable garnishes that are passed to other *parties*.

Pre-prepared and processed vegetables
Because this *Compendium* concentrates on the chef's craft as based on age-long principles, it should not be thought that these principles may not apply to the use of vegetables (and other commodities) prepared and processed in modern forms. Quick-frozen vegetables, for example, are widely used in the catering industry and the treatment outlined for fresh produce may be used for them provided that the preliminary steps in cooking are carried out in accordance with the processor's instructions given for the pack. In most case quick-frozen vegetables are already blanched and basic treatment by the chef involves subsequent immersion in boiling water and continuous cooking as for blanched vegetables. (See further notes on page 226.)

Canned vegetables, such as rarer items like artichoke bottoms and okra have long been in common use in professional kitchens. Dried pulses are similarly commonplace culinary items and kitchen craftsmen are also making use of dehydrated vegetables including the newer forms of accelerated freeze dry. What is important is that once reconstitution and basic cooking have taken place, a good finish, as outlined in the recipes, must equally be given to processed forms.

Guide to vegetable portioning. In using the following approximate quantities as a guide, it should be noted that the portioning policy must be determined in the light of cost and selling price. The quality of produce also affects the amount required to gauge net portions.

Vegetables	Gross Raw Portion	Net Raw Portion after Preparation
Artichokes	1 per portion	120 g (4 oz)
Asparagus, fresh	8 or 9 sticks per portion	
Beetroot	90 g (3 oz)	60 g (2 oz)

Vegetables	Gross Raw Portion	Net Raw Portion after Preparation
Broad Beans, fresh	180 g (6 oz)	120 g (4 oz)
Broad Beans, frozen	90 g (3 oz)	90 g (3 oz)
Broccoli, fresh	120 g (4 oz)	90 g (3 oz)
Broccoli, frozen	90 g (3 oz)	90 g (3 oz)
Brussels Sprouts, fresh	180 g (6 oz)	90 g (3 oz)
Brussels Sprouts, frozen	90 g (3 oz)	90 g (3 oz)
Button Onions	120 g (4 oz)	90 g (3 oz)
Cabbage, winter	240 g ($\frac{1}{2}$ lb)	90 g (3 oz)
Cabbage, spring	180 g (6 oz)	120 g (4 oz)
Cardoons	120 g (4 oz)	90 g (3 oz)
Carrots, old	120 g (4 oz)	90 g (3 oz)
Carrots, new	90 g (3 oz)	60 g (2 oz)
Cauliflower, fresh	120 g (4 oz)	90 g (3 oz)
Cauliflower, frozen	90 g (3 oz)	90 g (3 oz)
Celeriac	120 g (4 oz)	90 g (3 oz)
Celery	1 head: 2 portions	
Corn on cob	1 per person	
Corn salad	120 g (4 oz)	90 g (3 oz)
Cucumber	60 g (2 oz)	50 g (1$\frac{3}{4}$ oz)
Egg-Plant	90 g (3 oz)	90 g (3 oz)
Endive, Belgian	90 g (3 oz)	90 g (3 oz)
Fennel	120 g (4 oz)	90 g (3 oz)
Flageolets	180 g (6 oz)	120 g (4 oz)
French Beans, fresh	120 g (4 oz)	90 g (3 oz)
Jerusalem Artichokes	90 g (3 oz)	60 g (2 oz)
Kohl Rabis	180 g (6 oz)	90 g (3 oz)
Leeks	180 g (6 oz)	90 g (3 oz)
Lettuce, fresh (for serving as salad)	3 portions	
Lettuce (in cooking)	2 portions, depending on size	
Lettuce, cos	2 portions	
Lettuce, braised	1 portion	
Marrow	180 g (6 oz)	120 g (4 oz)

Vegetables	Gross Raw Portion	Net Raw Portion after Preparation
New Turnips	90 g (3 oz)	60 g (2 oz)
Onions	150 g (5 oz)	120 g (4 oz)
Parsnips	90 g (3 oz)	60 g (2 oz)
Peas, fresh, in pod	180 g (6 oz)	90 g (3 oz)
Peas, frozen	90 g (3 oz)	90 g (3 oz)
Pumpkin	180 g (6 oz)	120 g (4 oz)
Salsify	120 g (4 oz)	90 g (3 oz)
Scotch Kale	180 g (6 oz)	120 g (4 oz)
Sea-kale	120 g (4 oz)	90 g (3 oz)
Spinach, fresh	180 g (6 oz)	120 g (4 oz)
Spinach, frozen	120 g (4 oz)	90 g (3 oz)
Swedes	180 g (6 oz)	75 g (2½ oz)
Tomatoes	90 g (3 oz)	90 g (3 oz)
Turnip tops	120 g (4 oz)	60 g (2 oz)

EXAMPLES OF VEGETABLE GARNISHES
PREPARED BY THE ENTREMETTIER

754 Mixed vegetable garnishes

Guide to quantities for 4 covers

Bouquetière	Gross Raw Weight	Net Raw Weight
Turned carrots	120 g (4 oz)	75 g (2½ oz)
Artichoke bottoms	120 g (4 small)	120 g (4 small)
Turned turnip	120 g (4 oz)	75 g (2½ oz)
French beans	120 g (4 oz)	105 g (3½ oz)
Cauliflower	300 g (10 oz)	240 g (8 oz)

Served in small bouquets

Bourgeoise – Large turned vegetables		
Carrots	240 g (½ lb)	180 g (6 oz)
Button onions	240 g (½ lb)	180 g (6 oz)
Completed garnish includes lardons of bacon	180 g (6 oz)	135 g (4½ oz)

Brunoise   Ingredients as for Julienne but al
                             cut into fine dice.

Duxelle   120 g (¼ lb) [cooked weight]

Guide to quantities for 4 covers

Jardinière	Gross Raw Weight	Net Raw Weight
Bâtons of carrots	90 g (3 oz)	60 g (2 oz)
Bâtons of turnips	90 g (3 oz)	60 g (2 oz)
Peas	60 g (2 oz)	60 g (2 oz)
Lozenge French beans	60 g (2 oz)	50 g (1¾ oz)

Julienne		
Carrots	90 g (3 oz)	60 g (2 oz)
Celery	60 g (2 oz)	45 g (1½ oz)
Turnips	90 g (3 oz)	60 g (2 oz)
Leek	90 g (3 oz)	45 g (1½ oz)

Macédoine	As Jardinière but cut in dice.	
Primeurs	As Bouquetière using new or spring vegetables.	

Printanière		
Small turned carrots	120 g (4 oz)	75 g (2½ oz)
Small turned new turnips	120 g (4 oz)	75 g (2½ oz)
Lozenge French beans	90 g (3 oz)	75 g (2½ oz)
Fresh shelled peas	90 g (3 oz)	90 g (3 oz)

Tomates farcies		
4, 90 g (3-oz) tomatoes	360 g (¾ lb)	360 g (¾ lb)

755 Single vegetable and vegetable purée garnishes

Guide to quantities for 4 covers

In using this guide, note that weights depend on quality and on whether service is table d'hôte or à la carte, etc.

Garnish	Ingredients	Gross Weight	Approximate Cooked Weight
Argenteuil	Asparagus	750 g (1½ lb)	240 g (8 oz)
Bruxelloise	Brussels sprouts	500 g (1 lb)	300 g (10 oz)
Clamart	Fresh peas	300 g (10 oz)	180 g (6 oz)
Condé	Red beans	450 g (15 oz)	240 g (8 oz)
Conty	Lentils	240 g (8 oz)	180 g (6 oz)
Crécy	Carrots 150 g (5 oz) } Rice 60 g (2 oz)	210 g (7 oz)	180 g (6 oz)
Dubarry	Cauliflower	360 g (12 oz)	240 g (8 oz)
Esau	Lentils	240 g (8 oz)	180 g (6 oz)
Favorite	French beans	500 g (1 lb)	300 g (10 oz)
Florentine	Spinach	500 g (1 lb)	240 g (8 oz)

Garnish	Ingredients	Gross Weight	Approximate Cooked Weight
Freneuse	Turnip (with potatoes)	300 g (10 oz)	180 g (6 oz)
Maraîchère	Salsifis	360 g (12 oz)	240 g (8 oz)
Montagard	Chestnuts	660 g (22 oz)	180 g (6 oz)
Musard	Flageolets	300 g (10 oz)	240 g (8 oz)
Palestine	Jerusalem artichokes (with potatoes)	480 g (1 lb)	240 g (8 oz)
Parmentier	Potatoes	360 g (12 oz)	240 g (8 oz)
Piemontese	Cardoons 240 g (½ lb) and rice 60 g (2 oz)	300 g (10 oz)	180 g (6 oz)
Rachel	Artichoke bottoms	4 small	
Soubise	Onions } Rice }	120 g (4 oz) } 120 g (4 oz) }	240 g (8 oz)
St Germain	Peas	300 g (10 oz)	180 g (6 oz)
Vichy	Carrots, sliced	360 g (12 oz)	240 g (8 oz)

756 Boiling green vegetables

Green vegetables are cooked in boiling, salted water without lid or cover. Insufficient water is one reason why greens become yellow or brownish in colour; another cause of discolouration is over-long storing. To obtain good results, it is vital to use fresh vegetables and to cook and serve them promptly. When cooked, green vegetables should be drained of water, then returned to the pot, and put on the stove to dry-off any surplus moisture. Spinach is par-cooked and cooled under running water, and then gently squeezed in one hand to rid it of surplus water. Whether it is branch or purée spinach, it is stewed in butter to finish cooking. It is important that vegetables, to retain their full flavour, should not be over-cooked; preferably they should be firm. Finishing with butter completes the cooking.

756a Cooking quick frozen vegetables

Most packers of frozen vegetables indicate on the packs the recommended cooking method. These are normally sound. After basic cooking has been effected, 'finishing' and dressing may be completed in accordance with the general methods outlined throughout this book's vegetable section.

Whilst packers' instructions should not lightly be disregarded the following points may be generally useful. As for fresh vegetables, cooking in the minimum amount of boiling water usually renders best results. Frozen vegetables should *not* be defrosted prior to cooking. If defrosted inadvertently use as soon as possible and *never* re-freeze.

The following points regarding specific vegetables merely indicate the approach and are not exhaustive.

Purée of Spinach:	Cook briskly without water in a buttered pan.
Frozen Broccoli:	Cook in minimum amount of boiling salted water until tender. Drain well.

Frozen Peas:	Cook in the minimum of boiling salted water. Drain, toss in butter with a little sugar. The peas may also be cooked gently under cover without water.
Frozen French Beans:	Cook under cover without water or cook in the minimum amount of salted, boiling water. Drain and season.
Frozen Leaf Spinach:	Blanch in minimum amount of boiling salted water. Refresh. Drain well. Squeeze into portions. Sauté in butter and season.

757 Glazing carrots and turnips

Glazing helps to ensure the retention of flavour and also enhances presentation for service: carrots and turnips are placed in a pan and just covered with water, butter, and sugar.

Allow 60 g (2 oz) butter and 30 g (1 oz) sugar per 500 ml (pint), bring to the boil and cook until the water evaporates; this leaves a syrup formed by the sugar and butter, which gives a gloss to the vegetables.

758 Glazing button onions (à blanc)

Onions are taken out of the blanc (Recipe 759) just before they are cooked; the liquor is reduced to a glaze and the onions rolled in this before service.

758a Button onions (à brun)

The method is different here, the butter being melted in a sauté-pan first.
Put in the onions and lightly sprinkle with sugar.
Toss the onions until they acquire an even brown colour.
Cover with a lid and draw to the side of the stove.
Allow to cook slowly.

759 Blanc for vegetables

| 1 *l* (1 *qt*) *cold water* | *juice of* 1 *lemon* | 30 *g* (1 *oz*) *flour* |
| *salt* | | |

Whisk all ingredients in the pan.
Place on the stove and stir until boiling.
Place in the vegetables to be cooked.
When cooked, vegetables should be allowed to cool in blanc; leave until required.

Note. The purpose of the blanc is to retain the white quality of the vegetable being cooked. During preparation and cleaning, the vegetable is put into acidulated water to prevent its blackening or becoming discoloured. It should be clearly understood that cooking in blanc does not make the vegetable any whiter. It merely ensures that it does not lose any whiteness.

760 Braising vegetables

For braising, wash well and trim the vegetables, then blanch and refresh;

leeks, celery, and lettuces are squeezed gently by hand to express surplus water.

2 Line the bottom of a braising-pan with bacon or blanched pork-rind and then a bed of sliced carrots, onions, and bouquet garni (matignon); lay the vegetables on top, cover with a lid and place in the oven to sweat for 10 minutes. Cover with white stock, bring to the boil, and cook gently in the oven with the lid on.

3 When cool, express surplus juices by hand: celery and lettuce are cut in four or two, lengthwise, and folded.

4 Skim all fat from the cooking-liquor; reduce liquor to a glaze and add demi-glace to form a sauce; finish with lemon juice and butter.

VEGETABLE DISHES

761 Artichokes (to boil whole)

4 *whole artichokes*   *sauce as required*   *lemon*

1 Cut top off artichoke approximately one-third of height.
2 Trim all round, string them and rub bottom with lemon.
3 Cook in salted, boiling water.
4 Drain well. Remove string and heart and chokes (inner fibrous section).
5 Serve on napkin.

Note. Melted butter, hollandaise (Recipe 72) or mousseline sauce (Recipe 77) may be served separately. If cold, serve vinaigrette sauce.

761a Fonds d'artichauts – Artichoke bottoms

1 Using a stainless knife, remove stalk and all leaves to produce hollowed and rounded bottom-part.
2 Rub the artichoke bottoms with lemon juice to prevent discolouration and cook à blanc (Recipe 759).
3 Remove any remaining fibrous matter from the hollow of the fonds.

762 Artichauts barigoule

4 *fresh artichokes*   180 g (6 oz) *duxelle*   *prepared braising-pan*
4 *slices bacon*   (*Recipe 102*)

1 Trim artichoke tops and outer leaves.
2 Parboil (as Recipe 761), remove heart and chokes (the inner fibre section).
3 Season inside, and stuff with duxelles.
4 Wrap in bacon-slice and tie up.
5 Place in pan and braise gently.
6 When cooked, remove string and bacon.
7 Dress and pour over reduced and prepared braising-liquor.

763 Fonds d'artichauts provençale

8 *small artichokes*   ½ *lettuce*   *oil*
250 *ml* (½ *pt*) *shelled peas*   *seasoning*   *lemon*

1 Trim artichokes to bottoms and rub with lemon.
2 Place in pan containing hot oil to cover bottom.
3 Cover and allow to cook slowly (10 minutes).
4 Add peas and lettuce, coarsely-shredded.
5 Cover and finish cooking; season.

764 Fonds d'artichauts farcis – Stuffed artichoke bottoms

4 *moderately large artichokes*   ½ *lemon*   *melted butter*
240 g (½ *lb*) *duxelle* (*Recipe* 102)   *blanc*

1 Trim artichokes of leaves and chokes.
2 Trim bottoms and rub with lemon to prevent blackening.
3 Cook in a blanc, keep fairly firm.
4 Drain, remove any remaining fibrous matter and stuff with duxelle.
5 Place in buttered dish.
6 Sprinkle some breadcrumbs on top and a little melted butter.
7 Place in hot oven to form a gratin on top.

765 Fonds d'artichauts florentine

4 *medium-sized artichokes*   15 *ml spoon* [1 *tablespoon*] *velouté*
120 g (¼ *lb*) *spinach purée*   (*Recipe* 26)
   (*Recipe* 833)   10 *ml spoon* [½ *tablespoon*] *anchovy purée*
1 *clove crushed garlic*   125 *ml* (¼ *pt*) *mornay sauce* (*Recipe* 58)
seasoning   *grated cheese*

1 Prepare the bottoms as for stuffing (Recipe 764).
2 Dry spinach in pan on stove.
3 Season, add garlic, velouté, and anchovy.
4 Cook gently for 2 to 3 minutes.
5 Stuff bottoms with the above mixture.
6 Coat with mornay sauce and sprinkle with cheese.
7 Place in buttered dish and glaze in hot oven.

766 Fonds d'artichauts aux pointes d'asperges

4 *medium-sized artichokes*   62 *ml* (½ *gill*) *cream*   12 *asparagus tips*
125 *ml* (¼ *pt*) *mornay sauce*   *grated cheese*   *butter*
   (*Recipe* 58)   *seasoning*

1 Prepare artichokes as for bottoms.
2 Cook lightly in butter.
3 Bind asparagus tips with cream.
4 Place tips in bottoms.
5 Coat with mornay sauce.
6 Sprinkle with cheese and glaze in hot oven.

767 Fonds d'artichauts sautés

4 *artichokes*   *butter*   *fines herbes*

1 Prepare in usual manner.
2 Slice artichokes raw.
3 Season with salt and pepper.
4 Toss in butter, dish and sprinkle with herbs.

768 Fonds d'artichauts en purée – Purée of artichoke bottoms

> 4 *medium-sized artichokes*   *seasoning*   *butter*
> *mashed potatoes* (*Recipe* 896)

1 Trim artichokes as for bottoms. (Some prefer to remove 'choke' *after* cooking.)
2 Half-cook in a blanc and drain.
3 Complete cooking in butter.
4 Remove fibrous matter. Pass through a fine sieve.
5 Add mashed potatoes equal to half its bulk.
6 Mix well and serve with beurre noisette.

ASPERGES – ASPARAGUS

Premier-quality asparagus, especially in early season, is the lauris. The smaller green Parisian type used for tips is also known as sprew. Asparagus from Argenteuil is highly esteemed, therefore 'Argenteuil' on menus describes asparagus dishes. English asparagus is good but inclined to be small. Asparagus should be used as fresh as possible.
To prepare asparagus. Lightly scrape from the bottom of the flower downwards, wash and then tie in small bundles. Level the heads then cut the bundles at the foot. Place in plenty of salted, boiling water and cook gently.

769 Asperges au beurre fondu – Asparagus with melted butter

> 4 *bunches asparagus* (8 *or* 9 *stalks per bunch*)   120 *g* (¼ *lb*) *butter*

1 Cook asparagus as above.
2 Drain and place in serving dish.
3 Melt butter and serve separately.

Note.
 i Hollandaise (Recipe 72), or maltaise (Recipe 76), may be served.
 ii If cold, serve vinaigrette dressing (Recipe 118) or mayonnaise (Recipe 110).

770 Asperges au gratin

> 4 *bunches asparagus*   30 *g* (1 *oz*) *grated Parmesan*
> 250 *ml* (½ *pt*) *mornay sauce*   *cheese*
> (*Recipe* 58)

1 Dish asparagus in rows.
2 Coat with mornay sauce ⅓ down from heads.
3 Sprinkle with Parmesan cheese and glaze.

771 Asperges milanaise

  4 *bunches asparagus*   45 *g* (1½ *oz*) *grated Parmesan*
  120 *g* (¼ *lb*) *butter*   *cheese*

1 Butter serving-dish well.
2 Arrange asparagus in layers, in successive rows.
3 Sprinkle heads with cheese.
4 Cover heads with noisette butter and glaze under salamander.

772 Asperges polonaise

  2 *hard-boiled egg-yolks*   4 *bunches asparagus*   60 *g* (2 *oz*) *white*
    (*sieved*)   120 *g* (¼ *lb*) *butter*   *breadcrumbs*
  chopped parsley   *seasoning*

1 Dish asparagus (as Recipe 771).
2 Brown breadcrumbs in butter and season.
3 Add egg yolks and parsley.
4 Pour over asparagus and serve.

AUBERGINE – BRINJAL OR EGG-PLANT

773 Aubergines égyptienne

  10 *ml spoon* [½ *tablespoon*] *chopped onion*   2 *aubergines*   *seasoning*
  minced, cooked lean mutton   3 *tomatoes*   *oil, butter*

 1 Cut aubergines lengthwise into two.
 2 Criss-cross centre with a knife.
 3 Cook lightly in hot oil.
 4 Drain and withdraw the pulp.
 5 Cook onion in oil and add pulp chopped with an equal quantity of
   mutton.
 6 Place shells in buttered dish.
 7 Fill with prepared pulp.
 8 Place in oven for 10 to 15 minutes.
 9 A few slices of tomato cooked in oil are placed on top of each aubergine.
10 Sprinkle with chopped parsley.

774 Aubergines au gratin

  dry duxelle (*Recipe* 102)   *breadcrumbs*   2 *aubergines*
  demi-glace (*Recipe* 29)

1 Prepare as above.
2 Chop pulp and mix in equal quantity of dry duxelle.
3 Fill shells with preparation.
4 Sprinkle with crumbs and brown in oven.
5 Dish and serve a border of demi-glace sauce round the aubergines.

775 Aubergines frites

  2 *aubergines*   *flour* (*seasoned*)

1 Skin aubergines and cut into rounds; season and flour.
2 Deep-fry in hot oil.
3 Drain and serve on napkin immediately.

BETTERAVE – BEETROOT

776 Beetroot (to boil)

1 Trim off the green leaves (these may be treated as turnip tops), wash the
beets and boil until tender. Time varies according to age and size but will
certainly be more than 1 hour and may be as much as 3 to 4 hours.
2 Remove the skin carefully with blunt edge of knife or by even rubbing with
rough cloth.
3 Slice or dice according to mode of subsequent serving which may be, when
hot, à la crème or braised with piquant, red-wine sauce as well as cold for
salad use.

777 Blettes – Blett or strawberry spinach

Cook the leaves as for spinach and the stalks as for salsifis (see Recipe 944).

778 Brocoli – Broccoli

These are similar to cauliflower, though the purplish flowers are smaller and
more scattered. Recipes for cauliflower may be used.

779 Cardons – Cardoons

1 Cut off the outer green-leaf stalks and discard them.
2 Cut the white stalks into lengths of 6–8 cm (3 or 4 inches).
3 Rub with lemon and place in acidulated water.
4 Take out the fibrous part of the heart and treat the heart like the white
stalks.
5 Cook all à blanc (Recipe 759) for 1 to 1½ hours.

Note. Cardoons may be served with sauce bordelaise (Recipe 35), sauce
hollandaise (Recipe 72), cream, mornay sauce (Recipe 58), sauce italienne
(Recipe 42); or treated and served as for celery.

780 Cardons au Parmesan

30 g (1 oz) grated Parmesan cheese	blanc (Recipe 759)	750 g (1½ lb)
125 ml (¼ pt) demi-glace	240 g (½ lb) chopped	cardons
(Recipe 29)	veal fat	seasoning

1 Remove the green stalks and cut white ones into 6 cm (3-inch) lengths; peel,
and rub with lemon juice to keep white.
2 Remove the fibrous part from the heart and treat in the same manner.
3 Place the cardons in a boiling blanc and sprinkle the top with chopped veal
fat.
4 Simmer for 1½ hours; drain and toss in butter; build in layers and sprinkle
Parmesan cheese on each one; season each layer.
5 Cover with demi-glace sauce, sprinkle with Parmesan cheese and brown.

CAROTTES – CARROTS

781 Carottes glacées

750 g (1½ lb) peeled carrots   7 g (¼ oz) salt   15 g (½ oz) sugar
30 g (1 oz) butter per 500 ml (pt) of water

1 Cut carrots into 3 cm (1½-inch) lengths and quarter.
2 With a small knife trim them into barrel shapes.
3 Place in sauté pan and cover with cold water.
4 Add sugar, salt and butter, bring to boil.
5 Cook until water has evaporated, leaving a syrup glaze.

782 Carottes à la crème

1 As for carrottes glacées.
2 When cooked, lié with well-reduced cream.

783 Carottes Vichy

1 Slice carrots thinly on mandoline.
2 Finish as for carrottes glacées.

CELERIS – CELERY

784 Céleris braisés au jus

2 *heads of celery*   *bouquet garni*   1 *small carrot*
white stock (*Recipe* 6)   60 g (2 oz) *bacon rind*   1 *small onion*

1 Blanch and refresh celery and trim.
2 Cover bottom of pan with bacon rind.
3 Place sliced onions, carrots and bouquet garni on top.
4 Lay celery on top of vegetables.
5 Cover with lid and place in oven for 2 minutes.
6 Cover with stock, boil and cook in oven until tender.
7 Draw celery through hand to express surplus liquor.
8 Cut lengthwise in four, and fold.
9 Skim off fat from cooking-liquor.
10 Reduce and add some good jus lié (Recipe 30).
11 Coat celery with sauce.

785 Céleris au parmesan

1 Prepare as Recipe 784 then coat with demi-glace (Recipe 29).
2 Sprinkle with Parmesan cheese and glaze.

786 Céleris Mornay

1 Prepare as Recipe 785, using Mornay sauce (Recipe 58) instead of demi-glace.
2 Sprinkle with Parmesan cheese and glaze.

787 Céleris milanaise

Prepare as Recipe 785 but finish as for asparagus milanaise (Recipe 771).

788 Céleris à la moelle

Prepare as Recipe 787, then place a slice of poached beef marrow on each
piece of celery and coat with sauce bordelaise (Recipe 36).

789 Céleris with various sauces

1 Celery may be served with various sauces such as cream, hollandaise,
italienne, mousseline or bordelaise.
2 Sauce may be served separately or coated over the vegetable.

CÉLERI-RAVE – CELERIAC

790 Céleri-rave à la crème

62 ml ($\frac{1}{8}$ pt) cream sauce (Recipe 65)   480 g (1 lb) celeriac   62 ml ($\frac{1}{2}$ gill)
juice of $\frac{1}{2}$ lemon   1·25 ml spoon [$\frac{1}{4}$ tea-   cream
45 g (1$\frac{1}{2}$ oz) butter   spoon] vinegar   salt, pepper

1 Peel celeriac thinly and place in water acidulated with lemon juice to retain
colour.
2 Shape as for turned carrots; blanch in water with vinegar for about 5
minutes.
3 Sweat them in butter until tender, then mix with the sauce and cream, and
season.

791 Céleri-rave aux fines herbes

500 g (1 lb) celeriac   juice of $\frac{1}{4}$ lemon   60 g (2 oz) butter
4 g ($\frac{1}{8}$ oz) fines herbes   1·25 ml spoon [$\frac{1}{4}$ tea-   salt and pepper
(chopped parsley, thyme)   spoon] vinegar

1 Cook as for à la crème (Recipe 790) and drain well.
2 Finish the cooking in butter, add the fines herbes and season.

CHAMPIGNONS – MUSHROOMS AND OTHER FUNGI

Mushrooms (champignons), cèpes (flap mushrooms), morilles (morels), are all
treated similarly. White, cultivated mushrooms need not be peeled but should
be well washed to remove any sand which may adhere.

792 Cèpes bordelaise

15 ml spoon [1 tablespoon] $\frac{1}{4}$ lemon   62 ml ($\frac{1}{2}$ gill) oil
finely-chopped onion   15 g ($\frac{1}{2}$ oz) chopped   salt, pepper
15 ml spoon [1 tablespoon]   parsley
white breadcrumbs   500 g (1 lb) cèpes

1 Cut cèpes in collops and season.
2 Heat oil in pan, place in cèpes and sauté until well sizzled.

3 Add onions and cook for one or two minutes.
4 Finish with breadcrumbs.
5 When serving, squeeze lemon over and sprinkle with parsley.

793 Cèpes provençale

Prepare as bordelaise (Recipe 792) with the addition of garlic.

794 Champignons à la crème – Mushrooms in cream

500 g (1 *lb*) *mushrooms*	15 *ml spoon* [1 *tablespoon*]	250 *ml* (½ *pt*) *cream*
60 g (2 *oz*) *butter*	*finely-chopped onion*	*seasoning*

1 Fry onions in butter without colouring.
2 Add mushrooms, cover and cook.
3 Drain and cover with cream.
4 Boil slowly until cream is well reduced.

795 Champignons farcis

Large field mushrooms as required	*duxelle stuffing* (*Recipe* 102)	*white breadcrumbs* *butter*

1 Peel, wash, and dry mushrooms.
2 Place on well-buttered tray.
3 Fill with duxelle stuffing.
4 Sprinkle with breadcrumbs.
5 Place in oven to cook.

796 Champignons grillés

500 g (1 *lb*) *field mushrooms*	120 g (¼ *lb*) *parsley butter*	180 g (6 *oz*) *butter*
salt	(*Recipe* 89)	*pepper*

1 Peel, wash, and dry mushrooms.
2 Place in pan and season.
3 Coat with melted butter and grill gently.
4 When serving, place parsley butter in centre of each mushroom.

797 Purée de champignons

500 g (1 *lb*) *white mushrooms*	62 *ml* (½ *gill*) *cream*	*salt*
250 *ml* (½ *pt*) *Béchamel* (*Recipe* 51)	45 g (1½ *oz*) *butter*	*pepper*
nutmeg		

1 Wash and dry mushrooms.
2 Rub through a fine sieve.
3 Reduce Béchamel by one-third.
4 Add mushroom purée and cream.
5 Place on hot fire and reduce slightly.
6 Season and finish with butter.

798 Champignons tournés – Turned mushrooms

> *white mushrooms as required*

1 Cut stalks off flush with heads.
2 Groove head with point of small knife.
3 Wash well and cook quickly under cover in a little water acidulated with lemon juice together with a little butter.

799 Truffe – Truffle

To cook truffles:
1 Wash and brush, and soak in water for 3 hours.
2 Place in a cocotte, cover with sherry and add a few peppercorns.
3 Seal the lid with flour and water-paste and simmer in the oven for 30 minutes.
4 Place in a jar and strain the liquid on top.

CHOU – CABBAGE

800 Chou à l'anglaise

> 1½, 1 *kg* (2-*lb*) *cabbages*   *salt*

1 Trim the outer coarse leaves, and quarter cabbage.
2 Cut out coarse stalks.
3 Wash well and cook in plenty of boiling water (salted).
4 Drain and press between two plates
5 Cut in portions and serve.

800a Scotch kale and Curly kale

Other varieties of spring 'greens' may be prepared as cabbage.

801 Petit chou au beurre – Small cabbage with butter

1 Separate outer green leaves keeping them whole.
2 Quarter rest of cabbage.
3 Blanch and refresh.
4 Place outer green leaves on clean board and place quarter on top.
5 Gather into a clean cloth and squeeze into a ball.
6 Place in well-buttered pan and dot each ball with a piece of butter.
7 Season and cover with buttered paper.
8 Cover pan and cook in oven until tender.

802 Chou étuvé

1 Shred cabbage after trimming.
2 Wash well in cold water.
3 Drain and place in pan with a good knob of butter.
4 Add onion piqué, carrot and bacon rind.
5 Season with salt and pepper.

6 Cover with buttered paper and cover pan.
7 Cook in oven until tender.

803 Chou farcis braisé – Braised stuffed cabbage

1 *medium-sized cabbage*	120 g (¼ lb) streaky	seasoning
60 g (2 oz) fresh white bread-	bacon	7 g (¼ oz) chop-
crumbs	1 egg yolk	ped parsley
30 g (1 oz) finely-chopped onion	120 g (¼ lb) sausage-	250 ml (½ pt)
120 g (¼ lb) matignon (Recipe 3)	meat	white stock
125 ml (¼ pt) demi-glace	120 g (¼ lb) bacon rind	(Recipe 6)
(Recipe 29)		

1 Cut the cabbage in quarters and remove the core.
2 Wash well; blanch for 10 minutes and refresh; remove stalky parts.
3 Mince the bacon and mix with sausage-meat, crumbs, onions, parsley, and seasoning; bind with egg yolks.
4 Roll the stuffing into 4 balls and wrap the cabbage leaves neatly around each ball.
5 Place the stuffed cabbage on the matignon and cover with the bacon rind.
6 Add the stock; season and cook under cover in the oven until tender.
7 Strain the cooking-liquid off; boil and remove all fat; reduce the liquid, add to the demi-glace.
8 Dress the cabbage on an oval dish and coat with the sauce.
Note. To keep the cabbage in shape, pack tightly in the braising-pan.

CHOU DE MER OR CHOU MARIN

804 Chou de mer à la crème – Sea-kale in cream

62 ml (⅛ pt) cream sauce	500 g (1 lb) sea-kale	seasoning
(Recipe 65)	15 ml (⅛ gill) cream	

1 Wash and trim; tie in bundles.
2 Cook à blanc.
3 Drain well and pour a little cream sauce over the head before service.

805 Chou de mer hollandaise

500 g (1 lb) sea-kale   125 ml (¼ pt) sauce hollandaise (Recipe 72)

1 Prepare as chou de mer à la crème (Recipe 804).
2 Serve plain on a serviette with sauce hollandaise separately.

CHOU-RAVE – KOHLRABI

806 Choux-raves à la crème

62 ml (½ gill) sauce allemande	15 ml spoon [1 table-	500 g (1 lb)
(Recipe 54)	spoon] cream	kohlrabi
125 ml (¼ pt) white stock	salt, pepper and	30 g (1 oz) butter
(Recipe 6)	grated nutmeg	

1 Peel the kohlrabi thinly and shape as for turned carrots.
2 Blanch and refresh in salted water.
3 Stew them in butter till tender without colour.
4 Mix with the sauce and cream; adjust seasoning.

807 Choux-raves menagère

1 *kg* (1 *lb*) *kohlrabi*	30 *g* (1 *oz*) *butter* *salt*
250 *ml* (½ *pt*) *demi-glace* (Recipe 29)	*pepper* *nutmeg*

1 Peel thin and neatly turn into olive shapes.
2 Blanch and refresh in salted water.
3 Stew in butter until tender, drain and add the demi-glace.

CHOUX ROUGES – RED CABBAGE

808 Choux rouges flamande

240 *g* (½ *lb*) *bacon or pork rind*	500 *g* (1 *lb*) *red cabbage*	*bouquet garni*
120 *g* (¼ *lb*) *diced apples*	62 *ml* (½ *gill*) *wine-*	120 *g* (¼ *lb*)
(*net wt*)	*vinegar*	*butter*
15 *g* (½ *oz*) *caster sugar*	*salt*	*pepper*

1 Cut the cabbage in quarters, remove stumps and stalks and faded leaves; wash well in salted water.
2 Shred into rough julienne; season.
3 Place in a braising-pan with the butter and vinegar; cover with the bacon rind and cook under cover with the bouquet garni.
4 When 3-parts cooked, add the diced apples and sugar and finish off the cooking.
5 When cooked remove bouquet garni and bacon rind, adjust seasoning and serve in oval vegetable dish with a little of the cooking-liquor.

809 Choux rouges limousine

120 *g* (¼ *lb*) *diced apples* (*net wt*)	240 *g* (½ *lb*) *bacon or*	60 *g* (2 *oz*)
125 *ml* (¼ *pt*) *white stock*	*pork rind*	*butter*
(*Recipe* 6)	500 *g* (1 *lb*) *red*	*bouquet garni*
62 *ml* (½ *gill*) *wine-vinegar*	*cabbage*	30 *g* (1 *oz*) *pure*
120 *g* (¼ *lb*) *diced raw chestnuts*	15 *g* (½ *oz*) *caster sugar*	*lard*

1 Cut the cabbage in quarters, remove stump, stalks and faded leaves; wash well in salted water.
2 Shred into rough julienne and season.
3 Place the cabbage, chestnuts, pure lard, stock and bouquet garni into a braising-pan; cover with bacon or pork rind, and cook under cover in the oven.
4 When 3-parts cooked remove the bacon rind; sprinkle the cabbage with vinegar; add the diced apples and the sugar; replace the rind and finish off the cooking.
5 When cooked, remove the rind and bouquet garni; adjust seasoning and serve with a little of the cooking-liquor.

810 Pickled red cabbage

red cabbage	*250 ml ($\frac{1}{2}$ pt) spiced vinegar (Recipe 131)*	*salt*
pinch mixed herbs	*1 clove garlic*	*peppercorns*

1 Trim off outer leaves and cut off stalk.
2 Cut into quarters then in fine julienne.
3 Place on tray and sprinkle liberally with salt.
4 Leave for two days.
5 Drain and place in jar with herbs, peppercorns and garlic.
6 Cover with spiced vinegar and leave to marinade.

CHOUX DE BRUXELLES – BRUSSELS SPROUTS

811 Choux de Bruxelles à l'anglaise

500 g (1 lb) Brussels sprouts *boiling water* *salt*

1 Trim outer leaves of sprouts.
2 Cut a cross in the bottom of stem.
3 Wash well and drain.
4 Cook in plenty of boiling salted water.
5 Drain well and serve.

812 Choux de Bruxelles sautés

500 g (1 lb) Brussels sprouts *60 g (2 oz) butter*

1 Prepare and cook as above, Recipe 811.
2 Drain well.
3 Heat some butter in pan and sauté sprouts until they are slightly browned.

813 Purée de choux de Bruxelles

500 g (1 lb) Brussels sprouts *butter* *salt*
120 g ($\frac{1}{4}$ lb) mashed potato (Recipe 896)

1 Trim sprouts and wash well.
2 Three-parts cook, drain and finish cooking in butter.
3 Pass through sieve.
4 Add one-third of its bulk in mashed potato.
5 Mix well and add butter and salt.

814 Choux de Bruxelles limousine

1 Cook in salted water, strain well.
2 Toss in butter and garnish with pieces of cooked chestnuts.

815 Choux de Bruxelles polonaise

Finish as for chou-fleur polonaise (Recipe 821).

816 Choux de Bruxelles Mornay

1 Cook as for limousine (Recipe 814) but cover with mornay sauce (Recipe 58).
2 Sprinkle with cheese and brown under grill.

CHOU-FLEUR – CAULIFLOWER

817 Cauliflower (to boil)

1 Remove outer leaves.
2 Hollow out stalk with a small knife.
3 Wash well in salt water.
4 Cook steadily in plenty of boiling salted water.
5 The stalk should be tender and care must be taken not to break the flowers; drain well and finish according to the appropriate recipe, such as those listed below.

818 Chou-fleur nature, sauce hollandaise

360 g (¾ lb) *trimmed-weight cauliflower – approximately* 1 *medium-sized cauliflower*

1 Cook as Recipe 817 – drain well.
2 Serve on a vegetable dish with flower uppermost.
3 Hollandaise sauce served separately (Recipe 72).

Note. Alternatives for hollandaise are beurre fondu (Recipe 80) or sauce divine.

819 Chou-fleur Mornay (or chou-fleur au gratin)

360 g (¾ lb) *trimmed cauliflower*	190 ml (1½ gills) *Mornay sauce* (*Recipe* 58)	30 g (1 oz) *grated cheese*

1 Cook as for Recipe 817.
2 Drain well and place in buttered vegetable dish.
3 Coat with mornay sauce (Recipe 58).
4 Sprinkle with grated cheese.
5 Brown in hot oven.

Note. May also be prepared in individual portions.

820 Chou-fleur milanaise

360 g (¾ lb) *trimmed cauliflower*	45 g (1½ oz) *grated cheese*	60 g (2 oz) *butter*

1 Cook as Recipe 817.
2 Place in buttered vegetable dish.
3 Sprinkle with grated cheese.
4 Glaze under grill.
5 Finish with beurre noisette (Recipe 82).

821 Chou-fleur polonaise

360 g or ¾ *trimmed cauliflower*	60 g (2 oz) *white breadcrumbs*	120 g (¼ lb)
1 *hard-boiled egg* (*sieved*)	7 g (¼ oz) *chopped parsley*	*butter*

1 Cook as Recipe 817.
2 Place in buttered vegetable dish.
3 Place butter in frying-pan and melt.
4 Add breadcrumbs and fry until golden brown and frothy.
5 Add most of the sieved eggs and chopped parsley; season.
6 Pour over the cauliflower evenly and sprinkle with remaining sieved egg and parsley.

822 Chou-fleur sauté au beurre

360 g ($\frac{3}{4}$ *lb*) *trimmed cauliflower*   60 g (2 *oz*) *butter*

1 Cook as Recipe 817.
2 Cut into 4 equal portions.
3 Melt butter in frying-pan.
4 Add the cauliflower and colour evenly.
5 Season and serve in an oval vegetable dish.

823 Chou-fleur sauté aux fines herbes

To the above Recipe 822, when tossing in butter, add 15 g ($\frac{1}{2}$ oz) fines herbes.

CONCOMBRE – CUCUMBER

824 Concombres à la crème – Cucumbers in cream

360 g ($\frac{3}{4}$ *lb*) *cucumber*   62 ml ($\frac{1}{2}$ *gill*) *fresh cream*   30 g (1 *oz*) *butter*
salt and pepper

1 Peel, cut into 3 cm (1$\frac{1}{2}$-inch) sections and turn like olives.
2 Sweat in the butter without colouring.
3 Add the cream and simmer gently for 2 or 3 minutes; season and serve.

825 Concombres farcis – Stuffed cucumbers

360 g ($\frac{3}{4}$ *lb*) *cucumber*   120 g ($\frac{1}{4}$ *lb*) *duxelle* (*Recipe* 102)   *seasoning*
15 g ($\frac{1}{2}$ *oz*) *butter*   15 g ($\frac{1}{2}$ *oz*) *grated Parmesan cheese*

1 Peel the cucumber and cut into 4 cm (2-inch) lengths and cut them lengthways.
2 Remove the centre seeds and blanch and refresh in salted water.
3 Heat the duxelle and place in savoy-bag and pipe the mixture neatly in the centre.
4 Brush the top with melted butter, sprinkle with the cheese and brown lightly under the grill.
5 Sprinkle a little chopped parsley on top before serving.

826 Concombres glacés

Prepare as for carottes glacées (Recipe 781).

827 Courgettes – Vegetable marrows

Prepare and cook as cucumbers.

CROSNES DU JAPON – JAPANESE ARTICHOKES OR STACHYS

828 Crosnes du Japon milanaise

500 g (1 lb) Japanese arti-   30 g (1 oz) grated   45 g (1½ oz) butter
   chokes blanc (Recipe 759)   Parmesan cheese

1 To clean: wash and place them in a sack with bay salt and shake well to remove skins.
2 Re-wash and cook à blanc.
3 Drain, toss in butter, season.
4 Sprinkle with cheese and brown under grill.

829 Crosnes du Japon polonaise

500 g (1 lb) Japanese arti-   1 sieved hard-boiled egg   60 g (2 oz) butter
   chokes   120 g (¼ lb) breadcrumbs
7 g (¼ oz) chopped parsley

1 Cook stachys as for milanaise (Recipe 828).
2 Fry the crumbs golden brown in butter.
3 Add the eggs and parsley and coat over the stachys.
4 Sprinkle a little chopped parsley before service.

Note. May be used for fish garnish.

ENDIVE – CHICORY

830 Endive (to cook)

1 Wash, lay on buttered braising-pan, add salt and lemon juice.
2 Seal lid with flour and water paste.
3 Cook in moderate oven for 30 minutes.
4 No water is required as they contain sufficient in themselves.

831 Endive au jus

240 g (½ lb) endives   250 ml (½ pt) jus lié (Recipe 30)

1 Braise as Recipe 830.
2 When cooked, reduce cooking-liquor and add jus lié.
3 Coat over endives.

832 Endive Mornay

240 g (½ lb) endives   125 ml (¼ pt) mornay sauce   15 g (½ oz) grated
      (Recipe 58)   Parmesan cheese

1 Braise as Recipe 830.
2 Drain; coat with mornay sauce.
3 Sprinkle with cheese and brown.

ÉPINARDS – SPINACH

833 Épinards à la crème – Creamed spinach

125 ml (¼ pt) cream sauce   750 g (1½ lb) leaf spinach   60 g (2 oz)
(Recipe 65)   62 ml (½ gill) fresh cream   butter

1 Prepare and cook as for en branches (Recipe 836).
2 Pass through a sieve.
3 Put in pan with butter and dry on stove.
4 Add one-quarter of its bulk in cream sauce and simmer gently for 10 minutes.
5 Dish and sprinkle some fresh cream over.

Note. For boiling spinach see page 242.

834 Épinards à la Viroflay

Soubise d'épinards (as Recipe 61,   500 g (1 lb)   grated cheese
   quarter quantities)   blanched   melted butter
250 ml (½ pt) mornay sauce (Recipe 58)   spinach leaves

1 Place leaves on table.
2 Place soubise on each leaf and fold.
3 Place on buttered dish.
4 Coat with mornay sauce.
5 Sprinkle with cheese and melted butter.
6 Place in hot oven to glaze.

835 Épinards au gratin

750 g (1½ lb) leaf spinach   60 g (2 oz) grated cheese   90 g (3 oz) butter

1 Cook spinach and pass through sieve.
2 Place in pan with butter and dry on stove.
3 Add 30 g (1 oz) grated cheese.
4 Place in buttered dish and sprinkle with remaining cheese and melted butter.
5 Place in hot oven to glaze.

836 Épinards en branches – Spinach in leaf

750 g (1½ lb) leaf spinach   boiling salt water

1 Remove thick stalks from leaves.
2 Wash leaves well two or three times.
3 Half cook in plenty of boiling salted water.
4 Cool and squeeze in the hands to expel water.
5 Use as required.

837 Épinards en branches au beurre

750 g (1½ lb) leaf spinach   pinch of caster sugar   60 g (2 oz) butter
salt, pepper, grated nutmeg

1 Prepare and cook as Recipe 836.
2 Loosen leaves with a fork.
3 Melt butter in pan and finish cooking spinach in this.
4 Season with a pinch of sugar, salt, pepper and grated nutmeg.

838 Soufflé aux épinards

240 g (½ *lb*) *spinach purée*	30 g (1 *oz*) *Parmesan*	60 g (2 *oz*) *butter*
125 ml (¼ *pt*) *Béchamel sauce*	*cheese*	3 *eggs*
(*Recipe* 51)	12 *anchovy fillets*	*seasoning*

1 Heat spinach and Béchamel.
2 Add egg yolks and cheese; season.
3 Cool and add the beaten egg whites.
4 Place a layer of mixture in bottom of well-buttered soufflé dish.
5 Make a trellis of anchovy on top.
6 Build up successive layers, finishing with anchovies.
7 Cook as for ordinary soufflé.

839 Subric d'épinards

125 ml (¼ *pt*) *reduced*	60 g (2 *oz*) *butter*	62 ml (½ *gill*) *cream*
Béchamel (*Recipe* 51)	1 *egg*	2 *yolks*
750 g (1½ *lb*) *spinach purée*	*grated nutmeg*	*salt, pepper*

1 Heat the spinach purée and add butter.
2 Dry in hot oven.
3 Add Béchamel, cream, eggs, seasoning and mix well.
4 Heat some butter in frying-pan.
5 Drop some spinach from a spoon into the pan.
6 Cook both sides like a pancake.
7 Dish and serve.

840 Fenouil – Fennel

Same weight and cooking procedure as cardons – cardoons.

FÈVES – BEANS

841 Broad Beans – Grosses Fèves (to boil)

500 g (1 *lb*) *shelled broad beans*	*salted water*	*seasoning*
1 *small bunch savoury**		

1 Cook beans in salted water with savoury.
2 Drain and add savoury (chopped).

842 Fèves au beurre

Ingredients as for Recipe 841 with 60 g (2 oz) butter.
Cook beans as Recipe 841; drain and dry on fire and finish with butter.

 * This herb is also known as summer savoury.

843 Fèves à la crème

Ingredients as for Recipe 841 with 62 ml (½ gill) cream.
Prepare as Recipe 841 but lié with fresh cream.

844 Purée de fèves

Prepare as for purée of peas.

FLAGEOLETS

845 Flageolets – Small kidney beans (to boil)

> 500 g (1 *lb*) *flageolets*   *bouquet garni*
> 1 *small carrot*   *salted water*

1 Place all ingredients in pan and cover with cold water, salted.
2 Bring to boil and cook until tender.
3 Withdraw carrot, onion, and bouquet garni.
4 Drain beans and finish as required.

846 Flageolets au beurre

Prepare as Recipe 845 but finish with 60 g (2 *oz*) *butter*.

847 Flageolets en purée (or purée musard)

Prepare as for purée of peas (Recipe 885). Flageolet purée is also used for
thickening purée of French beans.

HARICOTS

848 Haricots blancs – Haricot beans (to prepare)

> 240 g (½ *lb*) *beans*   *bouquet garni*   1 *small onion*
> 750 *ml* (1½ *pt*) *cold water*   1 *small carrot*   *seasoning*

1 Soak beans for 12 hours and wash.
2 Place all ingredients in pan and cover with water.
3 Bring to boil and allow to cook slowly until tender.
4 Withdraw aromatics and dry beans on top of stove.
5 Treat as required.

849 Haricots blancs à l'américaine

> 125 *ml* (¼ *pt*) *tomato sauce* *bouquet garni*   250 *ml* (½ *pt*)
>   (*Recipe* 34)   120 g (¼ *lb*) *lean bacon*   *beans*
> 1 *small onion*   750 *ml* (1½ *pt*) *water*   1 *small carrot*

1 Prepare and cook as Recipe 848.
2 Cut bacon into dice and add to beans.
3 Bind beans with good tomato sauce.

850 Haricots blancs au beurre

1 Cook as for Américaine, Recipe 849, but without bacon.
2 Finish with 30 g (1 oz) butter.
3 Sprinkle with chopped parsley 4 g ($\frac{1}{8}$ oz).

851 Haricots blancs à la bretonne

Ingredients as for Recipe 849 with 120 *g* ($\frac{1}{4}$ *lb*) *tomato concassé*, 30 *g* (1 *oz*)
butter, 1 *clove garlic*, 125 *ml* ($\frac{1}{4}$ *pt*) *tomato sauce* (Recipe 34).

1 Prepare and cook as Recipe 848.
2 Drain and blend with the extra ingredients.

852 Haricots blancs en purée (or purée soissonnaise)

1 Prepare and cook in usual manner.
2 Drain and, while hot, pass through sieve.
3 Mix purée in pan with 45 g ($1\frac{1}{2}$ oz) butter and adjust consistency with hot
  milk.

853 Haricots rouges au vin – Red beans

    240 *g* ($\frac{1}{2}$ *lb*) *beans*   120 *g* ($\frac{1}{4}$ *lb*) *bacon*   125 *ml* ($\frac{1}{4}$ *pt*) *red wine*

1 Soak and prepare as Recipe 848.
2 Cook in a mixture of wine and water with the bacon.
3 Dice the bacon as a garnish.

854 Haricots verts au beurre – French beans

    500 *g* (1 *lb*) *French beans*   60 *g* (2 *oz*) *butter*   *salted water*

1 If necessary, remove string from beans.
2 Place beans in boiling salted water.
3 When cooked, beans should be slightly firm.
4 Drain and dry on stove.
5 Finish with butter and seasoning.

855 Haricots verts en purée (or purée favorite)

    360 *g* ($\frac{3}{4}$ *lb*) *French beans* 125 *ml* ($\frac{1}{4}$ *pt*) *purée of flageolets* (*Recipe* 847)

1 When cooked, drain and dry beans.
2 Place 45 g ($1\frac{1}{2}$ oz) butter in beans and stew slightly.
3 Pass beans through a sieve.
4 Mix flageolets purée 125 ml ($\frac{1}{4}$ pt) with French beans purée 250 ml ($\frac{1}{2}$ pt).

JETS DE HOUBLON

856 Jets de houblon – Hop sprouts (or shoots)

                        1 *lb for* 4 *covers*

1 Prepare as asparagus.
2 Serve with hollandaise sauce or melted butter.

LENTILLES

857 Lentilles – Lentils

Cook as for haricot beans.

LAITUE – LETTUCE

858 Laitues braisées – Braised lettuce

See Recipe 757 and dress as braised celery (Recipe 784).

859 Laitues farcies

Prepare as chou farci (Recipes 802 or 803) but riz pilaff (Recipe 366) may
also be used as forcemeat.

MAIS – CORN

860 Mais nature – Corn on the cob

4 *corn on the cob*	90 *g* (3 *oz*) *melted butter*	1 *l* (2 *pt*) *water*
10 *ml spoon* [½ *tablespoon*] *salt*	125 *ml* (¼ *pt*) *milk*	

1 Boil the water with the milk and salt.
2 Wash the corn and cook whole with the leaves.
3 Cooking time, 20 minutes.
4 Drain, serve with leaves drawn back on a serviette.
5 Melted butter or sauce hollandaise served separately.

Note. For certain garnishes the grains are separated from the stalk and treated
as required.

861 Mais à la creme – Creamed corn

4 *corn on the cob*	62 *ml* (⅛ *pt*) *cream*	*salt*
10 *ml spoon* [½ *tablespoon*] *caster sugar*	30 *g* (1 *oz*) *butter*	

1 Cook the corn and scrape off the ears.
2 Place the ears in a pan and sweat with butter; add the cream, sugar and salt.

Note. Creamed corn or sweetcorn may be bought prepared in cans.

MARRONS – CHESTNUTS

862 Chestnuts (to shell)

1 Split open the shell with a small, sharp knife.
2 Place in a hot oven for 5 minutes and remove the shells when hot.

863 Marrons braises – Braised chestnuts

500 g (1 *lb*) *marrons* (*gross weight*)	15 g (½ *oz*) *butter*	*salt*
190 *ml* (1½ *gills*) *brown veal stock* (*Recipe* 10)	*pinch sugar*	*pepper*

1 Place in sauté-pan with butter and sweat for a few minutes.
2 Moisten with veal stock and simmer under cover until tender.
3 Strain and keep the chestnuts hot while reducing the liquor to a glaze.
4 Roll the chestnuts in the glaze; serve in a casserole, sprinkle with chopped parsley before service.

864 Marrons etuves – Stewed chestnuts

1 With a pointed knife slit on side of the shell.
2 Place in frying-basket and plunge into hot fat.
3 Remove shell and skin.
4 Place in pan and cover with white stock (Recipe 6).
5 Stew gently until cooked.

865 Marrons glacés au jus – Glazed chestnuts

1 Prepare as Recipe 864.
2 Cook in strong veal stock (Recipe 10).
3 When almost cooked, remove chestnuts.
4 Reduce stock to a glaze.
5 Roll chestnuts in the glaze.

NAVETS – TURNIPS

866 Navets de Suède en purée – Swede purée or
Navets en purée – Turnip purée

750 g (1½ *lb*) *swedes or turnips*	*pepper*	60 g (2 *oz*) *butter*
salt		

1 Wash, peel and cut into large dice.
2 Place in cold water with salt and simmer until tender.
3 Drain and dry well.
4 Rub through a sieve; beat until creamy and blend in butter and seasoning.
5 Place in hot vegetable dish and ridge with palette knife.

Lunch service only.

867 Navets or navets de Suède glacés

As for carottes glacées (Recipe 781).

868 Turnip tops

Leaves of young turnip-tops may be treated and cooked as for choux verts à l'anglaise or as spinach.

OIGNONS – ONIONS

869 Oignons braisés – Braised onions

Prepare as for other braised vegetables, e.g., Recipe 760.

870 Oignons farcis – Stuffed onions

> duxelle stuffing   4 *large Spanish onions*   *prepared braising pan*
> (*Recipe* 102)

1 Peel and cut off top of onions.
2 Half-cook onions in water.
3 Drain and withdraw centre of onions.
4 Chop withdrawn section and mix with equal quantity of duxelles.
5 Stuff onions with this mixture.
6 Braise onions in usual manner.
7 Serve with sauce made by thickening (with fécule or roux), the cooking liquor.

871 Oignons frits à la française – French-fried onions

> 4 *fairly-large Spanish onions*   *milk*   *flour*
> salt

1 Slice onions into rings approximately 0·4 cm (one-fifth inch) thick.
2 Separate rings and place in milk.
3 Drain and dredge in flour.
4 Shake well in a cane colander or sieve.
5 Fry in deep fat until crisp and golden brown; season.

872 Petits oignons glacés (brun) – Brown-glazed button onions

Quantity. Allow 500 g–750 g (1 lb–1½ lb) for service as a principal vegetable accompaniment but only 250 g (½ lb) as garnish.

1 Carefully peel the onions.
2 Place butter in the bottom of a sauté-pan; heat and place in the onions.
3 Sprinkle some sugar on top.
4 Allow to cook slowly; the sugar caramelizes to give glaze and colour.

873 Petits oignons glacés (à blanc) – White-glazed button onions

Quantity. As Recipe 872.

1 Cover the peeled onions with white stock, adding 30 g (1 oz) butter per 250 ml (½ pint) of stock.
2 Cook onions slowly.
3 Drain, reduce cooking-liquor to give a glaze.
4 Roll the onions in this glaze before serving.

OKRA – GUMBO OR LADIES' FINGERS

874 Okra aux tomates

> 240 g (½ lb) tomato concassé ½ large tin of okra 30 g (1 oz) sliced onions
> 15 g (½ oz) butter salt, pepper

1 Stew the onions in butter.
2 Add the tomatoes and sweat for a few minutes.
3 Add the strained okra and stew for 10 minutes under cover; season.

875 Oseille – Sorrel

This astringent-tasting leaf is of the common dock family and may be prepared as spinach: it is used in soups and omelets as garnish rather than as a separate vegetable.

Preparation of sorrel for garnish:
1 Shred the leaves finely and wash thoroughly two or three times in cold water.
2 Place in a well-buttered braising-pan, cover with buttered greaseproof paper and cover with lid.
3 Bring to the boil then transfer to the oven to complete cooking.
4 When cooked, fill small jars with the sorrel and allow to cool.
5 When cold, cover with melted butter and keep in refrigerator until required.

PANAIS – PARSNIPS

876 Panais à la crème – Parsnips with cream

> 62 ml (½ gill) cream sauce 750 g (1½ lb) parsnips 62 ml (½ gill) cream
> (Recipe 65) seasoning lemon juice
> 30 g (1 oz) butter

1 Wash, peel and cut the parsnips into sections and turn as for carrots.
2 Cook in salted, acidulated water until tender.
3 Drain well, toss in butter, lié with the sauce and cream; season.

877 Panais au beurre

> 750 g (1½ lb) parsnips 60 g (2 oz) butter seasoning

1 Prepare and cook as for à la crème (Recipe 876).
2 Drain and toss in butter; season.

878 Panais aux fines herbes

> 750 g (1½ lb) parsnips 60 g (2 oz) butter 7 g (¼ oz) fines herbes

Prepare as for au beurre with addition of fines herbes.

PATATES (or *PATATES DOUCES*) – *SWEET POTATOES*

879 Patates en croquettes

500 *g* (1 *lb*) *sweet potatoes*	1 *egg yolk*	120 *g* (¼ *lb*) *white crumbs*
egg-wash	*flour*	*seasoning*
deep fat		

1 Peel potatoes by hand, thinly.
2 Prepare as for duchesse (Recipe 909) and make into small croquettes.
3 Fry in deep fat.

Note. Sweet potatoes may be prepared as duchesse, au four, or sauté, or plainly boiled and rolled in caramelized sugar.

PETITS POIS – PEAS

880 Petits pois à l'anglaise

500 *ml* (1 *pt*) *shelled peas*	30 *g* (1 *oz*) *butter*	*salt*

1 Cook in plenty of salt water; drain and season.
2 Add a pinch of sugar and toss in butter.

881 Petits pois à la bonne femme

6 *button onions*	*salt, sugar*	
250 *ml* (½ *pt*) *white stock*	60 *g* (2 *oz*) *diced bacon*	30 *g* (1 *oz*) *butter*
(*Recipe* 6)	500 *ml* (1 *pt*) *shelled peas*	15 *g* (½ *oz*) *flour*

1 Blanch and refresh bacon.
2 Put butter in pan and fry bacon lightly.
3 Add flour and cook slightly.
4 Moisten with stock and boil.
5 Add peas and onions and finish cooking.
6 Season with salt and sugar.

882 Petits pois à la française

500 *ml* (1 *pt*) *peas*	30 *g* (1 *oz*) *butter*	Beurre manié :
6 *button onions*	*salt, sugar*	30 *g* (1 *oz*) *butter*
½ *lettuce*	*pepper*	30 *g* (1 *oz*) *flour*

1 Shred lettuce.
2 Place in pan with rest of ingredients.
3 Half-cover with white stock or water.
4 Cover with lid and cook.
5 Lié with beurre manié.

883 Petits pois à la menthe

1 Same as for à l'anglaise (Recipe 880) but add a bunch of fresh mint.
2 Serve with blanched fresh mint leaves on top.

884 Petits pois flamande

    375 *ml* (¾ *pt*) *peas*   120 *g* (¼ *lb*) *carrots*

1 Prepare carrots as for glacé (Recipe 781) and par-cook.
2 Add peas. Complete the cooking. Adjust seasoning and serve.

885 Petits pois en purée – Purée of fresh peas

    few parsley leaves   *500 ml* (1 *pt*) *peas*   *sugar, salt*
    boiling water to cover   ½ *lettuce*   *butter*

1 Cover peas with water.
2 Add lettuce and parsley (tied).
3 Season with teaspoonful each of salt and sugar, and cook.
4 Drain peas and reduce cooking-liquor.
5 Pass through a sieve.
6 Add 60 g (2 oz) butter per litre (quart) of purée and finish with liquor; reduce to a glaze.

886 Petits pois mange tout

Mange tout, literally 'eat all', means that this type of pea is completely edible including the pod. The unshelled, but stalked, peas are simmered then dressed with butter.

PIMENTS DOUX – CAPSICUMS OR SWEET PEPPERS

The red and green sweet peppers are not really pimentoes, though often so called. True pimento yields the berry known as allspice. Although the seeds must be removed from both red and green peppers, it is not necessary to skin them though this is often done.

887 Piments doux farcis au riz – Peppers stuffed with rice

    4, 90 *g* (3-oz) *pimentoes*   190 *ml* (1½ *gills*) *brown*   7 *g* (¼ *oz*) *arrowroot*
    120 *g* (¼ *lb*) *rice pilaff*   *veal stock* (*Recipe* 10)   *seasoning*
    (*Recipe* 366)

1 If desired to remove the skins, brush with butter and expose under grill momentarily.
2 Remove all seeds from inside.
3 Fill with rice pilaff.
4 Braise in veal stock until tender.
5 When cooked, remove and dress in oval dish – season.
6 Reduce cooking-liquor, thicken with diluted arrowroot, strain and serve separately.

888 Peppers for salads and hors d'œuvre

Peppers, especially green ones, are widely used in salads; they may be shredded raw, mixed with onions and vinaigrette (Recipe 118) and served as hors d'œuvre.

POIREAUX – LEEKS

889 Poireaux au gratin

4, 180 g (6-oz) leeks   190 ml (1½ gills) Mornay   seasoning
15 g (½ oz) grated Parmesan cheese   sauce (Recipe 58)

1 Wash and trim the leeks.
2 Tie in a bundle and cook until tender in boiling salted water.
3 Drain well: fold in two.
4 Coat with mornay sauce, sprinkle with Parmesan cheese and brown under the grill.

890 Poireaux milanaise

22 g (¾ oz) grated   15 g (½ oz) butter blanc   4, 180 g (6-oz) leeks
   Parmesan cheese   (Recipe 759)

1 Prepare in bundles as Recipe 889.
2 Cook à blanc.
3 Place on a well-buttered dish.
4 Dress the leeks on top; sprinkle with cheese; brown under grill.

POMMES DE TERRE

Pommes de terre is the full French term for potatoes, and its literal translation is 'apples of the earth'. Usually, it is contracted to 'pommes'. As 'pommes' are apples, the context will indicate whether potatoes or apples are involved.

POMMES NOUVELLES – NEW POTATOES

891 Pommes nouvelles à l'anglaise

750 g (1½ lb) new potatoes   boiling salted water

1 Wash potatoes well, do not peel.
2 Place in pan and cover with boiling water, salted.
3 Bring to boil and cook slowly 20 to 25 minutes.
4 Drain and peel potatoes. Serve very hot.

892 Pommes nouvelles à la menthe – Minted new potatoes

750 g (1½ lb) new potatoes   boiling, salted water   2 or 3 sprigs mint

1 Cook as for à l'anglaise with mint added.
2 When peeled, dress potatoes with blanched mint leaf on top of each potato.

893 Pommes nouvelles persillées

750 g (1½ lb) new potatoes   boiling, salted water   7 g (¼ oz) chopped
45 g (1½ oz) butter   parsley

1 Prepare and cook as for à l'anglaise (Recipe 891).
2 When peeled, toss in butter.
3 Sprinkle with chopped parsley.

MAIN CROP OR 'OLD' POTATOES

894 Old potatoes (to boil)

1 Trim or turn to château (barrel) shape.
2 Cover with cold salted water.
3 Bring to boil and cook steadily (avoiding over-rapid, jostling boil which breaks up the structure).
4 May be dressed and served as above.

895 Pommes vapeur – Steamed potatoes

1 Trim to small château (large olive or barrel) shape.
2 Place on a tray preferably napkin-wrapped and cook in a steamer.
3 Serve with boiled fish, salmon, and turbot, etc.

896 Pommes en purée or pommes purées – Mashed potato

750 g (1½ lb) potatoes	cold, salted water	grated nutmeg
30 g (1 oz) butter	62 ml (⅛ pt) boiled milk	seasoning

1 Peel and quarter potatoes.
2 Cook as for à l'anglaise (Recipe 894).
3 Drain and dry potatoes.
4 Pass through sieve.
5 Place in pan and add milk and butter.
6 Season and beat until smooth and creamy over low heat.

897 Pommes en purée à la crème – Mashed potatoes with cream

750 g (1½ lb) peeled potatoes	30 g (1 oz) butter	30 ml (¼ gill) fresh
62 ml (⅛ pt) boiled milk	grated nutmeg,	cream
cold, salted water	pepper	

1 Prepare as for purée.
2 Dish potatoes on service dish.
3 Cover with cream which has been heated.

898 Pommes en purée au gratin

750 g (1½ lb) potatoes	cold, salted water	15 g (½ oz) grated cheese
62 ml (⅛ pt) boiling milk	30 g (1 oz) butter	grated nutmeg, pepper

1 Prepare as for purée (Recipe 896).
2 Dish on service dish.
3 Sprinkle with cheese.
4 Brown under the salamander.

899 Soufflé de pommes de terre – Potato soufflé

    750 g (1½ lb) peeled potatoes   62 ml (⅛ pt) boiled   grated nutmeg,
    30 g (1 oz) butter   milk   pepper
    cold, salted water   2 eggs

1 Prepare as for purée (Recipe 896).
2 Add the yolks of the eggs and beat well.
3 Whip the whites and fold into mixture.
4 Place in buttered soufflé-dish.
5 Cook as for ordinary soufflé.

Note. This method must not be confused with deep-fried pommes soufflées
(Recipe 931).

900 Pommes en robe de chambre – Steamed jacket-potatoes or belted potatoes

    8 *large, even-sized potatoes*

1 Wash potatoes well and dry with a cloth.
2 Cut half-inch ribbon of skin full circumference of potato.
3 Place on tray and cook in steamer.
4 Dress on serviette with branch parsley.

ROAST, OVEN-BROWNED, AND DERIVATIVE METHODS

901 Pommes rôties – Roast potatoes

    500 g (1 lb) even-sized potatoes (peeled)   60 g (2 oz) fat   salt

1 Heat fat in roasting-tray.
2 Place in potatoes and roll until they are coated with fat; sprinkle with salt.
3 Place in hot oven until cooked and golden brown; drain and serve.

902 Pommes château

    750 g (1½ lb) potatoes turned to   salt   60 g (2 oz) fat
       barrel-shape 4 cm (2 inches   30 g (1 oz) butter   7 g (¼ oz) chopped
       long)   parsley

Cook as Recipe 901, but drain and toss in butter and sprinkle with chopped
    parsley.

Note. Par-boiling for pommes château (and also pômmes rôties) is resorted
to in some kitchens to reduce oven-times, but the result is less satisfactory.

903 Pommes noisettes

          750 g (1½ lb) potatoes   60 g (2 oz) butter   salt

Cut potatoes to hazel-nut size with the special spoon-shaped cutter and cook
in butter until golden brown.

904 Pommes parisienne

    750 g (1½ lb) potatoes   60 g·(2 oz) butter   7 g (¼ oz) chopped .
    salt   meat glaze   parsley

1 Cut with parisienne spoon (or scoop) in similar style to Recipe 903, but larger.
2 Cook in the same manner.
3 Before serving, roll in melted meat-glaze and sprinkle with chopped parsley.

905 Pommes parmentier

750 g (1½ *lb*) *potatoes in* 1 *cm* (½-*inch*) *cubes*   60 g (2 oz) *fat*   *salt*

1 Heat fat in roasting-tray.
2 Place in potatoes and toss until coated with fat.
3 Cook in hot oven until brown.
4 Drain and season.

906 Pommes pavées

750 g (1½ *lb*) *potatoes in* 2 *cm* (1-*inch*) *cubes*   60 g (2 oz) *fat*   *salt*

Prepare as for Parmentier, Recipe 905.

907 Pommes sablées

As for Parmentier but just before completion of cooking, sprinkle liberally with 60 g (2 oz) white breadcrumbs; drain and serve.

908 Pommes olivette

750 g (1½ *lb*) *potatoes*   60 g (2 *oz*) *butter*   *salt*

Cut with special parisienne-type cutter in the shape of small olives and cook as for noisette.

DUCHESSE POTATOES AND DERIVATIVES

909 Pommes duchesse

750 g (1½ *lb*) *peeled potatoes*   30 g (1 *oz*) *butter*   *pepper*
2 *egg yolks*   *salt*   *grated nutmeg*

1 Boil potatoes until cooked.
2 Drain and dry well.
3 Mash potatoes and add butter and seasoning.
4 Beat in egg yolks.
4 Place potatoes in piping-bag with star-tube.
6 Pipe potatoes in rosette shape on to buttered tray.
7 Brush with egg-wash and brown in hot oven.
8 Finish by brushing with melted butter.

910 Pommes marquise

750 g (1½ *lb*) *pommes duchesse*   90 g (3 oz) *well-reduced tomato*
(*Recipe* 909)   *purée*

1 Beat purée of tomato into potatoes.
2 Pipe and finish as for pommes duchesse.
Note. Pommes marquise may be piped in the form of a nest and the cavity filled with tomato concassé.

911 Pommes St Florentin

> 750 g (1½ *lb*) *pommes duchesse*   90 g (3 *oz*) *chopped lean ham*
> (*Recipe* 909)   60 g (2 *oz*) *crushed vermicelli*

1 Mix duchesse with chopped ham, place on floured board and roll into cylinder.
2 Flatten into an oblong.
3 Slice into 60 g (2-oz) portions.
4 Dip in egg-wash and then in vermicelli. (Some chefs add also a little white breadcrumbs.)
5 Fry in deep fat.

912 Pommes Berny

> 750 g (1½ *lb*) *pommes duchesse* (*Recipe* 909)   *flaked almonds*   *egg-wash*
> 60 g (2 *oz*) *chopped truffles*

1 Mix truffles through potatoes.
2 Form potatoes the size and shape of an apricot.
3 Dip in egg-wash and roll in flaked almonds.
4 With the back of a small knife make a slight incision on top and insert a short piece of parsley stalk.
5 Fry in hot deep fat.

913 Pommes croquettes

> 750 g (1½ *lb*) *duchesse potato*   *egg-wash*   *flour and breadcrumbs*
> (*Recipe* 909)

1 Place potatoes on floured board.
2 Roll into long cylinder.
3 Cut off in cork-sized lengths 60 g (2 oz each).
4 Dip in egg-wash then breadcrumbs.
5 Place in basket; fry in hot deep fat.

DUCHESSE WITH CHOUX-PASTE

914 Pommes Dauphine

> 750 g (1½ *lb*) *pommes duchesse*   250 g (½ *lb*) *choux paste* (*Recipe* 999
> (*Recipe* 909)   *but unsweetened*)

Combine potatoes and choux paste.
Mould with tablespoons on greased paper and form into cylinders, 60 g (2 oz) each.
Fry in deep fat.

15 Pommes Lorette

> 750 g (1½ *lb*) *pommes Dauphine*   45 g (1½ *oz*) *grated Parmesan*
> (*Recipe* 914)   *cheese*

1 Mix cheese and potatoes.
2 Form into cigar shapes, 60 g (2 oz) each.
3 Fry in deep fat.

JACKET-BAKED AND DERIVATIVE

916 Pommes au four – Jacket-baked potatoes

   8 large potatoes   *45 g (1½ oz) butter*   *rock salt*

1 Wash potatoes and dry well with a clean cloth.
2 Cover bottom of tray with salt.
3 Place potatoes on top.
4 Bake in oven until tender.
5 Dress potatoes on serviette.
6 Make a cross-wise incision with pointed knife on potatoes.
7 Pull back potato-skin and place piece of butter in cavity.

917 Pommes Macaire

1 Prepare as for pommes au four (Recipe 916).
2 When cooked, scoop out pulp.
3 Season with salt and pepper.
4 Mash with fork and add 60 g (2 oz) butter.
5 Shape like fish cakes.
6 Fry in pan with butter, browning both sides.

918 Pommes Byron

1 Prepare as for pommes macaire (Recipe 917).
2 When fried, sprinkle with cream and grated cheese.
3 Glaze under salamander.

919 Pommes Robert

1 Prepare as for pommes macaire (Recipe 917) with the addition of 3 egg
   yolks and a good pinch of chopped chives per 500 g (pound) of potato.
2 Finish as for macaire.

920 Pommes de terre gratinées

1 Prepare as for pommes au four (Recipe 916) and when baked halve the
   potatoes lengthwise.
2 Withdraw the pulp and make as for pommes purée (Recipe 896).
3 With piping-bag refill the halves with the purée.
4 Sprinkle with grated cheese and brown in hot oven.
5 Serve on a serviette.

SAUTER OR SHALLOW-FRY

21 Pommes sautées

750 g (1½ *lb*) *unpeeled potatoes*

1 Wash potatoes well and cook in steamer.
2 Peel and cut in slices 0·5 cm (¼ inch) thick.
3 Sauté in oil in frying-pan until brown.
4 Drain well and season; sprinkle with chopped parsley.

22 Pommes sautées provençale

Prepare as sautées (Recipe 921) with the addition of chopped garlic.

23 Pommes sautées lyonnaise

Prepare as for pommes sautées (Recipe 921) with saturee-d onions mixed through.
Use one-third onions to potato.

DEEP FRIED

24 Pommes frites

1 kg (2 *lb*) *peeled potatoes*

Square off potatoes with knife.
Cut in 4 cm (2 inch) long batons 1 cm (½ inch) thick.
Wash well, drain, and fry in deep fat.
When cooked, drain and sprinkle with salt.

25 Pommes allumette

Prepare as pommes frites (Recipe 924) but cut in 3 cm (1½ inch) long batons 0·5 cm (¼ inch) thick. (**Pommes mignonette** are similar but slightly thicker.)

26 Pommes bataille

Prepare as pommes frites (Recipe 924) but cut in cubes of 1·5 cm (¾ inch).

27 Pommes chips – Game chips (or crisps)

Cut in thin slices on mandolin.
Wash well; drain, and dry.
Cook in hot fat until golden and crisp.
Sprinkle with salt.

28 Pommes Collerette

Trim potatoes in cylinder-shape.
Groove sides with channel knife.

3 Slice thinly on mandolin.
4 Finish as for pommes chips.

929 Pommes paille

1 Cut in julienne.
2 Wash well and cook in hot fat until golden and crisp.
3 Sprinkle with salt.

930 Pommes Pont-Neuf

Prepare as pommes frites (Recipe 924) but cut in 4 cm (2 inch) lengths 1·5 cm ($\frac{3}{4}$ inch) thick.

931 Pommes soufflées

1 Trim the potatoes square.
2 Cut the slice 0·3 cm ($\frac{1}{8}$ inch) thick.
3 Dry well on clean cloth.
4 Put into moderately hot fat.
5 When cooked they rise to the surface.
6 Drain into frying-basket.
7 Plunge into hot fat.
8 Fry until golden brown and soufflée-d; salt.

STEWED AND CASSEROLE

932 Pommes dauphinoise (gratin dauphinoise)

750 g (1½ lb) peeled potatoes	90 g (3 oz) grated	salt
500 ml (1 pt) boiled milk	Gruyère cheese	pepper
1 egg	1 clove garlic	grated nutmeg
30 g (1 oz) butter		

1 Slice potatoes thinly.
2 Mix milk, eggs and cheese, reserving 15 g (½ oz) cheese.
3 Mix potatoes with this mixture and season.
4 Rub an earthenware dish with garlic and butter.
5 Fill with potato mixture.
6 Sprinkle with cheese and butter.
7 Cook in moderate oven for 40 to 45 minutes.

933 Pommes savoyarde

750 g (1½ lb) peeled potatoes	salt	grated nutmeg
500 ml (1 pt) white stock (Recipe 6)	pepper	garlic
45 g (1½ oz) grated Gruyère cheese	butter	

Prepare as for pommes dauphinoise (Recipe 932).

934 Pommes Delmonico

750 g (1½ lb) potatoes cut in 1 cm (½-inch) cubes	white breadcrumbs	375 ml (¾ pt) milk
	salt	

1 Almost cover potatoes with milk.
2 Season, bring to boil, and cook in oven.
3 Sprinkle liberally with breadcrumbs on top before they are cooked giving them time to brown.

935 Pommes maître d'hôtel

750 g (1½ lb) medium-sized potatoes	cold salted water	salt
	7 g (¼ oz) chopped parsley	pepper
375 ml (¾ pt) boiling milk		

1 Cook potatoes in salted water.
2 Peel while still hot.
3 Cut into round slices.
4 Cover with boiling milk.
5 Season with salt and pepper.
6 Reduce the milk by half.
7 Place in service dish and sprinkle with chopped parsley.

936 Pommes maire

Prepare as for maître d'hôtel (Recipe 935) using cream instead of milk and omitting parsley.

937 Pommes boulangère

750 g (1½ lb) peeled potatoes	salt, pepper	60 g (2 oz) butter
240 g (½ lb) onions	white stock (Recipe 6)	
chopped parsley (optional)		

1 Slice potatoes and onions finely.
2 Fry onions in butter, slightly browning them.
3 Mix potatoes with onions and season.
4 Place in deep earthenware dish with bouquet garni.
5 Moisten with white stock and bring to boil.
6 Cook in oven until brown and stock has almost evaporated.
7 Withdraw bouquet garni; brush potatoes with melted butter.

FONDANT STYLE

938 Pommes fondantes

750 g (1½ lb) potatoes turned to barrel shape [5 cm (2½ inches long)]	salt, pepper	7 g (¼ oz) chopped parsley
	45 g (1½ oz) butter	white stock (Recipe 6)

1 Melt butter in tray.
2 Place in potatoes and toss until slightly browned.
3 Season, half cover with stock.
4 Bring to boil and place in oven.
5 Cook until golden brown and stock has almost evaporated.
6 Brush with melted butter and sprinkle with parsley.

939 Pommes berrichonne

750 g (1½ lb) château   120 g (¼ lb) diced   white stock (Recipe 6)
  potatoes   onions   7 g (¼ oz) chopped
  (Recipe 902)   120 g (¼ lb) lardons   parsley

As for pommes fondantes (Recipe 938).

ANNA AND DERIVATIVE STYLES

940 Pommes Anna

750 g (1½ lb) peeled potatoes   60 g (2 oz) melted butter   pepper
salt

1 Trim potatoes in cylinder-shape.
2 Well butter a pommes-Anna mould.
3 Slice potatoes thinly in circles.
4 Place potatoes in circles in bottom of mould overlapping each slice.
5 Butter and season each layer.
6 Build up layers until almost to the top of the mould.
7 Place in fairly hot oven and cook approximately for 30 to 40 minutes; turn
  out of mould.

941 Pommes Nana (for garnishes)

1 Prepare as for pommes Anna (Recipe 940) but cut into julienne.
2 Cook in well-buttered dariole moulds.

942 Pommes voisin

1 Prepare as for pommes Anna (Recipe 940).
2 Sprinkle each layer of potato with grated cheese.
3 Cook as for pommes Anna.

POTIRON – PUMPKIN

943 Potiron provençale

750 (1½ lb) pumpkin   62 ml (½ gill) oil   500 g (1 lb) tomato concasse
120 g (¼ lb) sliced   1 clove crushed   4 g (⅛ oz) chopped parsley
  onions   garlic   seasoning

1 Skin the pumpkin and remove seeds.
2 Cut into small collops.
3 Sauté the onions to golden brown.
4 Remove onions and drain well.
5 Quickly sauté the collops of pumpkin in the oil remaining from the onions;
  add the garlic and tomato concassé; season and add the cooked onions.
6 Serve with chopped parsley.

Note:

i Pumpkin may be plainly boiled and served with sauce hollandaise (Recipe 72), mornay sauce (Recipe 58) or with cream. In such cases, cut into sizes of 6 cm by 4 cm (3 by 2 inches).

ii Pumpkin is not a popular vegetable in this country but it is in demand in America for making pie.

SALSIFIS – SALSIFY OR OYSTER PLANT

944 Salsifis à la crème – Salsify in cream

1 Wash and peel salsify and place in acidulated water.
2 Cook à blanc.
3 Drain and dry; cut into 4 cm (2-inch) lengths.
4 Bind with cream sauce.

945 Salsifis sauté

1 Cook in blanc (Recipe 759) and cut in 4 cm (2-inch) lengths.
2 Sauté in butter until well browned.
3 Season and serve.

946 Salsifis poulette

500 g (1 lb) salsifis	blanc (Recipe 759)	30 g (1 oz) butter
125 ml (¼ pt) sauce poulette	seasoning	lemon juice
(Recipe 59)		

1 Wash well and scrape with peeler.
2 Place in lemon water as they are cleaned.
3 Cut into 4 cm (2-inch) lengths; cook à blanc.
4 Drain well; toss in butter, finish off in sauce poulette.

947 Salsifis aux fines herbes

500 g (1 lb) salsifis   60 g (2 oz) butter   7 g (¼ oz) fines herbes

1 Cook as for salsifis poulette (Recipe 946).
2 Drain well, toss in butter with the fines herbes; season.

948 Salsifis frit

500 g (1 lb) salsifis	2·5 ml spoon	125 ml (¼ pt) coating
62 ml (½ gill) oil	[½ teaspoon]	batter
seasoning	chopped parsley	(Recipe 1001)
62 ml (½ gill) vinegar	½ lemon	

1 Wash and scrape with peeler.
2 Cut into 4 cm (2-inch) lengths.
3 Cook in salt water with lemon juice.
4 Drain and place in oil, vinegar, and parsley for 20 minutes.
5 Drain and dip in batter; fry in deep fat; drain.
6 Garnish with fried parsley.

TOMATOES

949 Tomates concassées – Chopped tomato

> 4 *large tomatoes*   30 *g* (1 *oz*) *butter*   *pinch sugar*
> 1 *small finely-chopped onion*   *seasoning*

1 Blanch and skin tomatoes.
2 Cut in half.
3 Scoop out seeds and express juice.
4 Cut tomato in dice.
5 Sweet onions in butter without colouring them.
6 Add diced tomatoes and seasoning.
7 Cook for 5 minutes and finish with a small pinch of sugar.

950 Tomates farcies au gratin

> 4 *tomatoes*   120 *g* (¼ *lb*) *duxelle stuffing*   60 *g* (2 *oz*) *white*
> 30 *g* (1 *oz*) *butter*   (*Recipe* 102)   *breadcrumbs*

1 Blanch and peel tomatoes.
2 Cut off top of tomatoes and scoop out seeds.
3 Season inside with salt and pepper and fill with stuffing and brush with melted butter.
4 Sprinkle breadcrumbs on top; place on oiled tray and bake in oven.

951 Tomates farcies italienne

> 250 *ml* (½ *pt*) *rizotto Italienne*   4 *tomatoes*   15 *g* (½ *oz*) *grated cheese*
> (*Recipe* 367)

1 Prepare tomatoes as above but fill with rizotto italienne.
2 Sprinkle cheese on top and bake in oven.

952 Tomates farcies provençale

> 4 *tomatoes*   60 *g* (2 *oz*) *breadcrumbs*   *salt, pepper*
> 1 *clove crushed*   10 *ml spoon* [½ *tablespoon*]   *oil*
>   *garlic*   *chopped parsley*

1 Prepare as above but reserve seeds and pulp.
2 Place breadcrumbs in bowl and season adding the crushed garlic and parsley.
3 Strain tomato pulp over crumbs to moisten.
4 Fill tomatoes with breadcrumb mixture and cook in oil in oven.

953 Tomates grillées – Grilled tomatoes

> 4 *large tomatoes*   60 *g* (2 *oz*) *butter*   *seasoning*

1 Make an incision on the top in the form of a cross.
2 Brush liberally with butter, season.
3 Grill slowly under moderate heat.

954 Tomates sautées au beurre – Shallow-fried tomatoes

    4 *large tomatoes*   15 *g* ($\frac{1}{2}$ *oz*) *butter*

1 Cut in half and season.
2 Fry gently in butter flat-side down first, then turn over.

TOPINAMBOURS – JERUSALEM ARTICHOKES

955 Topinambours – Jerusalem artichokes (to boil)

1 Wash well and carefully peel thinly.
2 Place in acidulated water to retain whiteness.
3 Prepare à blanc (Recipe 759) and bring to the boil.
4 Add the artichokes and simmer until tender.
5 Drain well.

956 Topinambours à l'anglaise

    750 *g* (1$\frac{1}{2}$ *lb*) *topinambours*   240 *ml* ($\frac{1}{2}$ *pt*) *Béchamel*
    seasoning   (*Recipe* 51)

1 Trim and shape as for olives.
2 Cook lightly in blanc as Recipe 955.
3 Bind with thin Béchamel and season.

957 Topinambours aux fines herbes

    500 *g* (1 *lb*) *topinambours*   60 *g* (2 *oz*) *butter*   7 *g* ($\frac{1}{4}$ *oz*) *fines herbes*
    seasoning

1 Peel and trim the artichokes and toss in butter.
2 Add the fines herbes and season.
3 Place in oval vegetable-dish and sprinkle with fresh parsley before service.

958 Topinambours frits

    500 *g* (1 *lb*) *topinambours*   *Pâte à frire* (*Recipe* 1001)   *seasoning*
    60 *g* (2 *oz*) *butter*

1 Peel and slice topinambours.
2 Cook gently in butter.
3 When about to serve, dip in batter and fry in deep fat.

959 Topinambours en purée – Jerusalem artichoke purée

    500 *g* (1 *lb*) *topinambours*   120 *g* ($\frac{1}{4}$ *lb*) *mashed potatoes*   *seasoning*
    60 *g* (2 *oz*) *butter*   (*Recipe* 896)

1 Peel and slice topinambours.
2 Cook in butter.
3 Pass through sieve.
4 Season and add sufficient mashed potato to thicken mixture.

8. *Pastry and Sweets*

THE pâtisserie department of a large hotel or restaurant is a highly specialized one. Cooks who wish to become chef pâtissier (chief pastry-cook) usually turn their attention exclusively to this partie early in their careers. Nevertheless, in many establishments, and in other fields of catering, a good chef will consider it essential to have a sound basic knowledge of pâtisserie work.

In providing recipes for this section, selection (and exclusion) presented problems but the aim has been to cover the basics or fonds to allow for a wide range of work. These even permit the making of many desserts and sweets that have not been listed. For example, using the basic paste-recipes, it is possible to prepare a variety of fruit pies, tarts, and flans even though a full range of pies and tarts is not given. If correctly exploited, baked- and steamed-pudding mixes can also yield a diverse number of sweets such as Eve's, and other fruit puddings.

Simple scones and griddle goods have been omitted. Though useful as exercises during apprentice-training, these are seldom prepared within catering establishments today, but, like ice-cream, are purchased as required.

The Gâteaux and similar pastries that are represented should be regarded as examples, as there are so many variants and alternatives. Nevertheless from the recipes quoted within this section, a fair range of work for high-class service can be achieved.

BASIC PREPARATIONS IN THE PÂTISSERIE

SAUCES

960 Sauce abricot – Apricot sauce

> 240 g (½ lb) apricot purée   500 g (1 lb) sugar   15 ml spoon (⅛ gill) kirsch

1 Bring apricot purée and sugar to the boil, stirring occasionally to prevent burning.
2 When cool, add kirsch and reserve until required.

961 Sauce anglaise – Custard sauce

> 2 egg yolks   vanilla pod   250 ml (½ pt) milk
> 60 g (2 oz) sugar

1 Bring milk and vanilla pod to the boil; remove the pod, pour milk on to the egg yolks and sugar, stirring all the time.

2 Return to the stove and cook, but do not boil.
3 Continue cooking, without boiling, until the mixture coats the back of a spoon.

962 Sauce Arenberg or Mousseline sauce

2 *egg yolks*	45 *g* (1½ *oz*) *sugar*	500 *ml* (1 *pt*) *cream*
vanilla essence	62 *ml* (⅛ *pt*) *water*	

1 Whisk egg yolks, sugar, water and essence together over warm water until thick.
2 Whisk until cold, then add cream and continue whisking until it has the required light consistency.

963 Sauce caramel

500 *g* (1 *lb*) *loaf sugar*   125 *ml* (¼ *pt*) *water*

1 Boil sugar to a light caramel.
2 Add carefully 125 ml (¼ pt) hot water; sauce is then ready for use.

964 Sauce chocolat

120 *g* (¼ *lb*) *cocoa or*	250 *ml* (½ *pt*) *water*	360 *g* (¾ *lb*) *sugar*
chocolate powder		

1 Bring smoothly-mixed ingredients to the boil.
2 Sauce is ready for use.

965 Sauce citron – Lemon sauce

Juice and zest of	250 *ml* (½ *pt*) *water*	15 *g* (½ *oz*) *arrowroot*
1 *lemon*	60 *g* (2 *oz*) *sugar*	*egg colouring if desired*

1 Dissolve arrowroot in a little of the water.
2 Bring remainder of ingredients to the boil and whisk in the dissolved arrowroot; sauce is then ready for use.

966 Custard sauce (with powder)

240 *ml* (½ *pt*) *milk*   15 *g* (½ *oz*) *custard powder*   30 *g* (1 *oz*) *sugar*

1 Dissolve sugar and custard powder in a little of the milk.
2 Bring remainder of the milk to the boil and whisk in the dissolved powder.
3 Bring back to the boil and the sauce is then ready for use.

Note. This sauce is, of course, merely an inferior substitute for Sauce Anglaise (Recipe 961).

967 Sauce framboise – Raspberry sauce

240 *g* (½ *lb*) *raspberry purée*   240 *g* (½ *lb*) *sugar*   125 *ml* (¼ *pt*) *water*
colouring if necessary

Bring all ingredients to the boil and the sauce is then ready for use.

968 Sauce fraise – Strawberry sauce

Prepare as for sauce framboise substituting strawberry purée.

969 Jam sauce

150 g (5 oz) jam	5 ml spoon [½ dessertspoon]
62 ml (⅛ pt) water	arrowroot

1 Boil jam and water together and thicken with diluted arrowroot.
2 Re-boil, skim, and strain.

970 Melba sauce

120 g (¼ lb) raspberry purée	120 g (¼ lb)	240 g (½ lb)
cochineal (if required)	strawberry purée	caster sugar

Stir all ingredients together over heat to dissolve sugar; colour if necessary and use when cold.

Sauce Mousseline

(See Recipe 962).

971 Sauce Sabayon or **Zabaglione**

3 egg yolks	zest of ¼ lemon	125 ml (¼ pt) marsala
60 g (2 oz) caster sugar	62 ml (⅛ pt) white wine	

1 Whisk all the ingredients together over warm water until they rise to 3 or 4 times their volume.
2 Continue whisking until the mixture thickens; do not boil.

Note. Sabayon or Zabaglione can be served in glasses as a dessert or in sauceboats as an accompaniment to puddings such as soufflé.

972 Syrup sauce

60 g (2 oz) syrup	juice of ½ lemon	60 g (2 oz) sugar
125 ml (¼ pt) water	7 g (¼ oz) arrowroot	

1 Dissolve arrowroot in a little of the water.
2 Bring remainder of ingredients to the boil before whisking-in the dissolved arrowroot.
3 Re-boil to cook arrowroot.

972a Hard sweet sauces

Hard sauces for puddings such as Rum and Brandy Butters are, in effect, the sweet counterpart of the beurres composés, composed butters, referred to on page 23. Brandy butter, for example, may be made by creaming together 60 g (2 oz) butter and 60 g (2 oz) icing sugar and stirring in brandy [up to 62 ml (½ gill)] until blended. The sauce may be rolled and chilled for slicing or served creamy and non-chilled. Other types of liqueurs and essences may be used in similar proportions to provide variants.

GLAZES

973 Apricot glaze

240 g (½ *lb*) *apricot purée*   500 g (1 *lb*) *sugar* (*loaf*)   125 *ml* (¼ *pt*) *water*

1 Boil the sugar and water to 115°C (240°F).
2 Add the purée and re-boil until temperature reaches 110°C (230°F); strain.

974 Syrup glaze

125 *ml* (¼ *pt*) *water*   7 g (¼ *oz*) *arrowroot*   *egg colouring*
30 g (1 *oz*) *sugar*   *apple peelings and cores*

1 Dissolve arrowroot in a little water.
2 Boil remaining ingredients and strain.
3 Re-boil and whisk in arrowroot.

Note. Pear or peach trimmings can be used to make syrup.

975 Syrup for glazing petits fours

240 g (½ *lb*) *loaf sugar*   *juice of* ⅛ *lemon*   30 g (1 *oz*) *water*
30 g (1 *oz*) *glucose*

1 Boil sugar, glucose and water to 154°–157°C (310°F–315°F).
2 Add lemon juice and shake in thoroughly.
3 Pass fruits or marzipans through syrup with the aid of a fork and place on a lightly-oiled marble slab to cool and set.

ICINGS AND COVERINGS

976 American icing

240 g (½ *lb*) *loaf sugar*   1 *egg white*   *vanilla essence*
30 g (1 *oz*) *water*

1 Boil water and sugar to 120°C (245°F) and pour steadily on to the beaten egg white.
2 Add essence and continue beating until at the point of thickening.
3 Coat gâteaux or pastries.

977 Fondant

850 g (1¾ *lb*) *cube sugar*   120 g (¼ *lb*) *glucose*   125 *ml* (¼ *pt*) *water*

1 Boil sugar and water to 110°C (230°F).
2 Add glucose and re-boil to 115°C (240°F).
3 Pour out on to a marble slab surrounded by fondant bars.
4 Allow to cool slightly and work into a white mass with the aid of a spatula. Store in an earthenware jar or tin.

978 Royal icing

> 240 g (½ lb) icing sugar   lemon juice or cream   2 egg whites
> 1 drop ultra-marine blue   of tartar

1 Sieve icing sugar.
2 Add icing sugar gradually to whites of eggs, beating continuously with a wooden spatula.
3 Add lemon juice and colouring.

979 Water icing

> colouring and flavouring   240 g (½ lb) icing sugar   warm water
> as desired

Add warm water to icing sugar; add colouring and flavouring if desired and beat to required consistency.

980 Sucre filé – Spun sugar

> 240 g (½ lb) loaf sugar   15 g (½ oz) glucose   62 ml (⅛ pt) water
> juice of ⅛ lemon

1 Boil sugar, water and glucose to 155°C (312°F).
2 Add lemon juice.
3 Spin over an oiled wooden stick.

Note. Colouring may be added if desired.

981 Chocolate couverture

(a) Milk-chocolate couverture:
1 Grate the chocolate finely.
2 Place in a basin and warm to 45°C (112°F) over warm water stirring continuously with a spatula.
3 Cool to almost setting and re-warm to 31°C (88°F); the chocolate is then ready for moulding.

(b) Plain-chocolate couverture:
Prepare as above but warm to 46°C (115°F); cool to almost setting, and work at 32°–33°C (90° to 92°F).

CREAMS FOR FILLINGS

982 Crème d'amande – Almond cream

> 120 g (¼ lb) ground almonds   120 g (¼ lb) caster   120 g (¼ lb) butter
> almond essence if   sugar   30 g (1 oz) soft flour
>   necessary   3 eggs

1 Cream butter and sugar together.
2 Beat in eggs, one at a time.
3 Fold through flour and ground almonds.

Note. This lighter preparation is often preferred to frangipane sponge (Recipe 1037) as a filling for items such as gâteaux, tartelettes, and petits fours.

983 Crème au beurre-I – Butter cream

6 *egg yolks*	360 *g* (¾ *lb*) *creamed butter*	240 *g* (½ *lb*) *caster*
vanilla essence	60 *g* (2 *oz*) *water*	*sugar*

1 Whisk yolks, water, sugar and essence over warm water until they rise to become 3 to 4 times their original volume.
2 Continue beating until the mixture thickens and beat until cold.
3 Add the creamed butter to the mixture, a little at a time, beating continually with a wooden spatula until light and creamy.

983a Crème au beurre-II – Butter cream (alternative recipe)

500 *g* (1 *lb*) *butter*	1 *small egg*
500 *g* (1 *lb*) *icing sugar*	*vanilla essence*

Beat butter and sugar together, before adding egg and essence.

Note. For chocolate butter-cream incorporate 90 to 120 g (3 to 4 oz) melted chocolate. Similarly, coffee butter-cream may be made by adding essence to taste.

984 Crème Chantilly

Crème Chantilly is whisked cream with the addition of a little sugar and flavouring (if desired) e.g. vanilla, kirsch, Grand Marnier, etc.

985 Ganache

500 *g* (1 *lb*) *chocolate*	15 *ml spoon* (⅛ *gill*) *rum*
250 *ml* (½ *pt*) *cream*	*may be added if desired*

Bring the cream to the boil, pour on to melted chocolate and beat until cold and creamy.

Use as filling for gâteaux, etc.

986 Crème pâtissier

375 *ml* (¾ *pt*) *milk*	2 *egg yolks*	120 *g* (¼ *lb*) *sugar*
2 *eggs*	45 *g* (1½ *oz*) *flour*	*vanilla pod or essence*

1 Bring 250 ml (½ pint) of milk and vanilla essence to the boil and pour over remainder of the ingredients.
2 Return to the stove and whisk until the cream reaches the first boil.
3 Pour into a basin, cover with greaseproof paper and allow to cool.

987 Crème St Honoré

crème pâtissier (*Recipe* 986)	7 *egg whites*	60 *g* (2 *oz*) *caster sugar*

1 Whisk egg whites and sugar to a stiff snow.
2 Add beaten whites to boiling crème patissier (pastry cream) and mix thoroughly.
3 Pour into a basin, cover with greaseproof paper and allow to cool.

Used for Gâteaux St Honoré, Polka and Paris-Breste.

FURTHER FILLINGS AND FLAVOURINGS

988 Apricot marmalade

See Apricot Glaze (Recipe 973).

989 Caramel

250 g (½ lb) sugar   3 × 20 ml spoon (⅛ pt) water

1 Dissolve sugar and water; boil at approximately 170°C (340°F) until a light caramel is obtained.
2 Take care to brush down sides of sugar-boiler with cold water to prevent crystallization.
3 Carefully and slowly add 25 ml (1 fluid oz) hot water to the caramel to reduce the temperature to 115°C (240°F).
4 Pour into moulds and leave to set.
Used for caramel creams, lining dariole moulds, etc.

Note. When caramel is required for flavouring only, a slightly darker caramel may be used.

990 Marzipan

500 g (1 lb) caster sugar   125 ml (¼ pt) water   375 g (¾ lb) ground
30 g (1 oz) glucose   almonds

1 Bring sugar, water and glucose to 115°C (240°F).
2 Add the almonds and beat thoroughly with a wooden spatula until quite stiff.
3 Cover with a damp cloth and allow to cool.
4 Work to a smooth paste with icing sugar.

991 Praline

120 g (¼ lb) hazel nuts   125 ml (¼ pt) water   500 g (1 lb) loaf sugar
120 g (¼ lb) almonds

1 Toast nuts lightly in a cool oven.
2 Dissolve the sugar in the water and boil to a light caramel.
3 Add nuts and stir through with a wooden spatula and turn on to an oiled marble-slab.
4 When cold, crush with a rolling-pin and store in a sealed container.

992 Stock syrup

500 g (1 lb) loaf sugar   250 ml (½ pt) water

Bring sugar and water to boil and allow to cool.

Use for compôtes, etc. See also Syrup for Savarins and Rum Babas (Recipe 1010).

BASIC PASTES

993 Flaky and rough puff

240 g (½ lb) flour   125 ml (5 fluid oz) water   pinch salt
120 to 180 g (4   (approx.)   ¼ lemon juice
   to 6 oz) butter

Prepare as for pâte à feuilletage (Recipe 994) or with butter roughly distributed in lumps when forming dough followed by 6 turns (as in puff pastry-making).

Use for covering steak pies, puff pastries and gâteaux.

994 Pâte à feuilletage – Puff pastry

125 ml (5 fluid oz) water   240 g (½ lb) flour   pinch salt
  (approx.)   240 g (½ lb) butter   pinch cream of tartar
juice of ¼ lemon

1 Sieve flour on to a slab and form into a bay.
2 Add the water, salt, and lemon juice and mix to a smooth dough.
3 Allow to rest for 10 minutes.
4 Soften butter to similar consistency as dough.
5 Pin out the paste into a square, leaving it twice as thick in the centre.
6 Place the butter in the centre of the paste and envelop with the paste.
7 Pin out into an oblong, keeping the sides straight and the corners rectangular.
8 Give one half-turn; repeat this operation pinning to the open ends.
9 Allow the paste to rest for 15 to 20 minutes.
10 Repeat the above operation until the paste has had 6 half-turns.

Used for bouchées, vol-au-vents, covering steak pies, gâteaux, etc.

995 Pâte à foncer – Short pastry

120 g (¼ lb) flour   30 g (1 oz) lard   pinch salt
30 g (1 oz) butter   45 g (1½ oz) water

1 Rub the butter and lard lightly through flour until a fine sandy texture is obtained.
2 Form into a bay, pour in the water, add the salt and mix into a smooth dough; do not over-work.

Used for savoury flans, tartelettes, croustades. Sufficient for lining one 12 cm (6-inch) flan-ring.

996 Pâte sucrée – Sweet short-pastry

120 g (¼ lb) flour   30 g (1 oz) sugar   pinch salt
60 g (2 oz) butter   1 small egg

Mix egg and sugar for use as moistening, otherwise as for pâte à foncer (Recipe 995).

Used for flans, tartelettes. Sufficient for lining one 12 cm (6-inch) flan-ring.

997 Hot water paste

240 g (½ lb) flour	125 ml (¼ pt)	2·5 ml spoon [½ teaspoon]
75 g (2½ oz) butter or lard	water	salt

1 Add the salt to the flour and pass through a sieve.
2 Rub 30 g (1 oz) of fat in the flour.
3 Bring the water to the boil with the remainder of the fat.
4 Make a well in the centre of the flour; pour in the liquid partly-cooled and mix quickly with a wooden spoon.
5 Knead lightly with the hands into a ball-shape making sure the paste is smooth and free from cracks.
6 Roll the pastry 0·5 cm (¼ inch) thick, reserving sufficient to form a lid; keep warm and cover with a damp cloth until required; (it is, however, desirable to use it while still warm).

Used for raised and pork pies, etc. (normally prepared in the garde manger or larder).

Suet paste

See Recipe 743 (Steak and Kidney pudding).

998 Pâte à brioche – Brioche paste

240 g (½ lb) strong flour	2 eggs	95 ml (3¾ fluid oz) milk
15 g (½ oz) sugar	15 g (½ oz) yeast	pinch salt
60 g (2 oz) butter		

1 Same méthod as for savarin (Recipe 1000), i.e. prepare a batter with the yeast, milk and a little of the flour and when showing signs of collapse dough up with the remainder of the ingredients.
2 Allow to prove, i.e. double its volume.
3 Knock back and it is ready for use.

Used for pastries, rusks, etc.

Pâte à raviolis – Raviole paste

See Recipe 353.

Pâte à nouilles – Noodle paste

See Recipe 353.

999 Pâte à choux – Choux paste

190 ml (7½ fluid oz) water	120 g (4 oz) soft flour	pinch sugar
60 g (2 oz) butter	pinch salt	3 to 4 eggs

1 Bring water, salt, butter, and sugar to the boil.

2 Cast in the flour and beat with a wooden spatula until the mixture leaves the sides of the pan.

3 Allow to cool slightly and beat in the eggs one by one.

Used for éclairs, carolines, cream buns, gâteaux Polka, and St Honore, etc.

1000 Pâte à Savarin – Savarin paste

120 g (¼ lb) flour	7 g (¼ oz) yeast	pinch salt
2 eggs	30 g (1 oz) milk (84°F)	pinch sugar
30 g (1 oz) butter		

1 Dissolve yeast in the warmed milk.
2 Warm the flour slightly and form into a bay on the table.
3 Place in eggs, salt, and sugar, and mix together, bringing in a little of the flour.
4 Add the dissolved yeast and remaining flour to form into a smooth dough.
5 Place in a basin; distribute the butter evenly over the dough and allow to prove; cover with a cloth to prevent skinning.

Used for Savarins and Babas.

BATTERS

1001 Pâte à frire – Fritter batter

120 g (¼ lb) flour	7 g (¼ oz) oil	4 g (⅛ oz) yeast
125 ml (¼ pt) water (84°F)	15 g (½ oz) sugar	pinch salt

1 Dissolve the yeast in a little of the water.
2 Whisk the remaining ingredients together before adding the yeast.
3 Cover with a cloth and allow to prove for approximately 1 hour.

1002 Appareil à crèpe – Pancake batter

180 g (6 oz) soft flour	375 ml (¾ pt) milk	pinch salt
1 egg	45 g (1½ oz) oil	pinch sugar
2 egg yolks		

1 Whisk all ingredients together except half of the milk.
2 When smooth add remainder of milk.
3 Strain and set aside for use.

Used for crèpes au citron, crèpes Suzette, etc.

1003 Appareil à crèpe – Pancake batter (alternative)

250 ml (½ pt) milk	1 small egg	15 g (½ oz) browned butter (beurre
120 g (¼ lb) flour	pinch sugar	noisette) or oil
pinch salt		

1 Whisk all ingredients together with half of the milk.
2 When smooth add the remaining milk.
3 Strain if necessary.

MERINGUES

1004 Ordinary or cold meringue (Made by machine)

4 *egg whites*   240 g ($\frac{1}{2}$ *lb*) *caster sugar*   *pinch salt or lemon juice*

Note. When preparing by hand only half the amount of sugar can be beaten in; the remainder being gently folded in.

1 Whisk whites, salt and one-third of the sugar to a stiff snow.
2 Whisk in half of the remaining sugar.
3 Fold in remaining sugar.
4 Pipe onto greaseproof paper and bake without colouring (dry out) in very cool oven.

Used for meringue shells as in Recipes 1004a and b.

1004a Meringue Chantilly

Sandwiched with crème Chantilly (Recipe 984).

1004b Meringue glace

Filled with vanilla ice-cream in a sandwich style.

1005 Meringue italienne – Italian or boiled meringue

25 *ml spoon* (1 *fluid*   60 g (2 *oz*) *caster sugar*   180 g (6 *oz*) *loaf sugar*
oz) *water*   *lemon juice*   4 *egg whites*

1 Boil loaf sugar and water to 118°C (245°F).
2 Pour steadily onto the stiffly-beaten egg-whites and caster sugar.
3 Continue beating until cold.
4 Cook as Recipe 1004 or as indicated when an ingredient of a dish.
Used for vacherin, mushrooms, swans, etc.
Note. For meringue mix for Soufflées en Surprise, see Recipe 1161.

1006 Heavy hot meringue

4 *egg whites*   240 g ($\frac{1}{2}$ *lb*) *caster sugar*   *pinch salt*

1 Place sugar in oven to warm.
2 Add to the whites and salt.
3 Whisk until stiff.

Used for apple or lemon meringue pies, meringue rock cakes, topping Queen's pudding.

Œufs à la neige

See Recipe 1083.

1007 Vacherin

Italienne meringue (Recipe 1005).

1 Prepare meringue onto greaseproof paper in three separate rounds.
2 Bake in a cool oven 104°C (220°F) for approximately 2 hours.
3 When cold, sandwich with cream and decorate.

SAVARINS AND BABAS

1008 Savarin Chantilly

savarin paste *syrup (Recipe 1010)* *apricot purée*
(Recipe 1000) *whipped cream*

Soak savarin in syrup, brush with apricot purée and decorate with whipped cream.

1009 Savarin aux fruits

savarin paste *syrup (Recipe 1010)* *apricot purée*
(Recipe 1000) *whipped cream* *fruit*

1 Bake the savarin mix in the customary ring-savarin mould.
2 Soak in syrup (rum is not necessary in this instance), and brush with a little apricot purée.
3 Place on a round silver flat and decorate the centre with fruit; finish décor with whipped cream and garnish with cherries, angelica, rose petals, and grapes, etc.

1010 Syrup for Savarin and Rum Babas

250 *ml* (½ *pt*) *water* ½ *sliced lemon* 15 *ml spoon* (⅛ *gill*)
240 *g* (½ *lb*) *sugar* ¼ *cinnamon stick* *rum (when for Rum*
½ *sliced orange* 3 × 20 *ml spoon* (⅛ *pt*) *tea* *Baba)*

1 Bring all the ingredients except the rum to the boil.
2 Simmer for 10 minutes and strain; stir in rum.

Note. Rum is an essential ingredient when the syrup is for use with Rum Baba; for other savarins the rum may be omitted or another spirit or liqueur substituted.

1011 Baba au rhum

savarin paste (Recipe 1000)   *syrup (Recipe 1010)*
with the addition of: *apricot purée*
 30 *g* (1 *oz*) *currants*   *whipped cream*
 zest of ½ *lemon*
 30 *g* (1 *oz*) *sultanas*

1 Prepare a savarin mixture with the addition of the fruit and zest of the lemon; pour into individual dariole moulds and bake in hot oven.
2 Soak in syrup and brush with apricot purée.
3 When cold, split, and fill with cream.
4 Decorate with cherries, angelica, etc.

CHOUX PASTE

1012 Carolines

  choux pastry (Recipe 999)   *pastry cream (Recipe 986)*

Prepare small éclairs, fill with pastry cream and dip in chocolate or fondant.

1013 Choux au chocolat

  choux pastry (Recipe 999)   chocolate   crèmè pâtissier (Recipe 986)

1 Pipe in choux paste into rounds onto a baking-tray through 1 cm (½ inch) plain tube.
2 Egg-wash and bake in a hot oven.
3 Fill with crème pâtissier (Recipe 986) and dip in chocolate.

1014 Éclairs

  choux paste   crème pâtissier   chocolate or fondant
  (Recipe 999)   (Recipe 986)

1 Pipe in choux paste into rounds onto a baking-tray through 1 cm (½ inch) plain tube.
2 Egg-wash and mark with the back of a fork and bake in a hot oven.
3 When cold, fill with crème pâtissier (Recipe 986); dip in chocolate or coffee-flavoured fondant.

1015 Salambos

Same as Recipe 1012 but round in shape; these small spheres are used for savouries (hot or cold) and for sweet petit fours.

1016 Profiteroles

Small spheres of choux paste; they may be piped with filling of crème Chantilly or pâtissier, heaped and masked with chocolate sauce (profiteroles au chocolat) or, when baked plainly as extremely tiny spheres used as a garnish for clear soup (Consommé aux profiteroles).

1017 Beignets soufflés

  choux paste (Recipe 999)   caster sugar   apricot sauce (Recipe 960)

1 Prepare choux paste in small spheres on greased paper either (a) by moulding like quenelles between tablespoons or, (b) piping directly on to the greased paper.
2 Invert paper on surface of hot oil 121°C (about 250°F).
3 Remove paper and shake fritures in order that they may soufflé gradually, increasing temperature to 190°C (375°F) until they are a light-golden colour.
4 Drain well, roll in caster sugar.
5 Sauce apricot served separately (Recipe 960).

1018 Beignets soufflés en surprise

Prepare as above but before rolling in sugar, fill with hot jam or pastry cream (Recipe 986).

PUFF-PASTRY GOODS

1019 Amandines

    puff pastry (*Recipe* 994)   *almond cream* (*Recipe* 982)

1 Pin out puff pastry to 0·3 cm ($\frac{1}{8}$ inch) thick; place on baking sheet and spread 0·5 cm ($\frac{1}{4}$ inch) thick with almond cream.
2 Decorate with strips of puff pastry and bake in a moderate oven.
3 Ice when cold with water icing.

1020 d'Artois

    puff pastry (*Recipe* 994)   *almond cream* (*Recipe* 982)

1 Pin out paste 0·3 cm ($\frac{1}{8}$ inch) thick, in long bands 14 cm (7 inches) wide.
2 Egg-wash one side and place almond cream in the centre; fold over other two sides to enclose the almond cream as in a turnover.
3 Egg-wash, mark with the point of a knife and bake in a moderate oven.
4 When almost ready, dust with icing sugar and glaze.

1021 Chaussons Bruxellois – Vanilla turnovers

    puff pastry (*Recipe* 994)   *pastry cream* (*Recipe* 986)

1 Pin out puff pastry 0·3 cm ($\frac{1}{8}$ inch) thick and cut into squares.
2 Egg-wash corners and place pastry cream in centre.
3 Taking opposite corners, stretch and close in the middle on the pastry cream; egg-wash and bake in a hot oven.
4 Glaze with icing sugar.

1022 Chaussons à la confiture – Jam turnovers

Use same ingredients and method as for apple turnovers (Recipe 1023) but substitute jam for apples.

1023 Chaussons aux pommes – Apple turnovers

    puff pastry (*Recipe* 994)   *apples*   *cinammon*
    caster sugar

1 Pin out puff paste 0·3 cm ($\frac{1}{8}$ inch) thick and cut into rounds of the required size.
2 Egg-wash one side and place some finely-sliced apples, sugar, and cinnamon on it.
3 Fold over other side, and egg-wash; place on a baking-sheet and bake in a moderate oven.
4 When almost ready, dust with icing sugar and glaze.

1024 Fleurons – Small puff-pastry crescents

> *puff pastry (Recipe 994)*

1 Pin out puff pastry to 0·45 cm ($\frac{3}{16}$ inch) thick.
2 Lightly egg-wash and cut into small crescents.
3 Bake in a hot oven until golden brown.

Use as a garnish for poached fish dishes.

1025 Jalousies

> *puff pastry (Recipe 994)*   *raspberry or strawberry jam*

Prepare in the same manner as for d'Artois (Recipe 1020) using jam instead of almond cream.

1026 Palmiers – Pigs' ears

> *puff paste trimmings (Recipe 994)*   *caster sugar*

1 Pin out trimmings to 0·5 cm ($\frac{1}{8}$ inch) thick and 24 cm (12 inches) wide.
2 Brush with cold water and sprinkle with caster sugar.
3 Fold the paste from either side in three; then fold in two; cut into 1 cm ($\frac{1}{2}$-inch) pieces.
4 Place on a baking-sheet and bake in a hot oven.
5 When almost ready, turn over with palette knife and finish baking to a golden colour.

1027 Vol-au-Vents

> *puff paste (Recipe 994)*

Two slightly-differing methods are given below. The first is often called the English and the second the French method:

Method I.
1 Pin out the puff pastry to 1·5 cm ($\frac{3}{4}$ inch) thick and cut into rounds with a 12 cm (6 inch) cutter.
2 Place on a baking-tray, lightly egg-washed.
3 Make a circular incision with a 10 cm (5 inch) cutter halfway through the paste.
4 Allow to rest before baking in a hot oven 204°C (400°F).
5 Remove top, and remove soft paste from centre while still hot.

Method II.
1 Roll out puff pastry thinly 0·9 cm ($\frac{3}{4}$ inch thick).
2 Use a 12 cm (6 inch) damp cutter and cut two rounds of pastry and turn over
3 Place one round on a damp baking-tray and egg-wash the edges.
4 Using a small cutter approximately 2 cm (1 inch) less in diameter, make an incision on top of the second round of pastry and cut about halfway through
5 Place the second round on top of the first and seal well together.
6 Egg-wash the top only and bake for 15 to 20 minutes in a hot oven.
7 When cooked, remove the lid with a sharp pointed knife and remove any soft paste inside.

1028 Bouchées

Puff pastry (*Recipe* 994)

1 Pin out puff pastry from 0·7 cm to 1·0 cm ($\frac{1}{3}$ to $\frac{1}{2}$ inch) thick and cut into rounds with a 6 cm (3 inch) cutter.
2 Continue as for vol-au-vent (Recipe 1027).

1029 Petites bouchées or Bonne bouches

Puff pastry (*Recipe* 994)

1 Pin out puff pastry to 0·5 cm ($\frac{1}{4}$ inch) thick and cut into rounds with a 3 cm (1$\frac{1}{2}$ inch) cutter.
2 Continue as for vol-au-vent (Recipe 1027).

FLANS, TARTS, AND GÂTEAUX WITH SWEET OR SHORT PASTE

1030 Bande aux fruits

pâte sucre (*Recipe* 996)   *crème pâtissier* (*Recipe* 986)   *fruit*
syrup glaze (*Recipe* 974)

1 Pin out short pastry into a strip 24 × 10 × 0·5 cm (12 by 5 by $\frac{1}{4}$ inch thick) and decorate the edges with the aid of pastry pincers.
2 Egg-wash, stab the centre and bake in a moderate oven for 8 to 10 minutes.
3 When cold, spread pastry cream down the centre and decorate with appropriate fruit.
4 Mask with a syrup glaze and decorate with whipped cream.

Note. Bandes aux fruits are also sometimes made with ribbon strips of puff paste to form the side edges on the short-pastry base.

1031 Flan aux fruits

pâte sucre (*Recipe* 996)   *syrup glaze* (*Recipe* 974)   *fruit*
crème pâtissier

1 Line a flan ring with sweet short-paste and bake 'blind', i.e. with dried haricot beans as temporary filling to preserve shape.
2 When cold, half-fill with pastry cream.
3 Decorate the top with the appropriate fruit and glaze.

Use for pear flan – Flan aux poires, and soft fruit flans such as strawberry – Flan aux fraises, etc.

1032 Flan aux pommes – Apple flan

Apple purée:
2 *apples*, 60 g (2 oz) *sugar*
15 g ($\frac{1}{2}$ oz) *butter, cinnamon*

Additional ingredients:
1 *apple for decoration*
pâte sucrée (*Recipe* 996)
apricot glaze (*Recipe* 973)

1 Line a flan ring with sweet short-paste.
2 Place in apple purée and decorate with sliced, quartered apples in a circular fashion.
3 Bake for 20 to 25 minutes in a moderate oven 175°C (350°F).
4 One minute before taking flan from the oven, remove flan ring and lightly egg-wash outside border.
5 Return to oven for a minute.
5 When cool, glaze with apricot glaze.

1033 Pomme en robe – Baked apple dumplings

> *pâte sucrée (Recipe 996)*　　　*2 apples*　　　*puff-paste trimmings*

1 Core, peel, and halve apples.
2 Pin out paste to 0·5 cm ($\frac{1}{4}$ inch) thick and cut into 6 cm (3 inch) squares.
3 Place a half-apple in the centre of the square of paste and envelop.
4 Lightly egg-wash, then place a small round of puff-paste trimmings on top.
5 Bake for 15 to 20 minutes in a moderate oven.

1034 Tartelettes et barquettes de fruits

> *pâte sucrée (Recipe 996)*　　　*crème pâtissier (Recipe 986)*　　　*fruit*
> *syrup glaze (Recipe 974)*

Line tartelette or barquette moulds with sweet short paste and prepare as for fruit flan.

1035 Gâteau Alma

> *boiled meringue*　　　*fondant (Recipe 977)*　　　*raspberry jam*
> *(Recipe 1005)*　　　*pâte sucrée (Recipe 996)*　　　*15 g ($\frac{1}{2}$ oz) angelica*
> *frangipane (Recipe 1037)*

1 Prepare a Bakewell tart (Recipe 1036).
2 Prepare Italian meringue and build on Bakewell tart in a dome shape.
3 Dust with icing sugar and place in oven 177°C (350°F) for 10 minutes.
4 Allow to cool and mask with pink fondant.
5 Decorate with angelica.

1036 Bakewell tart

> *pâte sucrée (Recipe 996)*　　　*raspberry jam*　　　*icing sugar*
> *frangipane (Recipe 1037)*

1 Line one 12 cm (6 inch) flan-ring with sweet short-paste.
2 Spread the base of the flans with raspberry jam.
3 Two-thirds fill flans with frangipane sponge and decorate the tops with strips of sweet short-paste.
4 Bake in moderate oven 177°C (350°F) for 25 to 30 minutes.
5 Before taking from the oven, dust with icing sugar to give a glaze.
6 Serve on a d'oyley with custard sauce (Recipe 961 or 966) separately.

1037 Frangipane sponge mixture

> *almond essence if desired*   60 g (2 oz) butter   1 egg
> 45 g (1½ oz) ground almonds   60 g (2 oz) sugar   30 g (1 oz) flour

Sugar-butter method:

1 Cream butter and sugar thoroughly.
2 Beat through eggs, one by one.
3 Fold through sieved flour and almonds.
4 Add essence if necessary.

Use for Bakewell tart. This mixture (and also crème d'amande, Recipe 982) can be used for (a) Gâteau conversation (Recipe 1038); and (b) tartelette or gâteau Pithiviers (Recipe 1041).

GÂTEAUX WITH CHOUX, PUFF OR SHORT PASTES

1038 Gâteau conversation

> *almond cream*   *royal icing*   *puff paste* (*Recipe* 994)
> (*Recipe* 982)   (*Recipe* 978)

1 Pin out puff paste 0·3 cm (⅛ inch) thick and cut into rounds 16 cm (8 inches) diameter.
2 Place 1 round on a baking tray, egg-wash and spread almond cream in the centre (Frangipan sponge, Recipe 1037 may be substituted).
3 Cover with other round of paste, carefully sealing the edges.
4 Coat puff paste evenly with royal icing and decorate with strips of puff paste.
5 Bake in moderate oven 165° 177°C (330° to 350°F) for 30 to 35 minutes.

1039 Gâteau St Honoré

> *sweet short-pastry* (*Recipe* 996)   Crème St Honoré   *cherries*
> *choux pastry* (*Recipe* 999)   (*Recipe* 987)   *angelica*
> *boiled sugar* (*Recipe* 975)

1 Pin out short pastry 0·3 cm (⅛ inch) thick and cut into a round of 16 cm (8 inches) diameter.
2 Place on a baking sheet, slot with a fork, egg-wash and pipe a border of choux paste with 1 cm (½ inch) tube. Also pipe 16 small buns; egg-wash and bake in a moderate oven.
3 When cold, fill buns with crème St Honoré and dip in boiled sugar.
4 Place in circular fashion on border of gâteau with crème St Honoré.
5 Garnish buns with cherries and angelica.

1040 Gâteau mille feuilles

> 180 g (6 oz) *puff-pastry trimmings*   *raspberry jam*   *toasted almonds*
> (*Recipe* 994)   *fondant*   *apricot jam*
> *crème pâtissier* (*Recipe* 986)   (*Recipe* 977)

1 Pin out pastry 0·2 cm ($\frac{1}{16}$ inch) thick, cut into 3 rounds of 16 cm (8 inches) diameter.
2 Thoroughly stab and bake until light brown and crisp.
3 Sandwich the three layers together with the pastry cream and jam, making sure that the underside of the last ring is on top.
4 Lightly press together and coat sides with crème pâtissier and mask with toasted almonds.
5 Coat top with fondant and pipe a spiral of raspberry jam, apricot jam, and chocolate fondant from the centre.
6 Pull a knife across the top while the fondant is still soft to form pattern.

1041 Gâteau Pithiviers

puff-pastry (*Recipe* 994)   *crème d'amande* (*Recipe* 982)   *icing sugar*

1 Pin out puff pastry 0·3 cm ($\frac{1}{8}$ inch) thick, cut into two rounds of 16 cm (8 inches) diameter.
2 Place one round on a baking tray, egg-wash and spread almond cream in the centre (frangipane sponge, Recipe 1037, may be substituted).
3 Cover with the other round and press the edges together with the back of a knife.
4 Egg-wash the top and mark with knife in arcs from centre to outside edge of gâteau.
5 Bake in a moderate oven until almost ready and glaze with icing sugar.

1042 Gâteau Religieuse

choux pastry   *crème St Honoré*   *sweet short-pastry*
  (*Recipe* 999)   (*Recipe* 987)   (*Recipe* 996)
fondant icing (*Recipe* 977)   *whipped cream*

1 Line a flan ring with sweet short paste and bake 'blind'.
2 Prepare 4 éclairs, one end slightly thicker than the other.
3 When baked, fill with crème St Honoré and glaze with coffee and chocolate fondant.
4 Place remainder of crème St Honoré in flan, cone-shaped, and arrange éclairs against the cream.
5 Decorate between each éclair with whipped cream and finish the top with a chocolate-iced cream bun.

CAKES AND GÂTEAUX WITH CAKE MIXES

1043 Swiss roll sponge

butter cream (*Recipe* 983)   *90 g (3 oz) flour*   *3 eggs*
120 g (4 oz) caster sugar

1 Whisk eggs and sugar over hot water to ribbon stage.
2 Whisk until cold before folding through the sieved flour.
3 Spread on to a tray 28 × 40 cm (14 inches by 20 inches) lined with grease-proof paper.
4 Bake for 8 minutes – oven temperature 205°C (400°F).
5 Turn out on to a lightly-sugared cloth.

6 When cold, half spread with butter cream and roll up tightly: to give 1 Swiss roll.

Note. Other examples of fatless sponge are Recipes 1048 and 1055.

1044 Génoise (Sponge-butter method)

    30 *g* (1 *oz*) *melted butter*   60 *g* (2 *oz*) *sugar*   60 *g* (2 *oz*) *flour*
    2 *eggs*

1 Whisk eggs and sugar over hot water to ribbon stage.
2 Continue beating until cold before folding through the flour and finally the melted butter.
3 Bake immediately in a moderate oven for 25 minutes.

Used for gâteaux, and petit fours.

1045 Chocolate génoise

    2 *eggs*   60 *g* (2 *oz*) *sugar*   30 *g* (1 *oz*) *melted butter*
    7 *g* (¼ *oz*) *cocoa*   50 *g* (1¾ *oz*) *flour*

1 Sieve cocoa and flour together then follow method as for génoise (Recipe 1044).
2 Bake in a greased and floured gâteau-tin.

1046 Gâteau Mocha (or moka) – Coffee gâteau

    genoise (*Recipe* 1044)   *crème au beurre*   *coffee essence*
    roasted almond nibs   (*Recipe* 983)

1 Bake genoise mixture in a greased and floured gâteau-tin.
2 When cold, split and sandwich with coffee-flavoured butter cream.
3 Mask sides with toasted almond nibs and decorate top with butter cream.
4 Generally the word moka (or mocha) is written across the top of the gâteau.

1047 Gâteau Suchard – Chocolate gâteau

    chocolate genoise (*Recipe*   *chocolate butter*   120 *g* (¼ *lb*) *melted*
    1045)   *cream* (*Recipe*   *chocolate*
    chocolate vermicelli   983)

1 Bake genoise mixture in a greased and floured gâteau-tin and when cold, sandwich with chocolate butter cream.
2 Mask the sides with chocolate vermicelli.
3 Decorate the top with melted chocolate.

1048 Bûche de Noël – Christmas log

    vanilla butter cream   *marzipan leaves*   150 *g* (5 *oz*) *sugar*
    marzipan holly-berries   *chocolate butter cream*   5 *eggs*
    20 *ml spoon* [1 *fluid oz*]   120 *g* (4 *oz*) *flour*
    water

1 Use a biscuit à cuiller mix (Recipe 1055) for Swiss roll.
2 When prepared bake in an oblong tray on greaseproof paper.
3 When cold, form into a roll with vanilla butter cream.
4 Decorate with chocolate butter cream, marzipan leaves and holly-berries.

1049 Fruit cake – (Slab-cake style)

240 g (½ lb) butter	5 eggs	180 g (6 oz) currants
240 g (½ lb) sugar	300 g (10 oz) flour	180 g (6 oz) sultanas
60 g (2 oz) peel		

1 Cream butter and sugar.
2 Add the eggs one by one beating them in thoroughly.
3 Fold through flour, fruit, and peel.
4 Pour into a cake-tin lined with greaseproof paper and bake in slow oven for 1½ to 2 hours.

1050 Christmas cake

240 g (½ lb) sugar	240 g (½ lb) currants	15 ml spoon (⅛ gill)
240 g (½ lb) butter	240 g (½ lb) sultanas	rum
300 g (10 oz) soft flour	60 g (2 oz) minced peel	marzipan (Recipe 990)
5 eggs	7 g (¼ oz) spice	royal icing (Recipe 978)

1 Sugar-butter creaming method as for fruit cake (Recipe 1049).
2 When cold, mask with marzipan and decorate with royal icing.

1051 Wedding cake

600 g (1¼ lb) butter	480 g (1 lb) mixed peel	240 g (½ lb) ground almonds
600 g (1¼ lb) sugar	240 g (½ lb) glace cherries	750 g (1 lb 9 oz) soft flou
12 eggs	30 g (1 oz) mixed spice	marzipan (Recipe 990)
750 g (1½ lb) sultanas		royal icing (Recipe 978)
1·6 kg (3¼ lb) currants		

As for Christmas cake (Recipe 1050).

BISCUITS AND PETITS FOURS

1052 Petits fours

There are two principal categories of petits fours:

Petits fours glacés: Glazed petits fours include fruits dipped in sugar, fondant and petit choux glazed.
Additionally, there are fondant petits fours, exemplified by small pieces o genoise masked with fondant icing and which are, in effect, miniature Frenc cakes.

Petits fours secs: Dry petits fours are typically the various biscuits, macaroon and also meringue items and marzipan or almond paste dainties.

1053 Fruits glacés – Glazed fruits

Prunes:	Stone out and stuff with marzipan (Recipe 990).
Dates:	Stone out and stuff with marzipan (Recipe 990).
Cherries (glacés):	Stuff with marzipan (Recipe 990).
Cherries (fresh):	Keep in pairs, do not remove stalk.
Grapes:	Keep in pairs, do not remove stalk.
Oranges:	Peel and remove fillets without breaking the skin, dry out slightly overnight.
Strawberries:	Must be fresh and dry, hold by stalk of husk when glazing. Cochineal may be added to the syrup.

Note. To prepare syrup and for dipping see Recipe 975.

1054 Marzipan glacé

1 Condition marzipan (Recipe 990) by adding icing sugar, colour, and mould as desired.
2 Allow to dry out slightly before glazing (Recipe 975).

1055 Biscuits à la cuillère

2 *eggs*	60 g (2 oz) caster	60 g (2 oz) flour
15 *ml spoon* (½ *fluid oz*) *water*	*sugar*	

1 Whisk egg yolks, sugar, and water over a bain-marie to ribbon stage.
2 Whisk egg whites to a stiff snow.
3 Begin folding the flour through the egg yolks; sugar and water before adding the beaten egg whites.
4 Pipe on to greaseproof paper, 6 cm (3 inches) long, turn on to caster sugar and bake immediately in a hot oven (204°C (400°F) for approximately 6 minutes).

Used for pastries; lining a charlotte russe; serving with ices, bombes, etc. The mix may also be used whenever a fatless sponge is required.

1056 Langues de chat

60 g (2 oz) butter	90 g (3 oz) icing sugar	2 egg whites
60 g (2 oz) soft flour	vanilla essence	

1 Cream butter and sugar lightly.
2 Add egg whites one by one taking care not to curdle.
3 Finally, fold through flour and essence.
4 Pipe on to a well-greased baking tray through 0·3 cm (⅛ inch) plain tube, 4 cm (2 inch) length; bake in a hot oven.

1057 Palets de dames

Ingredients as for Langues de chat (Recipe 1056).

1 As for Langues de chat but pipe into rounds of 1 cm (½ inch) diameter.
2 When cold decorate with chocolate.

1058 Macaroon tartelettes

sweet short-pastry (Recipe 996)	120 g (¼ lb) ground	240 g (½ lb) caster
15 g (½ oz) ground rice or rice flour	almonds	sugar
		3 egg whites

1 Whisk whites lightly.
2 Add sugar, almonds, and ground rice, and beat thoroughly with a wooden spoon.
3 Line tartelette cases with sweet short-pastry.
4 Pipe in a little raspberry jam and cover with macaroon mixture.
5 Bake for 15 to 20 minutes at 165°C (330°F).

1059 Madeleines

60 *g* (2 *oz*) *butter*	90 *g* (3 *oz*) *caster sugar*	1 *to* 2 *eggs*
120 *g* (4 *oz*) *soda flour*	*vanilla essence*	

1 Sugar-batter method; pipe into greased dariole-moulds; bake for 15 minutes at 165°–177°C (330° to 350°F).
2 When cold, brush with raspberry purée and roll in coconut.
3 Pipe a dot of pink fondant on top.

Note. Dariole moulds produce 'Eiffel Tower' madeleines. Fluted coquille moulds are also accepted.

1060 Marquis biscuits

Langues de chat	*Praline* (*Recipe* 991)	*Ganache*
(*Recipe* 1056)		(*Recipe* 985)

Sandwich biscuits together with ganache and praline and pipe the word 'Marquis' on top with chocolate.

1061 Ratafia biscuits

15 *g* ($\frac{1}{2}$ *oz*) *ground rice or*	120 *g* ($\frac{1}{4}$ *lb*) *ground almonds*	3 *egg whites*
semolina	210 *g* (7 *oz*) *caster sugar*	

1 Lightly whisk egg whites and beat in remaining ingredients with a wooden spoon.
2 Pipe on to greaseproof paper to the size of a shilling.
3 Decorate with cherries, angelica, etc.; bake for 15 minutes at 160°C (320°F).

1062 Sables à la poche

120 *g* (4 *oz*) *sugar*	1 *egg yolk*	240 *g* ($\frac{1}{2}$ *lb*) *soft flour*
180 *g* (6 *oz*) *butter*	1 *egg*	*vanilla essence*

1 Cream butter and sugar until light in texture and colour.
2 Add yolk and egg one by one, beating thoroughly.
3 Fold through flour and essence lightly until smooth.
4 Pipe on to a greased and floured baking tray, using a star tube, into rosettes.
5 Decorate with cherry and angelica and bake in a moderate oven for 10 minutes approximately.

Sables

Miniature version of Sables à la poche (Recipe 1062).

1063 Shortbread

210 g (7 oz) soft flour	30 g (1 oz) rice flour	120 g (4 oz) butter
60 g (2 oz) sugar	1 small egg yolk	

1 Mix butter, sugar and egg yolk together.
2 Sieve flour and rice flour on to butter, sugar, etc., and knead.
3 Continue working on the table until smooth but do not oil.
4 Mould, stab and bake lightly; dust with caster sugar.

SOUFFLÉS AND PUDDING SOUFFLÉS

1064 Soufflé vanille – Vanilla soufflé (basic baked soufflé mix)

For 6 portions

60 g (2 oz) butter	90 g (3 oz) sugar	250 ml (½ pt) milk
60 g (2 oz) flour	4 egg yolks	1 vanilla pod
6 egg whites		

1 Butter and sugar soufflé dish.
2 Melt butter and add flour.
3 Add milk, vanilla pod, sugar and bring to the boil, remove vanilla pod.
4 Cool slightly, beat through egg yolks.
5 Fold through stiffly beaten egg whites.
6 Pour into soufflé case and two-thirds fill only; bake for 20 minutes in moderate oven 177°–188°C (350°–370°F).
7 Serve immediately.

1065 Soufflé Harlequin

Half vanilla and half chocolate soufflé (Recipes 1064 and 1066).

1066 Soufflé au chocolat – Chocolate soufflé

1 Soufflé vanille with the addition of 90 g (3 oz) grated or powdered chocolate which should be added to the milk.
2 Add an extra egg white as the chocolate tends to stiffen the appareil.

1067 Soufflé Grand Marnier

Soufflé vanille with the addition of 30 ml (¼ gill) Grand Marnier liqueur.

1068 Pouding soufflé vanille

vanilla pod or essence	60 g (2 oz) butter	4 eggs
60 g (2 oz) flour	190 ml (1½ gills) milk	60 g (2 oz) sugar

1 Boil milk, sugar and essence and pour into creamed butter and flour.
2 Return to the stove and re-boil.
3 Cool slightly and beat through egg yolks.
4 Fold through stiffly beaten egg whites.

5 Two-thirds fill buttered and sugared dariole moulds.
6 Cook in a bain-marie 20 minutes in moderate oven 177°C (350°F).

1069 Pouding soufflé à l'orange
Prepare as for Recipe 1068 plus juice and zest of 1 orange and ½ lemon in lieu of 25 ml (1 oz) of milk.

1070 Pouding soufflé Rothschild
Prepare as Recipe 1068 plus 15 g (½ oz) candied fruit and 15 ml spoon (⅛ gill) kirsch.

1071 Pouding soufflé Saxone
Prepare as for Recipe 1068 plus juice and zest of 1 lemon.

Cold soufflés
See Recipe 1129.

STEAMED AND BAKED PUDDINGS

1072 Steamed sponge pudding (basic mix)

120 g (4 oz) flour	60 g (2 oz) butter	60 g (2 oz) sugar
1 egg	25 ml spoon (1 fluid	7 g (¼ oz) baking powder
vanilla essence	oz) milk	

1 Cream butter and sugar, beat in egg. Fold through sieved flour and baking powder. Add milk to adjust to piping consistency.
2 Pipe into buttered dariole moulds and steam for 45 minutes.

1073 Chocolate sponge pudding

100 g (3½ oz) flour	15 g (½ oz) cocoa	60 g (2 oz) butter
60 g (2 oz) sugar	1 egg	30 g (1 oz) milk
7 g (¼ oz) baking powder		

As for Recipe 1072 with cocoa sieved with flour.

1074 Lemon sponge pudding
Prepare as Recipe 1072 without vanilla but plus juice and zest of ½ lemon.

1075 Pouding tunisien – Steamed date pudding

180 g (6 oz) breadcrumbs	180 g (6 oz) flour	180 g (6 oz) chopped suet
90 g (3 oz) syrup or 180 g	360 g (¾ lb) dates	1 to 2 eggs
(6 oz) sugar	zest of 1 lemon	7 g (¼ oz) spice
20 g (¾ oz) baking powder	zest of 1 orange	310 ml (12½ fluid oz) milk

1 Mix all dry ingredients together.
2 Form into a bay; add milk, eggs and syrup and form into a soft mixture.

3 Half fill buttered dariole moulds and steam for 1½ hours.

1076 Christmas pudding

For 100 portions

2 *kg* (4 *lb*) *sultanas*	720 *g* (1½ *lb*) *apples*	1·6 *kg* (3¼ *lb*) *flour*
2 *kg* (4 *lb*) *raisins*	1·6 *kg* (3¼ *lb*) *bread-*	360 *g* (¾ *lb*) *prunes*
2 *kg* (4 *lb*) *suet*	*crumbs*	240 *g* (½ *lb*) *ground*
2 *kg* (4 *lb*) *currants*	1·6 *kg* (3¼ *lb*) *brown*	*almonds*
22 *eggs*	*sugar*	120 *g* (4 *oz*) *ginger*
250 *ml* (½ *pt*) *milk*	30 *g* (1 *oz*) *salt*	1·5 *l* (3 *pints*) *stout*
zest of 2 *oranges*	250 *ml* (½ *pt*) *spirit*	45 *g* (1½ *oz*) *spice*
2 *kg* (4 *lb*) *peel*	*zest of* 2 *lemons*	

Soak fruit in spirit overnight and follow method for Recipe 1075.

Note. Steaming times depend on weight of puddings, but will be upward of 4 hours, i.e., 5 hours for 1 kg (2 lb) increasing to 6 hours for larger weights. It is customary to prepare and steam well in advance and to re-steam (approx. 3 hours according to size) on day of use.

1077 Baked sponge pudding

Prepare as Recipe 1072 but bake in a moderate oven 177°C (350°F) for 30 minutes.

MILK, CUSTARD AND KINDRED PUDDINGS

1078 Baked rice pudding

62 *ml* (½ *gill*) *rice*	500 *ml* (1 *pt*) *milk*	60 *g* (2 *oz*) *caster sugar*
15 *g* (½ *oz*) *butter*	*nutmeg*	*vanilla essence*

Butter a pie-dish and place in sugar and rice.
Pour in milk, add essence and grate a little nutmeg on top.
Bake for 1½ to 2 hours in a cool oven of 150°C (300°F).

1079 Semolina pudding

500 *ml* (1 *pt*) *milk*	62 *ml* (½ *gill*) *semolina*	60 *g* (2 *oz*) *sugar*
15 *g* (½ *oz*) *butter*	*nutmeg*	*vanilla essence*

Boil milk and essence, rain in semolina and cook gently at side of stove.
When cooked, add sugar, pour into buttered pie-dish; grate nutmeg on top and brown under salamander or in oven, sitting in bain-marie.

1079a Sago and tapioca puddings

Proceed as for semolina pudding (Recipe 1079) using 3 × 20 ml spoon (½ gill) *sago or tapioca* instead of semolina.

1080 Bread and butter pudding (for 12 portions)

1 *l* (1 *qt*) *milk*	30 *g* (1 *oz*) *currants*	60 *g* (2 *oz*) *butter*
120 *g* (4 *oz*) *sugar*	30 *g* (1 *oz*) *sultanas*	6 *slices bread*
4 *to* 5 *eggs*	*vanilla essence*	

1 Remove crusts and butter the bread, cut into triangles.
2 Butter a pie dish and sprinkle with half of the fruit.
3 Place in half of the buttered bread, the remainder of the fruit and top with the remaining bread.
4 Boil milk and essence, pour on to eggs and sugar; mix, strain and half fill pie-dish; allow to soak for 5 minutes before pouring in remainder of custard.
5 Cook in a bain-marie in a moderate oven at 175°C (350°F) for 45 minutes approximately.

1081 Cabinet pudding

500 *ml* (1 *pt*) *milk*	60 *g* (2 *oz*) *diced*	90 *g* (3 *oz*) *sugar*
vanilla pod	*genoise* (*Recipe*	60 *g* (2 *oz*) *ratafia biscuit*
30 *g* (1 *oz*) *cherries*	1044)	(*Recipe* 1061)
30 *g* (1 *oz*) *sultanas*	30 *g* (1 *oz*) *angelica*	30 *g* (1 *oz*) *currants*
3 *eggs*		

1 Lightly butter a charlotte mould.
2 Dice genoise, ratafia, cherries, and angelica; add sultanas and currants, and half fill charlotte mould.
3 Whisk eggs and sugar together; add warm milk which has been infused with vanilla pod; strain.
4 Half fill charlotte mould with custard and let stand for 10 minutes.
5 Add remainder of custard; sit in a bain-marie of hot water and cook in a moderate oven for 30 to 40 minutes; do not allow water to boil.
6 Turn out and serve a jam or sabayon sauce (Recipe 970).

1082 Pudding Diplomate (cold)

270 *g* (9 *oz*) *milk*	60 *g* (2 *oz*) *caster sugar*	3 *egg yolks*
15 *g* (½ *oz*) *gelatine*	60 *g* (2 *oz*) *water*	270 *g* (9 *oz*) *cream*
(*powdered*)	30 *g* (1 *oz*) *sultanas*	30 *g* (1 *oz*) *glacé cherrie*
30 *g* (1 *oz*) *currants*	15 *g* (½ *oz*) *angelica*	125 *ml* (1 *gill*) *stock*
2 × 15 *ml spoon*	8 *savoy biscuits* (*Recipe*	*syrup* (*Recipe* 992)
(¼ *gill*) *kirsch*	1055)	

1 Lightly oil charlotte or dariole moulds and decorate with cherries and angelica.
2 Soak currants, sultanas and savoy biscuits in kirsch-flavoured syrup.
3 Prepare sauce anglaise as in Recipe 961.
4 Add dissolved gelatine to custard and strain.
5 When on point of setting, fold through stiffly beaten cream and place in mould in alternate layers with soaked savoy biscuits and fruit.
6 Allow to set in refrigerator.
7 When set, turn out and decorate with cream.

1083 Œufs à la neige

500 *ml* (1 *pt*) *milk*	120 *g* (4 *oz*) *sugar*	*additional* 180 *g* (6 *oz*)
4 *eggs*	*vanilla essence*	*sugar for meringue*

1 Prepare meringue with egg whites and 180 g (6 oz) sugar (Recipe 1004) and poach in warmed milk and essence; (mould meringues between two spoons).
2 Prepare a sauce anglaise (Recipe 961) with yolks of eggs and sugar and allow to set in a salad bowl.
3 Sprinkle meringue with flaked almonds; brown under grill and float on sauce anglaise.

1084 Pouding à la reine – Queen's pudding or Queen of puddings

250 ml (½ pt) milk	2 eggs	60 g (2 oz) raspberry
60 g (2 oz) sugar	45 g (1½ oz) cake crumbs	jam
15 g (½ oz) butter	30 g (1 oz) apricot jam	icing sugar

1 Butter a pie-dish, spread with 30 g (1 oz) raspberry jam and sprinkle with cake crumbs (or bread crumbs).
2 Prepare an egg custard and half fill pie-dish allowing crumbs to soak.
3 Pour in remainder of custard, sit in bain-marie and bake for 45 minutes.
4 Prepare a meringue with whites of egg and sugar (Recipe 1006) and pipe on to custard; brown in oven before decorating the top by piping with alternate squares of jam (raspberry and apricot).

1085 Pouding soufflé samaritaine

190 ml (1½ gills) milk	30 g (1 oz) semolina	45 g (1½ oz) caster
7 g (¼ oz) butter	zest of ½ lemon	sugar
90 g (3 oz) loaf sugar for	3 egg whites	2 egg yolks
caramel (Recipe 989)		

1 Boil milk, butter, lemon zest, and sugar; rain in semolina and allow to cook at the side of stove.
2 Prepare a caramel and line 4 dariole moulds with it.
3 Allow semolina and milk to cool slightly; beat through egg yolks.
4 Fold through stiffly-beaten egg whites and fill two-thirds of dariole moulds.
5 Sit in bain-marie and bake for 20 minutes.
6 Turn out on to entrée-dish and serve immediately.

Note. Additional caramel sauce (Recipe 963) can be served if desired.

SWEET OMELETS

Although omelets (including sweet ones) are made by the chef entremettier rather than by the chef pâtissier in a large professional kitchen, a few examples are listed here for convenience.

1086 Omelette à la confiture – Jam omelet

120 g (¼ lb) strawberry	30 g (1 oz) (approx.)	8 eggs
jam (warmed)	butter, clarified	
1 poker or heated iron bar	120 g (¼ lb) caster sugar	

1 Prepare omelet as Recipe 327.
2 Before folding, fill with warm jam.

3 When dished, sprinkle top copiously with sugar.
4 Burn sugar with hot poker, making any simple design as desired.

1087 Omelette au rhum – Rum omelet

    8 *eggs*   30 *g* (1 *oz*) (*approx.*)   125 *ml* ($\frac{1}{4}$ *pt*) *rum*
    120 *g* ($\frac{1}{4}$ *lb*) *caster sugar*   *butter, clarified*

1 Make omelet (as Recipe 327), seasoning with a little sugar.
2 Sprinkle top with sugar.
3 Pour rum over sugar and set alight to serve.

1088 Soufflé omelette

    8 *eggs*   *pinch of salt*   30 *g* (1 *oz*) (*approx.*) *butter*
    60 *g* (2 *oz*) *sugar*

1 Beat yolks separately from whites.
2 Beat whites and add sugar.
3 Fold whites into yolks.
4 Pour into hot buttered pan.
5 Place in oven or under grill to cook.

CRÊPES – PANCAKES

1089 To prepare pancakes (Pannequet – alternative name for Crêpe):

1 Heat oil or clarified butter in pan and pour away.
2 Heat sufficient batter (Recipes 1002 or 1003) to coat base of pan thinly and evenly.
3 Cook until lightly coloured, toss and cook other side likewise.
4 It is then ready for service, plain or otherwise as below.

1090 Crêpes au citron – Pancakes with lemon

Crêpes folded in four and accompanied by lemon quarters.

1091 Crêpes au confiture

Rolled with filling of warmed jam.

1092 Crêpes couvente

Filling of diced or purée of pears.

1093 Crêpes Normande

With apple purée filling.

1094 Crêpes parisienne

Prepare with the addition of 30 g (1 oz) cream and 30 g (1 oz) crushed biscuits to crêpe batter (Recipe 1002 or 1003).

1095 Blinis – Unsweetened pancakes (for caviar)

10 g (⅜ oz) yeast ⎫ for	180 g (6 oz) buck-	2 egg yolks
125 ml (¼ pt) warm milk ⎬ ferment	wheat flour	salt
2 egg whites (beaten stiff)	250 ml (½ pt) warm milk	

1 Sift the flour and make a bay.
2 Pour the 125 ml (¼ pint) warm milk and yeast in the bay, sprinkle with flour and allow to ferment.
3 Keep in a warm place for ¾ hour.
4 Make into a batter with the 250 ml (½ pint) of milk and egg yolks and allow to stand for 30 minutes.
5 Fold in the egg whites.
6 Make into small pancakes (as Recipe 1089 but about 7 to 8 cm (3½ to 4-inch) diameter).

Note. When serving blinis with caviar, accompany with sour cream.

BEIGNETS – FRITTERS

Beignets soufflés

See Recipe 1017.

1096 Fruit for fritters (to prepare)

Apples: Core, peel and cut in rings. Flour before passing through batter (Recipe 1001).
Pears: Peel, halve and remove core. Cut into quarters depending on size. Flour before passing through batter.

Note. For soft fruit, pineapples, peaches, etc., flour before passing through batter.

1097 Fruit fritters (to cook)

1 Prepare fruit as necessary (e.g. stone, peel, and core), and if sliced, cut 0·5 cm (¼-inch) thick.
2 Flour, pass through batter (Recipe 1001) and remove excess batter before frying in hot fat.
3 Turn during cooking process.
4 Drain on cooling-wire and dust with caster sugar and glaze under salamander.
5 Serve apricot sauce or custard separately.

1098 Beignets de bananes – Banana fritters

Allow 2 bananas per portion depending on size:

1 Skin and lightly flour the bananas.
2 Pass through warm frangipane cream (Recipe 1099).
3 Allow to set before passing through batter (Recipe 1001).
4 Finish as for fruit fritters (Recipe 1097).

1099 Frangipane cream (for fritters)

250 *ml* (½ *pt*) *milk*	45 *g* (1½ *oz*) *flour*	3 *egg yolks*
1 *egg*	45 *g* (1½ *oz*) *sugar*	7 *g* (¼ *oz*) *butter*
1 *vanilla pod*		

1 Boil milk, butter and vanilla pod.
2 Mix remainder of ingredients together to a smooth paste.
3 Add boiling milk to paste mixing smoothly.
4 Return to pan and bring to boil whisking continuously.
5 Pour in basin, cover with greased paper.

FRUIT COMPÔTES – STEWED OR POACHED FRUIT

1100 Syrup for compôtes

500 *g* (1 *lb*) *loaf sugar*   625 *ml* (1¼ *pt*) *water*

1 Bring sugar and water to boil.
2 Syrup should register 20° when tested by saccharometer.

1101 Compôte de pommes – Stewed apples

660 *g* (22 *oz*) *apples*   250 *ml* (½ *pt*) *syrup* (*Recipe* 1100)

1 Quarter, core, and peel apples.
2 Place into boiling syrup.
3 Return to boil and immediately remove from stove.
4 Cover with a lid and allow to cool.

1102 Compôte de pêches – Poached peaches

1 Blanch and skin peaches.
2 Cook in syrup until stone feels loose.
3 When cold, they are ready for service.

1103 Compôte de poires – Poached pears

500 *g* (1 *lb*) *pears*   250 *ml* (½ *pt*) *syrup* (*Recipe* 1100)

Prepare as for apples (Recipe 1101).

1104 Compôte de cerises – Stewed cherries

1 Place 360 g (¾ lb) cherries (with stalk removed) in boiling syrup.
2 Return to boil and allow to cool.

1105 Compôte de prunes – Plum compôte

Place 360 g (¾ lb) plums in boiling syrup and poach gently in the oven in a covered saucepan.

1106 Compôte de reine-Claudes – Greengages

1106a Compôte d'abricots – Apricots
1106b Compôte de mirabelles – Mirabelle plums
1106c Compôte de groseilles verts – Gooseberries

May be prepared as for plums; allow 300–360 g (10 oz to 12 oz) fruit for 4 covers.

1107 Compôte de framboise – Raspberry compôte

1 Place 360 g (12 oz) raspberries in boiling syrup.
2 Return to boil and allow to cool.

1108 Compôte de fraises – Strawberries

1108a Compôte de groseilles rouges – Red currants
1108b Compôte de cassis – Black currants

Prepare similar quantities in same manner as for raspberries (Recipe 1107).

1109 Compôte de rhubarbe – Stewed rhubarb

1 Peel and cut 500 g (1 lb) rhubarb into equal lengths and place in a baking tin.
2 Sprinkle with sugar and a little water and red colouring if necessary.
3 Cover with wet greaseproof paper and poach until tender in a moderate oven.

1110 Compôte de pruneaux – Stewed prunes

500 g (1 *lb*) *prunes*	¼ *stick cinnamon*	15 *ml spoon* [1 *tablespoon*] *treacle*
120 g (¼ *lb*) *sugar*	*zest of* ½ *lemon*	250 *ml* (½ *pt*) *water*

1 Soak prunes overnight.
2 Refresh, cover with cold water and add sugar, cinnamon, zest of lemon, and treacle.
3 Allow to simmer for ½ hour.
4 Ready to serve when cold.

1111 Compôte de figues – Stewed figs

As for prunes, Recipe 1110, omitting treacle.

FRESH FRUIT SALAD

1112 Macédoine de fruit

Apples and *pears:*	Peel, core and slice evenly
Grapes:	Peel and stone
Oranges:	Remove cap of skin from top and bottom, and remove skin from sides in a circular manner. Cut out quarters which should not contain any skin.

Peaches:	Quarter and slice evenly
Pineapple:	Peel and cut rounds into eighths
Strawberries:	Remove husk and if large, cut into quarters
Bananas:	Skin and slice not too finely

Place in a silver timbale, add sugar, lemon juice and moisten with stock syrup (Recipe 992).

WARM FRUIT DISHES

1113 Charlotte aux pommes – Apple Charlotte

620 g (1¼ *lb*) *apples* ⎫
15 g (½ *oz*) *margarine* ⎪
45 g (1½ *oz*) *sugar* ⎬ purée
1 *clove* ⎪
lemon zest ⎭

500 g (1 *lb*) *bread*
120 g (¼ *lb*) *butter*
250 ml (½ *pt*) *apricot sauce* (*Recipe* 960)

1 Prepare a purée with the apples and other listed ingredients.
2 Line dariole moulds with buttered bread then fill with apple purée.
3 Bake in a moderate oven for 20 to 30 minutes.
4 Serve with apricot sauce (Recipe 960).

1114 Poire bourdalous

30 g (1 *oz*) *crushed macaroons*
  (*Recipe* 1058) *or*
30 g (1 *oz*) *flaked almonds*

120 g (¼ *lb*) *frangipane*
  cream (*Recipe* 1099)

4 *pears*
15 g (½ *oz*) *butter*

1 Poach pears in syrup and drain.
2 Halve pears and coat with frangipane cream.
3 Sprinkle with crushed macaroons or flaked almonds and melted butter.
4 Glaze under salamander and serve hot.

Note. Apricots, bananas, peaches, apples and nectarines may be prepared similarly.

1115 Poires au vin rouge – Pears in red wine

4 *pears*
125 *ml* (¼ *pt*) *red wine*

¼ *stick cinnamon*
½ *lemon*

60 g (2 *oz*) *sugar*
125 *ml* (¼ *pt*) *water*

1 Prepare a syrup with water, wine, cinnamon, lemon, and sugar and allow pears to poach in it.
2 Pears should be served warm but not hot.
3 Serve with ratafia biscuits (Recipe 1061).

JELLIES, CREAMS, AND COLD RICE SWEETS

In the preparation of jellies and creams, it is possible to produce many different kinds by changing the flavours. This can be achieved by including different fruits, their pulp and juice, and liqueurs. Basic recipes for jelly, bavarois (Bavarian cream), mousse of cold soufflé should, therefore, be fully exploited.

1116 Basic jelly I – for warm-weather use

60 g (2 oz) gelatine   120 g (4 oz) sugar   750 ml (1½ pt) water or milk

1116a Basic jelly II – for cold-weather use

870 ml (1¾ pt) water or   60 g (2 oz) gelatine   150 g (5 oz) sugar
milk (including cream, etc.)

To both these jellies add fruit, flavouring, purée, and cream as required.

1117 Gelée au citron – Lemon jelly

750 ml (1½ pt) cold water   60 g (2 oz) gelatine   1 bay-leaf
120 g (4 oz) sugar   3 egg whites   ¼ stick cinnamon
juice of 2 to 2½ lemons   zest of ½ lemon   coriander seeds

1 Mix all ingredients together and bring slowly to the boil, stirring continuously.
2 Allow to simmer for ½ hour.
3 When straining, ladle from side of saucepan carefully.
4 Pass through a jelly bag.

1118 Gelée à l'orange – Orange jelly

750 ml (1½ pt) water   juice and zest of 1 orange   cochineal
60 g (2 oz) gelatine   juice and zest of 1 lemon   ¼ stick cinnamon
3 egg whites   coriander seeds   1 bay-leaf

Prepare for lemon jelly (Recipe 1117).

1119 Fruit jellies

Raspberry, strawberry, etc., are prepared in a similar manner to lemon and orange jellies (Recipes 1117 and 1118).

1120 Liqueur and wine jellies

Add kirsch, maraschino, white wine, etc., to lemon jelly (Recipe 1117) and colour accordingly.

BAVAROIS AND DERIVATIVE DISHES

1121 Bavarois à la vanille – Vanilla bavarois or basic Bavarian cream

500 ml (1 pt) milk   120 g (4 oz) sugar   30 g (1 oz) gelatine (leaf)
4 eggs   125 ml (¼ pt) cream   vanilla essence

1 Prepare a sauce anglaise (Recipe 961).
2 Add soaked gelatine and dissolve in the sauce anglaise.
3 Strain and place on ice, when on point of setting fold through beaten cream followed by stiffly-beaten egg whites.
4 Ladle into moulds before the preparation sets.

Note. Egg white need not be added; in which case the whipped cream may be proportionately increased (i.e. up to double the amount).

1122 Bavarois aux framboises I – Raspberry bavarois

1 Ingredients and method as for Recipe 1121 but replace 125 ml ($\frac{1}{4}$ pint) of the milk with a 125 ml ($\frac{1}{4}$ pint) of raspberry purée and the juice of $\frac{1}{2}$ lemon and colouring, if necessary.
2 Purée is added before folding through the cream and egg whites.

1123 Bavarois aux framboises II

120 g (4 *oz*) *raspberry purée*	7 g ($\frac{1}{4}$ *oz*) *gelatine*	*red colouring*
75 g (2$\frac{1}{2}$ *oz*) *sugar*	125 ml ($\frac{1}{4}$ *pt*) *cream*	*juice of $\frac{1}{4}$ lemon*

1 Dissolve all ingredients together except the cream.
2 When dissolved, allow to cool and when almost setting, fold through the beaten cream.

1124 Bavarois au chocolat

Vanilla bavarois with the addition of 120 g ($\frac{1}{4}$ lb) grated or powdered chocolate (Recipe 1121).

1125 Bavarois rubané – Ribboned (or tri-coloured) bavarois

Three layers of bavarois preparation, i.e.,

  i Chocolate – Vanilla – Raspberry
             or
  ii Coffee – Raspberry – Chocolate

1126 Charlotte royale

Swiss roll (Recipe 1043)   *Vanilla bavarois (Recipe* 1121)
125 *ml* ($\frac{1}{4}$ *pt*) *fruit jelly (Recipe* 1119)

1 Set 1 cm (half-inch) of raspberry or strawberry jelly on bottom of charlotte mould.
2 Line the charlotte mould with slices of Swiss roll and fill with vanilla or strawberry bavarois.
3 Turn out when set.

1127 Charlotte russe

Savoy biscuits (Recipe 1055)   *Vanilla bavarois (Recipe* 1121)

1 Line a Charlotte mould with savoy biscuits and fill with vanilla or strawberry bavarois.
2 Turn out when set.

1128 Mousses I

Vanilla bavarois (Recipe 1121), omit 125 ml (¼ pt) milk and replace it with
125 ml (¼ pt) cream.

1128a Mousses II

¼ *lemon juice*	60 *g (2 oz) sugar*	125 *ml (¼ pt) fruit*
250 *ml (½ pt) cream*	*colouring if desired*	*purée*

1 Lightly whisk cream and sugar together and fold through the remaining
  ingredients.
2 Pipe into frosted goblets.
3 Serve with biscuits à cuillère (Recipe 1055).

SOUFFLÉS FROID – COLD SOUFFLÉS

1129 Soufflé milanaise

125 *ml (¼ pt) cream*	120 *g (¼ lb) sugar*	2 *eggs*
1 *lemon*	*pistachio nuts*	*toasted almonds*
7 *g (¼ oz) gelatine*		

1 Surround a soufflé case with greaseproof paper.
2 Dissolve gelatine in the juice of ½ lemon.
3 Whisk egg yolks, sugar and lemon juice to ribbon stage over warm water.
4 Add dissolved gelatine and allow to cool.
5 When cold fold through whipped cream followed by beaten whites.
6 Pour into soufflé case and allow to set.
7 Remove paper, coat sides with almond nibs, decorate with whipped cream
  and blanched pistachio nuts.

CUSTARD CREAMS

1130 Crème caramel – Caramel cream

60 *g (2 oz) loaf sugar* ⎫ *Caramel*	*All ingredients as for Crème*	
30 *g (1 oz) water* ⎭ (*Recipe* 989)	*Renversée (Recipe* 1131)	

1 Prepare a caramel and cover the bottom of a charlotte mould.
2 When set, strain and continue in the same manner as for Crème Renversée
  (Recipe 1131).
3 When cold, turn out on to a round silver flat.

1131 Crème renversée

250 *ml (½ pt) milk*	2 *eggs*	60 *g (2 oz) sugar*
1 *vanilla pod*		

1 Bring the milk and vanilla pod to the boil and pour over eggs and sugar.
2 Strain into a pie-dish or charlotte mould; place in a bain-marie and cook in the oven until set.
3 When cold, it is ready to serve.
4 Carefully turn out from mould and decorate with cream, if desired.

1132 Petits pots de crème au café

Crème renversée (Recipe 1131) with the addition of 45 g (1½ oz) coffee essence.
As for petits pots de crème vanille (Recipe 1134).

1133 Petits pots de crème au chocolat

crème renversée (Recipe 1131)   45 *g* (1½ *oz) chocolate or*
                        21 *g* (¾ *oz) cocoa powder*

As for petits pots de crème vanille (Recipe 1134).

1134 Petits pots de crème à la vanille

Crème renversée (Recipe 1131)

1 Prepare a Crème renversée and ladle into individual cocottes.
2 Bake in a bain-marie.

COLD SWEETS WITH MILK AND CREAM

1135 Junket

10 *ml spoon* [1 *dessert-*   30 *g* (1 *oz) sugar*   250 *ml* (½ *pt) milk*
spoon] essence of rennet   *grated nutmeg*

1 Warm milk and sugar to blood heat.
2 Pour over essence.
3 Place a little grated nutmeg on top.
4 Leave to set.

1136 Syllabub

250 *ml* (½ *pt) cream*   *zest and juice of* ½ *lemon*   30–60 *g* (1 *to* 2 *oz)*
125 *ml* (¼ *pt) white wine*   *sugar*

1 Lightly whisk cream and add wine, zest, lemon juice, and sugar to taste.
2 Place on a sieve to remove excess moisture.
3 Place a little wine in frosted goblets and pour the syllabub on top.

Note. Red wine or brandy can be used.

1137 Fruit fools

250 *ml* (½ *pt) fruit purée*   125 *ml* (¼ *pt) cream*   6 *egg whites*
60 *g* (2 *oz) sugar*

1 Lightly whip the cream.
2 Whisk whites to a stiff snow.
3 Fold all ingredients together.
4 Add colouring if necessary.

TRIFLE

1138 Fruit trifle

sponge cake	*custard sauce*	*syrup* {240 g (½ lb) sugar
raspberry jam	*whipped cream*	{375 ml (¾ pt) water
angelica, cherries		

1 Sandwich sponge with jam and place in a salad bowl.
2 Add the fruit and moisten with syrup.
3 Cover with custard sauce.
4 When cold, decorate with whipped cream, cherries, angelica, etc.

1139 Sherry trifle

120 g (¼ lb) sponge or	60 g (2 oz) ratafia	125 ml (¼ pt) cream
génoise (Recipe 1044)	biscuits (Recipe 1061)	250 ml (½ pt) milk
2 egg yolks	or macaroons (or	1 vanilla pod
60 g (2 oz) sugar	both mixed)	15 ml (⅛ gill) sherry
62 ml (⅛ pt) stock syrup	30 g (1 oz) raspberry	blanched almonds
(Recipe 992)	jam	cherries, angelica

1 Prepare a sauce anglaise with the milk, sugar, egg yolks, and vanilla pod
   (Recipe 961).
2 Halve the genoise, spread with jam and cut into dice.
3 Place diced sponge and a few ratafia biscuits in a salad bowl and moisten
   with sherry and stock syrup.
4 Napper with custard and leave to cool.
5 Decorate with stiffly-beaten cream, split blanched almonds, cherries and
   angelica, and remaining ratafia biscuits.

COLD RICE SWEETS

1140 Rice for Condé

625 ml (1¼ pt) milk	120 g (¼ lb) sugar	120 g (¼ lb) rice
60 g (2 oz) butter	250 ml (½ pt) cream	vanilla essence

1 Boil milk and essence and rain in rice; bake in the oven for 1 hour approximately.
2 When soft, add sugar, butter and allow to cool.
3 When cold, fold through 250 ml (½ pint) of whipped cream.
4 Mould as required.

1141 Apricot Condé

1 Prepare as for condé (Recipe 1140).

2 Place rice neatly in salad bowl and arrange appropriate poached fruit on top.
3 Glaze with kirsch-flavoured apricot sauce (Recipe 960).
4 Decorate with whipped cream, cherries, angelica, etc.

1142 Riz à l'impératrice

> *rice (Recipe 1140)*   *vanilla bavarois (Recipe 1121)·*
> *orange or strawberry jelly*   *Melba sauce (Recipe 970)*

1 Set jelly, 0·5 cm (¼ inch) thick in dariole or charlotte moulds.
2 Pour in vanilla bavarois containing the cooked rice.
3 When set turn out on to silver, masked with jam sauce.

1143 Rice for créole

> 500 *ml (1 pt) milk*   15 *g (½ oz) gelatine*   60 *g (2 oz) sugar*
> 62 *ml (½ gill) rice*   125 *ml (¼ pt) cream*   2 *egg whites*
> *vanilla essence*

1 Boil milk and essence, add rice and bake in oven until tender.
2 When cooked, add sugar and gelatine, place on ice to cool.
3 When on point of setting, fold through beaten cream and stiffly-beaten egg whites; mould as desired.

1144 Ananas créole – Pineapple creole

1 Prepare rice as Recipe 1143.
2 Mould rice in form of a pineapple, cut lengthwise.
3 Criss-cross to resemble pineapple skin.
4 Surround with half-rings of pineapple.
5 Glaze pineapple with apricot sauce (Recipe 960).
6 Decorate with angelica to resemble pineapple top.

ICES AND DESSERTS INCORPORATING ICE-CREAMS

1145 American ice-cream

> 250 *ml (½ pt) milk*   ½ *can condensed milk*   180 *g (6 oz) sugar*
> 250 *ml (½ pt) cream*   1 *sheet gelatine*   *vanilla essence*

1 Dissolve gelatine and sugar in fresh milk.
2 Add essence – strain and cool.
3 Add remaining ingredients and freeze.

1146 Glace vanille – Vanilla ice-cream or Custard ice

> 500 *ml (1 pt) milk*   4 *egg yolks*   90 *to* 120 *g (4 to 5 oz)*
> *vanilla pod or essence*   *sugar*

1 Bring milk and vanilla pod to the boil.

2 Pour on to yolks and sugar; return to the stove and cook until custard coats the back of a spoon.
3 Strain, cool, and freeze.

Note.

 i For *Glace au café* – Coffee ice, add coffee essence to the custard mix.
 ii For *Glace au chocolat* – Chocolate ice, add 120 g ($\frac{1}{4}$ lb) grated chocolate to milk before boiling to make custard.
 iii Strawberry, raspberry and fruit-flavoured ices may similarly be made by flavouring with fruit pulp or purée and colouring if necessary.

1147 Biscuit glacé

 pâte à bombe (Recipe 1149)   6 *egg whites*   310 *ml* ($\frac{5}{8}$ *pt*) *cream*

1 Line the mould with greaseproof paper by cutting the paper to the size of lids and interior.
2 Place lid and paper on the bottom of one side and fill in the mixture evenly, taking care to prevent air bubbles.
3 Replace top lid with paper and place in deep-freeze cabinet to set.
4 For service, turn out on to a dish with wafers to form a base.
5 Tastefully decorate the top with crème Chantilly and appropriate fruit such as Tutti Fruitte, Ananas, Framboise, Fraises.

Note. Biscuits glacés are normally cut by the waiter at the service table.

1148 Bombes

Ice bombs are usually made in a shaped mould, shell-shaped rather than the older-fashioned bomb-like sphere originally used. They may contain various layers of flavoured ice-cream or biscuit ices and when served are usually decorated with cream, crystallized fruits, violets, rose petals, etc.

1149 Pâte à bombe – Ice-bombe mix

 3 *eggs*   90 *g (3 oz) sugar*   3 × 20 *ml spoon* (2$\frac{1}{2}$ *fluid oz*)
 190 *ml* (1$\frac{1}{2}$ *gills) cream*   *flavouring*   *water* ($\frac{1}{8}$ *pt*)

1 Whisk yolks, sugar, and water together over a bain-marie until stiff.
2 Remove from heat and whisk until cold.
3 Add flavouring and fold through beaten cream.
4 Mould as desired.

1150 Bombe andalouse – Apricot ice-cream

 vanilla biscuit ice-cream   250 *ml* ($\frac{1}{2}$ *pt) apricot purée*   *whipped cream*
  (Recipe 1147)   *juice of* $\frac{1}{2}$ *lemon*   *half apricots*
 custard ice (Recipe 1146)

1 Prepare a custard ice (Recipe 1146) and when partly frozen add 250 ml ($\frac{1}{2}$ pt) apricot purée plus the juice of $\frac{1}{4}$ lemon.

2 Fill bombe mould, freeze.
3 When frozen, hollow centre and fill with vanilla biscuit ice.
4 Freeze.
5 To turn out: plunge into tepid water and set on to a silver lined with wafers.
6 Decorate with cream and apricots.

1151 Bombe Nesselrode

vanilla ice-cream	120 g (¼ lb) glacé chestnuts	190 ml (1½ gills)
(*Recipe* 1146)	(*purée-d*)	*cream*

1 Prepare a custard ice and clothe the bombe mould.
2 Fill with lightly beaten cream and purée of chestnuts.
3 Freeze – turn out and decorate with half-chestnuts and whipped cream.

1152 Parfaits

Parfait nowadays describes a single-flavoured unclothed ice made from biscuit glacé preparation. *Parfait au Rhum* for example, is made as for biscuit glacé (Recipe 1147) with the addition of 50 ml (¹⁄₁₆ pt) rum and moulded in a bombe mould. Alternatives may be prepared with cognac or other liqueurs, and also *Parfait aux Café* (strong essence of coffee to flavour).

1152a Parfait praline

This is a biscuit glacé with praline (Recipe 991).

COUPES

Coupes are in fact the cups or silver goblets in which garnished ices are presented. The following are but a few examples:

1153 Coupe Alexandra

fruit salad	*kirsch*	*strawberry ice-cream*

1 Place fruit salad, flavoured with kirsch into a coupe.
2 Place a rocher (scooped portion) of strawberry ice-cream on top of fruit and decorate with cream and cherry or strawberry.

1154 Coupe Andalouse

orange fillets	*maraschino*	*lemon ice-cream*

1 Place orange fillets soaked in maraschino in coupes.
2 Place a rocher (scoop portion) of lemon ice-cream on top; decorate accordingly.

1155 Coupe Edna May

cherries	*vanilla ice-cream*	*whipped cream*
Melba sauce (*Recipe* 969)		

Coat ice-cream and cherries with Melba sauce and decorate with cream.

1156 Coupe Jacques

fruit salad (Recipe 1112)   *maraschino*   *lemon ice-cream* '
sugar   *strawberry*   *whipped cream*

1 Soak fruit in maraschino and sugar and place into coupes.
2 Place ice-cream on top of fruit and decorate with whipped cream.

1157 Coupe Jamaïque

rum-flavoured   *coffee ice-cream*   *sliced pineapple*
apricot sauce (Recipe 960)   *whipped cream*   *crystallized violet*

1 Soak pineapple in rum-flavoured apricot sauce.
2 Rocher of coffee ice.
3 Decorate with cream and crystallized violet.

1158 Poire belle Hélène

Poached pear with vanilla ice-cream and with hot Sauce chocolat (Recipe 964) served separately.

1159 Pêche Melba

1 Blanched, skinned, and poached whole peaches.
2 Vanilla ice-cream and peaches coated with sauce Melba (Recipe 970).

1160 Pêche ou Poire Pear Dame Blanche – Peach or Pear

4 *rochers vanilla ice-cream*   2 *peaches or* 2 *pears*   *whipped cream*
mousseline (or Arenberg)   *crushed violet*
sauce (Recipe 962)

1 Place 4 rochers of vanilla ice-cream in a timbale.
2 Place, between the ice-cream, 4 halves or 4 whole peaches, or pears, and coat with mousseline sauce.
3 Decorate with cream and crushed violet.

Note. Mousseline sauce is almond-flavoured.

OMELETTE SOUFFLÉ OR SOUFFLÉ EN SURPRISE

1161 Meringues for omelettes soufflés en surprise

8 *egg whites*   *pinch salt or cream of*   180 *g* (6 *oz*) *caster*
(*one egg yolk if desired*)   *tartar*   *sugar*

Whisk all ingredients together into a stiff snow before adding the yolk.

Note. Some chefs add a little pâte à bombe to the prepared meringue.

1162 Omelette soufflé or Soufflé en surprise

genoise	*ice-cream*	*meringue (Recipe* 1161)
cherries	*angelica*	15 *g* (½ *oz) caster sugar*

1 Hollow out a piece of genoise and moisten with fruit syrup and kirsch.
2 Place on ice-cream: half vanilla, half strawberry.
3 Mask with meringue, decorate with cherries, angelica, and sprinkle with caster sugar.
4 Brown off in a hot oven or under the salamander.

1163 Omelette soufflé Alaska

Recipe 1162 using only vanilla ice-cream on genoise but topped with méringue.

1163a Omelette soufflé Paquita

As for soufflé Alaska with the addition of macédoine of fruit (Recipe 1112).

1163b Omelette or soufflé My Lord

Same as Paquita using pears.

1163c Omelette or soufflé My Lady

As for My Lord using peaches.

BREADS, ROLLS, AND DANISH PASTRY

1164 Pâte à croissant – Crescent paste or dough

240 *g* (½ *lb) flour*	15 *g* (½ *oz) yeast*	62 *ml* (2½ *fl oz) milk*
2 *eggs*	60 *g* (2 *oz) butter*	15 *g* (½ *oz) salt*
15 *g* (½ *oz) sugar*	Plus 60 *g* (2 *oz) butter or* 90 *g* (3 *oz) puff paste (Recipe* 994)	

1 Same method as for pâte à savarin (Recipe 1000).
2 When proved, beat through butter and pin out into an oblong.
3 Place on butter or puff paste to cover two-thirds of the paste.
4 Give four half-turns as for puff paste; dough is then ready for use.

1165 Vienna rolls and bread

120 *g* (¼ *lb) soft flour*	7 *g* (¼ *oz) lard*	4 *g* (⅛ *oz) sugar*
120 *g* (¼ *lb) strong flour*	7 *g* (¼ *oz) milk powder*	100 *ml* (4 *fluid oz)*
7 *g* (¼ *oz) yeast*	4 *g* (⅛ *oz) salt*	*water (approx.)*

1 Dissolve the yeast in a little of the water.
2 Place the flour on to the table and form into a bay.
3 Cream the lard, sugar and salt in the centre of the bay before adding the remainder of the ingredients.
4 Work into a smooth dough.
5 Cover with a cloth and allow to prove, for 2 hours approximately; scale as required.

1166 Bridge roll dough

45 g (1½ oz) strong flour   15 g (½ oz) sugar   60 g (2 oz) butter
200 g (6½ oz) soft flour   7 g (¼ oz) salt   90 ml (3½ fluid oz)
15 g (½ oz) yeast   2 egg yolks   milk

1 Prepare a batter with 45 g (1½ oz) strong flour, the yeast and a little milk; leave aside to prove for ½ hour approximately.
2 Work the remainder of the ingredients in to a smooth dough until it does not adhere to the hands or basin.
3 Add fermented sponge or batter to the dough and set aside in a warm place to prove (double its volume) for ½ hour approximately.

1167 Tea-bread dough

45 g (1½ oz) strong flour   15 g (½ oz) sugar   7 g (¼ oz) salt
200 g (6½ oz) soft flour   60 g (2 oz) butter   90 ml (3½ fluid oz)
15 g (½ oz) yeast   2 eggs   milk

Prepare sponge and dough as for Bridge rolls (Recipe 1166).

1168 Doughnut dough

240 g (½ lb) soft flour   30 g (1 oz) sugar   120 g (4 oz) milk
7 g (¼ oz) baking powder   1 egg   (approx.)
30 g (1 oz) butter   pinch salt   zest of ½ lemon

1 Sieve flour and baking powder together.
2 Rub butter lightly through the flour.
3 Form into a bay; add remainder of ingredients and knead to a smooth dough.
4 Pin out to 0·5 cm (¼ inch) thick and cut into rings using 6 cm (3-inch) and 3 cm (1½-inch) cutter.
5 Fry to golden brown and toss in sugar.
6 Serve either hot or cold.

1169 Danish pastry

625 g (1¼ lb) flour   60 g (2 oz) sugar   2 eggs
250 ml (½ pt) milk   60 g (2 oz) yeast   420 g (14 oz) butter
7 g (¼ oz) spice

1 Dissolve the sugar in cold milk and add the crumbled yeast.
2 Stir in the egg until it is well mixed.
3 Sieve the flour and spice together into the liquid and mix to a dough.
4 Place in the refrigerator for ½ hour.
5 Roll the dough into a rectangular shape.
6 Spread the butter in walnut-size pieces over two-thirds of the surface of dough.
7 Fold over the remaining dough and then over again so that 3 layers of dough enclose 2 layers of fat.
8 Roll out the pastry keeping the shape rectangular, brush off surplus flour and fold in three.
9 Half-turn the pastry, roll again and fold into three.

10 Cover paste with damp cloth and place in refrigerator for 1 hour.
11 Repeat the rolling and folding process again, so that the paste has been rolled and folded 4 times.

Note. Keep the paste very cold during manipulation.

1170 Danish pockets

Ingredients as for Recipe 1169.

1 Roll out basic paste into a sheet 0·5 cm ($\frac{1}{4}$ inch) thick and cut into squares 7 × 8 cm (3½ by 4 inches).
2 Place almond paste, with sultanas worked in it, in the centre of the squares; fold the corners and press each tip well down in the middle of the almond paste.
3 Egg-wash and prove slowly; bake at 215° C (420° F).

1171 Danish butterflies

Ingredients as Recipe 1169.

1 Roll out basic paste 0·3 cm ($\frac{1}{8}$ inch) thick and 24 cm (12 inches) wide.
2 Wash surface with melted butter.
3 Sprinkle with caster sugar and roasted almond-nibs and roll the paste cylindrically.
4 Cut into pieces 1·5 cm ($\frac{3}{4}$ inch) wide.
5 Open out the folds to right and left by pressing with the back of a knife down the centre.
6 Arrange on trays, egg-wash, prove slowly, and bake at 205° C (400° F).
7 Brush with apricot glaze.

9. Savouries and Supplementary Breakfast Dishes

SAVOURIES

SAVOURIES for service as a final course to complete a meal have long been in demand in Britain. French chefs, though they helped to develop many of them, tend to be somewhat contemptuous of savouries and do not include them among items prepared in the continental tradition. Just as cheese is nowadays sometimes served before the pudding or dessert so there has been a tendency also to serve a savoury in that menu position. Favoured especially by men-diners, however, its original purpose was to leave the diner with a savoury tang after eating. For that reason the canapé, croûte or other items need not be large and, indeed, neatness and daintiness are essential features of this kind of dish.

1172 Anges à cheval – Angels on horseback

4 *oblongs toast* 6 *cm* × 4 *cm* (3″ × 2″)   15 *g* (½ *oz*) *butter*   12 *oysters*
12 *bacon rashers*

1 Butter the toast.
2 Flatten the bacon and wrap a slice round each oyster.
3 Skewer and grill.
4 Garnish with a few straw potatoes and watercress.

1173 Beignets soufflés au parmesan

60 *g* (2 *oz*) *flour*	2 *eggs*	125 *ml* (¼ *pt*) *water*
15 *g* (½ *oz*) *grated*	*pinch salt*	*fat for deep frying*
Parmesan cheese	30 *g* (1 *oz*) *butter*	

1 Boil water and butter.
2 Sift flour and salt and mix into the water and butter.
3 Cook until mixture leaves the side of the pan.
4 Add the eggs one by one beating well; add the cheese.
5 Pipe on to greased paper.
6 Fry in deep fat; drain well.

1174 Buck rarebit

Method and ingredients as Welsh rarebit (Recipe 1194) but each portion topped with a well-rounded, soft-poached egg.

1175 Canapé Chang Wang

4 slices tomato	Welsh rarebit mix	4 bacon rashers, rolled
15 g (½ oz) chutney	(Recipe 1194)	4 rounds of toast

1 Prepare as for Welsh rarebit and place a slice of tomato on top of each before glazing; add a little chutney to each portion and place a bacon roll on top.
2 Glaze slowly; garnish with parsley.

1176 Canapé des gourmets

4 small rounds of toast	240 g (½ lb) finely-chopped ham	10 ml spoon [½ tablespoon] cream
30 g (1 oz) mustard butter	15 g (½ oz) butter	paprika

1 Butter toast, which has been cut with a round 6 cm (3 inch) cutter.
2 Heat the ham with the mustard butter (Recipe 91) and cream and flavour with a little paprika.
3 Heap evenly on the buttered toast; brush with butter and pass under the grill.
4 Garnish with sprigs of parsley.

1177 Canapé Diane

4 oblongs toast 6 cm × 4 cm (3″ × 2″)	240 g (½ lb) chicken-liver 12 bacon rashers	15 g (½ oz) butter

1 Butter the toast.
2 Flatten the bacon and wrap a slice round each piece of liver.
3 Skewer and grill.
4 Remove skewer and place 3 on each piece of toast.
5 Garnish with a few straw potatoes and watercress.

1178 Canapé écossais – Scotch woodcock

8 eggs	8 fillet anchovies	15 ml spoon (⅛ gill) cream
30 g (1 oz) butter	4 rounds of toast	16 capers

1 Butter toast, which has been cut with a round 6 cm (3 inch) cutter.
2 Prepare scrambled egg (Recipe 300) add cream.
3 Heap the mixture evenly on toast.
4 Garnish with criss-cross of anchovy.
5 Place a caper in each section.
6 Garnish with parsley.

1179 Canapé Ivanhoe

240 g (½ lb) findon haddock	4 small grilled mushrooms	cayenne pepper
	15 g (½ oz) butter	seasoning
3 × 20 ml spoon (½ gill) Béchamel (Recipe 51)	10 ml spoon [½ tablespoon] cream	250 ml (½ pt) milk
		4 rounds of toast

1 Cook haddock in milk (Recipe 1206).
2 Skin and chop very fine.
3 Sweat in butter, bind with Béchamel, add cream and season.
4 Heap evenly on buttered toast, cut with a round 6 cm (3 inch) cutter.
5 Place a grilled mushroom on top of each.
6 Pass under salamander.
7 Garnish with parsley.

1180 Canapé Quo Vadis

4 *oblongs toast* 6 cm × 4 cm (3″ × 2″)	125 ml (¼ pt)	30 g (1 oz) butter
4 *grilled mushrooms*	milk	240 g (½ lb)
120 g (¼ lb) flour	seasoning	herring roes

Prepare as for Laitances sur croûte (Recipe 1187) but with a garnish of grilled mushrooms.

1181 Canapé yorkaise

Prepare as for Croûte Derby (Recipe 1184) with grilled mushroom on top.

1182 Croûte anchois – Anchovy toast

4 *oblongs toast* 6 cm × 4 cm (3″ × 2″)	15 g (½ oz) butter	parsley
60 g (2 oz) fillet anchovies	½ lemon	paprika

1 Butter the toast.
2 Lay the anchovies lengthwise on the toast.
3 Brush with butter and heat under the salamander.
4 Dust with paprika, garnish with small pieces of lemon and picked parsley.

1183 Croûte baron

4 *small rounds of toast*	8 *large, grilled*	15 g (½ oz) butter
8 *slices beef-bone marrow*	mushrooms	parsley
7 g (¼ oz) white breadcrumbs	4 rashers streaky bacon	

1 Butter toast, which has been cut with a round 6 cm (3 inch) cutter.
2 Place grilled mushrooms on toast.
3 Grill bacon and place on mushrooms.
4 Heat the marrow in a little stock; drain and place on the bacon.
5 Sprinkle lightly with breadcrumbs and pass under the salamander.
6 Garnish with sprig parsley.

1184 Croûte Derby

4 *small rounds of toast*	15 ml spoon [1 table-	2 pickled walnuts
240 g (½ lb) finely-chopped ham	spoon] cream	15 g (½ oz) butter

1 Butter toast, which has been cut with a round 6 cm (3 inch) cutter.
2 Heat the ham in butter, add the cream and season with paprika.

3 Heap the mixture on the toast and garnish each one with half a walnut.
4 Pass under the salamander.
5 Garnish with parsley.

1185 Croûte Windsor

This is the alternative name for canapé yorkaise (Recipe 1181).

1186 Diables noirs or Diables à cheval – Black devils or devils on horseback

| 4 *oblongs toast* 6 *cm* × 4 *cm* (3″ × 2″) | 12 *cooked* | 15 *g* (½ *oz*) *chutney* |
| 12 *slices streaky bacon* | *prunes* | 15 *g* (½ *oz*) *butter* |

1 Stone prunes and fill with chutney.
2 Flatten bacon and wrap a slice round each stuffed prune.
3 Skewer and grill.
4 Remove skewer and place 3 on each piece of toast.
5 Garnish with parsley.

1187 Laitances sur croûtes – Soft roes on toast

4 *oblongs toast* 6 *cm* × 4 *cm* (3″ × 2″)	120 *g* (¼ *lb*) *flour*	30 *g* (1 *oz*) *butter*
240 *g* (½ *lb*) *herring roes* (*soft*)	*paprika*	125 *ml* (¼ *pt*)
pepper	*salt*	*milk*

1 Soak the roes in milk, drain and dust with flour.
2 Place evenly on buttered tray and brush butter on each one and season.
3 Grill for 5 minutes.
4 Dress lengthwise on buttered toast.
5 Dust with paprika and garnish with parsley.

1188 Paillettes d'or – Cheese straws

60 *g* (2 *oz*) *flour*	*little water*	1 *small egg yolk*
30 *g* (1 *oz*) *Parmesan cheese*	30 *g* (1 *oz*) *butter*	*salt*
cayenne pepper		

1 Sift flour, salt and pepper.
2 Rub in the butter.
3 Blend in the cheese.
4 Add the egg yolk and water to make a firm dough.
5 Roll out 0·3 cm (⅛ inch) thick.
6 Cut 6 cm (3 inch) long and 0·5 cm (¼ inch) wide.
7 Twist the straws.
8 Lay on greased baking sheet.
9 Bake in moderate oven for 7 minutes.
10 Sprinkle with salt.

Note. Cheese straws are also as frequently made with puff paste.

1189 Quiche Lorraine

Paste:

120 g (¼ lb) flour
30 g (1 oz) butter
30 g (1 oz) lard
1 egg yolk
pinch salt
2 or 3 × 10 ml spoon (1–1½ fluid oz) water

Filling:

30 g (1 oz) diced bacon
½ clove chopped garlic
1 egg
125 ml (¼ pt) milk
seasoning
21 g (¾ oz) grated Gruyère cheese

Paste:

1 Sift flour and salt.
2 Rub in the fat.
3 Make a bay, add egg yolks and water; work to a paste.
4 Line a 14 cm (7-inch) flan-ring and allow to stand.

Filling:

1 Boil the milk with the garlic.
2 Beat the eggs and seasoning.
3 Add the milk and mix well.
4 Fry the diced bacon and garnish the bottom of the flan.
5 Strain liquid over the top.
6 Sprinkle with cheese.
7 Cook in moderate oven until firm, serve hot.

1190 Ramequins au gruyère

4 croustades (tartlet cases of pastry)   125 ml (¼ pt) milk   seasoning
21 g (¾ oz) Gruyère cheese (grated)   1 egg

1 Boil the milk.
2 Beat the eggs and seasoning, and combine with cheese.
3 Add the milk, mix well.
4 Strain into the cooked croustades.
5 Cook in moderate oven until set.

1191 Ramequins suisse

Ingredients as Recipe 1190 with the addition of 30 g (1 oz) diced, cooked mushrooms, 1 sherry-glass white wine.

1 Add the sherry-glass of white wine to the above recipe (1190).
2 Garnish bottom of croustades with diced, cooked mushrooms.

Note. Ramequin-style savoury-tartlets may be prepared in barquettes or other shaped pastry-cases.

1192 Sardines sur croûte – Sardines on toast

1 small can sardines   4 oblongs toast 6 cm × 4 cm (3″ × 2″)   paprika
15 g (½ oz) butter   ½ lemon

1 Skin both sides of sardines.

2 Lay 2 sardines on each piece of toast; brush with butter and heat under salamander.
3 Garnish with small pieces of lemon and parsley.

1193 Soufflé parmesan – Cheese soufflé

190 *ml* (1½ *gills*) *stiff* *Béchamel* (*Recipe* 51) 3 *egg whites*	15 *g* (½ *oz*) *butter* 21 *g* (¾ *oz*) *grated* *Parmesan cheese*	2 *egg yolks* 1 *small soufflé* *case*

1 Heat Béchamel.
2 Beat in the egg yolks and cheese; season.
3 Allow to cool slightly.
4 Beat the egg white stiffly.
5 Fold into the mixture gently.
6 Grease the soufflé-case and dust with Parmesan cheese.
7 Pour in the mixture.
8 Bake in hot oven for 20 minutes.

Note. Variant savouries may be made by cooking this mixture in barquettes or croustades.

1194 Welsh Rarebit (or Welsh Rabbit)

120 *ml* (¼ *pt*) *stiff Béchamel* (*Recipe* 51) 5 *ml spoon* [½ *dessertspoon*] *Worcester sauce* 120 *ml* (¼ *pt*) *beer*	1·25 *ml spoon* [¼ *teaspoon*] *mustard* 1 *egg yolk* *seasoning*	4 *rounds toast cut with* 6 *cm* (3-*inch*) *round* *cutter* 240 *g* (½ *lb*) *grated* *Cheddar or Cheshire* *cheese*

1 Make a reduction of the beer and mustard.
2 Add the Béchamel and melt the cheese into a smooth paste; add the Worcester sauce.
3 Bind the mixture with the egg yolk, and season.
4 Allow to cool.
5 Butter the toast and cover like a pyramid with the Welsh rarebit.
6 Set to glaze slowly at the bottom of the grill.

Note. Béchamel is added to stabilize and ensure creamy texture; traditionalists may prefer to prepare Welsh rarebit without this aid.

1195 Hot club sandwiches

In addition to the foregoing croûtes and canapés listed amongst savouries, there is a certain demand in hotels and restaurants for the hot sandwich or club sandwich as a light snack or savoury. This type of sandwich is made from sandwich-loaf bread, with crust removed, and toasted and buttered. Club sandwiches may be made in one or two layers garnished with slices of ham, chicken, mushrooms, bacon, minute steaks, and sausages.

1196 Open hot sandwiches

Also in addition to the named canapés there are more substantial open sandwiches made from one slice of toast and topped with various types of cheese, canned fish, shell-fish, liver and meat pâté, eggs, salpicon, and so on.

1197 Cold sandwiches

The chef garde manger is responsible for the preparation of whatever open, cold sandwiches or canapés are required. The range of both types is infinite. Small bridge rolls and petit pains may also be used for such dishes.

BREAKFAST COOKERY

The preparation and cookery of simple breakfast dishes are tasks customarily left to a subordinate cook rather than to a fully-trained chef de partie. Many of the dishes in the preceding chapters are, however, suitable for breakfast service. This is especially so of the following: preliminary breakfast items such as half-grapefruit, tomato and fruit juices, and similar appetizers already mentioned in the section on hors d'oeuvre; Macédoine of fruit and fruit compôtes listed among the recipes in Chapter 8; simple fish dishes from Chapter 5. All these have application to breakfast service.

Moreover, vegetables may accompany many fried and grilled items from Chapter 6 including offal, such as kidney, liver, and sausages. Plainer methods from the vegetable recipes of Chapter 7 may be used. Potatoes, tomatoes and mushrooms, particularly in shallow-fried and grilled modes are especially suitable.

Breakfast cookery is little used in continental systems but in Great Britain, the Commonwealth and America there is still a demand for cooked courses. For breakfast in the American manner, the customary grills and fried dishes of bacon, sausage, and meats, and the usual fish dishes are also augmented by specialities such as corned-beef hash (see Recipe 728), by pancakes and by American-style biscuits.

While chefs in charge of kitchens will interest themselves in beverages accompanying meals, the making of items such as tea, coffee, and chocolate is normally carried out in the still-room under the supervision of the maître d'hôtel or restaurant manager. Other than toasts which may be prepared for canapés and hot open sandwiches, toast is normally prepared in the still-room and not by the chef. Toast split and re-toasted is known as toast Melba.

EGGS
(See Chapter 4 for range of egg dishes)

1198 Œufs à la coque – Eggs (to boil)

Though precise cooking-times depend on the size of the egg, large, high-grade eggs are cooked by plunging into boiling water as follows:
1. Hard-boiled: 8–10 minutes.
2. Soft-boiled: 5 minutes
3. Lightly soft-boiled: 3½–4 minutes.

1199 Coddled eggs

There is a small demand for eggs lightly-boiled. This is done by immersion of the egg in boiling water for 1 minute, withdrawing the pan from the heat, retaining tight covering on the vessel, and allowing the cooking to be completed by standing for a further 5 minutes.

FISH

(See Chapter 5 for further range of fish dishes)

1200 Harengs grillés – Grilled herrings

4 *herrings*	120 g (¼ *lb*) *seasoned*	*seasoning*
60 g (2 *oz*) *melted butter*	*flour*	

1 Clean the herrings by gutting, scaling, trimming tails and fins and removing head.
2 Ciseler both sides of herring.
3 Pass through seasoned flour.
4 Brush with melted butter on both sides; season.
5 Grill both sides under moderate heat for approximately 5 minutes.
6 Served with mustard sauce or mustard butter (Recipes 67, 91).

1200a Herring meunière

Prepare as for mackerel meunière (Recipe 1202).

1201 Oatmeal herrings

4 *boned herrings*	120 g (¼ *lb*) *butter*	*seasoning*
240 g (½ *lb*) *fine oatmeal*	*chopped parsley*	

1 Dip herrings in melted butter and then into the seasoned fine oatmeal.
2 Shallow-fry in butter and sprinkle with a little chopped parsley before serving.

1202 Mackerel meunière – Maquereau meunière

4 *mackerel*	*chopped parsley*	1 *lemon*
120 g (¼ *lb*) *butter*	120 g (¼ *lb*) *seasoned flour*	125 *ml* (1 *gill*) *oi*

1 Prepare as for grilling herrings (Recipe 1200).
2 Pass through seasoned flour.
3 Shallow-fry in hot fat.
4 Garnish with lemon slices.
5 Cover with a beurre noisette (Recipe 82).
6 Add a dash of lemon juice.
7 Sprinkle with chopped parsley.

1202a Grilled mackerel

Prepare as grilled herrings (Recipe 1200).

1203 Fish kedgeree

4 *hard-boiled eggs*   180 *g* (6 *oz*) *plain boiled* 250 *ml* ($\frac{1}{2}$ *pt*) *curry*
240 *g* ($\frac{1}{2}$ *lb*) *white cooked*   *rice* (*Recipe* 362)   *sauce* (*Recipe* 32)
    fish or cooked Finnan haddock

1 Place the rice in silver dish and make a hollow in the centre.
2 Mix the cooked fish with the curry sauce and add the sliced, hard-boiled eggs and place in the centre of the rice.

1204 Fishcakes

240 *g* ($\frac{1}{2}$ *lb*) *cooked white*   240 *g* ($\frac{1}{2}$ *lb*) *dry mashed*   120 *g* ($\frac{1}{4}$ *lb*) *white*
    fish   *potato*   *breadcrumbs*
15 *g* ($\frac{1}{2}$ *oz*) *melted butter*   2·5 *ml spoon* [$\frac{1}{2}$ *teaspoon*] *seasoning*
60 *g* (2 *oz*) *seasoned flour*   *anchovy essence*   1 *egg* (*beaten*)

1 Break fish into small pieces removing all skin and bone.
2 Mix with the dry mashed potatoes and bind with the beaten egg, season.
3 Cut into even-sized pieces and form into neat cakes.
4 Pass through seasoned flour, egg-wash, and crumbs.
5 Fry in deep fat or shallow-fry.

1205 Salmon fishcakes

Ingredients and method as Recipe 1204 substituting cooked or canned salmon for white fish.

Note. Croquettes or cutlets of fish or salmon may be made from the two preceding recipes.

1206 Finnan haddock in milk

4 *small findons*   375 *ml* ($\frac{3}{4}$ *pt*) *milk*   *pepper*
60 *g* (2 *oz*) *butter*

1 Trim off the lugs and tail.
2 Butter a dish large enough to hold the fish flat.
3 Lay the fish skin-side down.
4 Cover with milk and sprinkle with butter.
5 Cover with greased kitchen paper.
6 Cook in moderate oven for 10 minutes.
7 When cooked, remove vertebrae.
8 Reduce cooking-liquor slightly.
9 Pour over the Finnan before serving.

1207 Haddock Monte Carlo

Prepare as Recipe 1206 with the addition of a poached egg on top of each portion.

1208 Arbroath smokies in milk

For these smoked haddock – a speciality of Arbroath – ingredients and method are the same as for Finnan haddock in milk (Recipe 1206).

1209 Grilled Arbroath smokies

4 *smokies*   90 g (3 oz) *butter*

1 Brush with melted butter.
2 Grill for 3 minutes on each side.

1210 Smoked cod fillet

500 g [1 *lb fish* (120 g *or* 4 oz *per person*)]   120 g (4 oz)   750 ml (1½ pt)
pepper   *butter*   *milk*

Treat as Finnan in Milk (Recipe 1206).

1211 Grilled kipper

8 *kippers*   90 g (3 oz) *butter*

1 Remove head and tail and brush with butter.
2 Grill slowly for approximately 4 minutes.
3 Remove bone before serving and again brush with butter.

1212 Bloaters

8 *bloaters*   90 g (3 oz) *butter*

Trim as for grilled herring then treat as kippers or alternatively place in a pan with little water and butter, cooking quickly under cover.

1213 Grilled turbot steak

4, 180 g (6-oz) *steaks*   62 ml (½ gill) *oil*   60 g (2 oz) *seasoned flour*
½ *lemon*   *parsley*   *seasoning*

1 Pass the steaks through the seasoned flour.
2 Brush with oil.
3 Grill both sides.
4 Remove centre bone and black skin before service.
5 Brush with melted butter.
6 Garnish with lemon slices and sprigs of parsley.

1214 Grilled, fried, and meunière fish

Most white fish as well as those listed above are suitable, when cooked in a simple style, for breakfast services, especially whiting, cod, plaice, fresh haddock, and halibut; trout is also an acceptable fish.

1215 Potatoes for breakfast

Sauté potatoes (Recipe 921) and croquettes (Recipe 913) are examples of potatoes suitable to accompany breakfast items such as grilled bacon and eggs. Even composite forms of hashed potatoes such as Bubble and Squeak (with cooked cabbage) can also be used.

Glossary

CULINARY jargon still includes much 'kitchen French' quite apart from the precise language of the French menu. This brief list defines terms used in the compendium together with others encountered in the professional kitchen. Many words whose meaning is made apparent in the titles of recipes or in the text have not been included.

Abats.	Offal.
Ail.	Garlic.
Ailerons de volaille.	Chicken winglets used, for example, as a garnish for clear soup (e.g. petit marmite) or rizotto. For consommé: singe and trim tips, then cook in white stock. When cooked, bones may be removed.
Allemande, à l'.	In German style. It often signifies sauerkraut garnish.
Anglaise, à l'.	Plainly cooked: usually boiled, steamed, or plain roasts or friends.
Animelles.	Lamb's fry.
Appareil.	The food items or mixture for preparing a dish: hence, appareil à crèpes – pancake batter.
Aromates.	Aromatics: sweet-smelling herbs and spices.
Au bleu.	Method of boiling live fish (especially trout) in plain court-bouillon.
Au four.	In the oven: thus, pommes au four – jacket potatoes.
Au gras.	Richly-cooked or dressed.
Au naturel.	Plainly-cooked and served.
Bain-marie.	Double saucepan or bath of hot water for slow cooking or keeping hot.
Ballotine.	Boned and stuffed form of poultry or game birds.
Bande.	Band or strip, hence bande aux fruits, strip-type flan.
Bard, to.	To cover with slices of fat (e.g. in roasting game birds).
Barquette.	Boat-shaped pastry tartlet.
Batarde.	Rudimentary white sauce of water (or stock) thickened with white roux or flour and used as 'extender' to increase the volume of a sauce.
Bâton.	Stick-shaped garnish or stick-like French bread.
Blanch.	Foods are blanched by being covered with cold water, brought to the boil, drained and refreshed by being

plunged again into cold water. The term is, however, also used loosely to indicate processes like plunging tomatoes in boiling water and peeling and the preliminary par-frying of pommes frites.

Bombay duck.	Dried Indian fish served as accompaniment to curry.
Bouquet garni.	Bundle of herbs, usually thyme, bay-leaf, and parsley tied within strips of celery or leek.
Broche, à la.	On the spit (roasted).
Brochette.	Skewer: thus, à la brochette – cooked on a skewer.
Brûlé.	Burnt.
Brunoise.	Mixed vegetable garnish cut into tiny dice.
Carmine.	Red colouring.
Casserole, en.	Cooked in casserole (or vessel for oven use).
Chapelure.	Browned breadcrumbs.
Chaud-froider.	To coat with chaud-froid sauce.
Chemiser.	To line a mould with jelly (including aspic).
Chiffonade.	Fine ribbon-cut of lettuce or sorrel for soup or sauce garnish.
Chinois.	Conical strainer not unlike Chinese coolie hat in shape.
Choesels.	An offal dish primarily composed of oxtail and sweetbreads cooked en daube.
Ciseler.	To cut gashes on: e.g., incising herring for grilling, or to slice finely.
Clouter.	To pierce and stick with, for example, cloves or truffle fragments.
Cocotte, en.	In small oven-proof dish.
Concasser.	To chop; especially used of peeled and pipped tomatoes.
Contiser.	To incise (meat, fish, poultry); to insert truffle slice, clove of garlic, etc.
Coquille.	Shell.
Cordon.	Ribbon; refers also to ribbon or thread of sauce circling a dish.
Créole.	In Creole style: tradition of cookery from the southern states of the U.S.A. usually implies with rice.
Croustadine.	Flat puff-paste bouchées of various shapes.
Cru.	Raw.
Cuit.	Cooked.
Darioles.	Small baba-shaped moulds.
Daube, or Daubière.	Oven cooking-pot: hence, en daube – oven-stewed or -braised.
Demidoff knife.	Grooving cutter used to channel decorative strips of vegetable subsequently cut into serrated roundels for Demidoff garnish.

Dépouiller.	To remove scum and fat by skimming during slow bringing-to-boil, and during cooking.
Dorure.	Egg-wash for gilding pastry.
Doux, douce.	Sweet.
Ébarber.	To beard; to remove inedible fringe from shellfish, e.g. oysters and mussels.
Émincer.	To cut into small pieces.
Escalope.	Collop or slice.
Espagnole, à l'.	In Spanish style often with onion: a Spanish-style omelet is flat.
Faire revenir.	To fry quickly; to give colour without cooking through.
Faire suer.	To sweat (q.v.).
Fécule.	Starch flour (fécule de riz – rice flour; fécule de pommes de terre – potato flour).
Feuille.	Leaf; hence, mille feuilles (literally, thousand leaves) describes a puff-pastry gâteau.
Feuilletage.	Puff pastry.
Fines herbes.	Finely-chopped mixed herbs such as parsley, chives, tarragon, and chervil.
Flamande, à la.	Flemish style, with Flamande garnish.
Flamber.	To flame (flambé, flamed).
Fouetté.	Whipped; hence, crème fouettée – whipped cream.
Française, à la.	Cooked in the French style; for example, vegetables in butter.
Frappé.	Iced.
Friandises.	Small dainties (particularly, nowadays, sweet items). Alternative name for petits fours.
Friture.	Deep-frying vessel or bath (also food which has been deep-fried).
Gaufrette.	Wafer: wafer biscuit served with ice.
Girofle.	Clove; hence, clou de girofle (literally, stud of clove) when piercing onion for onion clouté.
Glacé.	Iced, frozen or glazed with glossy sauce, jelly, etc.
Grecque, à la.	In Greek style, usually with rice garnish.
Gros sel.	Coarse salt, freezing salt.
Hâtelet.	Small skewer, usually decorative and of silver.
Hongroise.	Hungarian style; usually signifies use of paprika.
Huile.	Oil (hence à l'huile, cooked or dressed with oil).
Indienne, à l'.	Indian style, usually indicates garnish of curry sauce and rice.

Irlandaise, à l'.	Irish style, probably with potatoes as garnish.
Italienne, à l'.	In Italian style, usually signifies garnish of pasta with tomato sauce.
Julienne.	Cut into match-size strips.
Larde (Fr.).	Bacon or salt fat pork.
Lardons.	Dice of bacon.
Lyonnaise, à la.	In Lyon style, usually with onions.
Macédoine.	Mixed fruit or vegetables cut in dice [about 0·5 cm (¼ inch) cubes].
Macerer.	To macerate; e.g., to steep fruit in sugar and flavouring liquors.
Madère.	Madeira; fortified wine of Madeira is extensively used in cooking.
Mandoline.	Implement incorporating a blade within a frame to make fine slicing possible.
Manié.	Literally, handled, manipulated; hence beurre manié (butter worked into flour).
Marmite.	Soup pot or stock pot (petite marmite: small earthenware soup pot).
Mask, to.	Cover with sauce or aspic.
Médaillons.	Medallions: round, flat pieces of meat or fish, or preparations of meat or fish.
Mélange.	Mixture.
Mexicaine.	Mexican style, possibly with pimento.
Mijoter.	To simmer slowly.
Mille-feuille.	Literally, a thousand leaves: a puff-pastry gâteau.
Miroton.	A dish of cooked meat, sliced and re-heated in sauce
Moelle.	Beef-bone marrow.
Monter au buerre.	To enrich a sauce by tossing while adding small pieces of butter.
Moulin.	Mill (pepper mill).
Napper.	To coat or mask with sauce or aspic.
Noques.	French version of Gnocchi.
Normande, à la.	In Normandy style, usually with apple or cider or calvados.
Panaché.	Mixed.
Pané.	Breadcrumbed.
Panure.	As chapelure: browned breadcrumbs.
Passer.	To pass, to sieve, or strain.
Pastillage.	Sugar-and-gum paste used by pâtissier for sugar boxes and cake decoration, etc.

Paysanne, à la.	In peasant (or simple) style: vegetables (or other items) sliced in small pieces for garnish.
Pluches.	Leaves or shreads (e.g., of chervil).
Poivrade.	Peppery dish.
Poivre.	Pepper, hence au poivre with pepper as predominant flavouring.
Polonaise, à la.	In Polish style, possibly with beetroot, sour cream and red cabbage accompanying.
Portugaise, à la.	Portuguese style, usually cooked in oil with tomato and onion.
Potage.	Soup.
Provençale.	In southern French style, usually cooked in oil with garlic and tomato flavouring.
Rascasse.	Mediterreanean fish, 'hog-fish'.
Ravier.	Small dish for hors d'œuvre items.
Rechauffer.	To re-heat.
Recherché.	Unusually fine.
Reduce.	By rapid open boiling to evaporate a sauce or liquor; to concentrate and make richer.
Reduction.	The result of reducing.
Rissole.	Minced meat in deep-fried paste cases. Commonly (but less correctly) used to describe medallions of left-over minced meat.
Rissoler.	To toss rapidly in hot fat to colour.
Rocher.	Literally rock, used to denote portion of ice-cream in coupes and similar dishes.
Royale.	An unsweetened custard; cut into dice as garnish for soup (usually clear soup).
Sable.	Literally, sand; used to describe a type of shortbread.
Saccharometer.	Measuring instrument to test sugar content.
Saindoux.	Lard (pork dripping).
Salamandre.	A top fired grill for glazing or to make gratins; originally a portable metal utensil made hot and passed above a dish.
Sec, sèche.	Dry.
Sel.	Salt.
Spatule.	Spatula: a flat, spoonlike implement of wood or metal for stirring and mixing.
Suer.	To sweat (q.v.).
Suprême.	Alternative name for fillet, fine cut of game, poultry, meat or fish.
Sweat, sweat on.	To cook in fat without colouring.
Tamis.	Sieve or strainer; a tammy.
Tasse.	Cup: therefore, en tasse – served in cup.

Terrine. Earthenware dish used for pâtés of meat, liver, and game, etc. Therefore, used as an alternative name for pâtés.

Timbale. A deep circular dish.

Tomaté. Tomatoed, i.e. flavoured with tomato or tomato purée.

Tomber. To reduce (q.v.), therefore, tomber à glace; to reduce to a glaze.

Tourner. See *turn.*

Truffle essence. Liquor in which truffles are canned or cooked.

Turn. To turn (vegetables, mushrooms etc). is to trim with small knife to regular shape.

Vert-pré. Green stuff: watercress.

Vin. Wine.

Vinaigre. Literally, sour wine. True wine vinegar is to be preferred for all culinary and table purposes.

Voiler. To veil or cover with spun sugar.

Xérès, vin de. Sherry wine.

Zeste. Rind of orange or lemon.

Index

References are to recipe numbers, not page